CONTENTS

QUICK REFERENCE DATA

CHAPTER ONE
GENERAL INFORMATION..1

Service hints
Tools
Expendable supplies
Safety first

CHAPTER TWO
TUNE-UP...5

Engine washdown
Compression test
Carbon removal
Spark plugs
Breaker points
Ignition timing (breaker point models)
Capacitor discharge ignition
Air cleaner
Carburetor adjustment
Oil pump adjustment
Clutch adjustment

CHAPTER THREE
ENGINE, TRANSMISISON, AND CLUTCH.................................29

Operating principles
Engine lubrication
Engine removal
Cylinders and cylinder heads
Piston, piston pin, and piston rings
Left crankcase cover
Engine sprocket
Alternator
Right crankcase cover
Clutch and release mechanism
Primary drive gear
Gearshift mechanism
Crankcase
Crankshaft
Transmission
Kickstarter

CHAPTER FOUR
ELECTRICAL SYSTEM..72

Battery ignition system
KH500 and H1 capacitor discharge ignition system
H2 ignition system
Spark plugs
Alternators
Rectifier
Solid state voltage regulator
Electromagnetic voltage regulator--H1
Battery
Lights
Horn

CHAPTER FIVE
CARBURETORS 94

Carburetor operation
Carburetor overhaul
Carburetor adjustment
Carburetor components
Miscellaneous carburetor problems

CHAPTER SIX
CHASSIS, SUSPENSION, AND STEERING 107

Frame
Handlebar
Wheels and tires
Front disc brakes
Drum brakes
Front forks
Steering system
Shock absorbers
Swinging arm
Rear sprocket
Fuel and oil tanks
Kickstand and centerstand
Exhaust pipes and mufflers
Drive chain
Hydraulic steering damper
Frame repair

CHAPTER SEVEN
PERIODIC SERVICE AND MAINTENANCE 156

CHAPTER EIGHT
TROUBLESHOOTING 158

Operating requirements
Troubleshooting instruments
Emergency troubleshooting
Charging system
Engine
Engine noises
Excessive vibration
Fuel system
Clutch slip
Transmission
Poor handling
Brakes
Lighting system
Troubleshooting guide

APPENDIX
SPECIFICATIONS 164

S1
KH250
S2
S3
KH400
H1
KH500
H2

U.K. SUPPLEMENT 173

INDEX 177

WIRING DIAGRAMS 180

FLOYD CLYMER - 2025 EDITION
KAWASAKI TRIPLES

250cc
S1 & KH250

350cc
S2

400cc
S3 & KH400

500cc
H1 & KH500

750cc
H2

WORKSHOP MANUAL 1968 to 1980

A Floyd Clymer Publication - 2025 VelocePress.com

PREFACE

TRADEMARKS & COPYRIGHT

Kawasaki® (Motorcycle Division) is a subsidiary of Kawasaki Heavy Industries, Ltd. (KHI). This publication is not sponsored by or endorsed by the trademark owner. We recognize that some words, model names and designations, for example, mentioned herein are the property of the trademark holder. We use them for identification purposes only. This is not an official publication however; it may include non-copyright works of the trademark owner.

INTRODUCTION

Welcome to the world of digital publishing ~ the book you now hold in your hand was printed using the latest state of the art digital technology. The advent of print-on-demand has forever changed the publishing process, never has information been so accessible and it is our hope that this book serves your informational needs for years to come. If this is your first exposure to digital publishing, we hope that you are pleased with the results. Many more titles of interest to the classic automobile and motorcycle enthusiast, collector and restorer are available via our website at www.VelocePress.com. We hope that you find this title as interesting as we do.

NOTE FROM THE PUBLISHER

The information presented is true and complete to the best of our knowledge. All recommendations are made without any guarantees on the part of the author or the publisher, who also disclaim all liability incurred with the use of this information. As this manual covers all sixteen variants of eight different Kawasaki models, the reader is encouraged to review each section in its entirety prior to commencing any repairs or adjustments in order to ensure they select the data that is appropriate for the specific model under repair.

INFORMATION ON THE USE OF THIS PUBLICATION

This manual is an invaluable resource for those interested in performing their own maintenance. However, in today's information age we are constantly subject to changes in common practice, new technology, availability of improved materials and increased awareness of chemical toxicity. As such, it is advised that the user consult with an experienced professional prior to undertaking any procedure described herein. While every care has been taken to ensure correctness of information, it is obviously not possible to guarantee complete freedom from errors or omissions or to accept liability arising from such errors or omissions. Therefore, any individual that uses the information contained within, or elects to perform or participate in do-it-yourself repairs or modifications acknowledges that there is a risk factor involved and that the publisher or its associates cannot be held responsible for personal injury or property damage resulting from the use of the information or the outcome of such procedures.

WARNING!

One final word of advice, this publication is intended to be used as a reference guide, and when in doubt the reader should consult with a qualified technician.

QUICK REFERENCE DATA

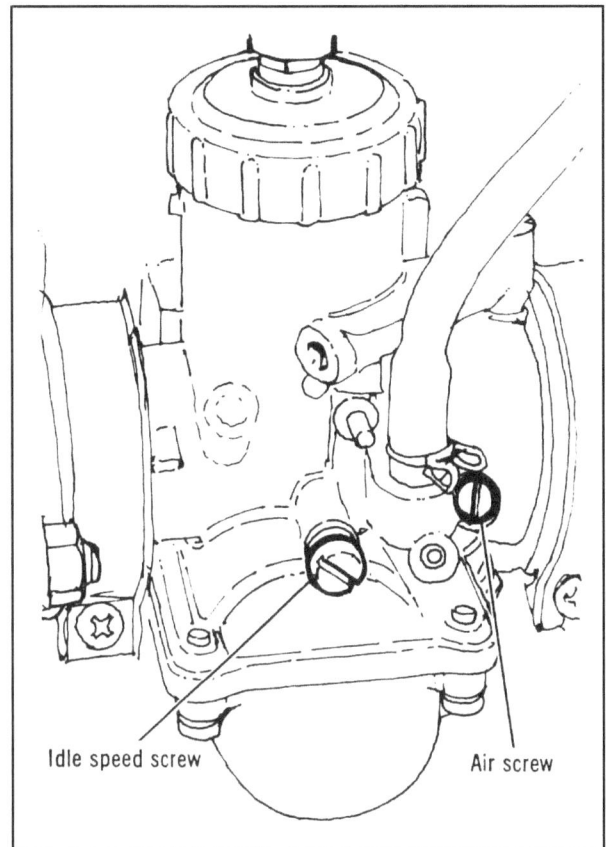

SPARK PLUG GAP

Model	Gap
S series	0.024-0.028 in. (0.6-0.7mm)
KH series (no CDI)	0.024-0.028 in. (0.6-0.7mm)
KH series (CDI)	0.035-0.039 in. (0.90-1.00mm)
H1 (no CDI)	0.020 in. (0.50mm)
H1 (CDI)	0.035-0.039 in. (0.90-1.00mm)
H2	0.035-0.039 in. (0.90-1.00mm)

IDLE SPEED

Model	Idle RPM
S1	1,300-1,500
KH250	1,200-1,300
S2	1,300-1,500
KH400	1,100-1,200
S3	1,100-1,200
KH500	1,300-1,500
H1 (CDI)	1,150-1,250
H1 (no CDI)	1,150-1,250
H2	1,150-1,250

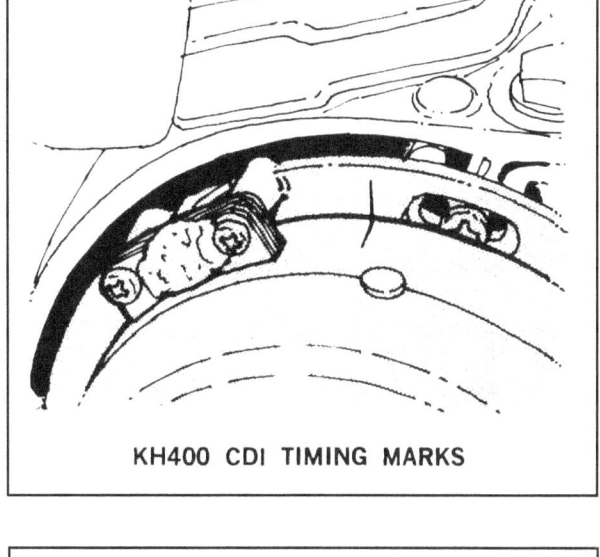

KH400 CDI TIMING MARKS

H1E AND KH500 CDI TIMING MARKS

AIR SCREW SETTING

Model	Turns
S1	$1\frac{3}{4}$
KH250	$1\frac{1}{2}$
S2	$1\frac{1}{2}$
KH400	$1\frac{1}{4}$
S3	$1\frac{3}{4}$
KH500	$1\frac{1}{2}$
H1 (CDI)	$1\frac{1}{4}$
H1 (no CDI)	$1\frac{1}{2}$
H2	$1\frac{1}{2}-1\frac{3}{4}$

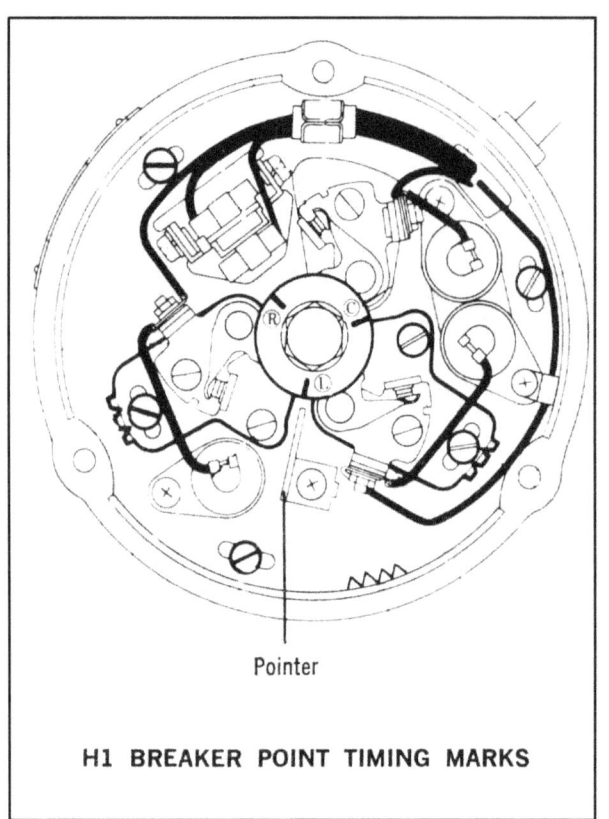

Pointer

H1 BREAKER POINT TIMING MARKS

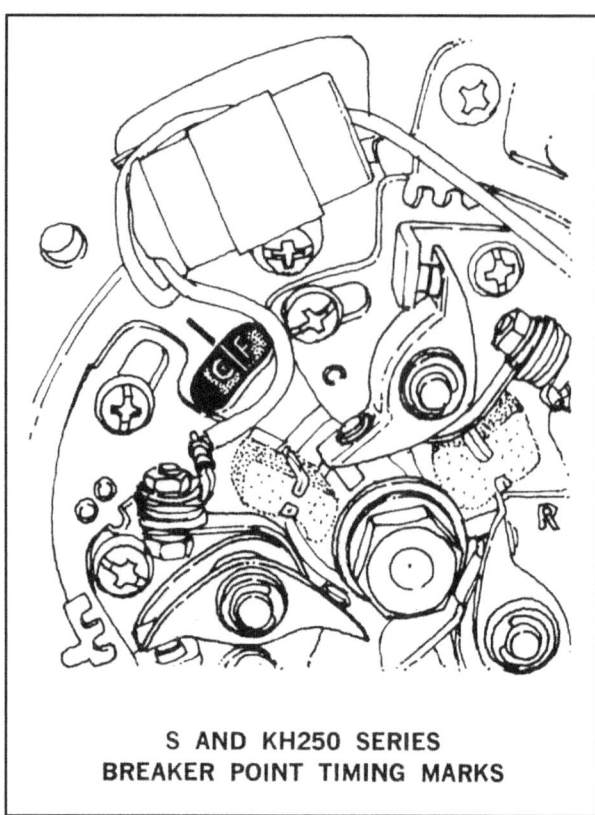

S AND KH250 SERIES BREAKER POINT TIMING MARKS

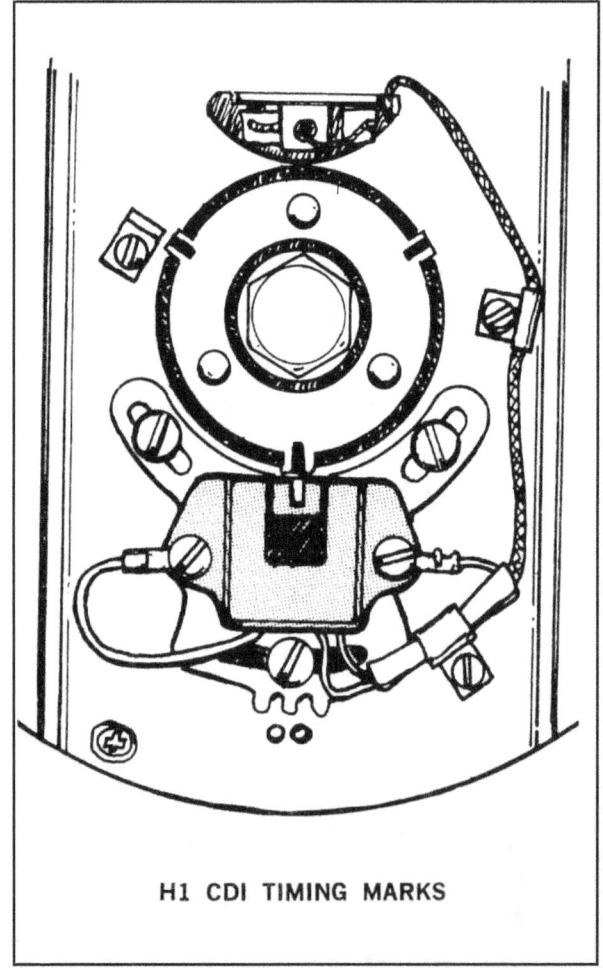

H1 CDI TIMING MARKS

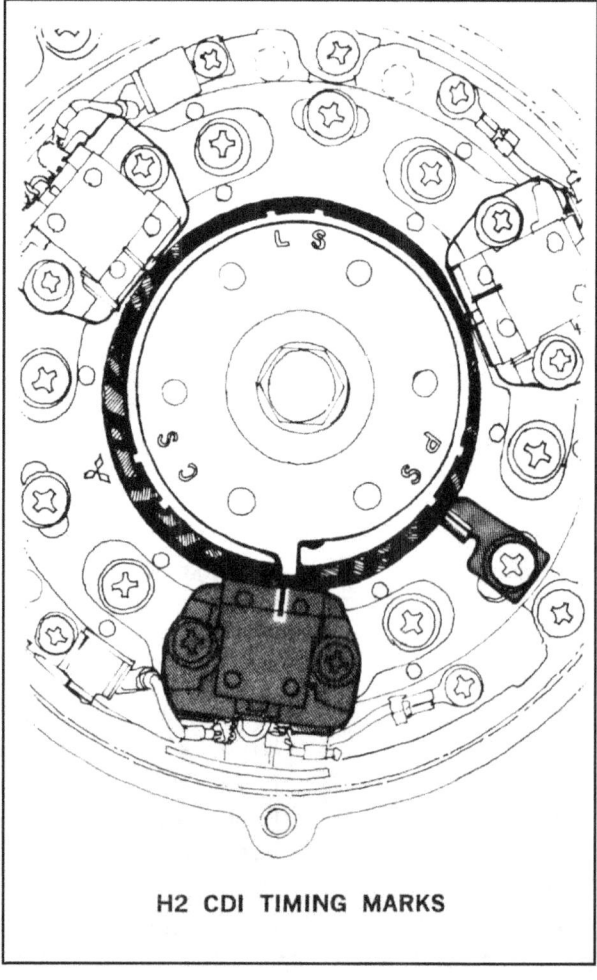

H2 CDI TIMING MARKS

CHAPTER ONE

GENERAL INFORMATION

This book provides maintenance and repair guidance to owners of Kawasaki triple cylinder motorcycles. Coverage includes all H, KH, and S series models.

SERVICE HINTS

Most of the service procedures covered are straightforward, and can be performed by anyone reasonably handy with tools. It is suggested however, that you consider your own capabilities before attempting any operation involving major disassembly of the engine. Some procedures require precision measurements. Unless you have the skills and equipment to make these measurements it would be better to have a motorcycle shop make them for you.

Repairs go much faster and easier if your machine is clean before you begin work. There are special cleaners for washing the engine and related parts. Just brush or spray on the cleaning solution, let it stand, then rinse it away with a garden hose. Clean all oily or greasy parts with cleaning solvent as you remove them. *Never use gasoline as a cleaning agent.* Gasoline presents an extreme fire hazard. Be sure to work in a well ventilated area when you use cleaning solvent. Keep a fire extinguisher, rated for gasoline fires, handy just in case.

Special tools are required for some service procedures. These may be purchased at Kawasaki dealers. If you are on good terms with the dealer's service department, you may be able to borrow their tools.

Much of the labor charge for repairs made by dealers is for removal and disassembly of other parts to reach the defective one. It is frequently possible to do all of this yourself, then take the affected subassembly in for repair.

Once you decide to tackle the job yourself, read the entire section in this manual which pertains to it. Study the illustrations and the text until you have a good idea of what's involved. If special tools are required, make arrangements to get them before you start. It is frustrating to get partly into a job and then find that you are unable to complete it.

TOOLS

Every motorcyclist should carry a small tool kit with him, to make minor roadside adjustments and repairs. A suggested kit, available through most dealers, is shown in **Figure 1**.

An assortment of ordinary hand tools is also required. As a minimum, have the following available.

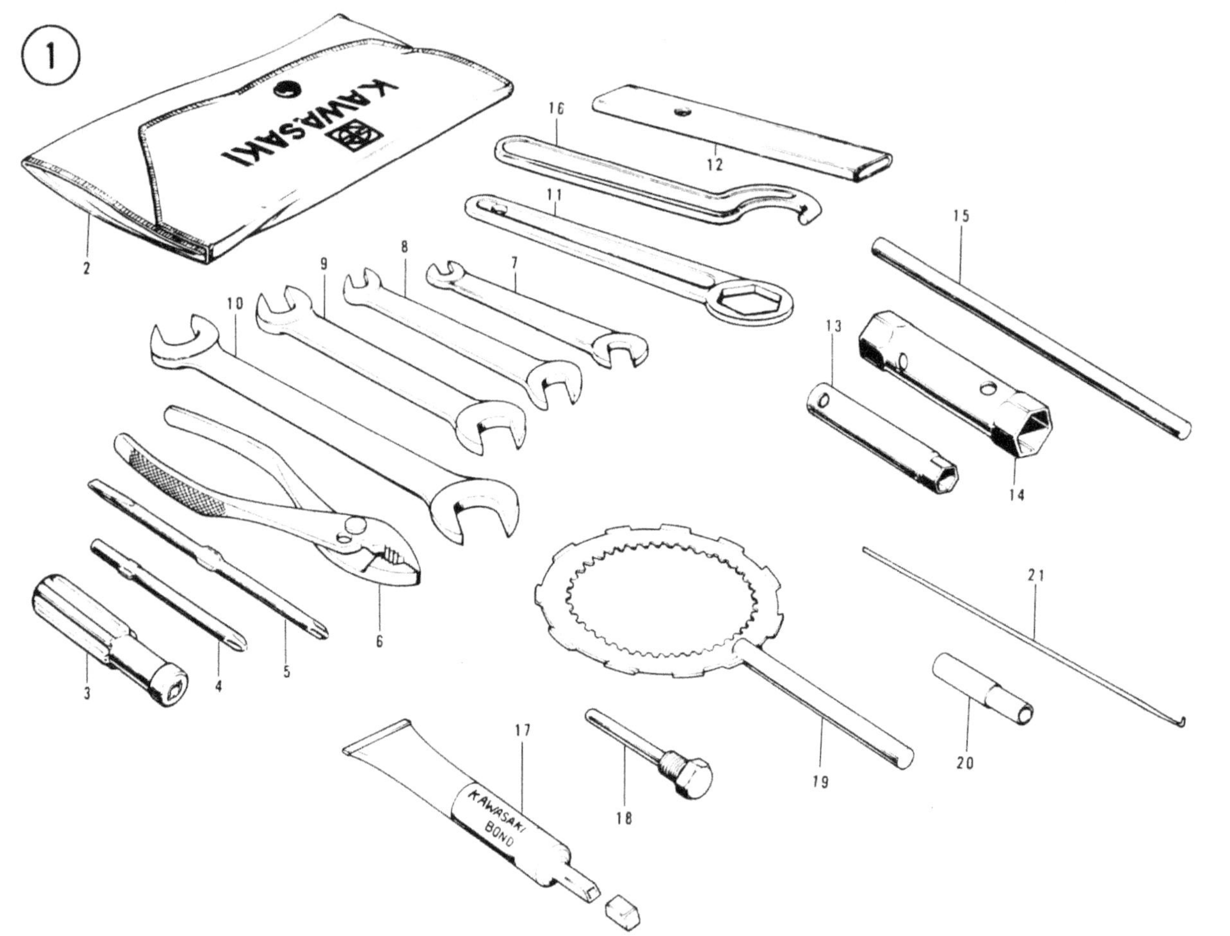

SUGGESTED TOOLS

1. Tool kit	8. Wrench	15. Wrench bar
2. Tool bag	9. Wrench	16. Wrench
3. Screwdriver handle	10. Wrench	17. Liquid gasket
4. Screwdriver	11. Wrench	18. Rotor puller
5. Screwdriver	12. Wrench bar	19. Clutch holder
6. Pliers	13. Wrench	20. Boot stopper remover
7. Wrench	14. Wrench	21. Boot remover

1. Combination wrenches
2. Socket wrenches
3. Assorted screwdrivers
4. Pliers
5. Spark plug wrench
6. Plastic mallet
7. Small hammer

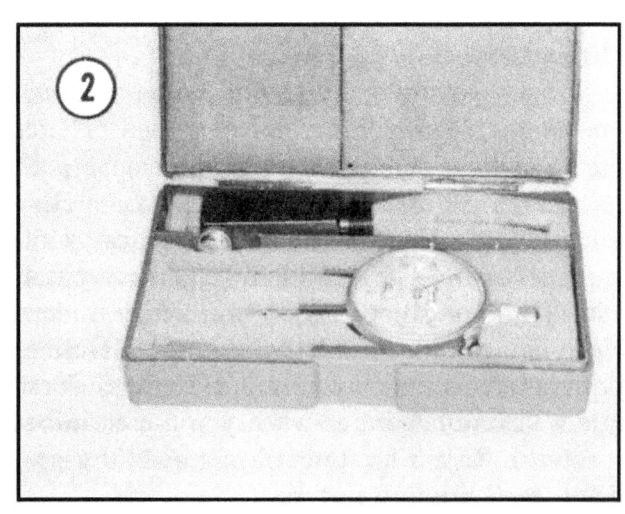

Advanced tune-up and troubleshooting procedures require a few more tools.

1. *Timing gauge* (**Figure 2**). Some early models require that ignition timing be set by adjusting

each set of points so that they just begin to open when each piston is at some specified distance below top dead center. By screwing this instrument into the spark plug hole, piston position may be determined. The tool shown costs about twenty dollars, and is available from larger dealers and mail order houses. Cheaper ones, which utilize a vernier scale instead of a dial indicator, are also available. They are satisfactory, but are not quite so quick and easy to use.

2. *Hydrometer* (**Figure 3**). This instrument measures state of charge of the battery, and tells much about battery condition. Such an instrument is available at any auto parts store and through most larger mail order outlets. A satisfactory one costs less than three dollars.

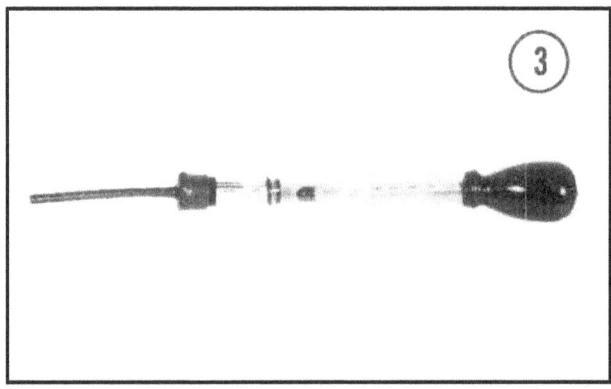

3. *Multimeter* or VOM (**Figure 4**). This instrument is invaluable for electrical system troubleshooting and service. A few of its functions may be duplicated by locally fabricated substitutes, but for the serious hobbyist, it is a must. Its uses are described in the applicable sections of this book. Prices start at around ten dollars at electronics hobbyist stores and mail order outlets.

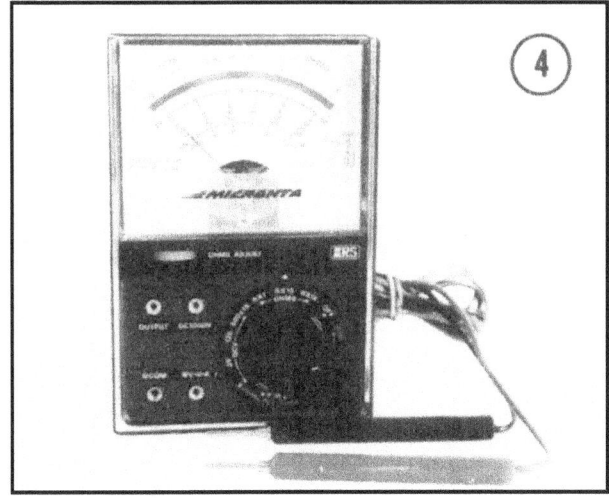

4. *Compression gauge* (**Figure 5**). An engine with low compression can not be properly tuned and will not develop full power. A compression gauge measures engine compression. The one shown has a flexible stem, which enables it to reach cylinders where there is little clearance between the cylinder head and frame. Cheap ones start around three dollars, available at auto accessory stores or by mail order from large catalog order firms.

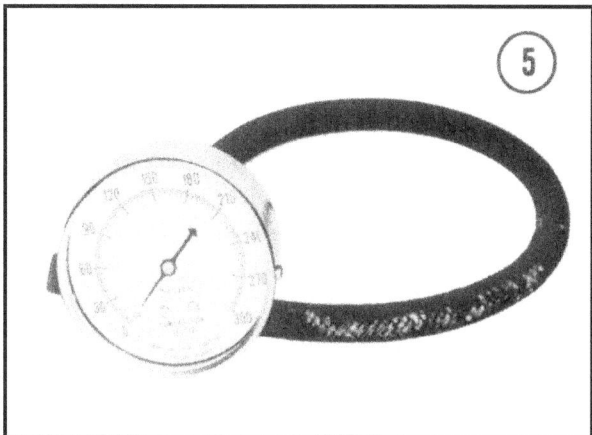

5. *Impact driver* (**Figure 6**). This tool might have been designed with the motorcyclist in mind. It make removal of engine cover screws easy, and eliminates damaged screw slots. Good ones run about twelve dollars at larger hardware stores.

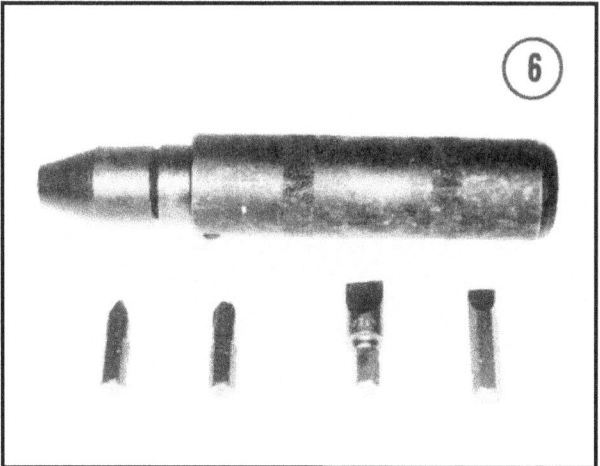

6. *Ignition gauge* (**Figure 7**). This tool measures point gap on machines so equipped, or rotor air gap on models with CDI. It also has round wire gauges for measuring spark plug gap.

A few special tools may also be required for major engine service. They are available at Kawasaki dealers.

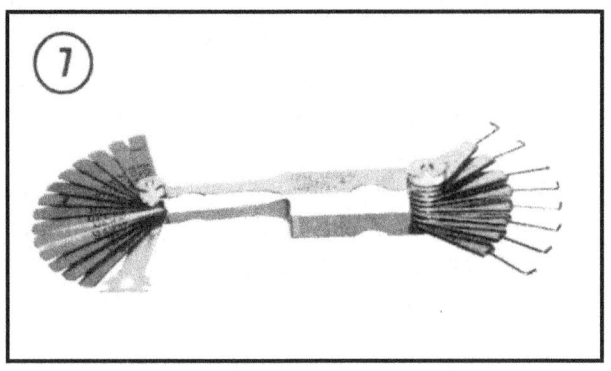

EXPENDABLE SUPPLIES

Certain expendable supplies are also required. These include grease, oil, gasket cement, wiping rags, cleaning solvent, and distilled water. Cleaning solvent is available at many service stations. Distilled water, required for battery service, is available at every supermarket. It is sold for use in steam irons, and is quite inexpensive.

SAFETY FIRST

Professional mechanics can work for years without sustaining serious injury. If you observe a few rules of common sense and safety, you can enjoy many safe hours servicing your machine. You can also hurt yourself or damage the bike if you ignore these rules.

1. Never use gasoline as a cleaning solvent.

2. Never smoke or use a torch near flammable liquids, such as cleaning solvent in open containers.

3. Never smoke or use a torch in an area where batteries are charging. Highly explosive hydrogen gas is formed during the charging process.

4. If welding or brazing is required on the machine, remove the fuel tank to a safe distance, at least 50 feet away.

5. Be sure to use properly sized wrenches for nut turning.

6. If a nut is tight, think for a moment what would happen to your hand should the wrench slip. Be guided accordingly.

7. Keep your work area clean and uncluttered.

8. Wear safety goggles in all operations involving drilling, grinding, or use of a chisel.

9. Never use worn tools.

10. Keep a fire extinguisher handy. Be sure that it is rated for gasoline and electrical fires.

CHAPTER TWO

TUNE-UP

Proper attention to engine tune-up will pay rich dividends in performance and engine life. It frequently happens that minor problems found during an engine tune-up are easily corrected at the time, but which could lead to serious trouble later if left uncorrected. For purposes of this book, we will define a tune-up as a general adjustment and/or service of all service items to ensure continued peak operating efficiency of a motorcycle engine. We will further extend that definition to include related service procedures such as clutch and oil pump adjustment.

As part of a proper tune-up, some service procedures are essential. The following paragraphs discuss details of these procedures. Note that for some machines, a few items are not applicable. For example, the section on breaker point adjustment does not apply to those models with CDI.

ENGINE WASHDOWN

Begin by thoroughly cleaning the engine. Do-it-yourself car washes are good for this purpose. Be sure not to direct the spray where it can short out any electrical components. Also avoid the air cleaner intake. Brush-on or spray-on engine cleaners are good also. They turn any grease or oil into a soap which may be washed off with a hose.

COMPRESSION TEST

An engine with low compression cannot be properly tuned and will not develop full power. If compression is low, it is necessary to find and correct the cause before proceeding. To make a compression test, proceed as follows:

1. Start the engine, then ride the bike long enough to warm it thoroughly.
2. Remove each spark plug.
3. Screw the compression gauge into the spark plug hole, or if a press-in type gauge is used, hold it firmly in position.
4. With the ignition switch OFF and the throttle wide open, crank the engine briskly with the kickstarter several times. The compression gauge indication will increase with each kick. Continue to crank the engine until the gauge indicates no more increase, then record the compression gauge reading.

Example:

1st kick	90 psi
2nd kick	125 psi
3rd kick	140 psi
4th kick	150 psi
5th kick	150 psi

5. Repeat this procedure for each remaining cylinder. Normal compression should be ap-

proximately 140 pounds per square inch (10 kilograms per square centimeter) for all models. If there is more than 14 pounds per square inch (1.0 kilogram per square centimeter) difference between any 2 cylinders, or if compression pressure is less than 100 pounds per square inch (7 kilograms per square centimeter) in any cylinder, make repairs as necessary.

A difference of 20 percent between successive readings on any cylinder over a period of time, if made under identical conditions, is also an indication of trouble. An example for a single cylinder is given in **Table 1**.

Table 1   COMPRESSION HISTORY

Mileage	Compression Pressure
New	140
2,000	140
4,000	135
6,000	135
8,000	105

Note that a one-time compression test taken at 8,000 miles might be considered normal, but compared with past history of the engine, it is an indication of trouble.

It is for the reasons outlined in the foregoing paragraphs that the serious motorcycle hobbyist will want to own and use his own compression gauge, and also keep a permanent record of its findings. It should be pointed out, however, that readings taken with different gauges are not necessarily conclusive, because of production tolerances, calibration errors, and other factors.

CARBON REMOVAL

Two-stroke engines are particularly susceptible to carbon formation. Deposits form on the inside of the cylinder head, on top of the pistons, and within the exhaust ports. Combustion chamber deposits result in an increase in compression ratio, which can cause overheating, preignition, and possible severe engine damage. Carbon depots within the exhaust ports, exhaust pipes, and mufflers restrict engine breathing, thus causing loss of power.

Remove carbon from the engine every 4,000 miles, or more often if necessary. To do so, proceed as follows:

1. Allow the engine to cool thoroughly to prevent cylinder head warpage. Starting with one cylinder head, loosen each retaining nut a half turn at a time until the nuts are free. Follow a crisscross loosening sequence.

2. Remove the cylinder heads and head gaskets (**Figure 1**). If any one doesn't come off easily, tap it lightly with a rubber mallet. Do not pry it off; doing so may cause damage to its sealing surface.

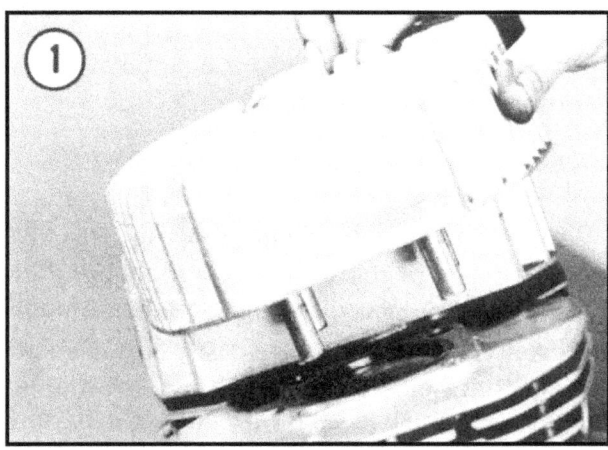

3. Carefully lift the cylinder from its studs (**Figure 2**). It may be necessary to tap around the exhaust ports with a rubber mallet to loosen the cylinder.

An easy method for removing cylinder head deposits is to use the rounded end of a hacksaw blade as a scraper, as shown in **Figure 3**. Be very careful not to cause any damage to the sealing surfaces.

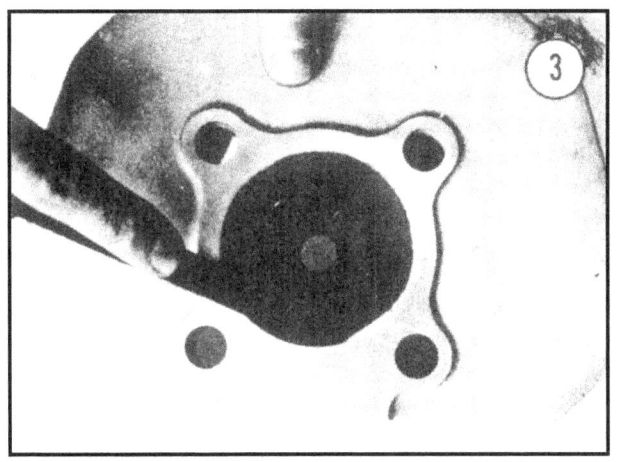

The same tool may be used for removing carbon deposits from piston heads (**Figure 4**). After removing all deposits from the piston head, clean all carbon and gum from the piston ring grooves, using a ring groove cleaning tool or broken piston ring (**Figure 5**). Any deposits left in the grooves will cause the piston rings to stick, thereby causing gas blow-by and loss of power.

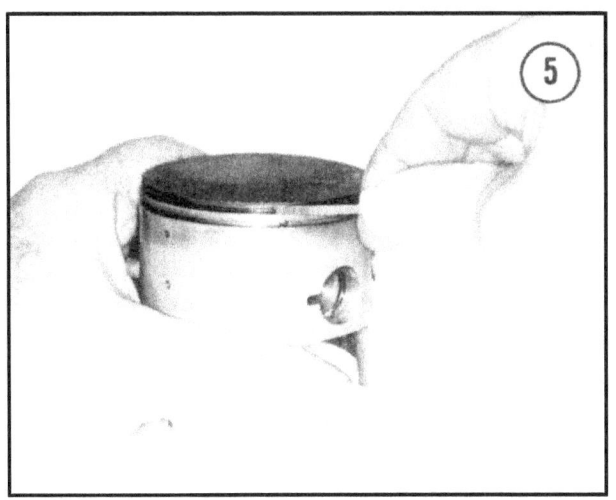

Finally, scrape all carbon deposits from the cylinder exhaust port, as shown in **Figure 6**. A blunted screwdriver is a suitable tool for this job.

Note that when replacing the cylinder, it is necessary to compress each piston ring as it enters the cylinder. A ring compressor tool makes the job easier, but the rings may also be compressed by hand. A screw type hose clamp tightened around the rings makes an excellent ring compressor. Lubricate each piston and cylinder liberally when installing cylinders.

Reverse the removal procedure to install the head. Always use new cylinder head gaskets, except, of course, on engines which do not use them. Torque cylinder head nuts to 16 ft.-lb. (2.2 mkg) upon installation in crisscross order.

SPARK PLUGS

Among the first steps to be done during any tune-up is to remove and examine the spark plugs. Be sure to note which plug came from which cylinder, because used spark plug condition can tell much about engine condition and carburetion to a trained observer.

To remove a spark plug, first clean the area around its base to prevent dirt or other foreign material from entering the cylinder. Then unscrew the spark plug, using a 13/16 inch deep socket. If difficulty is encountered removing a spark plug, apply penetrating oil to its base and allow some 20 minutes for the oil to work in. It may also be helpful to rap the cylinder head lightly with a rubber or plastic mallet; this procedure sets up vibrations which helps the penetrating oil to work in.

When installing new plugs or used plugs with new gaskets, screw them in finger-tight, then tighten an additional ½ turn with a spark plug wrench. If gaskets are not replaced, screw the plugs in finger-tight, then tighten an additional ⅛ turn (18-22 ft.-lb.).

Figure 7 illustrates various conditions which might be encountered upon plug removal.

Normal condition—If plugs have a light tan or gray colored deposit and no abnormal gap wear or erosion, good engine condition, carburetion, and ignition condition are indicated. The plug in use is of the proper heat range, and may be serviced and returned to use.

Carbon fouled—Soft, dry, sooty deposits are evidence of incomplete combustion and can usually be attributed to rich carburetion. This condition is also sometimes caused by weak ignition, retarded timing, or low compression. Such a plug may usually be cleaned and returned to service, but the condition which causes fouling should be corrected.

Oil fouled—This plug exhibits a black insulator tip, damp, oily film over the firing end, and a carbon layer over the entire nose. Electrodes will not be worn. Common causes for this condition are:

    a. Improper fuel/oil mixture
    b. Wrong type of oil
    c. Idle speed too low
    d. Idle mixture too rich
    e. Clogged air filter
    f. Weak ignition
    g. Excessive idling
    h. Oil pump out of adjustment
    i. Wrong spark plugs (too cold)

Oil-fouled spark plugs may be cleaned in a pinch, but it is better to replace them. It is important to correct the cause of fouling before the engine is returned to service.

Gap bridging—Plugs with this condition exhibit gaps shorted out by combustion chamber deposits fused between electrodes. Any of the following may be the cause:

    a. Improper fuel/oil mixture
    b. Clogged exhaust
    c. Oil pump misadjusted

Be sure to locate and correct the cause of this spark plug condition. Such plugs must be replaced with new ones.

Overheated—Overheated spark plugs exhibit burned electrodes. The insulator tip will be light gray or even chalk white. The most common cause for this condition is using a spark plug of the wrong heat range (too hot). If it is known that the correct plug is used, other causes are lean fuel mixture, engine overloading or lugging, loose carburetor mounting, or timing advanced too far. Always correct the fault before putting the bike back into service. Such plugs cannot be salvaged; replace with new ones.

Worn out—Corrosive gases formed by combustion and high voltage sparks have eroded the electrodes. Spark plugs in this condition require more voltage to fire under hard acceleration; often more than the ignition system can supply. Replace them with new plugs of the same heat range.

Preignition—If electrodes are melted, preignition is almost certainly the cause. Check for carburetor mounting or intake manifold leaks, also overadvanced ignition timing. It is also possible that a plug of the wrong heat range (too hot) is being used. Find the cause of preignition before placing the engine back into service.

Spark plugs may usually be cleaned and regapped, which will restore them to near new condition. Since the effort involved is considerable, such service may not be worth it, since new plugs are relatively inexpensive.

For those who wish to service used plugs, the following procedure is recommended:

1. Clean all oily deposits from the spark plug with cleaning solvent, then blow dry with compressed air. If this precaution is not taken, oily deposits will cause gumming or caking of the sandblast cleaner.

SPARK PLUG CONDITIONS

NORMAL USE

OIL FOULED

CARBON FOULED

OVERHEATED

GAP BRIDGED

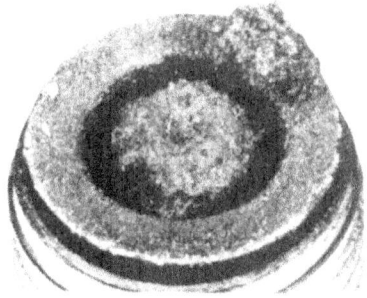

SUSTAINED PREIGNITION

WORN OUT

Photos courtesy of Champion Spark Plug Company.

2. Place the spark plug in a sandblast cleaner and blast 3 to 5 seconds, then turn on air only to remove particles from the plug.

3. Repeat Step 2 as required until the plug is cleaned. Prolonged sandblasting will erode the insulator and make the plug much more susceptible to fouling.

4. Bend the side electrode up slightly, then file the center electrode so that it is no longer rounded. The reason for this step is that less voltage is required to jump between sharp corners than between rounded edges.

5. Adjust spark plug gap to the value specified for the bike in question, using a round wire gauge for measurement (**Figure 8**). Always adjust spark plug gap by bending the outer electrode only. **Table 2** lists proper spark plug gaps.

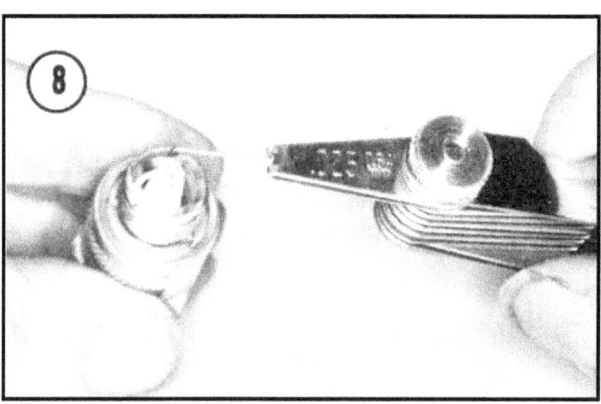

Table 2   SPARK PLUG GAP

Model	Gap
S series	0.024-0.028 in. (0.6-0.7mm)
KH series (no CDI)	0.024-0.028 in. (0.6-0.7mm)
KH series (CDI)	0.035-0.039 in. (0.90-1.00mm)
H1 (no CDI)	0.020 in. (0.50mm)
H1 (CDI)	0.035-0.039 in. (0.90-1.00mm)
H2	0.035-0.039 in. (0.90-1.00mm)

BREAKER POINTS

On machines so equipped, breaker points are among the most important items requiring service. They should be serviced every 2,000 miles and replaced whenever their condition is doubtful. Remove the breaker point cover to gain access to the points.

Servicing Breaker Points

Normal use of the motorcycle causes the breaker points to burn and pit gradually. If they are not too pitted, they can be dressed with a few strokes of a clean point file. Do not use emery cloth or sandpaper, as particles can remain on the points and cause arcing and burning. If a few strokes of the file do not smooth the points completely, replace them.

Oil or dirt may get on the points, resulting in premature failure. Common causes for this condition are defective crankshaft seals, improper breaker cam lubrication, or lack of care when the breaker point cover is removed.

To clean the points, dress them lightly with a point file, then remove all residue with lacquer thinner. Close the points on a piece of clean white paper, such as a business card. Continue to pull the card through the closed points until no discoloration or particles remain on the card. Finally, rotate the engine and observe the points as they open and close. If they do not meet squarely, replace them.

As a final test of breaker point condition, connect the positive test lead of a voltmeter to the terminal with the wire to the condenser. Connect the negative test lead to a good ground. Turn the engine over until the points are closed, then turn the ignition switch to ON. With the voltmeter set to its lowest range, it should not indicate more than approximately 0.12 volt. If it does, point resistance is excessive, and the points should be replaced. Repeat this step for both remaining sets of points.

If the points are OK, they may be adjusted and returned to service.

Point Adjustment

1. Turn the engine over until one set of points is open to their widest distance apart. This operation will be easier if all spark plugs are removed first.

2. Measure point gap, using a clean feeler gauge as shown in **Figure 9**. Be sure that no oil from your fingertips gets onto the feeler gauge and then onto the points. If point gap is 0.012-0.016 in. (0.30-0.40mm), no gap adjustment is required.

3. If point gap is not as specified, refer to **Figure 10**. Loosen point mounting screw (A) slightly, then adjust gap to 0.014 in. (0.35mm) with a screwdriver inserted into pry slots (B).

4. Retighten the mounting screw and recheck the adjustment.

5. Repeat Steps 1 through 4 for each remaining set of points.

6. Apply a very small amount of breaker cam lubricant to the breaker cam.

Point Replacement

To replace breaker points it is only necessary to remove the mounting screw, then disconnect the wire which goes to the condenser. Reverse the removal procedure for installation. Be sure to adjust point gap and set ignition timing after replacement.

**IGNITION TIMING
(BREAKER POINT MODELS)**

Any time after the breaker points are serviced or replaced, it is necessary to adjust ignition timing. If the spark plug fires too early, severe engine damage may result. Overheating and loss of power will result if the spark occurs too late. There are 2 timing procedures for models with breaker points. The first is used on S and KH series models. The other method is used on H1 models with breaker points. Note that timing must be set separately for each cylinder.

S and KH Series Timing

1. Turn the engine over until the "F" mark for any cylinder (A in **Figure 11**) aligns with stamped line (B) on the stator assembly.

2. Connect a buzz box, voltmeter, or other continuity indicator across the points associated with the timing mark (R, L, or C). If a voltmeter or test light is used, turn ignition switch to ON.

3. Loosen both timing plate screws (A) slightly (**Figure 12**) so that the timing plate may be moved.

4. Insert a screwdriver into the pry slots (B), then move the timing plate until the continuity tester indicates that the points just begin to open. This situation is indicated by the test lamp

12

lighting or the voltmeter indicating battery voltage. If a commercial point tester is used, follow its manufacturer's operating instructions.

5. Retighten the timing plate screws.

6. Check the adjustment by turning the engine clockwise slightly to close the points, then turn it slowly counterclockwise. The timing marks should align just as the points open.

7. Repeat Steps 1 through 6 for both remaining cylinders.

Note that it is also possible to adjust timing using a commercial timing light. Connect the light to each spark plug in turn and adjust the associated timing plate with the engine running.

H1 Timing

Any change in point gap, including that which results from normal wear of the point surfaces and rubbing blocks, affects ignition timing. To adjust ignition timing on H series models with breaker points, proceed as follows:

1. Insert a dial gauge into the left cylinder spark plug hole.

2. Slowly rotate the engine in its normal direction until the left piston is at top dead center, as determined by the dial gauge.

3. Set the dial indicator to zero.

4. Rotate the engine in reverse to lower the piston about ½ inch.

5. Connect a test lamp, buzzer, or other continuity tester across the points for the left cylinder (B and ground).

6. Slowly rotate the engine in its normal running direction until piston is 0.086 in. (2.33mm) from TDC if new points are installed, or 0.115 in. (2.94mm) for old points.

7. Refer to **Figure 13**. Loosen clamp screws (A) just enough so that base plate may be moved.

8. Insert a screwdriver into pry slots (C). Rotate the base plate slowly, so that the points for the left cylinder just open, as indicated by the continuity tester.

9. Tighten clamp screws (A).

10. Recheck the adjustment by turning the engine backward to lower the piston slightly, then

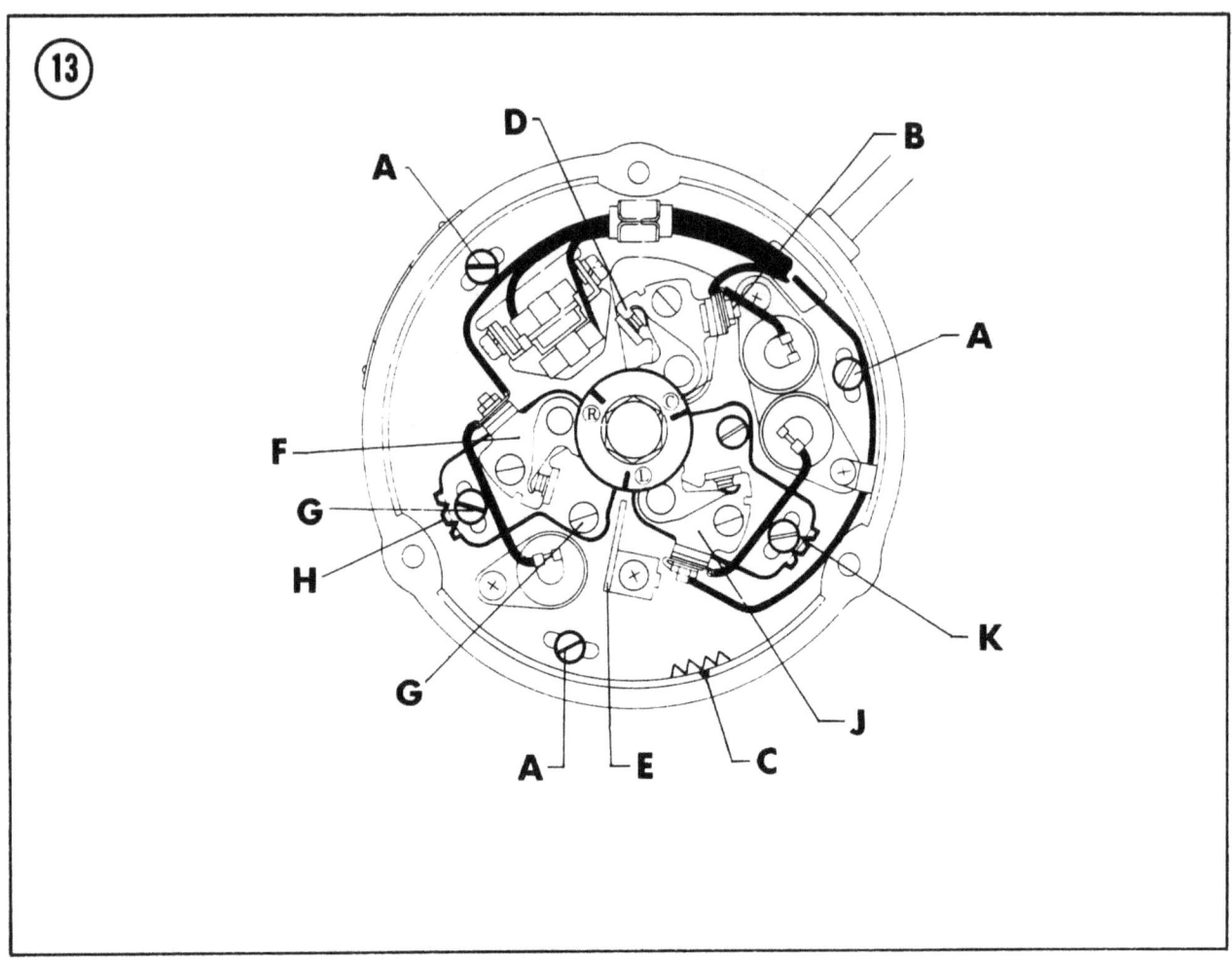

turning it forward very slowly. The points for the left cylinder should just open as the dial gauge indicates the distance specified in Step 6.

11. Loosen the screw on timing pointer (E) and adjust the pointer (only) so that it aligns with left cylinder timing mark (L) on the rotor.

12. Rotate the engine until right cylinder timing mark (R) aligns with timing pointer (E).

13. Loosen timing plate clamp screw (G). Connect the continuity tester across the right-hand cylinder points (F and ground).

14. Move the timing plate with a screwdriver in slots (H) as required so that the points just begin to open, as indicated by the continuity tester. Tighten clamp screw (G).

15. Recheck the adjustment by turning the engine backward slightly, then very slowly turning it forward. The points should just begin to open as right cylinder timing mark (R) and timing pointer (E) align.

16. Repeat Steps 12 through 15 for the center cylinder.

CAPACITOR DISCHARGE IGNITION

H2 models and some H1 models are equipped with a capacitor discharge ignition (CDI) system. There are no breaker points or other moving parts to get out of adjustment, so ignition timing is the only adjustment required. Once set, timing should not change for the life of the bike, but it should be checked periodically.

H2 CDI Timing

To adjust ignition timing, proceed as follows:
1. Set each spark plug gap to 0.035-0.039 in. (0.9-1.0mm).
2. Remove the left engine cover.
3. Refer to **Figure 14**. Using a feeler gauge, check the gap between each signal generator pickup coil and the projection on the rotor. Correct gap is 0.020-0.031 in. (0.5-0.8mm). Loosen coil mounting screws (A) and move the coil by hand to adjust the gap if necessary (**Figure 15**).

15

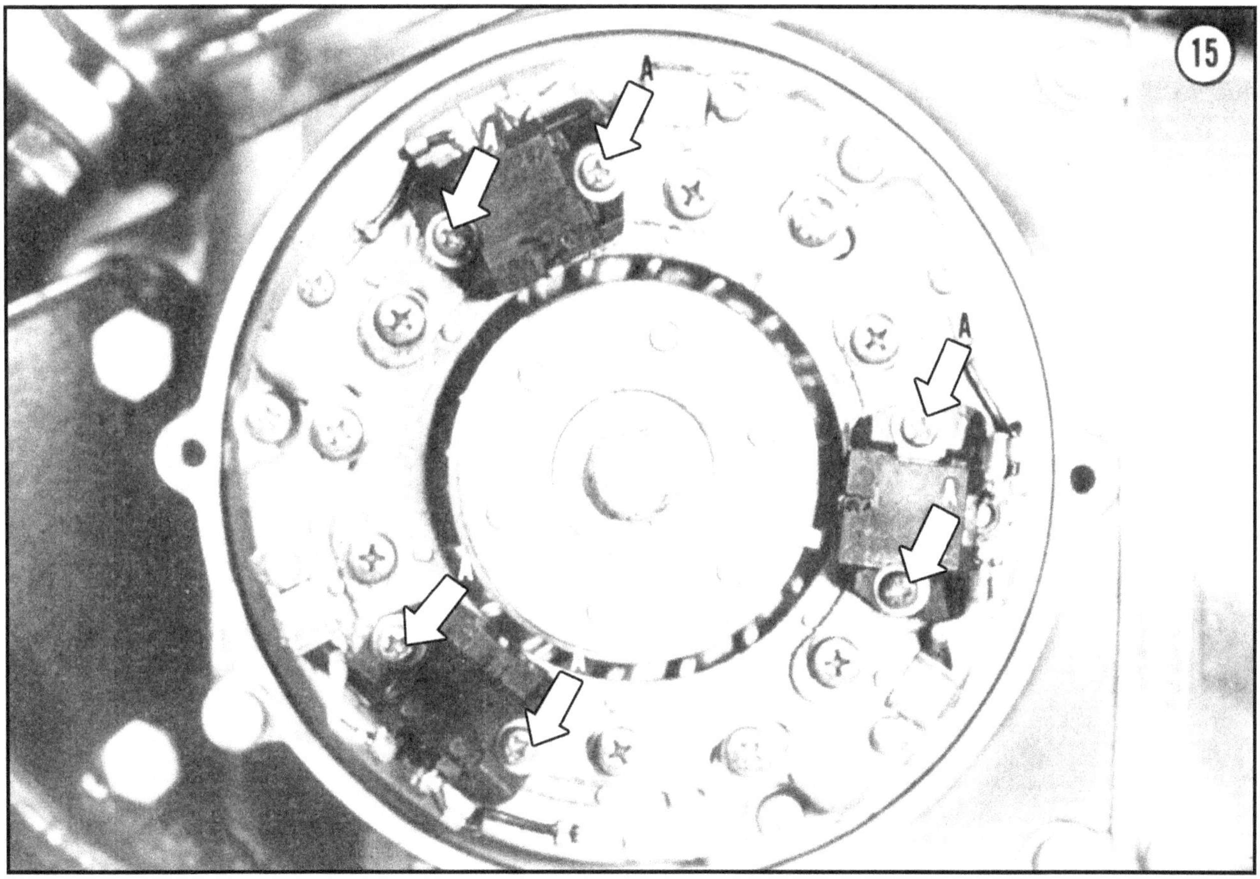

CAUTION
Do not pry on the coil housing with any tool. Such action may break the coil housing.

4. Remove the spark plug.

5. Mount a dial gauge in the right cylinder spark plug hole.

6. Slowly turn the engine until the piston is at top dead center. Zero the dial gauge.

7. Turn the engine backward to lower the piston approximately ¼ in. (6mm).

8. Very slowly turn the engine in its normal direction until the dial gauge indicates that the piston is 0.123 in. (3.13mm) below top dead center.

9. Refer to **Figure 16**. Bend the pointer on the stator so that it coincides with the "R" mark on the rotor.

10. Turn the rotor slightly counterclockwise to align the nearest "S" mark with the pointer.

11. Refer to **Figure 17**. See if the trailing edge of the rotor magnet projection coincides with the mark on top of the right signal generator coil housing. If it does not, loosen coil *base* mounting screws (A in **Figure 18**), then move the base right or left as required. Do not pry on the coil. Be sure to retighten the screws.

12. Repeat Steps 9 and 10 for the remaining cylinders.

13. Install the spark plugs, and connect a timing light to the right cylinder spark plug.

14. Start the engine and run it at 4,000 rpm. Direct the timing light at the pointer. The pointer and "R" mark should align. If not, stop the engine and readjust right cylinder timing.

15. Repeat Steps 13 and 14 for each of the remaining cylinders.

H1E and KH500 CDI Ignition Timing

1. Remove the cover from the left side of the engine.

2. Turn engine until projection on rotor aligns with projection on pickup coil.

3. Measure air gap (**Figure 19**). Air gap should be 0.02-0.03 in. (0.5-0.8mm).

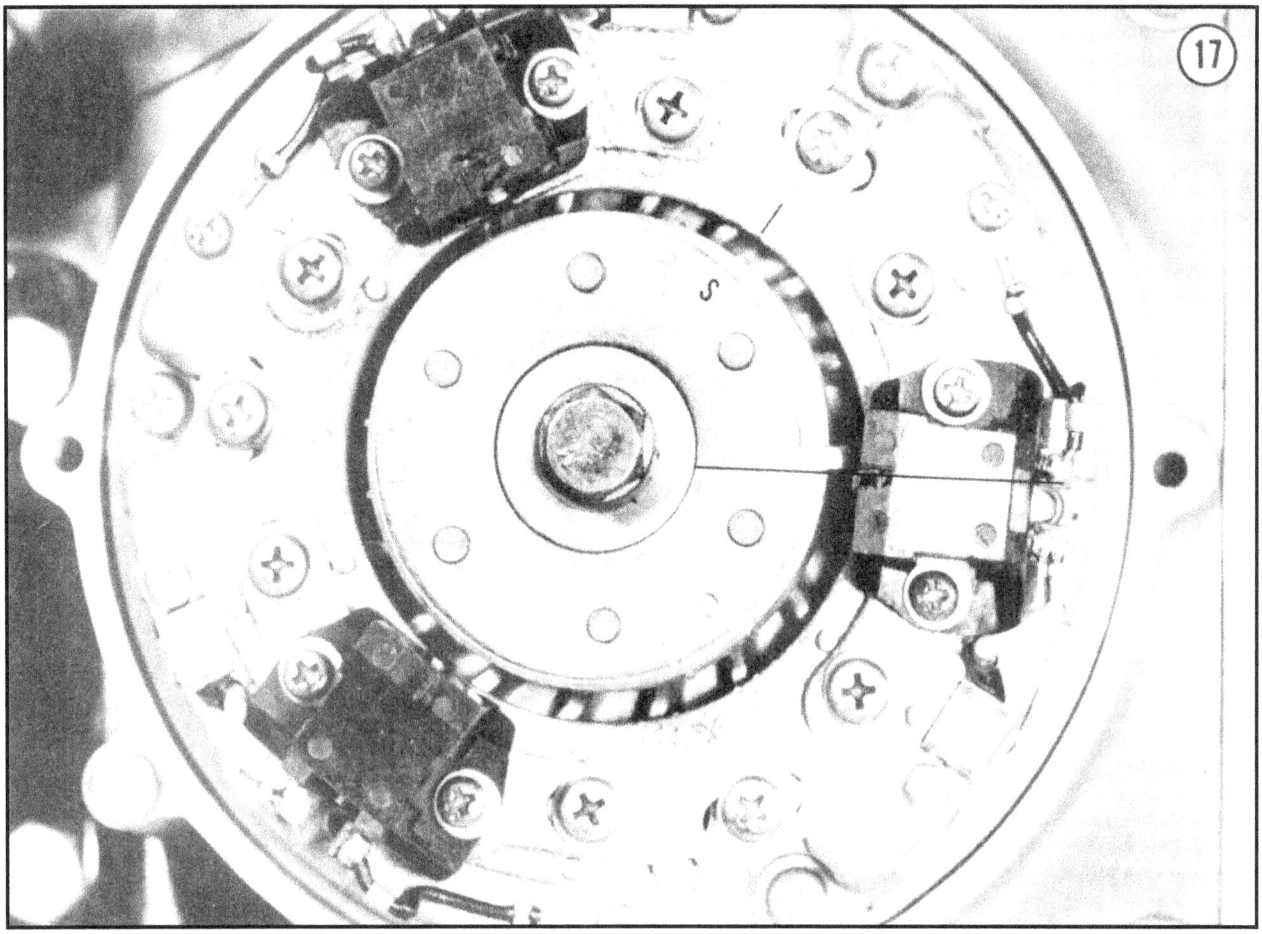

17

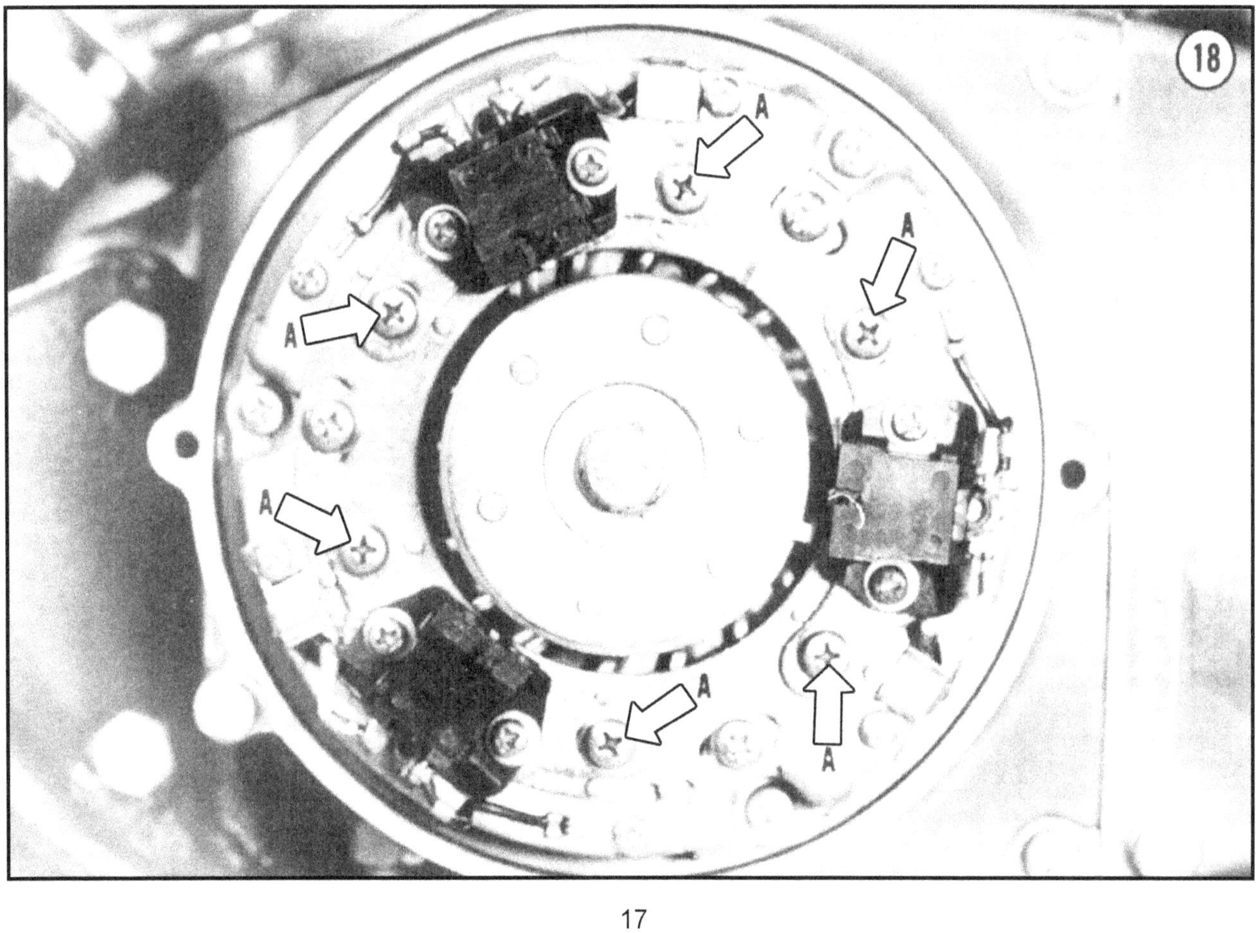

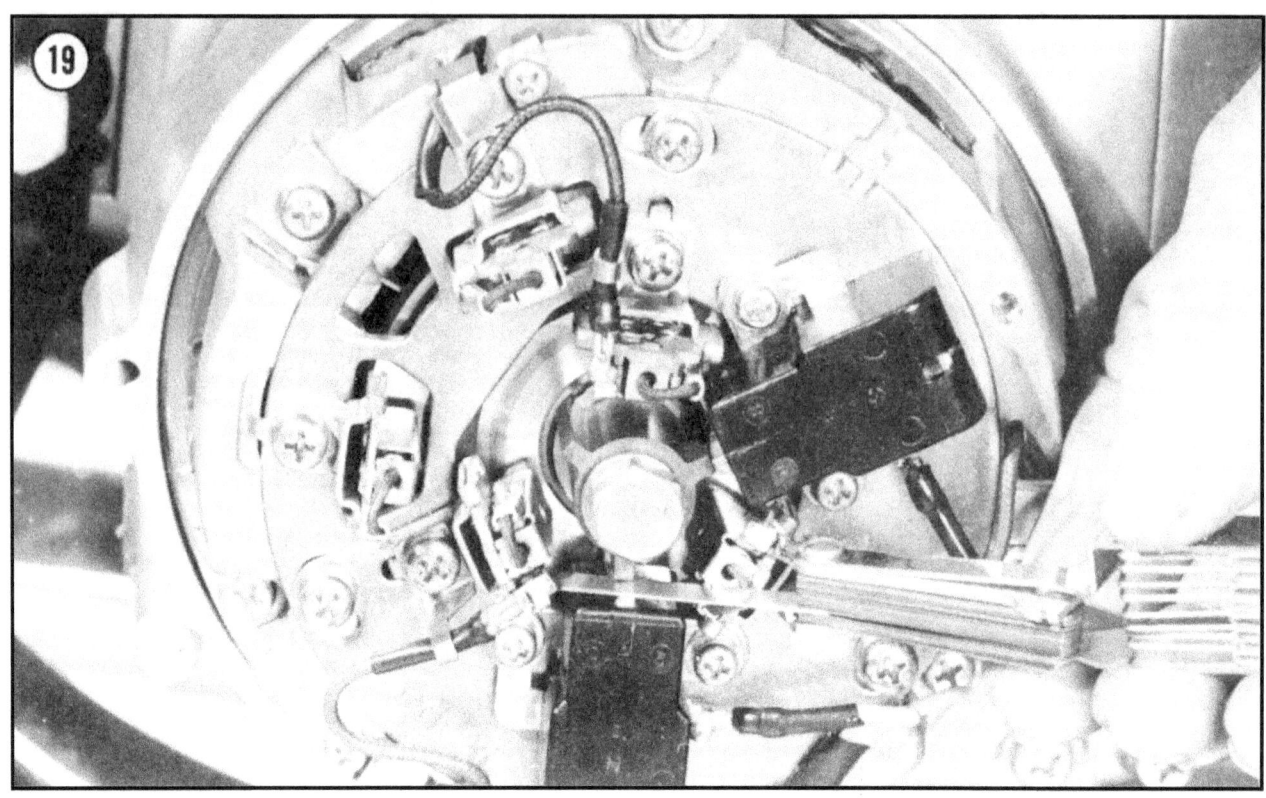

4. If gap is incorrect, refer to **Figure 20**. Slightly reloosen screws (A), then move coil (B) as required.

5. Tighten both screws, and recheck gap. Readjust if necessary.

6. Repeat Steps 2 through 5 for the other coil.

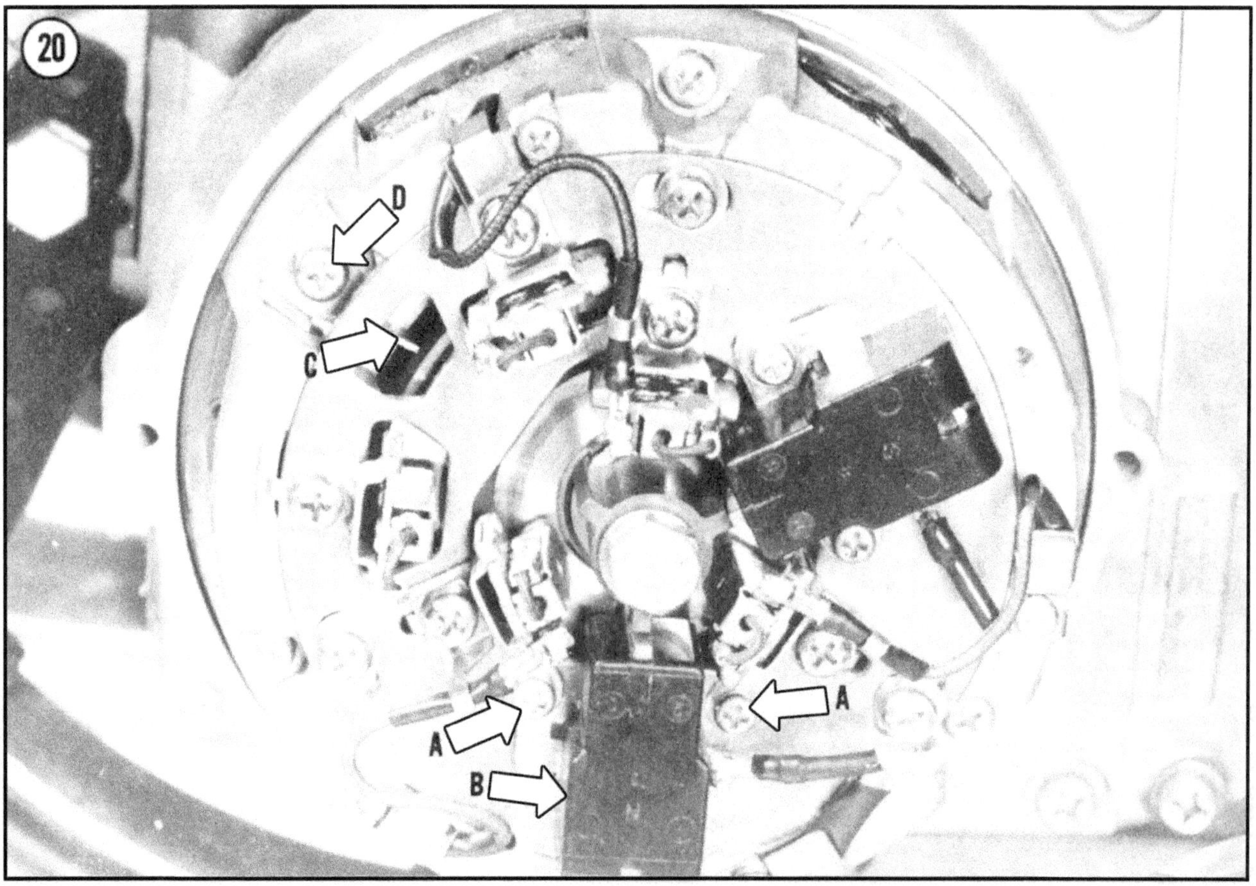

7. Remove left cylinder spark plug, then insert a dial gauge so that piston position can be determined.

8. Turn engine until piston is at top dead center, then turn it backward until piston is 0.116 in. (2.94mm) below top dead center.

9. Check that pointer (C) aligns with notch on rotor. If not, loosen setscrew (D), then move pointer as required. Tighten screw (D).

10. Turn engine counterclockwise until second notch on rotor aligns with pointer. Trailing edge of lower rotor projection should be aligned with leading edge of lower pickup coil (**Figure 21**).

11. If timing is incorrect, refer to **Figure 22**. Slightly loosen screws (A), insert a screwdriver into pry slots (B), and then turn entire stator plate as required until rotor and pickup are aligned as shown in Figure 21. Tighten screws (A).

12. Check that alignment between the other pickup and rotor is similar to that in Figure 21. If not, loosen both coil mounting screws (A in **Figure 23**), then move coil as required. Be sure that air gap remains in tolerance.

13. Replace spark plug.

H1 CDI Ignition Timing

1. Remove the ignition cover from the left side of engine.

2. Turn engine until the projection on the signal generator rotor aligns with the projection on the pickup coil.

3. Measure air gap (**Figure 24A**); it should be 0.016-0.024 in. (0.4-0.6mm). If not, loosen the mounting screws (1 and 2, **Figure 24A**) and adjust as required.

4. Remove the left cylinder spark plug and in-

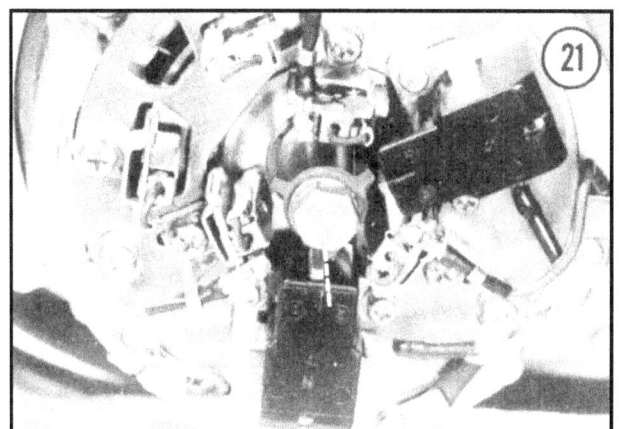

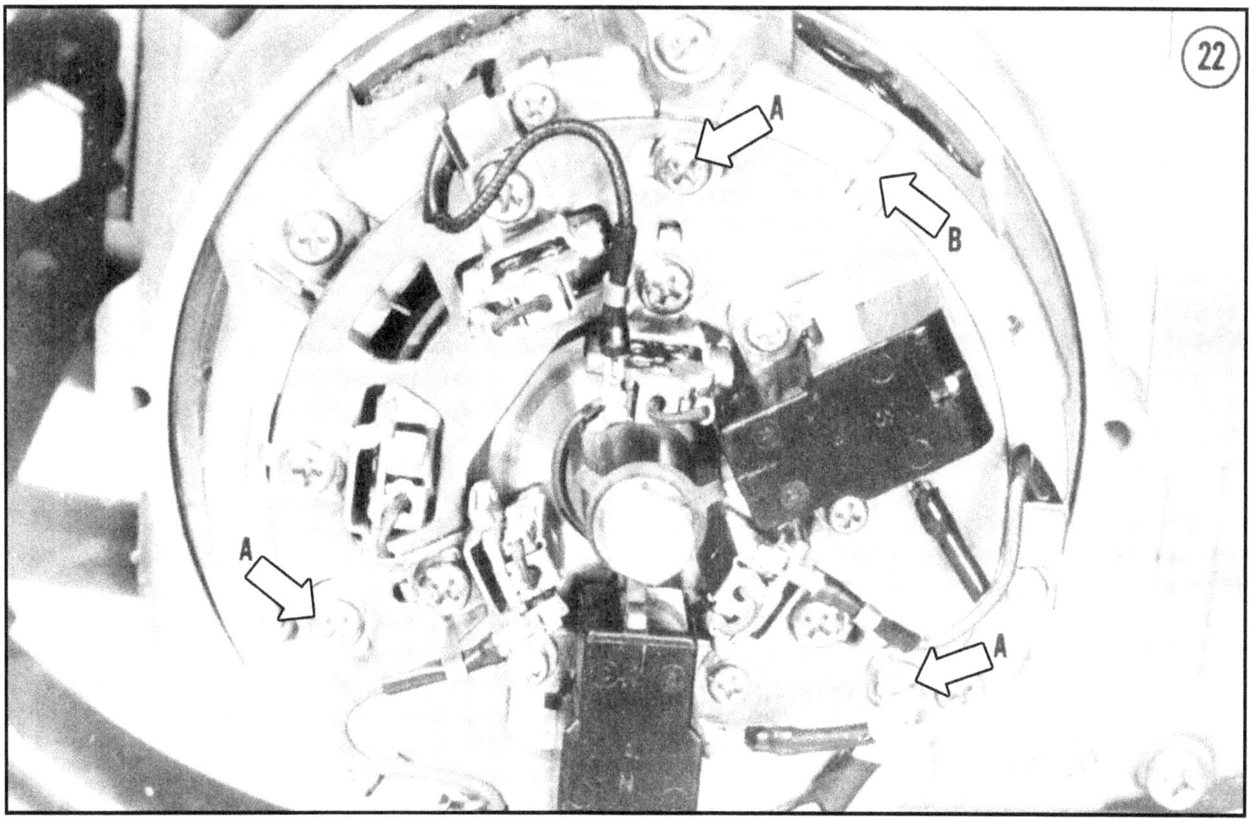

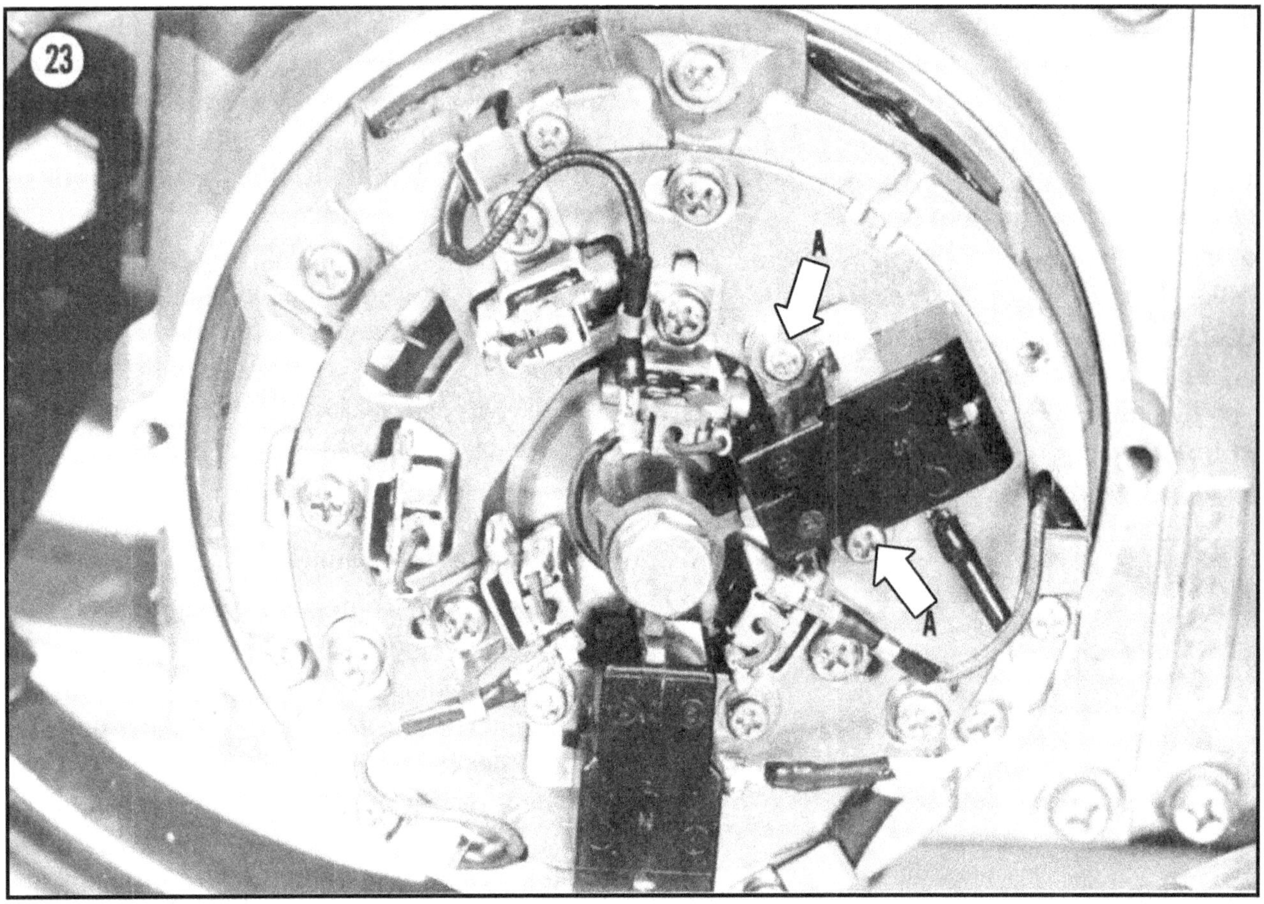

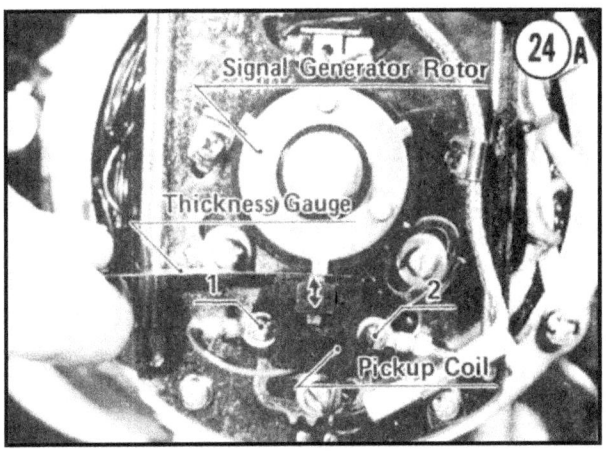

stall a dial gauge so that piston position can be determined.

5. Turn engine until piston is at top dead center, then turn it backwards until the piston is 0.136 in. (3.45mm) below top dead center.

6. Check that the marks (**Figure 24B**) on the signal generator rotor and pickup coil align. If not, loosen the 3 mounting screws (3, 4, and 5, **Figure 24B**), align the marks and tighten the screws.

7. Align the pointer (6, **Figure 24C**) with the

next mark on the signal generator rotor. Rotate the engine and check that any 2 pointers will coincide with the pickup mark and the pointer, respectively. This can then be used for a future reference mark to reset the timing or adjust the air gap, thus eliminating the need to perform Steps 4 and 5 each time.

8. Recheck that the air gap is still correct; readjust if necessary.

9. Remove the dial indicator and install the spark plug and ignition cover.

KH400 Ignition Timing

1. Remove ignition cover from left crankcase.

2. Check that mark on stator plate aligns with mark on crankcase (**Figure 25A**).

3. If marks do not align, refer to **Figure 25B**. Remove flywheel. Loosen stator plate screws (A) slightly, then turn stator plate as required until marks align. Tighten screws (A). Replace the flywheel.

4. Connect a timing light to the left spark plug lead.

5. Start engine and run it at 4,000 rpm. Direct the timing light at the flywheel. Timing marks on flywheel and stator plate should align (**Figure 26**). If not, loosen stator plate screws, then turn stator plate as required.

6. Install ignition cover.

AIR CLEANER

The air cleaner prevents dirt and dust from entering the engine and causing piston, ring, and cylinder wear. If the air cleaner becomes clogged, its filtering efficiency is reduced, causing poor gas mileage and reduced engine power. Clean the air filter every 2,000 miles, or more often under dusty conditions.

Removal, H1 and KH500

1. Remove side cover (**Figure 27**).

2. Loosen air duct clamps, remove air cleaner mounting screw (**Figure 28**), then remove the air ducts.

3. Undo clips, then pull element out through left side of frame (**Figure 29**).

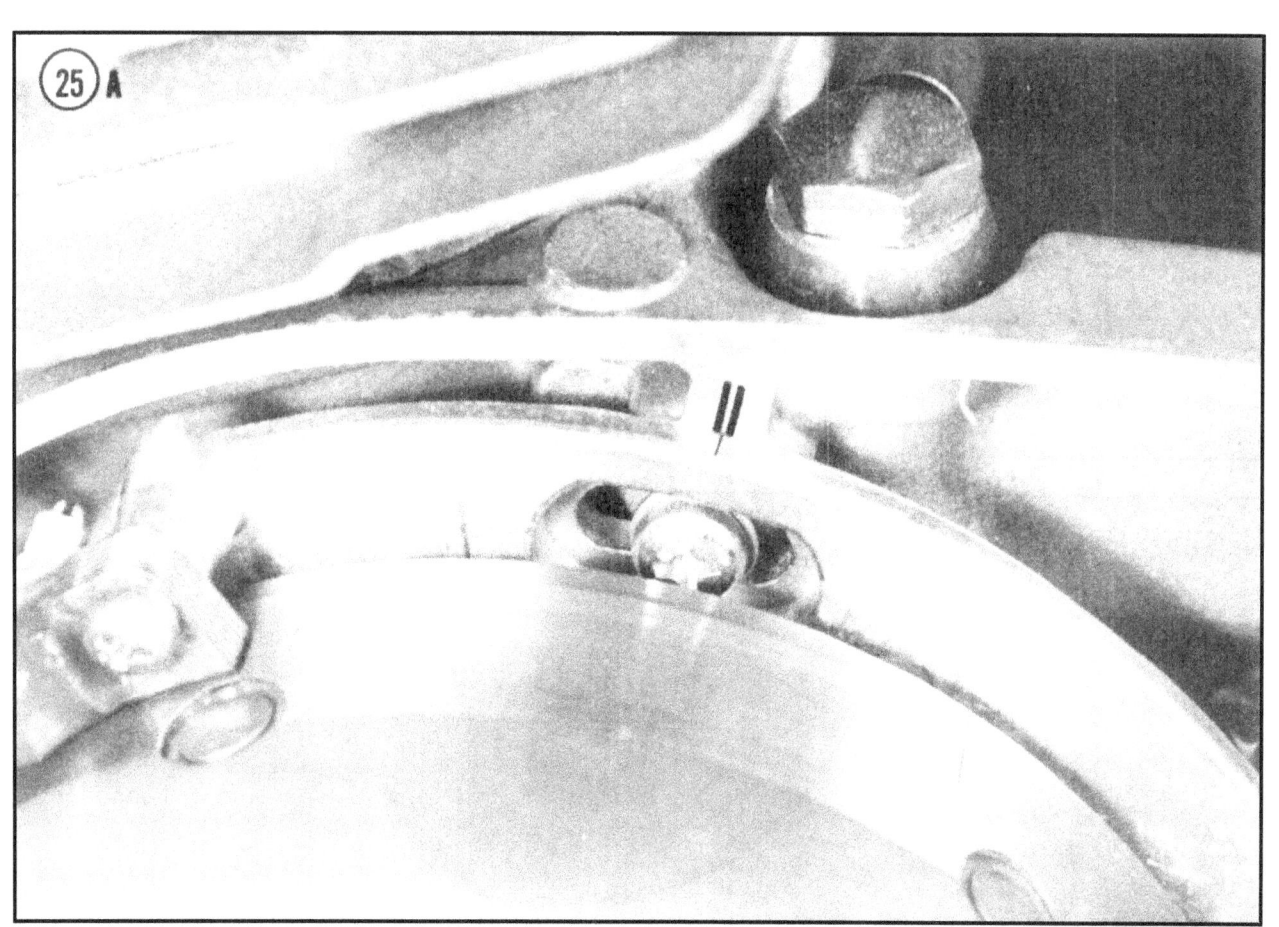

25
B
A
A
A

26

27
MACH III 500

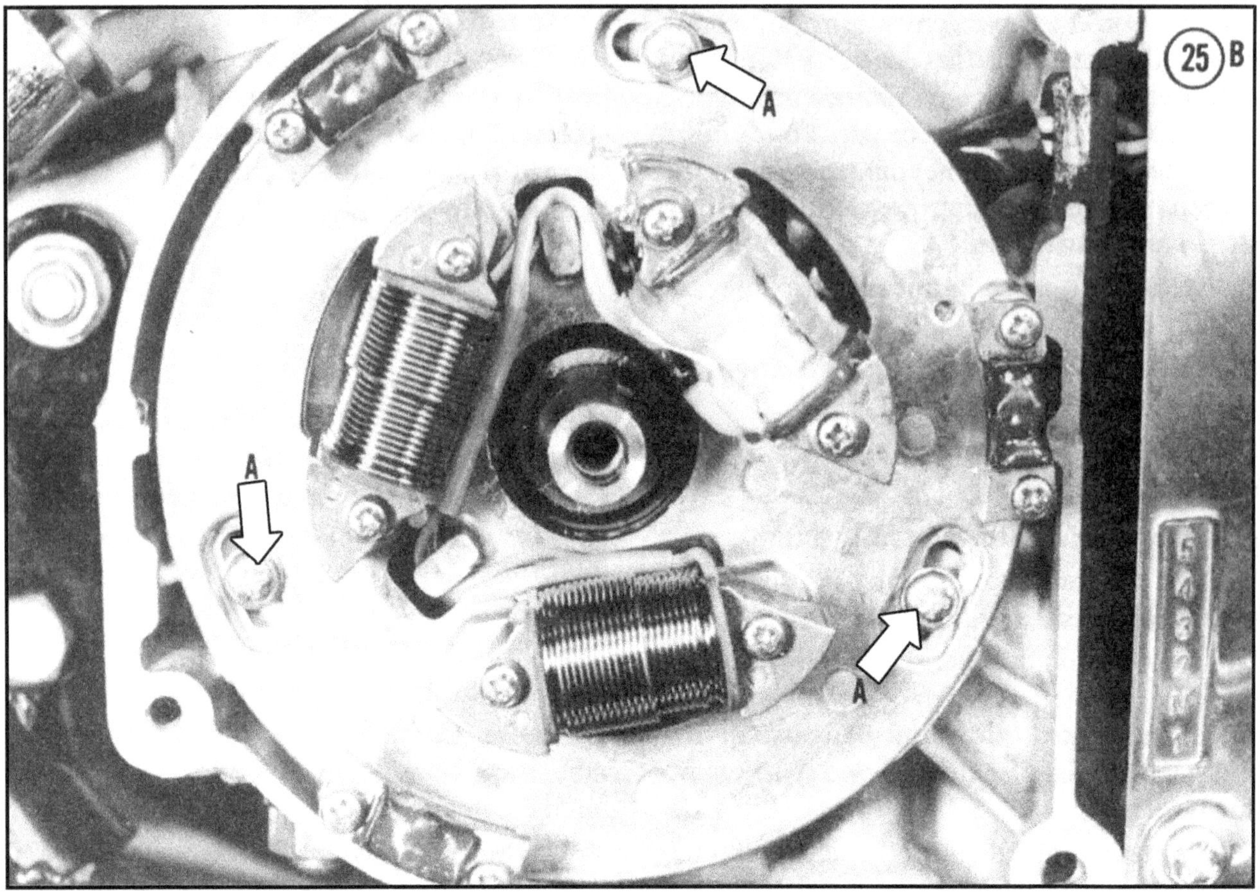

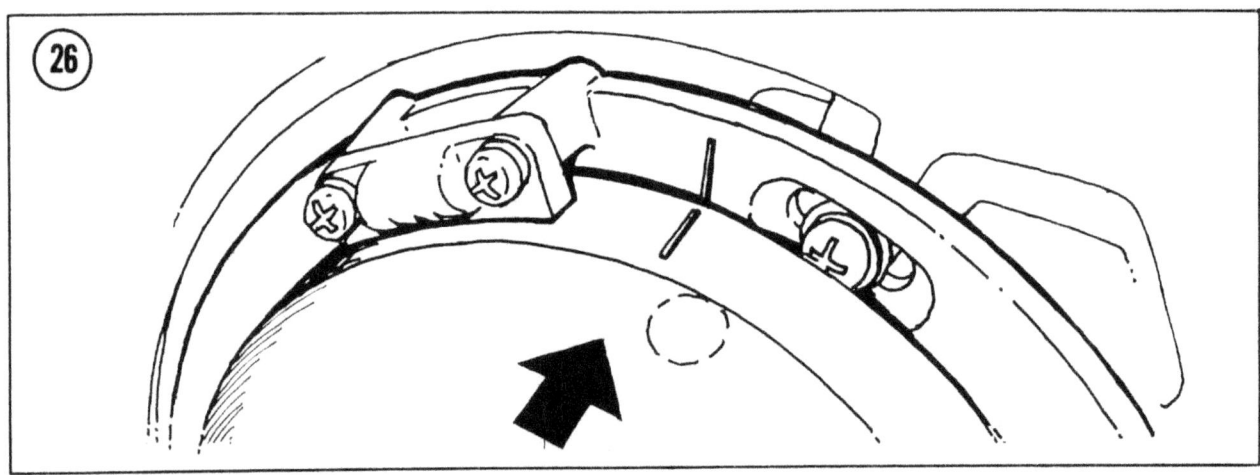

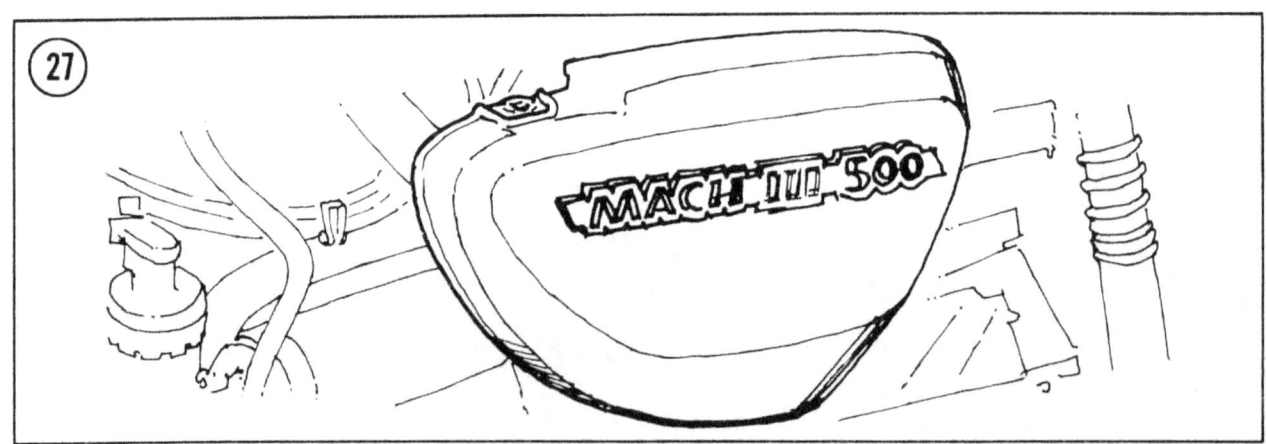

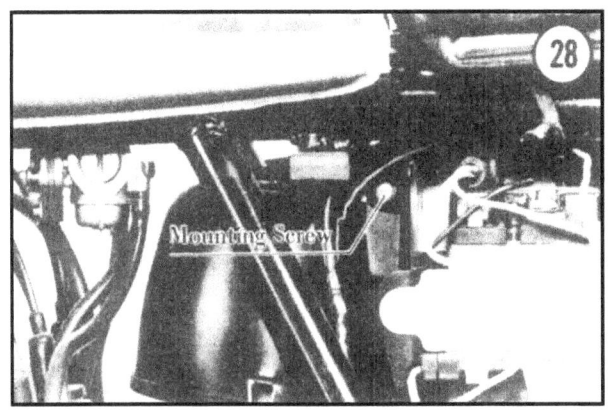

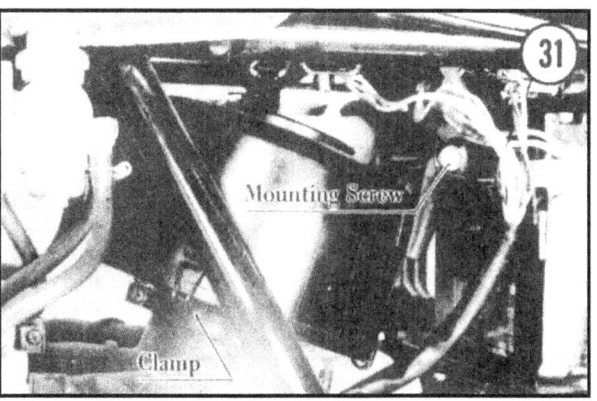

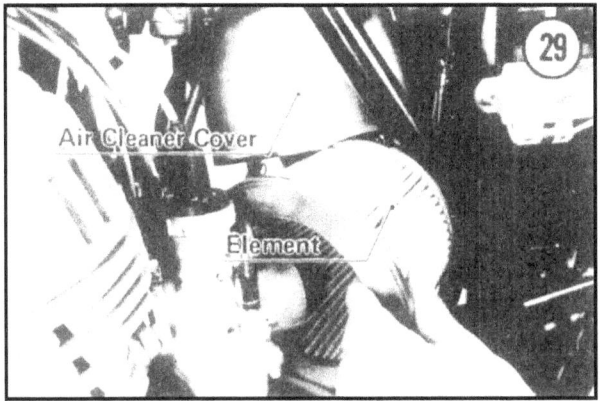

Removal, Model H2

The air cleaner element on H2 models can be removed alone, but it is easier to remove the element and housing together after first removing the left side cover mounting bracket.

1. Remove left side cover. Then lift seat and remove rubber silencer (**Figure 30**).

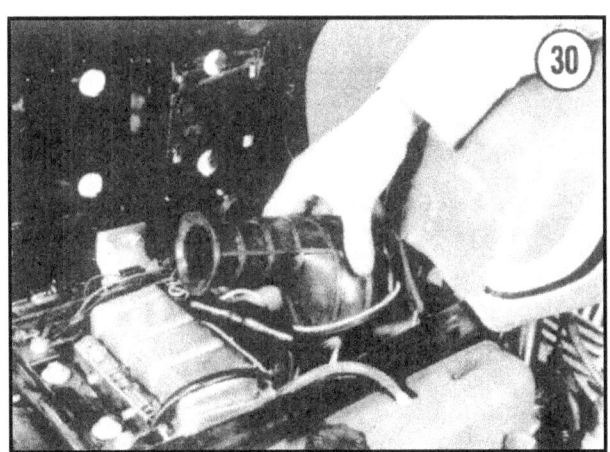

2. Loosen air duct clamp, then remove air cleaner mounting screw (**Figure 31**).

3. Remove left cover mounting bracket, then push air ducts forward and pull out air cleaner (**Figure 32**).

Removal, S and Smaller KH Series

1. Remove side cover (**Figure 33**).
2. Loosen thumb screw (**Figure 34**).

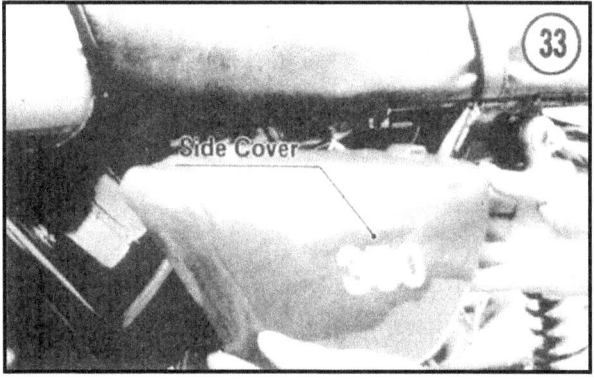

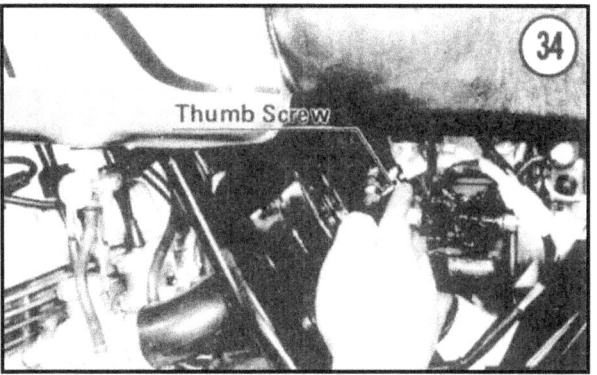

23

3. Pull out air cleaner assembly through left side of frame (**Figure 35**).

4. Remove mounting screws (**Figure 36**) to remove element from its housing.

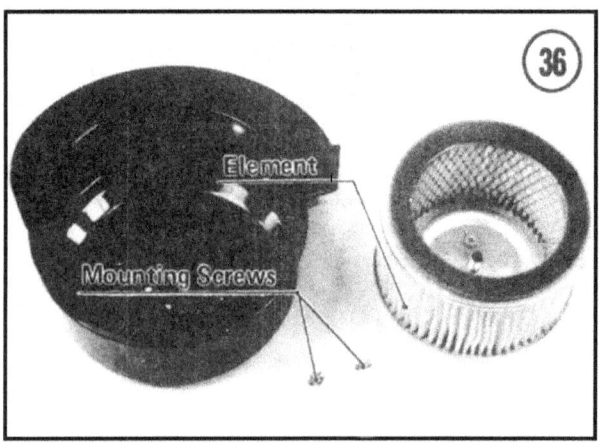

Cleaning

Clean the element in solvent, or replace if necessary. Do not permit any oil to get on the element. Clean the felt portion also, and wet with a small quantity of oil. Make sure that no oil gets on the element. If the felt is loose, glue it back into place.

CARBURETOR ADJUSTMENT

On any multicylinder engine, the carburetors must be adjusted equally to achieve proper idling performance. Follow the adjustment procedure in the order specified.

Control Cable Adjustment

Refer to **Figure 37**. There is a throttle cable which goes to each carburetor. In order for all cables to move together, it is necessary that all cables be adjusted to zero play with the throttle fully closed.

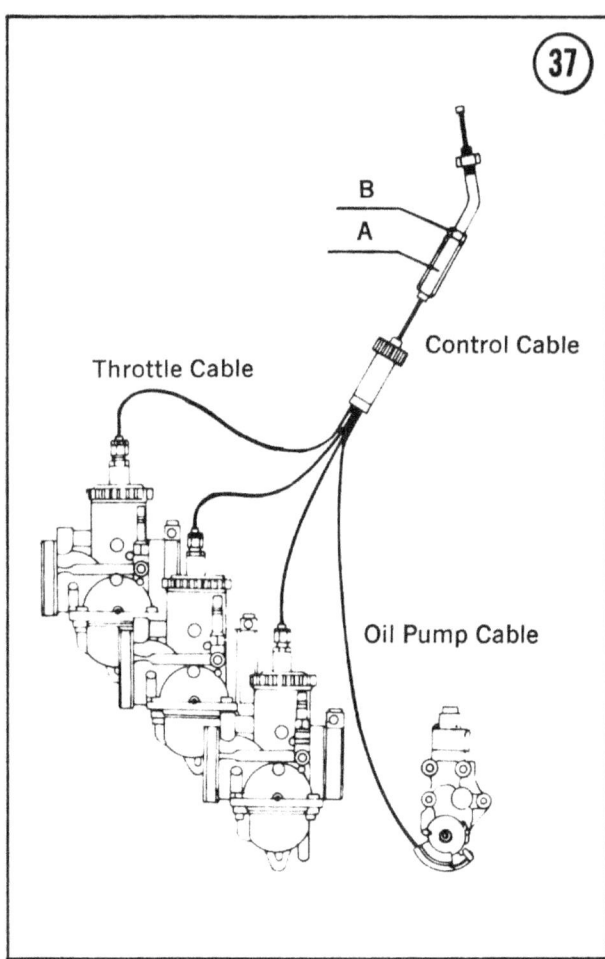

1. Refer to **Figure 38**. Loosen locknut (B) and turn cable adjuster (A) to provide slack in the cable at the throttle grip.

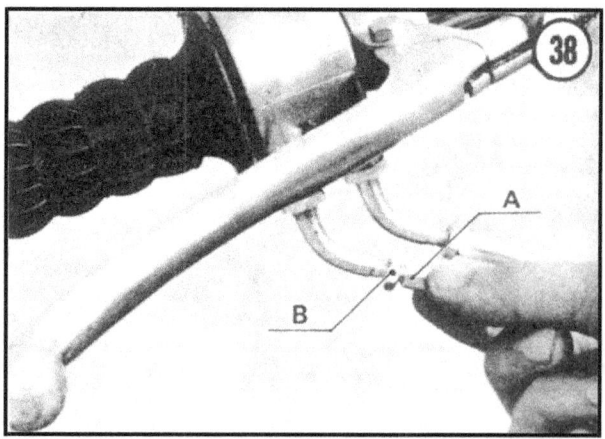

2. On some models, the idle speed screw is on top of the carburetor (**Figure 39**); on others it is on the side (**Figure 40**). Turn each idle speed screw until the throttle valves are fully closed.

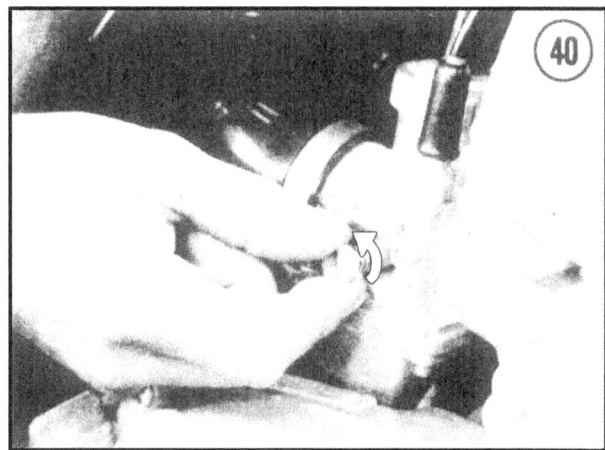

3. With all throttle valves fully closed, adjust the outer sleeve of each cable for zero play. Refer to **Figure 41**. Loosen locknut (D), turn throttle cable adjuster (C) right or left as required until no play is felt when the cable sleeve is moved up and down. Be sure to tighten locknut (D) after adjustment. Repeat for each carburetor.

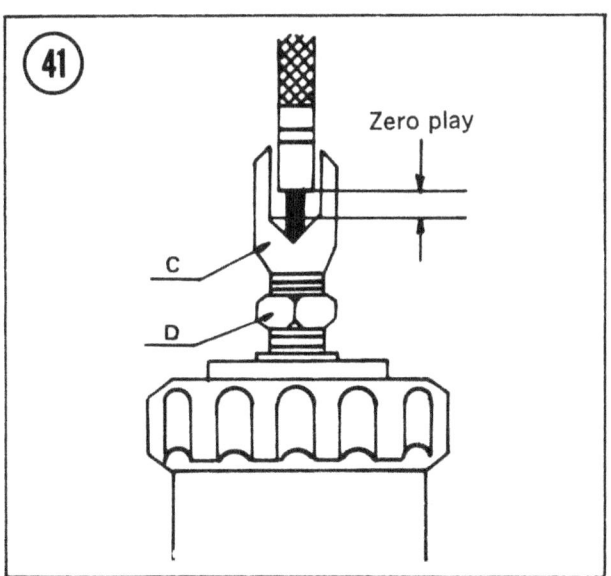

Air Screw and Idle Speed

These adjustments are so related that they are considered together. As an initial setting, turn in each air screw until it seats lightly, then back it out the number of turns specified in **Table 3**.

Table 3 AIR SCREW SETTING

Model	Turns
S1	1¾
KH250	1½
S2	1½
KH400	1¼
S3	1¾
KH500	1½
H1 (CDI)	1¼
H1 (no CDI)	1½
H2	1½-1¾

1. Start the engine and run it for a few minutes until it is thoroughly warm.

2. With the engine running, turn each idle speed screw equally to achieve the idle speed specified in **Table 4**.

Table 4 IDLE SPEED

Model	Idle RPM
S1	1,300-1,500
KH250	1,200-1,300
S2	1,300-1,500
KH400	1,300-1,500
S3	1,100-1,200
KH500	1,300-1,500
H1 (CDI)	1,150-1,250
H1 (no CDI)	1,150-1,250
H2	1,150-1,250

3. Hold a hand behind each muffler to check that exhaust pressure from each cylinder is equal. Make individual corrections as necessary with idle speed and air screws.

A more sensitive adjustment may be obtained as follows:

1. With the engine warm, remove the spark plug leads from the center and right cylinders, then

reconnect those leads to spare spark plugs and place them on the cylinder heads.

2. Start the engine and run it on the left cylinder alone.

3. Turn the idle speed screw until the engine runs slower and begins to falter (**Figure 42**).

4. Adjust the idle air screw as required to make the engine run smoothly.

5. Repeat Steps 3 and 4 to achieve the lowest stable idle speed.

6. Using the idle speed screw, adjust idle speed to the lower of the values given in Table 4.

7. Repeat Steps 2 through 6 for each of the remaining cylinders. Be sure that a spark plug is connected to each spark plug lead going to the "dead" cylinders.

> NOTE: *It may happen that spark plugs in the "dead" cylinders may become fouled during this procedure. Avoid prolonged running on one cylinder.*

8. After idle speed and mixture are adjusted equally for each cylinder, reconnect each cylinder to its spark plug lead. Then start the engine and turn each idle speed screw equally to achieve the proper idle speed.

Throttle Grip

Refer to **Figure 43**. Loosen locknut (B), then turn adjuster (A) to provide 0.08 to 0.12 in. (2 to 3mm) cable play at the throttle grip. Be sure to tighten the locknut after adjustment.

> CAUTION
> *Always check oil pump adjustment after adjusting carburetors.*

Starter Cable Adjustment

Figure 44 is a diagram of the starter cables. Refer to this illustration during the following procedure.

1. Loosen locknut (B in **Figure 45**), then turn starter lever adjuster (A) until there is some play in the starter lever.

2. With all starter plungers fully closed, adjust the outer sleeve of each starter cable at the carburetors to provide 0.04-0.08 in. (1-2mm) play

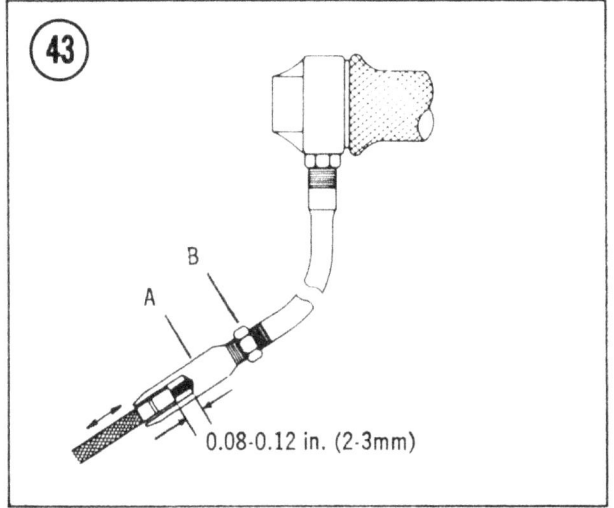

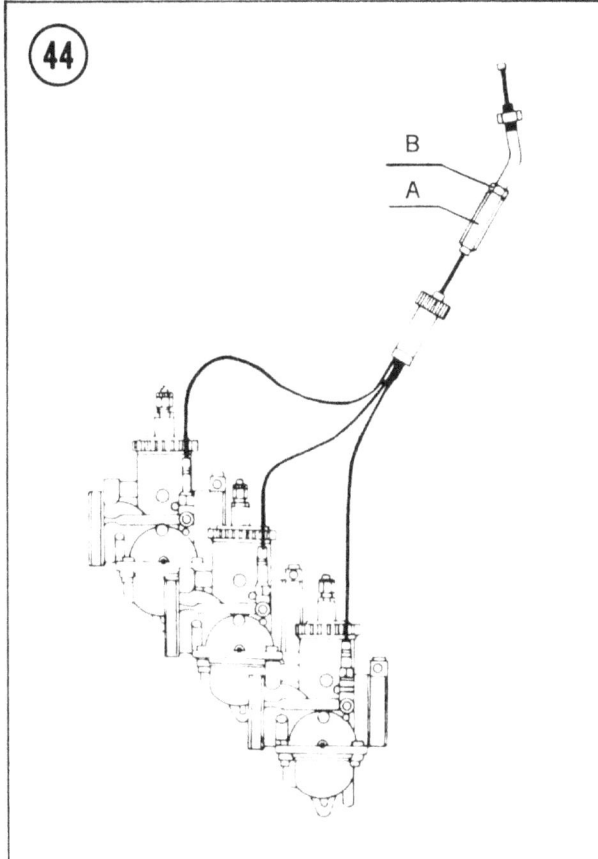

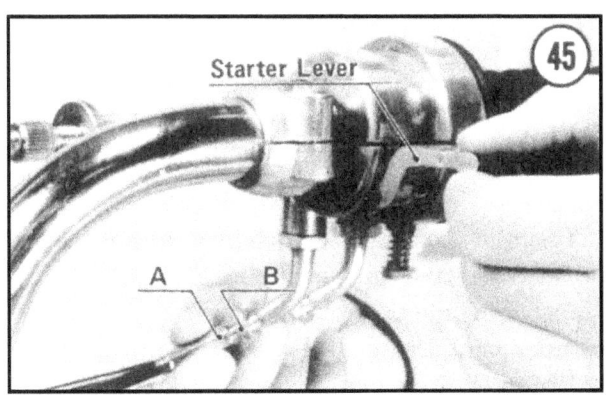

(**Figure 46**). To do so, loosen locknut (D), then turn adjuster (C) while moving the cable sleeve up and down until only a little play is felt. Be sure to tighten locknut (D).

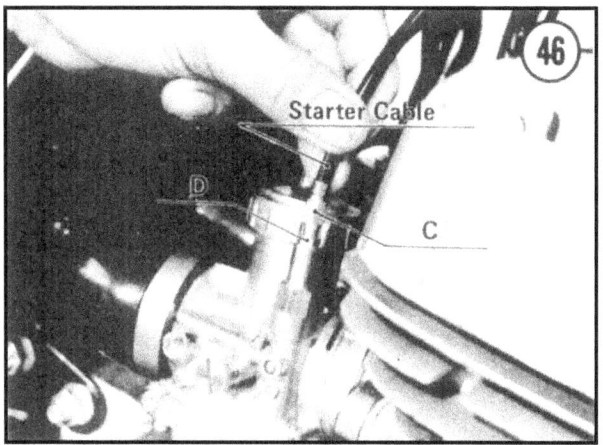

3. Finally, adjust play at the starter lever (**Figure 47**). Turn adjuster (A) to provide 0.12-0.16 in. (3-4mm) play at the starter lever. Be sure to tighten locknut (B).

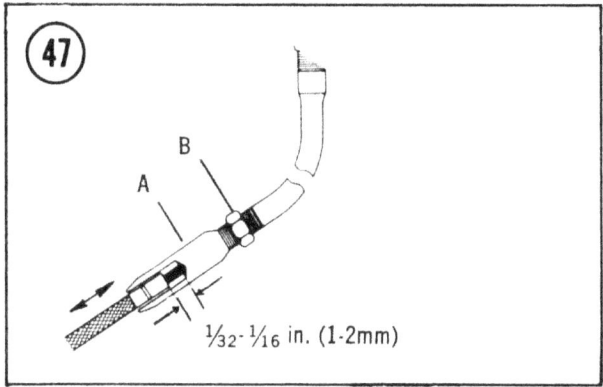

OIL PUMP ADJUSTMENT

The oil pump must increase and decrease oil flow in accordance with engine speed and load. Turn the oil pump cable adjuster so that the mark on the oil pump control lever aligns with the mark on the lever stop (**Figure 48**) when the throttle is fully closed. On some models, the cable adjuster is in the cable; on others the adjuster is at the oil pump.

CLUTCH ADJUSTMENT

Because clutch plates wear with use and clutch cables stretch with time, it is necessary to adjust the clutch every 2,000 miles.

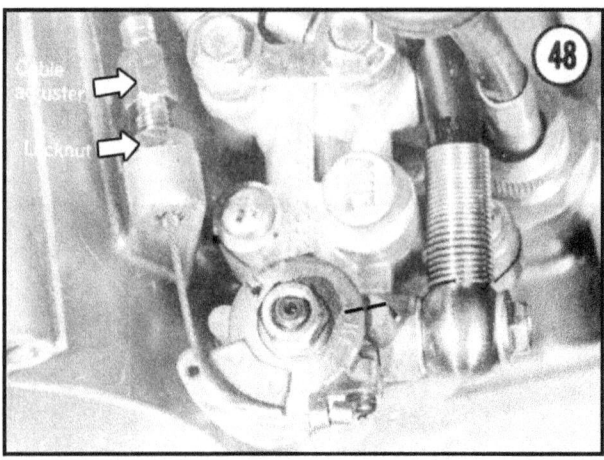

1. Refer to **Figure 49**. Loosen locknut (B), then back out screw (A) until clutch release lever moves freely.

2. Refer to **Figure 50**. Loosen locknut (D), then turn adjuster (C) until there is approximately ¼ inch (6-7mm) thread length between the adjuster and locknut.

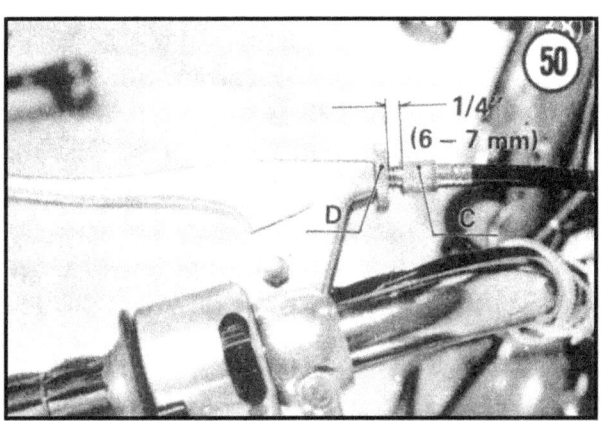

3. Refer to **Figure 51**. Loosen locknut (F), then turn cable adjuster (E) until the clutch release lever makes a 100-degree angle with its mounting screws. Be sure to tighten the locknut.

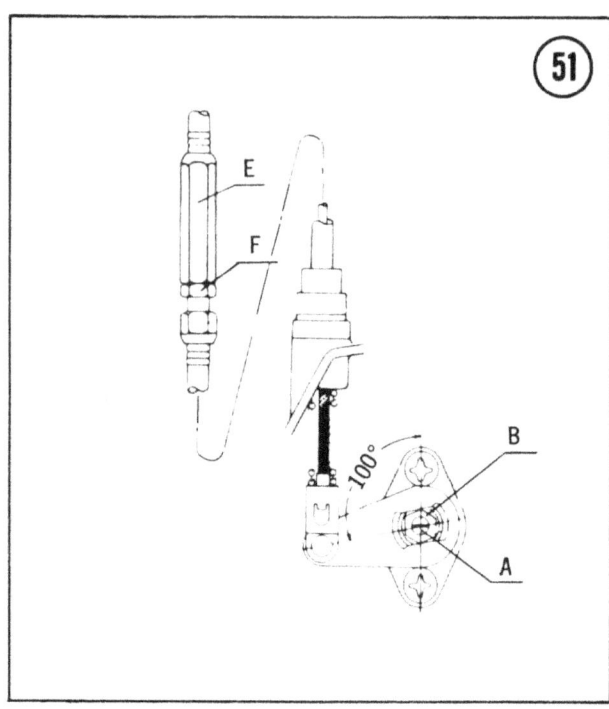

4. Turn adjustment screw A (Figure 49) in until it seats lightly. Do not continue turning past this point. Hold the screw in this position, then tighten its locknut.

5. Refer to **Figure 52**. Turn clutch hand lever adjuster (C) to provide 0.125 in. (3mm) play at the clutch lever. Be sure to tighten locknut (D).

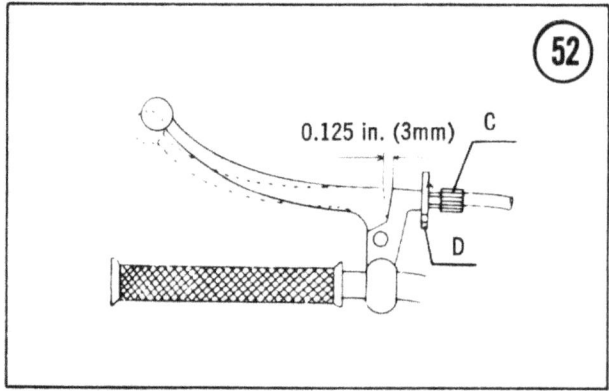

OTHER OPERATIONS

Certain other maintenance procedures should be accomplished at the time of engine tune-up. Refer to Chapter Seven for a list of recommended maintenance services to be performed at the time of engine tune-up.

CHAPTER THREE

ENGINE, TRANSMISSION, AND CLUTCH

This chapter describes removal, disassembly, service, and reassembly of the engine, transmission, and clutch. It is suggested that the engine be serviced without removing it from the chassis except for overhaul of the crankshaft assembly, transmission, gearshift mechanism, or bearings. Operating principles of piston port 2-stroke engines are also discussed in this chapter.

OPERATING PRINCIPLES

Figures 1 through 4 illustrate operating principles of 2-stroke engines. During this discussion, assume that the crankshaft is rotating counterclockwise. In **Figure 1**, as the piston travels downward, a scavenging port (A) between the crankcase and the cylinder is uncovered. Exhaust gases leave the cylinder through exhaust port (B), which is also opened by downward movement of the piston. A fresh fuel/air charge, which has previously been compressed slightly, travels from crankcase (C) to the cylinder through scavenging port (A) as the port opens. Since the incoming charge is under pressure, it rushes into the cylinder quickly and helps to expel the exhaust gases from the previous cycle.

Figure 2 illustrates the next phase of the cycle. As the crankshaft continues to rotate, the piston

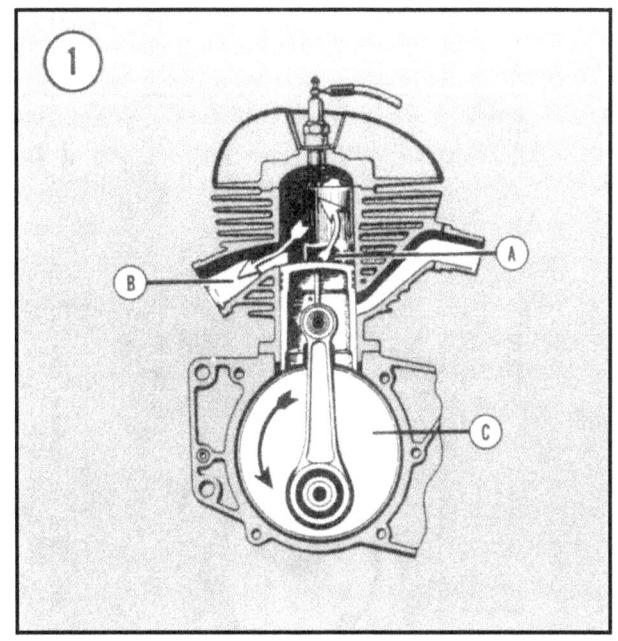

moves upward, closing the exhaust and scavenging ports. As the piston continues upward, the air/fuel mixture in the cylinder is compressed. Notice also that upward movement of the piston creates a low pressure area in the crankcase at the same time. Further upward movement of the piston uncovers intake port (D). A fresh fuel/air charge is then drawn into the crankcase through the intake port because of the low pressure created by upward piston movement.

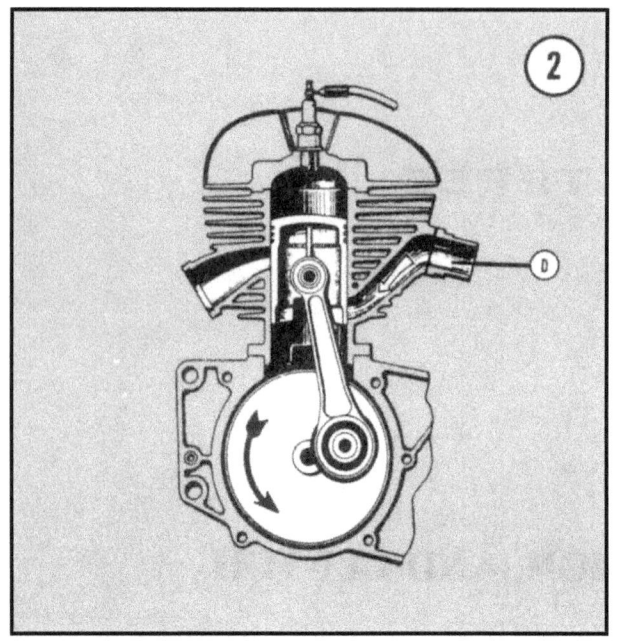

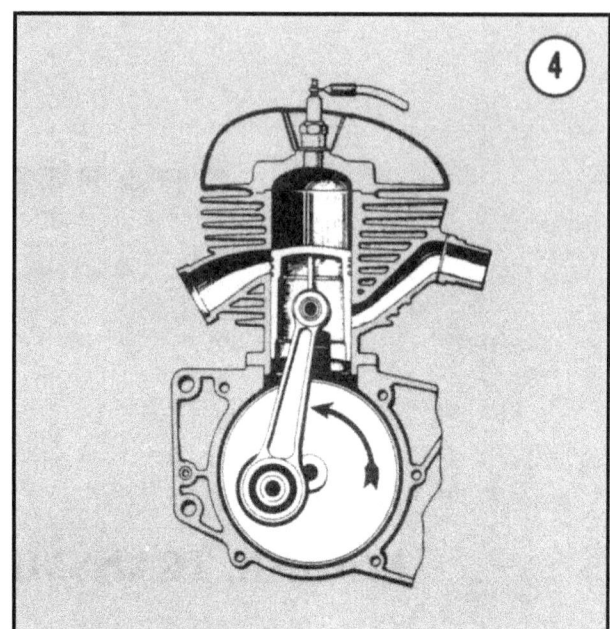

The third phase is shown in **Figure 3**. As the piston approaches top dead center, the spark plug fires, igniting the compressed mixture. The piston is then driven downward by the expanding gases.

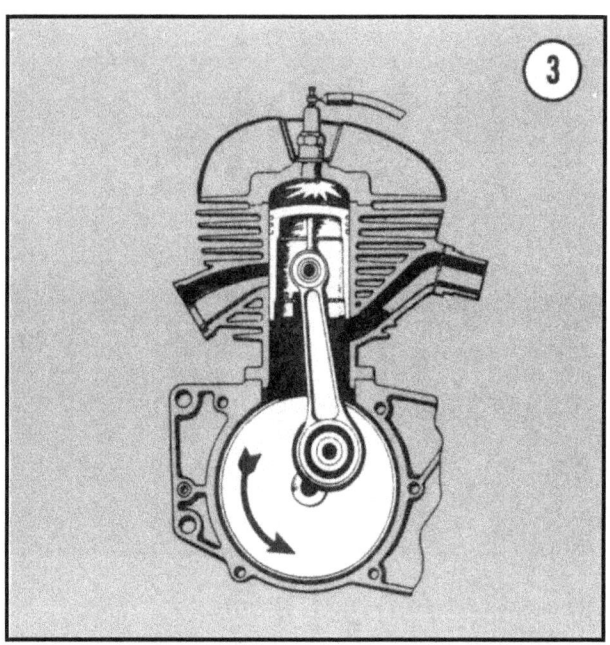

When the top of the piston uncovers the exhaust port, the fourth phase begins, as shown in **Figure 4**. The exhaust gases leave the cylinder through the exhaust port. As the piston continues downward, the intake port is closed and the mixture in the crankcase is compressed in preparation for the next cycle.

It can be seen from the foregoing discussion that every downward stroke of the piston is a power stroke. Three-cylinder engines are so arranged that a cylinder fires for each 120 degrees rotation of the crankshaft, thus producing 3 power strokes for each crankshaft revolution.

The conventional piston port engine has a design limitation in that the scavenging ports cannot be made large enough to completely clear the cylinder of exhaust gases because of the position of the intake and exhaust ports. This condition results in contamination of the fresh mixture by residual exhaust gases.

To overcome this limitation, Kawasaki triple-cylinder machines have 2 additional scavenging ports, shown in **Figure 5**, which permit more complete removal of exhaust gases which would otherwise remain in the cylinder.

The additional scavenging ports are placed to the rear of the conventional scavenging ports, and are so designed to direct the fresh fuel/air charge to the area containing the remaining exhaust gases. The action of these ports result in more efficient operation over the entire engine operating range.

ENGINE LUBRICATION

A conventional 2-stroke engine cannot receive its lubrication from an oil supply in the crankcase. Oil splash in the crankcase would be carried into the cylinder with the fuel/air charge, resulting in high oil consumption and spark plug

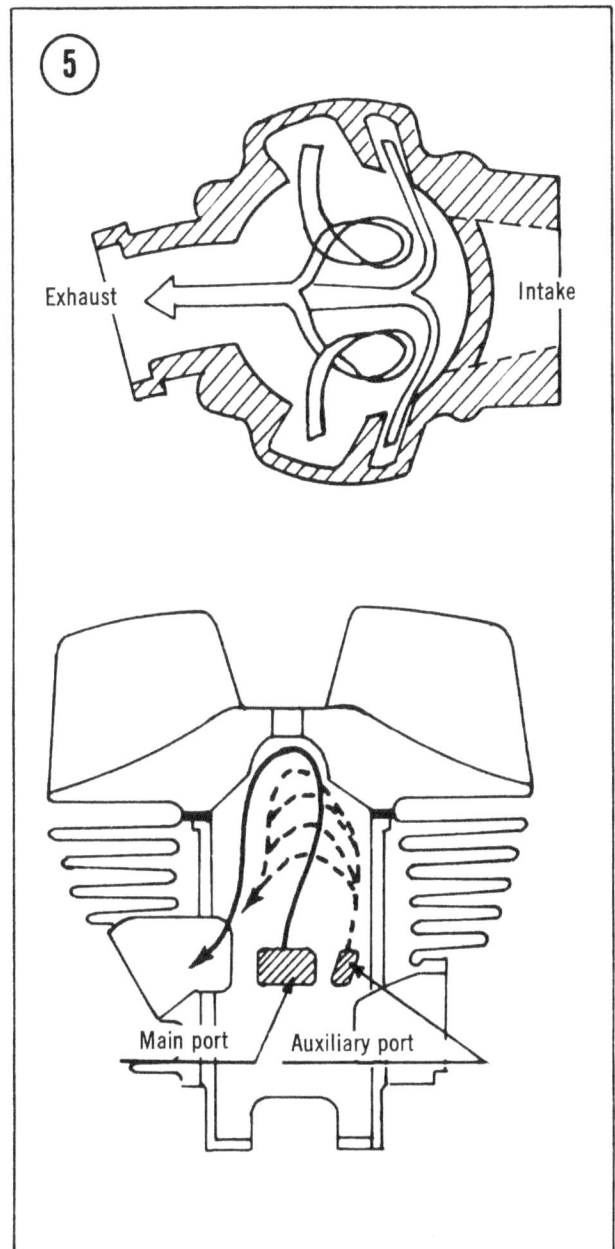

Injectolube System

The injectolube system, used on H series models, is similar to the Superlube system in that it supplies oil to the engine in varying quantities to meet engine needs. The oil pump has an additional output, however, which supplies oil under pressure to the main and connecting rod bearings (**Figure 6**) in the engine.

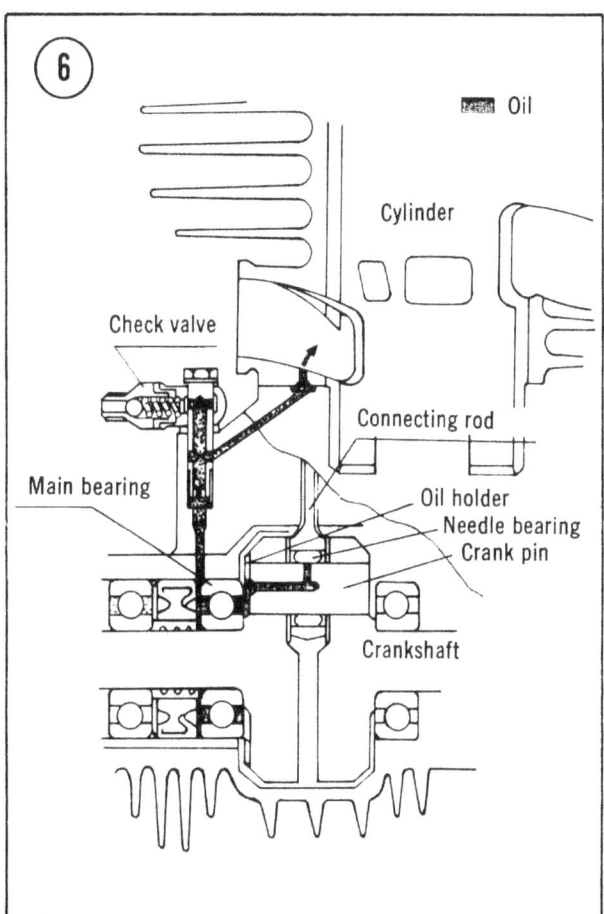

fouling. Triple-cylinder Kawasaki 2-stroke engines use one of two methods for engine lubrication.

Superlube System

This system is used on KH250, KH400, and S series machines. A separate engine-driven oil pump supplies lubricating oil from an oil tank to the engine induction tract. Output from the pump is controlled not only by engine speed, but also by throttle position, which is closely related to engine load. Therefore, the engine is supplied with the proper amount of oil under all operating conditions.

Oil Pump

Figure 7 illustrates a typical oil pump. The pump is a precision assembly; never attempt to disassemble it. Should a malfunction occur, replace it.

To check the condition of the pump, proceed as follows.

1. Mix sufficient 2-stroke oil with the fuel in the tank to produce an approximate 20 to 1 mixture, for example.

Fuel	*Oil*
1 gallon	6.4 ounces
4 liters	200 cubic centimeters

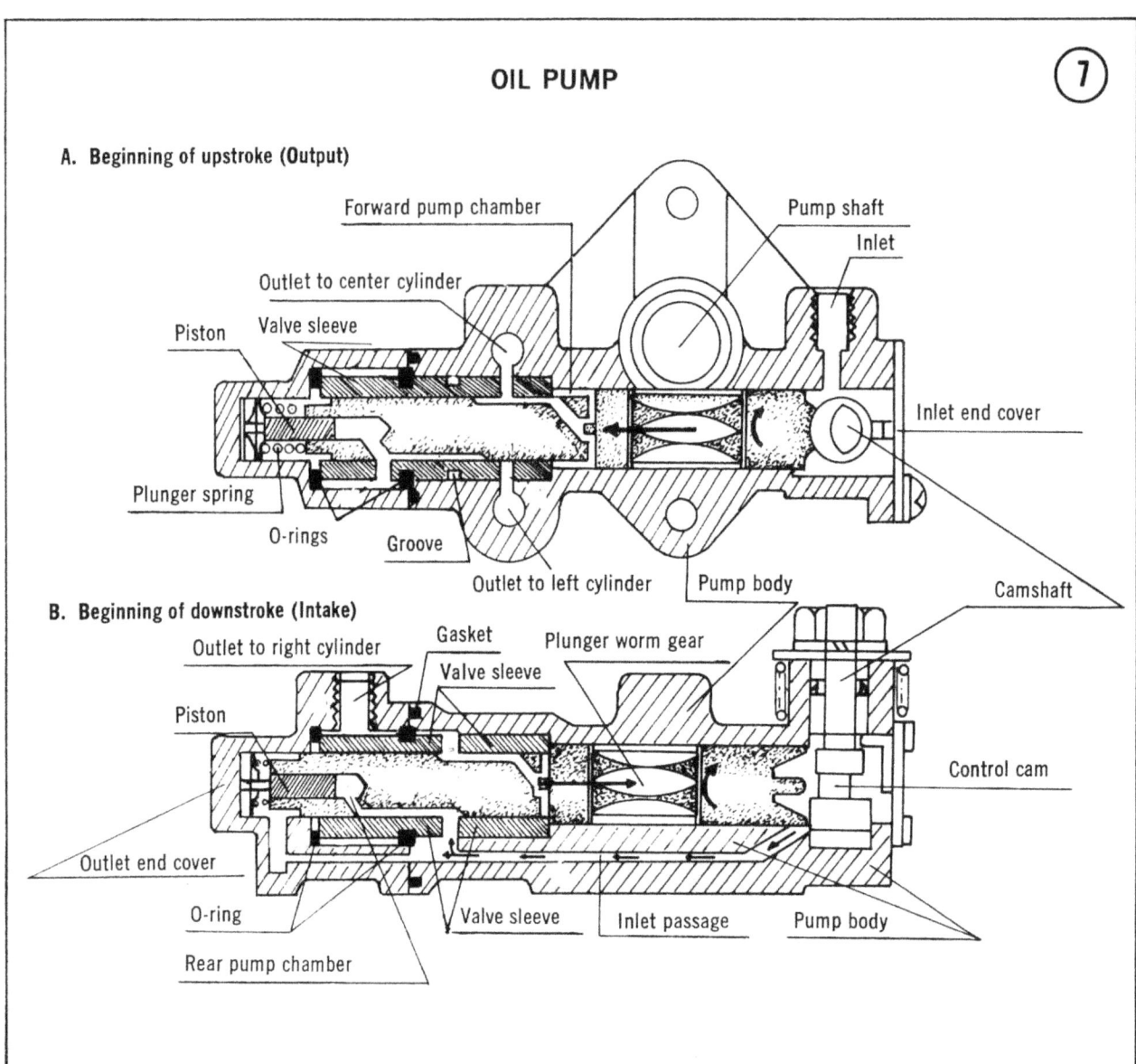

2. Remove the check valve at the crankcase. Connect the outlet from the pump to a collecting vessel by means of a suitable piece of tubing.

3. Start the engine and run it at 2,000 rpm.

4. Pull the control lever on the pump fully upward.

5. Measure the quantity of oil pumped in 3 minutes. Proper quantities are listed in **Table 1**.

Oil pump adjustment is described in Chapter Two.

ENGINE REMOVAL

1. Thoroughly clean the engine exterior of dirt, oil, and foreign material, using one of the cleaners formulated for the purpose.

2. Be sure to have the proper tools for the job. See the general information in Chapter One.

Table 1   OIL PUMP OUTPUT

Model	Oil Quantity Ounce	(Cubic Centimeters)
S1, S2*	0.108–0.128	(3.20–3.79)
S2, KH250	0.127–0.150	(3.75–4.43)
S3, KH400	0.109–0.128	(3.21–3.79)
KH500, H1	0.171–0.197	(5.05–5.83)
H2	0.228–0.255	(6.75–7.53)

*Pumps marked "S1" or "S2" on lever.

3. As you remove parts from the engine, clean them thoroughly in solvent and place them in trays in order of their disassembly. Doing so will

make reassembly faster and easier, and will ensure correct installation of all engine parts.

The procedure for removing the engine is generally similar for all models. The following steps are set forth as a guide:

1. If the engine runs, start it and let it run for a few minutes to warm the oil. Then remove the drain plug and drain transmission oil.

2. Turn fuel petcock off. Disconnect fuel lines at carburetors.

3. Remove exhaust pipes.

4. Remove oil pump cover.

5. Remove tachometer cable.

6. On machines so equipped, remove the distributor cap.

7. Remove carburetor air inlet tubes.

8. Remove carburetors.

9. Remove oil pump cable at oil pump. It is first necessary to remove the oil pump lever cover on model H1.

10. Remove oil inlet tube at oil pump. To prevent loss of oil, remove the banjo fitting from tube end, then insert a screw into end of tube.

11. Remove gearshift pedal and its associated linkage as an assembly.

12. Remove the front chain cover.

13. On S and H1 models, remove master link, then remove drive chain. When reconnecting master link, be sure that its clip is installed as shown in **Figure 8**.

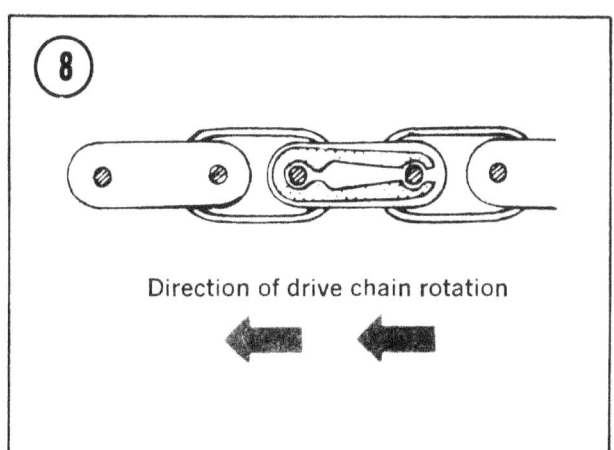

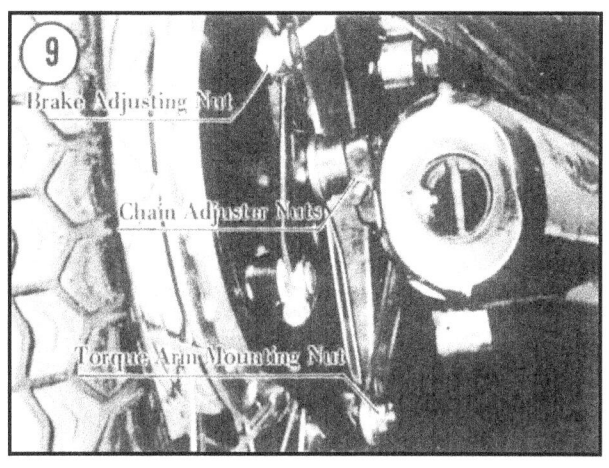

14. On H2 models, refer to **Figure 9**. Loosen rear torque arm mounting nut, brake adjustment nut, rear axle nut, and both chain tension adjusters. Then move rear wheel forward to slacken drive chain enough for removal.

15. Loosen clutch release locknut, then turn clutch adjustment nut at clutch lever to allow sufficient play to remove clutch cable from clutch release lever.

16. Disconnect alternator wiring.

17. Examine engine carefully. Make sure that there are no more cables on other attachments between it and the frame.

18. Remove engine mounting bolts. Bolt locations are shown in **Figure 10**.

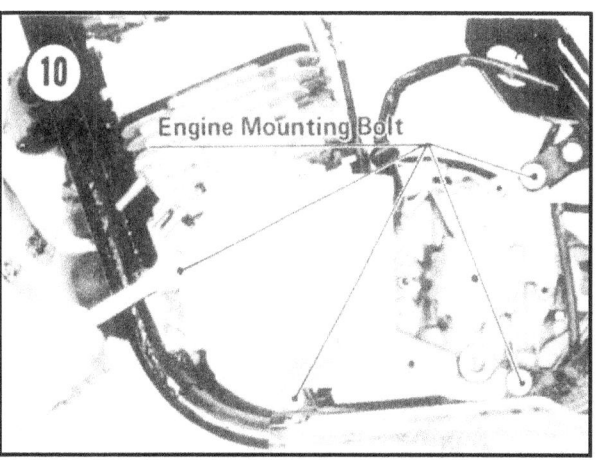

19. Straddle motorcycle, then lift engine from frame.

20. Reverse the removal procedure to install the engine. Be sure to check the following items before you start the engine.

    a. Oil supply
    b. Transmission oil level
    c. Clutch adjustment
    d. Oil pump and throttle cables

e. Drive chain adjustment
f. Engine mounting bolts
g. Ignition timing

CYLINDERS AND CYLINDER HEADS

Figure 11 is an exploded view of a typical cylinder and cylinder head assembly. Cylinders are cast from lightweight aluminum alloy, and are lined with cast iron sleeves. **Figure 12** illustrates cylinder construction. Note that the cylinder sleeve is of sufficient thickness to permit boring and honing after long usage or a piston seizure.

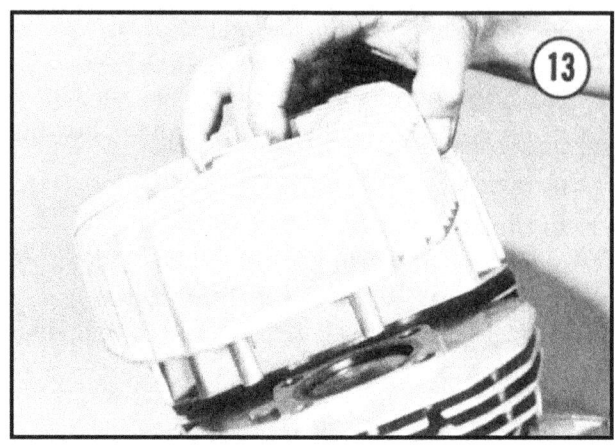

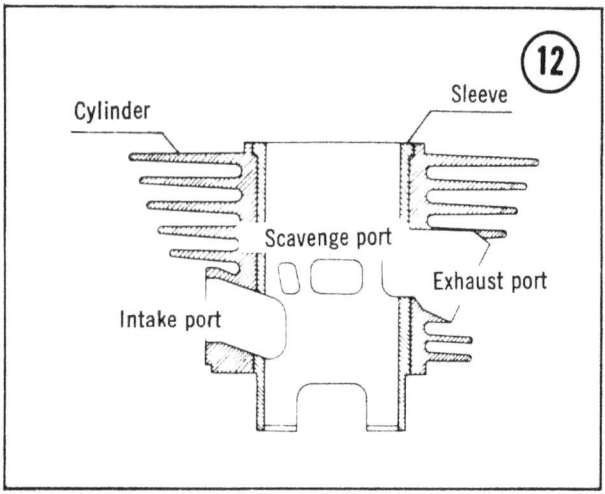

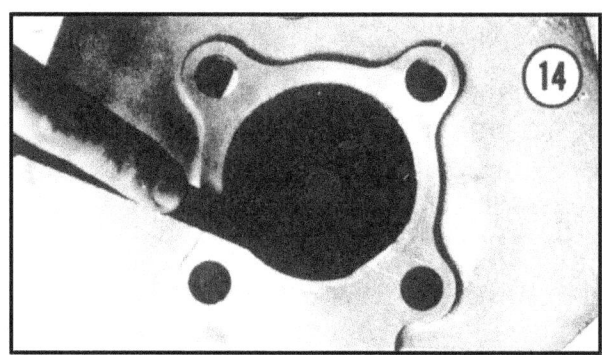

ure 14. Be careful not to damage the gasket surface.

Cylinder Head Removal and Installation

Allow engine to cool thoroughly, then loosen each cylinder head nut a little bit at a time, in crisscross order, until each one turns freely. Then remove all nuts. Lift off each cylinder head and its gasket (**Figure 13**). It may be necessary to tap cylinder heads lightly with a rubber mallet to loosen them; if so, take care not to break any cooling fins.

Always use new gaskets upon reassembly. Torque cylinder head nuts in crisscross order, a little bit at a time, to 16 ft.-lb. (2.2 mkg).

Removing Carbon Deposits

Carbon deposits in the combustion chamber result in an increase in compression ratio and can cause preignition, overheating, and excessive fuel consumption. To remove these deposits, scrape them off with the rounded end of a hacksaw blade or a screwdriver, as shown in Fig-

Cylinder Removal and Installation

With the cylinder head removed, tap the cylinder around the exhaust port with a plastic mallet, then pull it away from the crankcase (**Figure 15**). Stuff clean rags into the crankcase openings to prevent entry of any foreign material. Before installing cylinders, be sure that each piston ring end gap is aligned with the locating pin in the ring groove. Lubricate the piston and cylinder, then insert the piston into the lower end of the cylinder. It will be necessary to compress each piston ring as it goes into the cylinder. **Figure 16** illustrates this operation. Always use new cylinder base gaskets upon reassembly.

Be sure that gasket sealer does not block the lubrication hole in the base of cylinders (**Figure 17**), or the corresponding holes in the cylinder base gasket or crankcase casting.

Checking Cylinders

Measure cylinder wall wear at the locations shown in **Figure 18** with a cylinder gauge or inside micrometer. Position the measuring instrument parallel and then at right angles to the

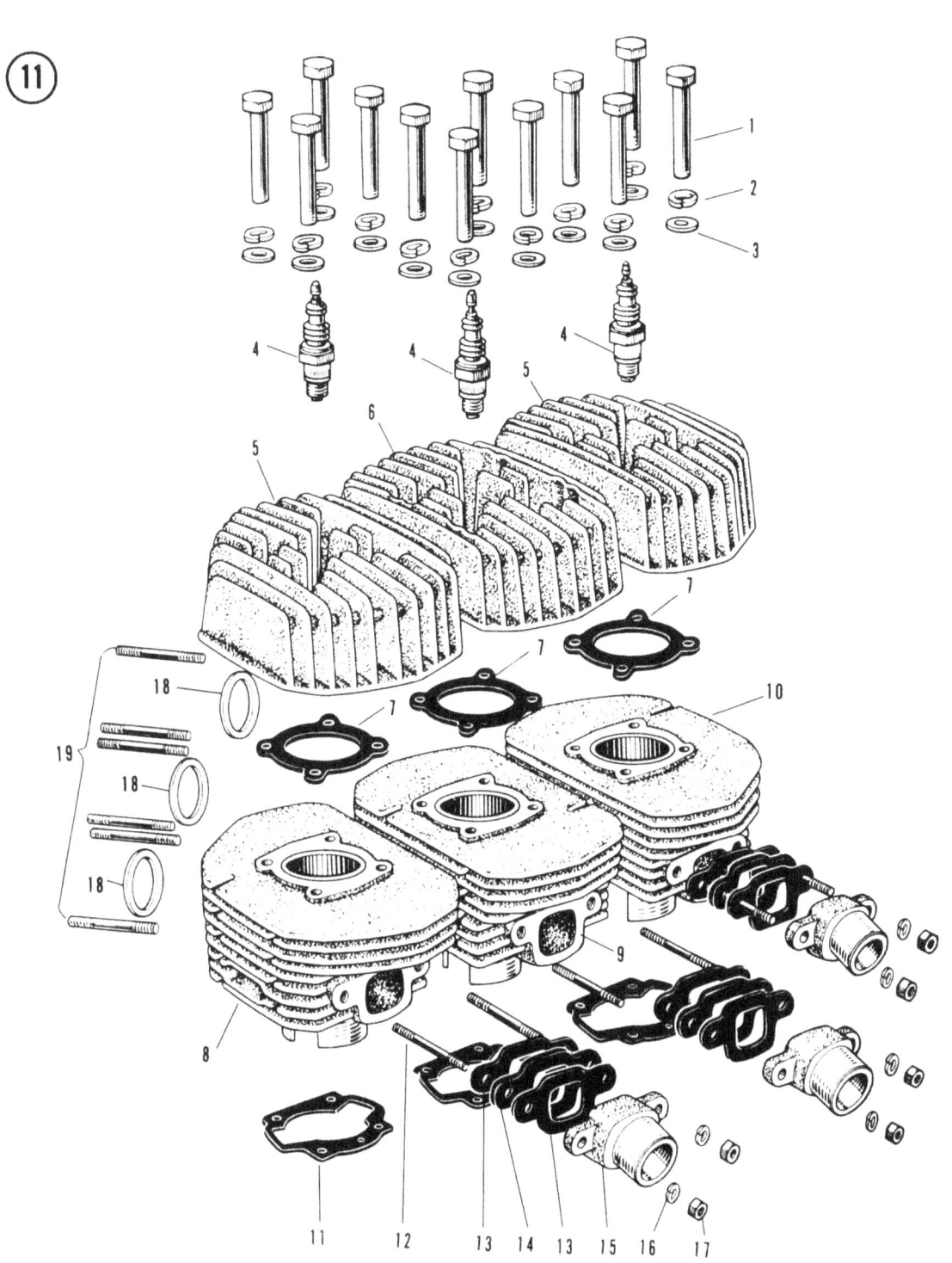

CYLINDER AND CYLINDER HEAD

1. Nut
2. Spring washer
3. Plain washer
4. Spark plug
5. Cylinder head
6. Cylinder head
7. Cylinder head gasket
8. Cylinder with Helisert insert or stud
9. Cylinder with Helisert or stud
10. Cylinder with Helisert insert
11. Cylinder base gasket
12. Stud
13. Air inlet gasket
14. Heat insulator
15. Air inlet
16. Spring washer
17. Nut
18. Exhaust pipe gasket

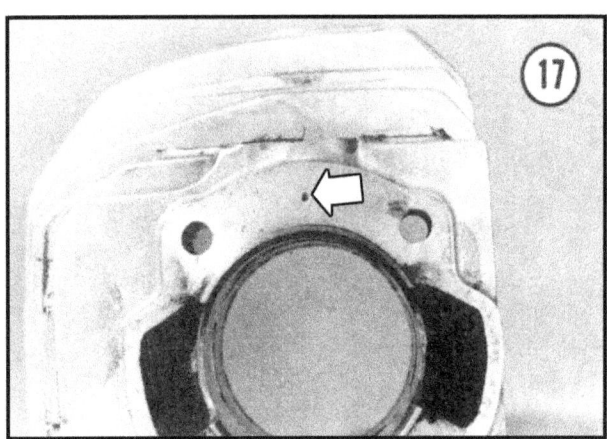

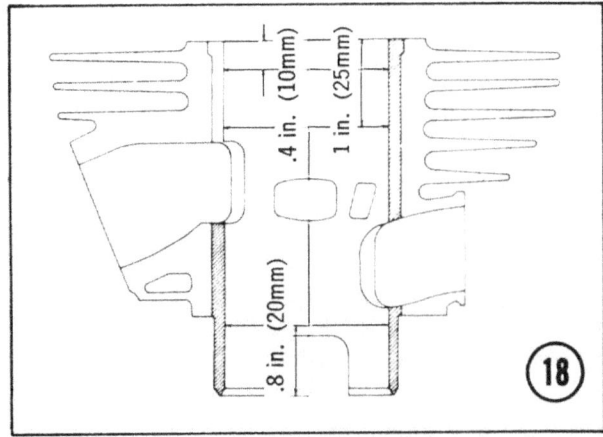

crankshaft at each depth. If any measurement exceeds the service limit, or if the difference between any 2 measurements exceeds 0.002 in. (0.05mm) rebore and hone the cylinder to the next oversize, or replace the cylinder. Pistons are available in oversizes of 0.02 in. (0.50mm) and 0.04 in. (1.00mm). After boring and honing, the difference between maximum and minimum diameters must not be more than 0.0004 in. (0.01mm). Standard measurements and service limits are listed in **Table 2**.

Table 2 CYLINDER STANDARDS

Model	Standard Dimension Inches	(mm)	Service Limit Inches	(mm)
S1	1.772	(45.00)	1.778	(45.15)
KH250	1.772	(45.00)	1.778	(45.15)
S2	2.086	(53.00)	2.093	(53.15)
S3	2.244	(57.00)	2.250	(57.15)
KH400	2.244	(57.00)	2.250	(57.15)
H1	2.362	(60.00)	2.368	(60.15)
KH500	2.362	(60.00)	2.368	(60.15)
H2	2.795	(71.00)	2.801	(71.15)

Removing Carbon Deposits

Scrape the carbon deposits from around the cylinder exhaust port. The rounded end of a hacksaw blade is a suitable tool for carbon removal.

PISTON, PISTON PIN, AND PISTON RINGS

Removing the Piston Pin

Remove the clips at each end of the piston pin with needle nose pliers (**Figure 19**). Then pull out the piston pin (**Figure 20**).

> CAUTION
> *Mark the top of the pistons so that they can be reinstalled in the same cylinder.*

Replacing Piston Rings

Remove the piston rings by spreading the top ring with a thumb on each end, as shown in **Figure 21**. Then remove the ring from the top of the piston. Repeat the procedure for the remaining ring. The expander ring (**Figures 22 and 23**)

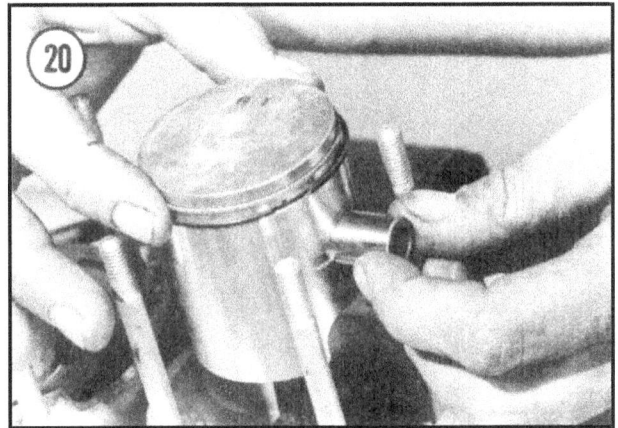

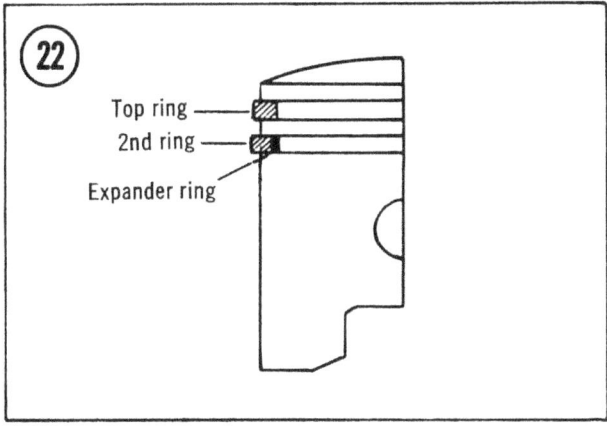

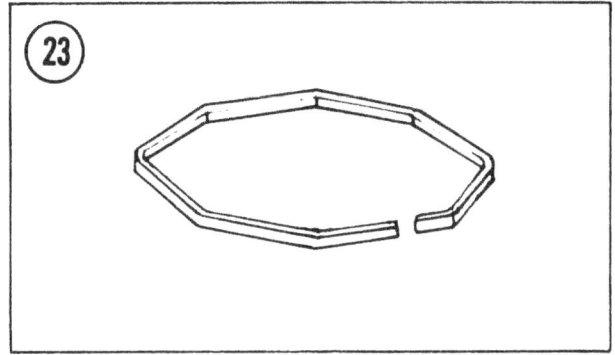

may be removed easily by prying the ends apart with a narrow screwdriver.

Scrape the carbon from the head of the piston (**Figure 24**). Then clean all carbon and gum from the piston ring grooves (**Figure 25**) using a broken piston ring, or a ring groove cleaning tool. Any deposits left in the grooves will cause the rings to stick, thereby causing gas blow-by and loss of power.

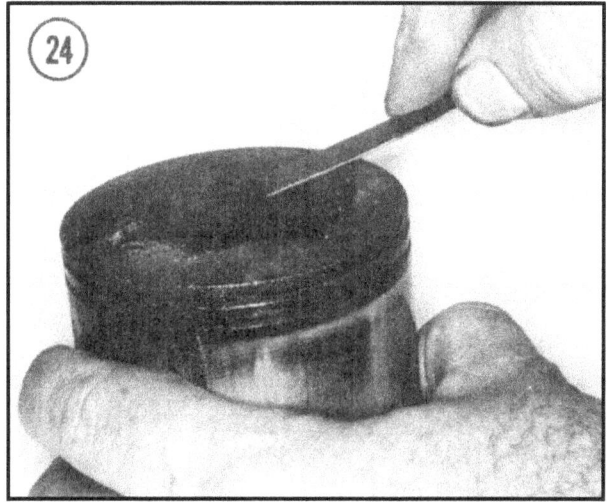

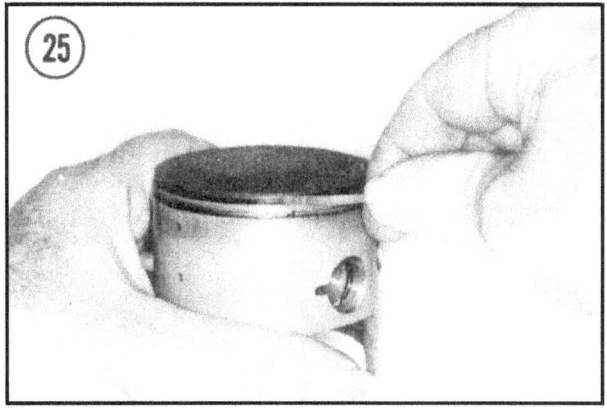

Measure each ring for wear as shown in **Figure 26**. Insert the ring 0.2 in. (5mm) into the cylinder, then measure ring gap (a) with a feeler

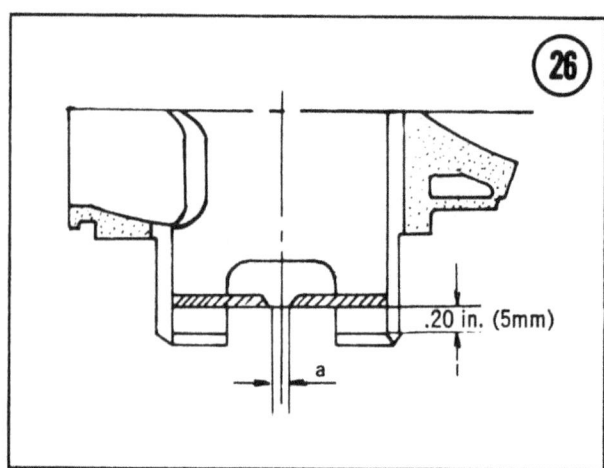

calipers at measurement locations shown in **Figure 28**. Measurements should be as specified in **Table 3**.

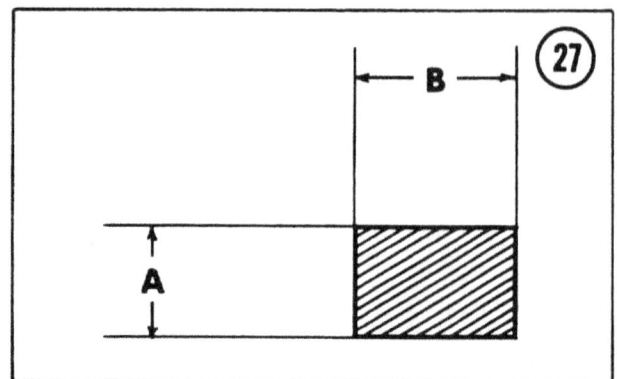

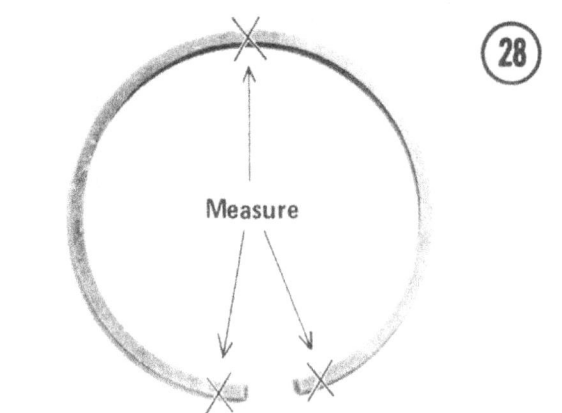

gauge. To ensure that the ring is positioned squarely in the cylinder, push it into place with the head of the piston. Standard gap for models S, KH250, and KH400 is 0.006-0.014 in. (0.15-0.35mm). If the gap exceeds 0.028 in. (0.7mm), replace all rings. Standard gap for H1 models is 0.008-0.012 in. (0.2-0.3mm) and H2 models is 0.008-0.016 in. (0.2-0.4mm). If the gap exceeds 0.031 in. (0.8mm), replace all rings.

There is a difference in tension between the center and ends of the piston ring, and consequently a difference in wear. Therefore, measure "A" and "B" (**Figure 27**) with vernier

Table 3   PISTON RING STANDARDS

Model		"A" Inch	(Millimeters)	"B" Inch	(Millimeters)
S1	(top)	0.059	(1.5)	0.083	(2.1)
	(bottom)	0.059	(1.5)	0.083	(2.1)
KH250	(top)	0.059	(1.5)	0.083	(2.1)
	(bottom)	0.059	(1.5)	0.083	(2.1)
S2	(top)	0.059	(1.5)	0.091	(2.3)
	(bottom)	0.059	(1.5)	0.091	(2.3)
S3	(top)	0.059	(1.5)	0.094	(2.4)
	(bottom)	0.059	(1.5)	0.079	(2.0)
KH400	(top)	0.059	(1.5)	0.094	(2.4)
	(bottom)	0.059	(1.5)	0.079	(2.0)
H1	(top)	0.059	(1.5)	0.098	(2.5)
	(bottom)	0.059	(1.5)	0.075	(1.9)
KH500	(top)	0.059	(1.5)	0.098	(2.5)
	(bottom)	0.059	(1.5)	0.075	(1.9)
H2	(top)	0.059	(1.5)	0.118	(3.0)
	(bottom)	0.059	(1.5)	0.106	(2.7)

Piston rings must have enough tension so that they bear snugly against the cylinder wall to prevent compression leakage. However, too much tension results in rapid wear and may result in piston seizure. Check for proper piston ring tension by measuring the gap between the ends of the ring, with the ring unrestrained. Ring gaps should be as specified in **Table 4**.

To check the fit of the piston ring in its groove, slip the outer surface of the ring into the groove next to the locating pin, then roll the ring completely around the piston (**Figure 29**). If any binding occurs, determine and correct the cause before proceeding. Then measure clearance between each ring and its groove at several places around the piston, as shown in **Figure 30**. Replace the piston and/or the ring if clearance exceeds the service limits specified in **Table 5**.

When replacing piston rings, install the lower one first. Be sure that any printing on the ring is toward the top of the piston. Spread the rings carefully with your thumbs, just enough to slip them over the piston. Align the end gaps with the locating pin in each ring groove. The top ring can be identified by its chromed outer surface.

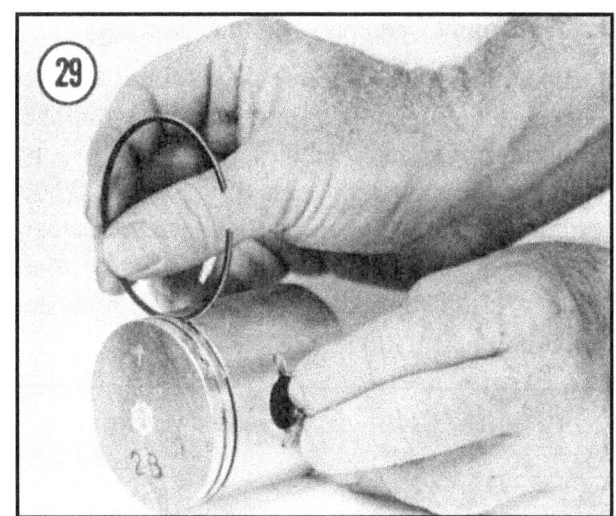

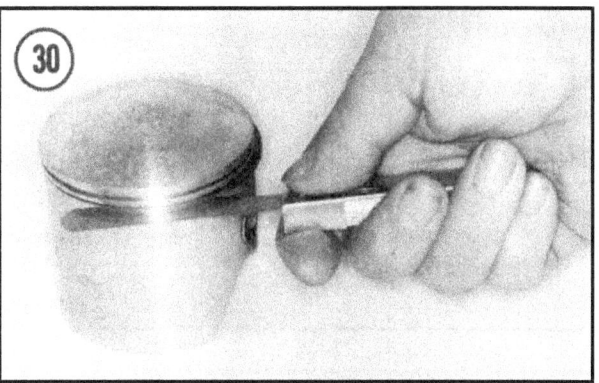

Table 4   PISTON RING GAP

Model	Top Ring Gap Inch	(Millimeters)	Bottom Ring Gap Inch	(Millimeters)
S1	0.24	(6.0)	0.24	(6.0)
KH250	0.24	(6.0)	0.24	(6.0)
S2	0.26	(6.5)	0.26	(6.5)
S3	0.24	(6.0)	0.34	(8.5)
KH400	0.24	(6.0)	0.34	(8.5)
H1	0.28	(7.0)	0.37	(9.5)
KH500	0.28	(7.0)	0.37	(9.5)
H2	0.32	(8.0)	0.32	(8.0)

Table 5   RING CLEARANCE SPECIFICATIONS

Ring	Standard Clearance Inch	(Millimeter)	Service Limit Inch	(Millimeter)
Top	0.0035-0.0051	(0.09-0.13)	0.0067	(0.17)
Bottom	0.0020-0.0035	(0.05-0.09)	0.0047	(0.12)

Checking and Correcting Piston Clearance

Piston clearance (**Figure 31**) is the difference between the maximum piston diameter and the minimum cylinder diameter. Measure the outside diameter of the piston skirt (**Figure 32**) at right angles to the piston pin. The measurement should be made 0.2 in. (5mm) from the bottom of the piston. Proper piston clearances are listed in **Table 6**.

Table 6 PISTON CLEARANCE

Model	Piston Clearance Inch	(Millimeters)
S1*	0.0010	(0.025)
S1 and KH250	0.0006	(0.016)
S2	0.0012	(0.031)
S3 and KH400	0.0032	(0.082)
1973 H1	0.0026	(0.066)
1974 H1	0.0024	(0.061)
H2	0.0029	(0.074)

*S1 engine No. 0-04593

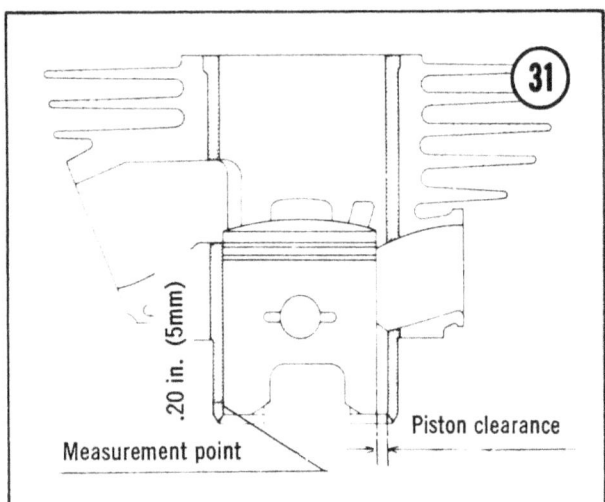

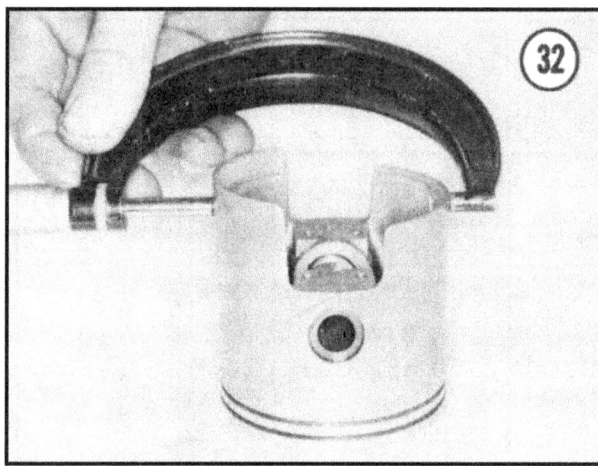

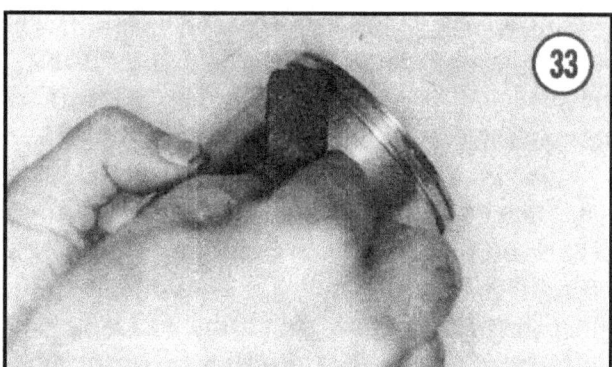

A piston showing signs of seizure will result in noise, loss of power, and damage to the cylinder wall. If such a piston is reused without correction, another seizure will develop. To correct this condition, lightly smooth the affected area with No. 400 emery paper or a fine oilstone (**Figure 33**). Replace the piston if it is deeply scratched.

Small End Bearing

Assemble the piston pin, needle bearing, and connecting rod. Then measure radial play. Replace the bearing and/or the piston pin if clearance is over the service limit, or if there are scratches on the piston pin. Standard clearance for all models is 0.00012-0.00088 in. (0.003-0.022mm). The service limit for all models is 0.004 in. (0.10mm).

Piston Installation

Install the piston with the arrow mark pointing toward the front of the machine. This is important because the hole for the piston pin is offset slightly to prevent piston slap, as shown in **Figure 34**. Be sure that each piston pin snap ring is installed so that its opening does not face either piston groove (**Figure 35**). Always use new snap rings upon assembly. If pistons are reused, they must be installed in their original positions.

LEFT CRANKCASE COVERS

On the left side of the engine are the left cover and front chain case cover. Under these covers are the engine sprocket, alternator, and clutch release mechanism.

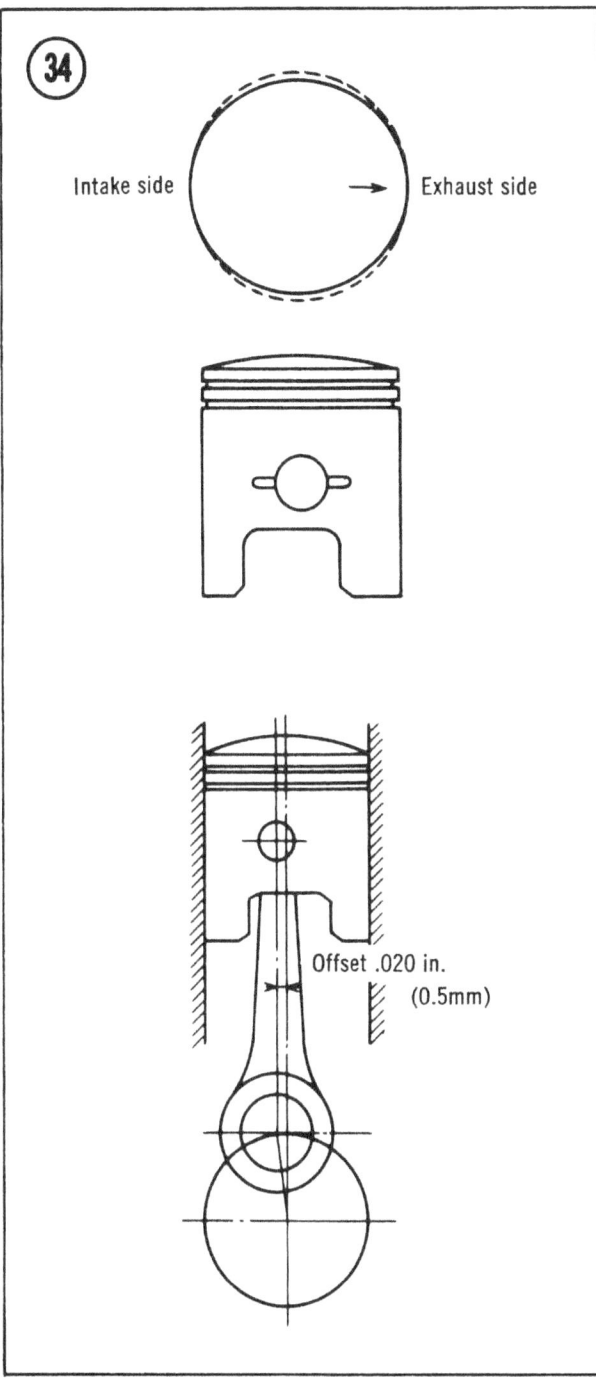

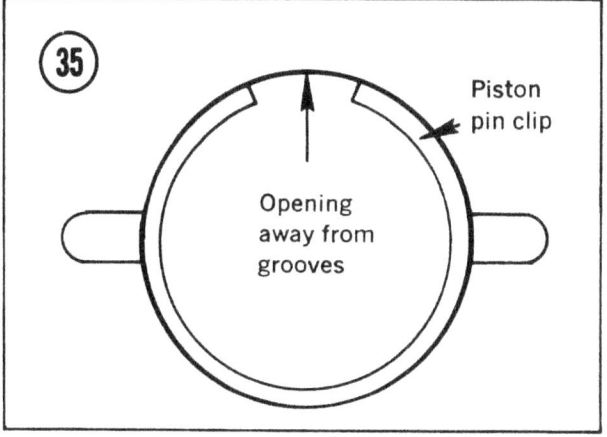

To disassemble the engine left side, first remove the front chain case cover and gearshift pedal if they have not already been removed. Then remove the attaching screws and pull off the left cover (**Figure 36**).

Reverse the disassembly procedure to reassemble the left engine cover.

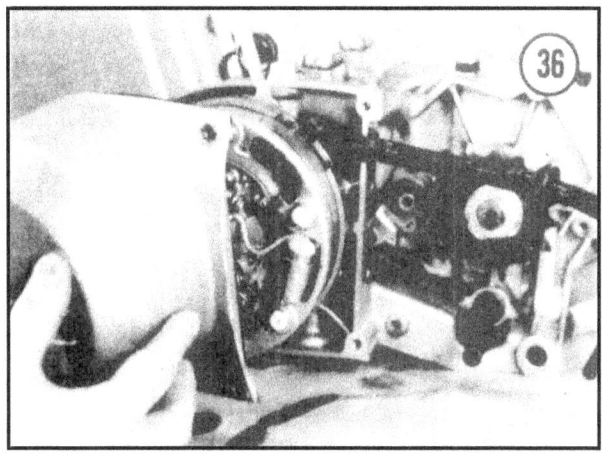

ENGINE SPROCKET

The engine sprocket is subject to wear and abrasion from sand and dust, which tend to collect on the sprocket. To minimize wear, the sprocket is made from abrasion resistant steel.

Removal

1. Straighten the tab on the lockwasher, using a small hammer and chisel (**Figure 37**).

2. Hold the sprocket in position (**Figure 38**), then remove the sprocket nut and sprocket.

Inspection

A worn sprocket results in excessive chain noise, and will shorten the life of the chain.

Measure the root diameter, as shown in **Figure 39**. Replace the sprocket if it shows any defects, or if the root diameter is less than specified in **Table 7**.

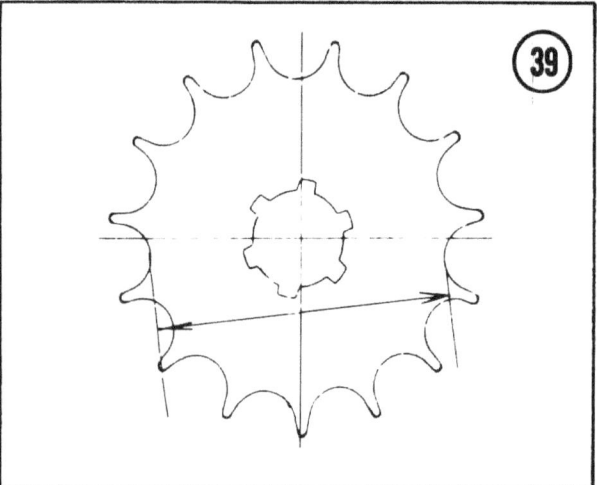

Installation

Reverse the removal procedure to install the sprocket. Use a new lockwasher, and be sure to bend up the tab.

ALTERNATOR

All 3-cylinder models are equipped with alternators as the source of electrical power. Removal and installation only are discussed in this section. For details of alternator troubleshooting and service, refer to Chapter Four.

Removal

1. Restrain crankshaft from turning. If a suitable tool is not available, feed a rolled-up rag between the primary drive and primary driven gears under the right engine cover.

2. Remove wire from the neutral indicator switch (**Figure 40**).

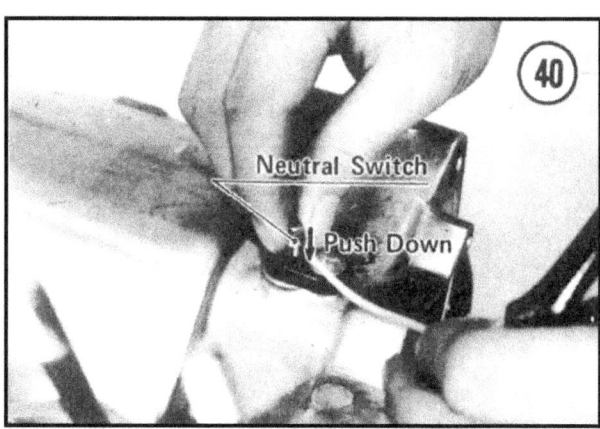

3. Remove mounting bolt, then pull off signal generator rotor (CDI models only), as shown in **Figure 41**.

Table 7   ENGINE SPROCKET SPECIFICATIONS

Sprocket Teeth	Standard Dimension		Wear Limit	
	Inches	(Millimeters)	Inches	(Millimeters)
14	2.41	(61.2)	2.38	(60.4)
15	2.59	(65.8)	2.56	(65.0)
16	2.80	(71.2)	2.77	(70.4)

4. Remove timing cam bolt on models without CDI, as shown in **Figure 42**.

5. Remove stator assembly (**Figure 43**).
6. Remove rotor retaining bolt (**Figure 44**).
7. Using a suitable puller, remove alternator rotor (**Figure 45**).
8. Remove shaft key.

Installation

Reverse the removal procedure to install the alternator. On CDI models, make sure that the

key slot is aligned with the crankshaft key. Also, align the signal generator rotor slot with the signal generator rotor alignment pin, as shown in **Figure 46**.

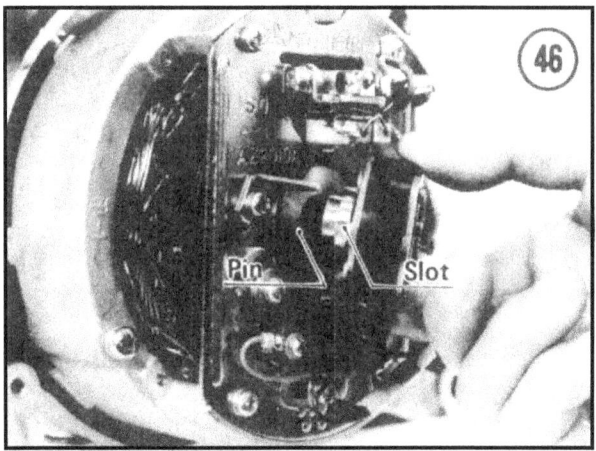

On models without CDI, align the timing cam pin with the rotor key slot (**Figure 47**).

RIGHT CRANKCASE COVER

Under the right crankcase cover are the oil pump, tachometer drive, and distributor on models so equipped. Additionally, the right crankcase cover forms the outer part of the clutch housing.

Cover Removal

1. Remove the oil pump cover, oil pump cable, oil pump inlet tube, and tachometer cable if these items have not been removed previously. Refer to the section on engine removal.

2. Remove the kickstarter pedal.

3. On models so equipped, remove the distributor cap clamp, then pull off the distributor cap (**Figure 48**).

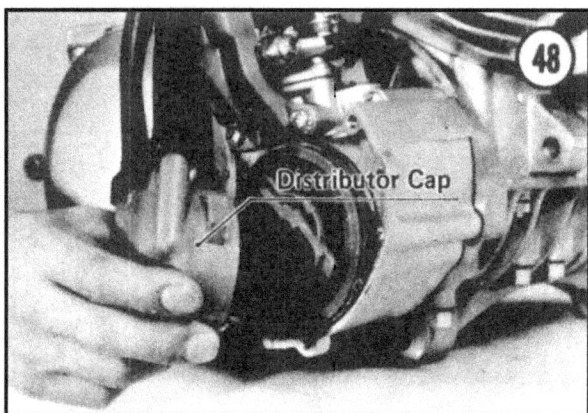

4. Remove banjo bolts, then remove oil outlet tubes (**Figure 49**).

5. Drain the transmission oil if it has not been drained previously.

6. Remove the attaching screws, then pull off the crankcase cover (**Figure 50**).

Cover Inspection

Examine the sealing surface of the cover for any damage. If the sealing surface is damaged,

oil will leak. Do not remove the oil seals from the kickstarter or gearshift shafts unless they are damaged or leaking.

Cover Installation

Reverse the removal procedure to install the cover. Always use new gasket upon installation.

Distributor Removal

To remove the distributor on CDI models, proceed as follows:

1. Hold rotor to prevent distributor shaft from turning, remove distributor pinion mounting nut (**Figure 51**), then pull gear from its shaft.

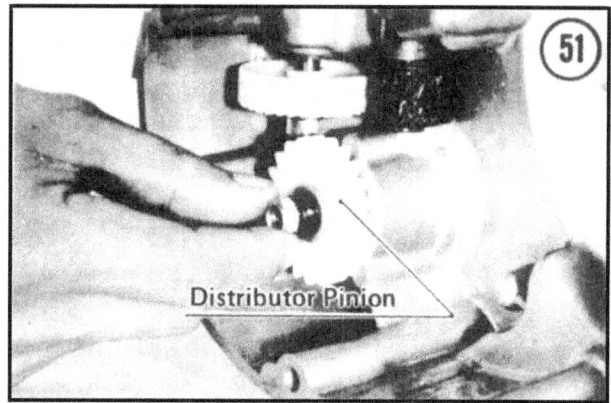

2. Pull distributor rotor from its shaft (**Figure 52**).

3. Remove distributor insulator from right crankcase cover.

4. Remove pin from distributor shaft (**Figure 53**).

5. Tap the distributor shaft lightly with a plastic mallet to remove it.

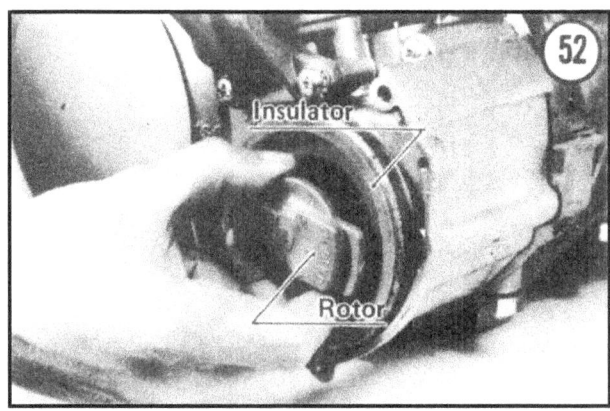

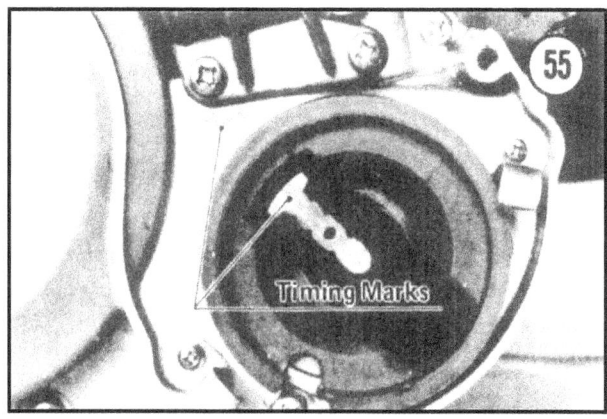

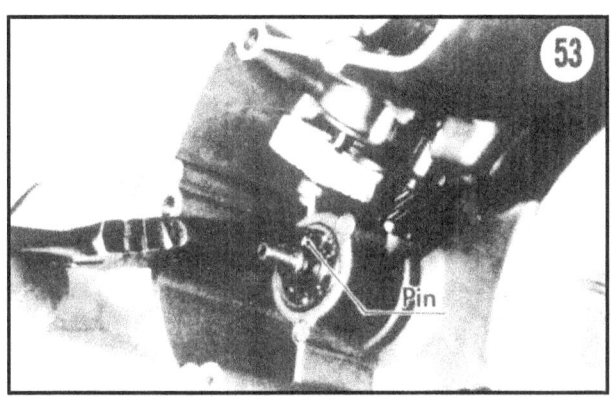

Distributor Installation

Reverse the removal procedure to install the distributor. Pay particular attention to the following points:

1. Mount a dial indicator to determine piston position in right-hand cylinder, as shown in **Figure 54**.

2. Turn engine until right-hand piston is at top dead center.

3. Turn distributor rotor until timing mark on rotor aligns with "T" mark on right cover, as shown in **Figure 55**. It may happen that the mark on the rotor does not align exactly with the center of "T" mark. In such case, its position is satisfactory as long as the line on the rotor falls within the tolerance marks on either side of the "T" mark.

Tachometer Gear

On S series and smaller KH series models, pull out tachometer gear assembly with pliers (**Figure 56**).

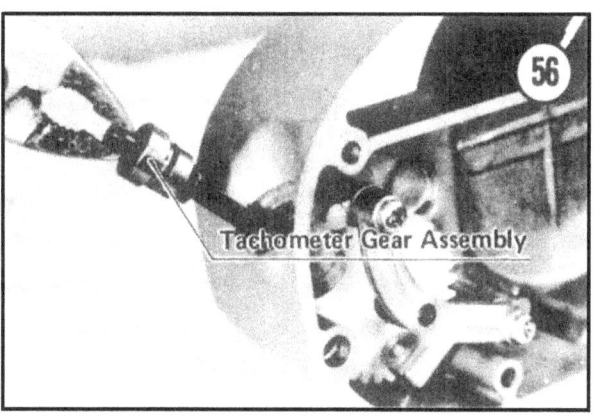

On H series and KH 500 models, pull shaft and guide bushing from tachometer cable opening (**Figure 57**). Then remove tachometer gear and thrust washer.

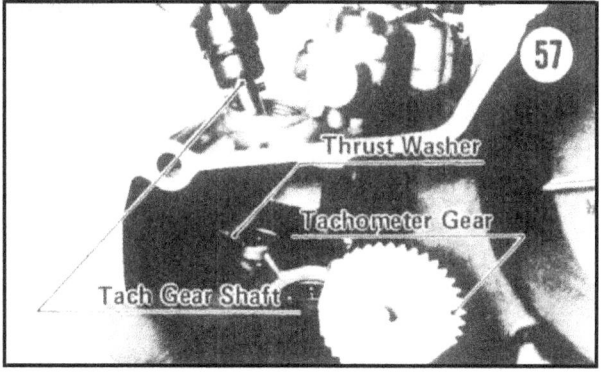

Reverse the removal procedure to install the tachometer gear.

H Series and KH500 Oil Pump

1. Remove mounting screws (**Figure 58**), then pull off pump.

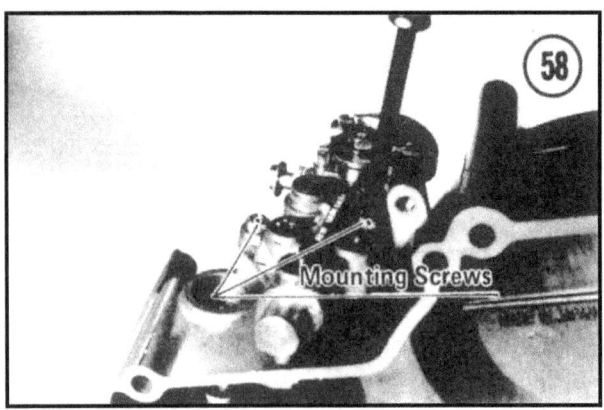

2. Pry end of guide bushing to remove it (**Figure 59**).

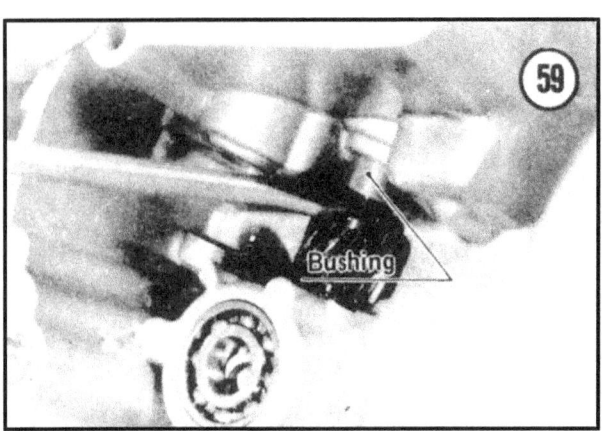

3. Remove oil pump shaft and thrust washer (**Figure 60**).

4. Reverse the removal procedure to install the pump.

S Series and Smaller KH Series Oil Pump Removal

1. Remove mounting screws, then pull off oil pump (**Figure 61**).

2. Remove tachometer gear mounting bracket screws, then remove bracket, oil pump gear, shaft, and thrust washer.

3. Reverse the removal procedure to install the oil pump.

Bushings

Be careful that you don't damage the lip on either the oil pump or tachometer bushings. To install the bushings, tap them in as far as they will go (**Figure 62**).

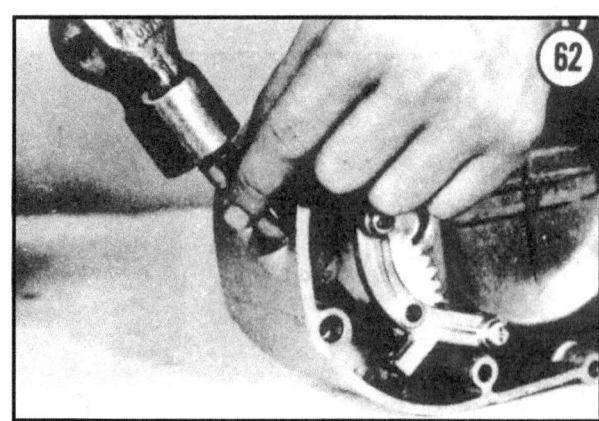

CLUTCH AND CLUTCH RELEASE MECHANISM

Figure 63A is an exploded view of the H2 clutch and clutch release. **Figure 63B** shows the clutch for the H1 and KH500, and **Figure 63C** shows the clutch for the S and KH400 series.

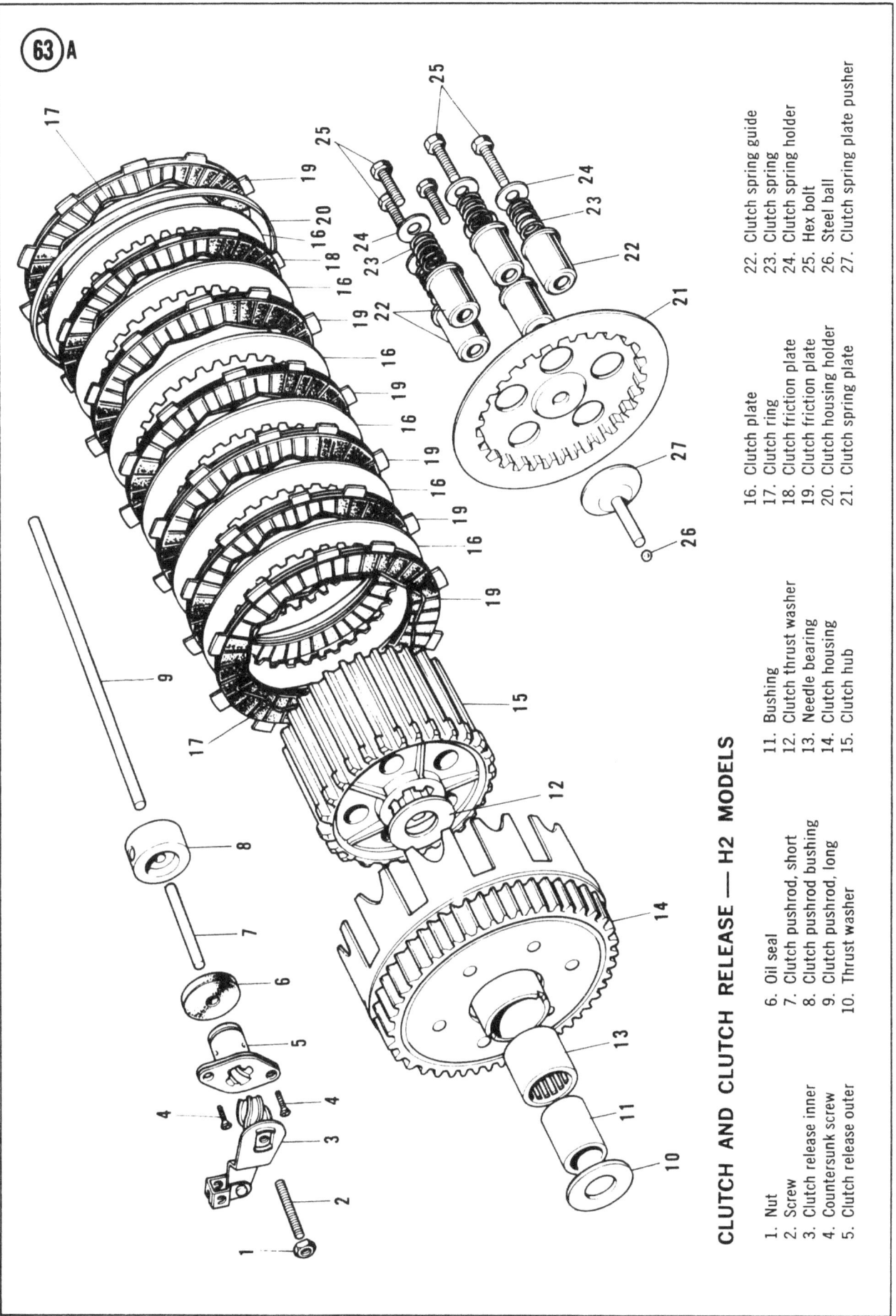

CLUTCH AND CLUTCH RELEASE — H2 MODELS

1. Nut
2. Screw
3. Clutch release inner
4. Countersunk screw
5. Clutch release outer
6. Oil seal
7. Clutch pushrod, short
8. Clutch pushrod bushing
9. Clutch pushrod, long
10. Thrust washer
11. Bushing
12. Clutch thrust washer
13. Needle bearing
14. Clutch housing
15. Clutch hub
16. Clutch plate
17. Clutch ring
18. Clutch friction plate
19. Clutch friction plate
20. Clutch housing holder
21. Clutch spring plate
22. Clutch spring guide
23. Clutch spring
24. Clutch spring holder
25. Hex bolt
26. Steel ball
27. Clutch spring plate pusher

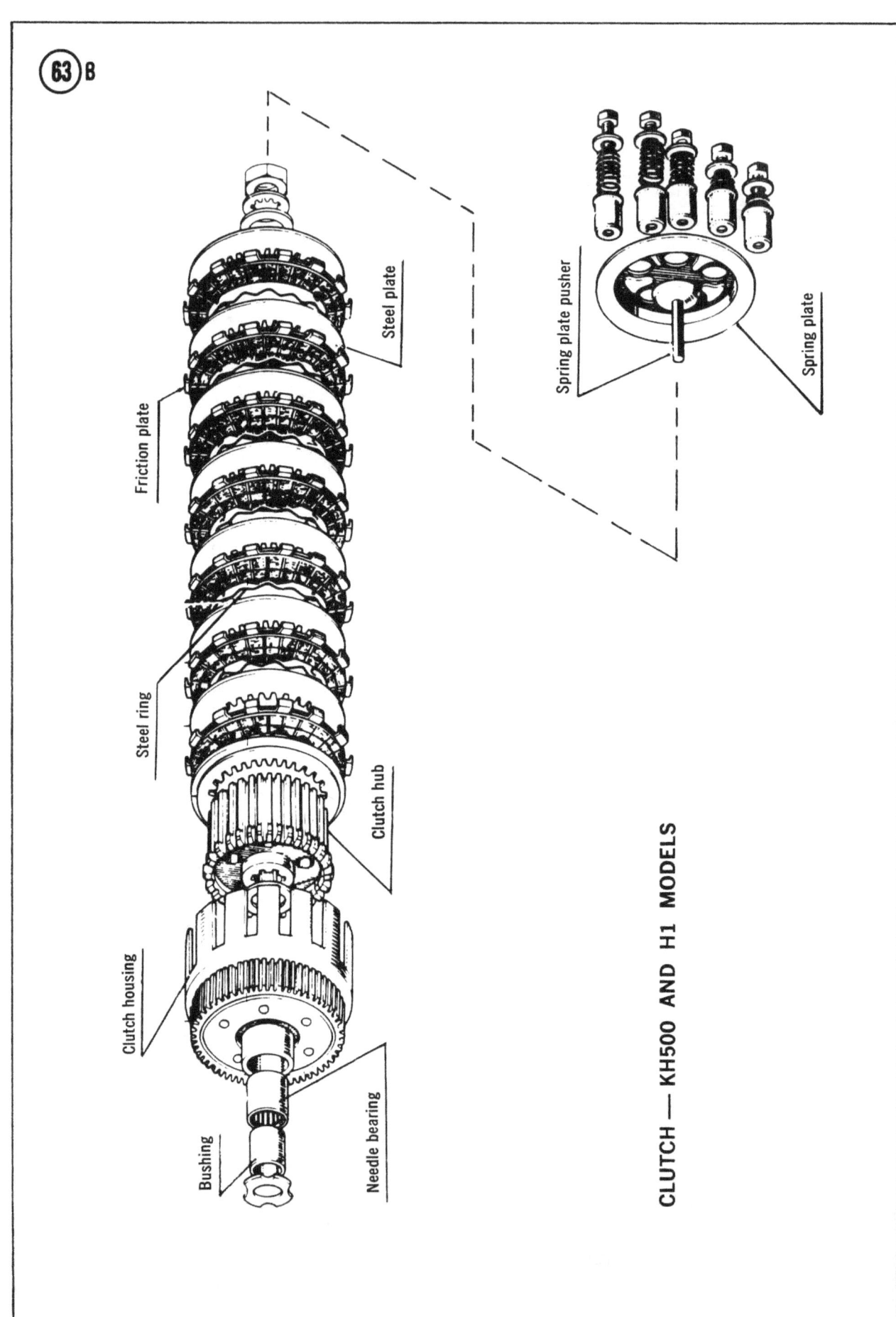

CLUTCH — KH500 AND H1 MODELS

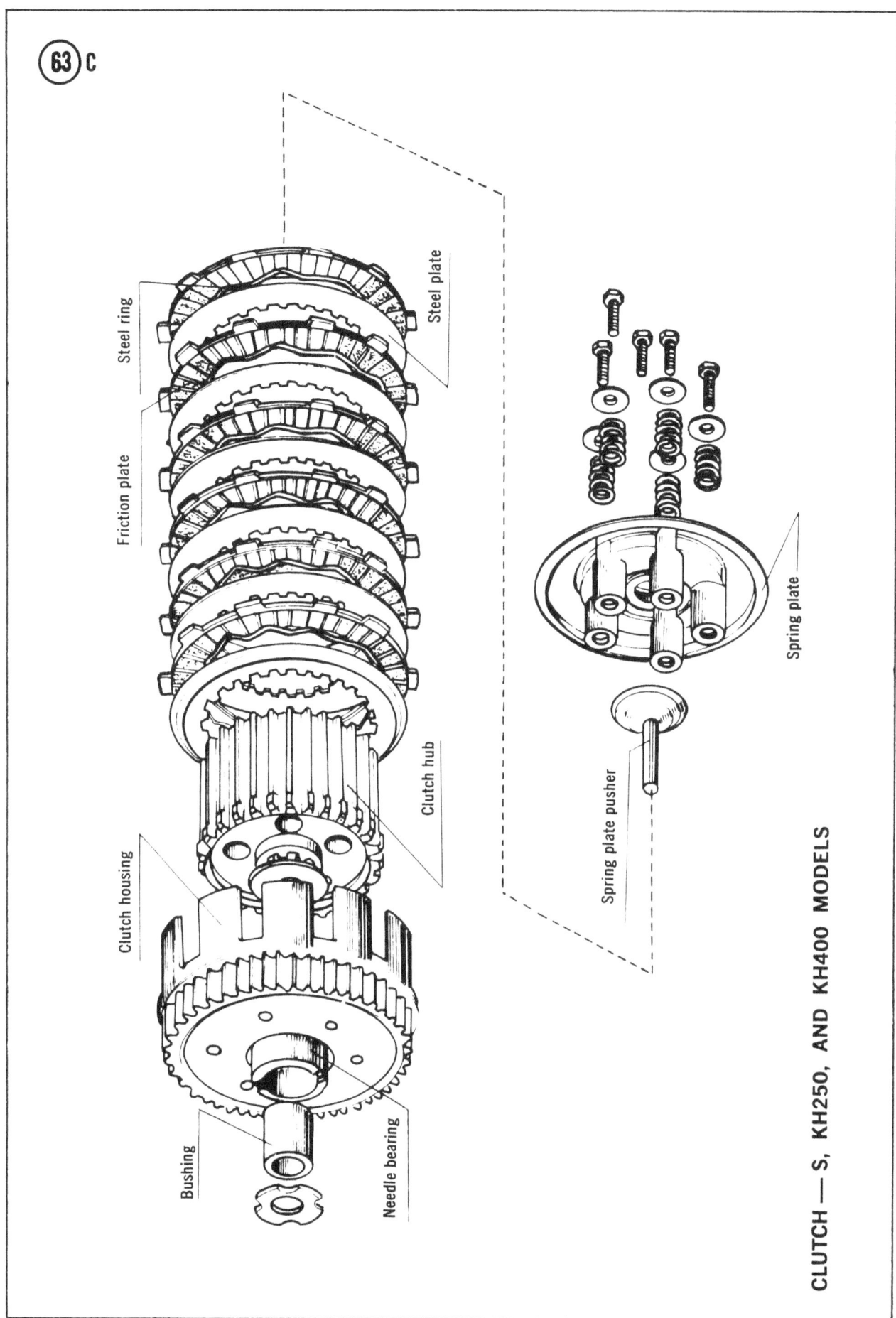

CLUTCH — S, KH250, AND KH400 MODELS

Clutch Operation

As the rider operates the clutch lever, the clutch cable pulls release lever (3), causing it to rotate in release housing (5). As the release lever rotates, helical splines force the lever to move away from the release housing. As the release lever moves, short (7) and long (8) pushrods move with it, and disengage the clutch. Screw (2) and locknut (1) are used to adjust the clutch.

Clutch Disassembly

Clutch disassembly is not difficult, but it is important to take careful note of the order of disassembly.

1. Loosen each bolt in turn, a little at a time, until all are loose. Then remove all bolts (**Figure 64**).

2. Remove clutch springs (**Figure 65**).
3. Remove spring guides (**Figure 66**).
4. On model H2, remove retaining ring.
5. Remove spring plate (**Figure 67**).

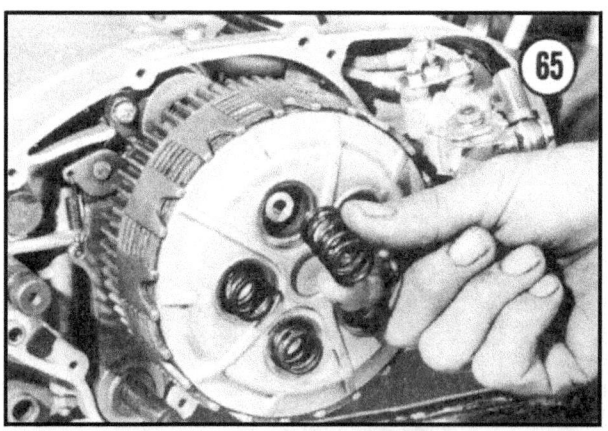

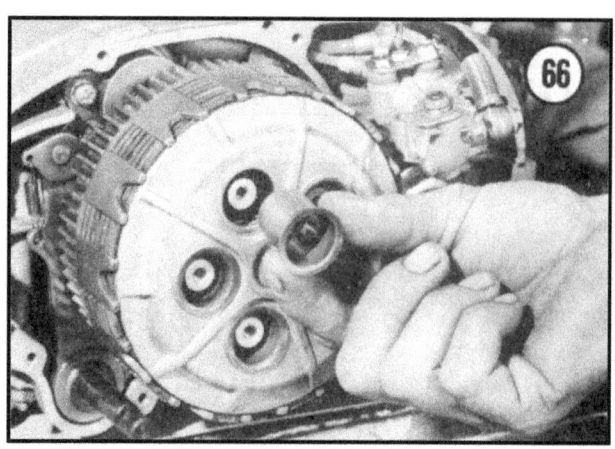

6. Remove push crown (**Figure 68**).
7. Remove friction plates (**Figure 69**).
8. Remove clutch hub nut (**Figure 70**). It may be necessary to fabricate a suitable tool, similar to that shown in **Figure 71**, to prevent the clutch hub from turning.
9. Remove lockwasher and flat washer, then remove clutch hub (**Figure 72**).
10. Remove thrust washer (**Figure 73**).
11. Pull clutch housing from shaft (**Figure 74**).

12. Remove bushing (**Figure 75**).

13. Remove remaining thrust washer (**Figure 76**).

14. Remove clutch release mechanisms (**Figure 77**).

15. Pull out both pushrods (**Figure 78**).

> NOTE: *It is necessary to disassemble the crankcase to remove the pushrod bushing and oil seal. Refer to the applicable section.*

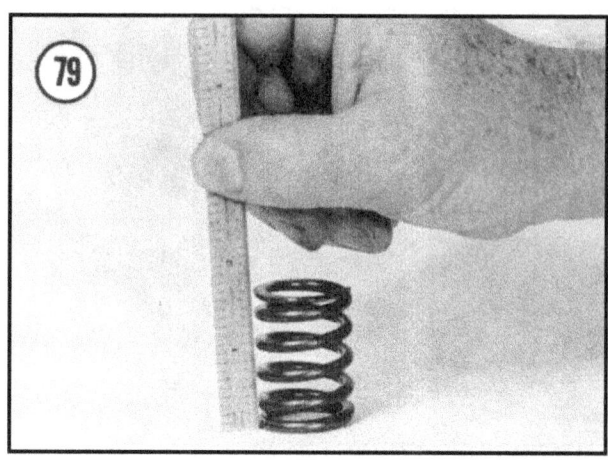

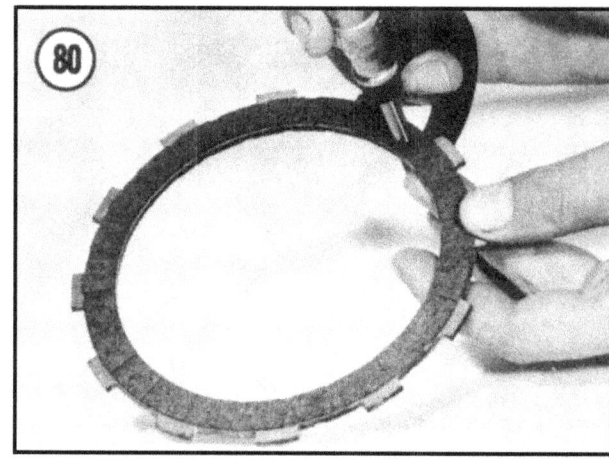

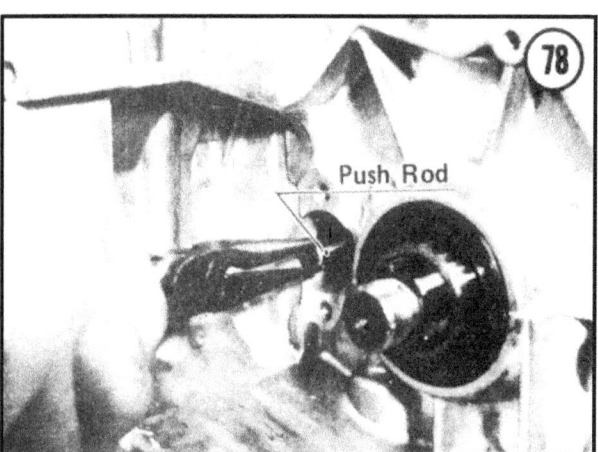

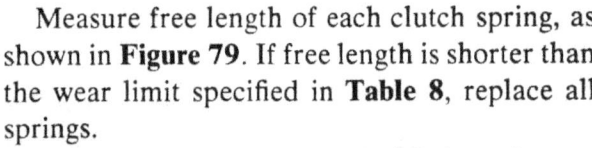

Clutch Inspection

Measure free length of each clutch spring, as shown in **Figure 79**. If free length is shorter than the wear limit specified in **Table 8**, replace all springs.

Measure thickness of each friction plate at several places, as shown in **Figure 80**. Replace any plate that is worn unevenly, or more than the wear limit listed in **Table 9**.

Measure gap (B) between the splines on the clutch friction plates and the clutch housing (**Figure 81**), using a feeler gauge. Replace the friction plates if the gap exceeds that specified in **Table 10**.

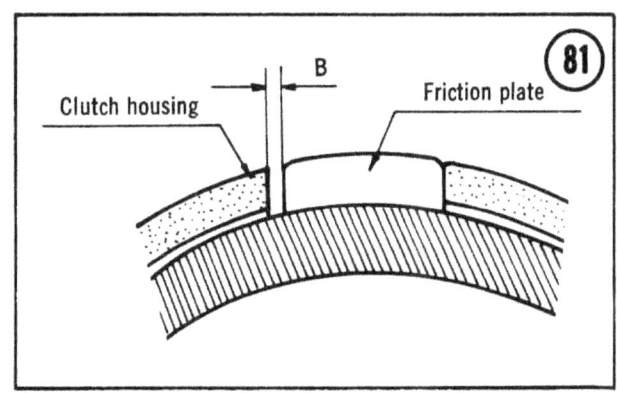

Check the gear teeth on the clutch housing for burrs, nicks, or damage. Smooth any such defects with an oilstone. If the oilstone doesn't smooth out the damage, replace the clutch housing.

Table 8 CLUTCH SPRING SPECIFICATIONS

Model	Standard Length Inches	(Millimeters)	Wear Limit Inches	(Millimeters)
S1	1.36	(34.5)	1.28	(32.5)
KH250	1.36	(34.5)	1.28	(32.5)
S2	1.13	(28.7)	1.05	(26.7)
S3	1.13	(28.7)	1.05	(26.7)
KH400	1.13	(28.7)	1.05	(26.7)
H1	1.42	(36.0)	1.34	(34.0)
KH500	1.42	(36.0)	1.34	(34.0)
H2	1.26	(32.0)	1.18	(30.0)

Table 9 FRICTION PLATE SPECIFICATIONS

Model	Standard Thickness Inch	(Millimeters)	Wear Limit Inch	(Millimeters)
S series	0.118	(3.0)	0.106	(2.7)
KH250	0.118	(3.0)	0.106	(2.7)
KH400	0.118	(3.0)	0.106	(2.7)
H1	0.110	(2.8)	0.098	(2.5)
KH500	0.110	(2.8)	0.098	(2.5)
H2	0.110	(2.8)	0.098	(2.5)

Table 10 FRICTION PLATE GAP

Model	Gap Inch	(Millimeter)
S series	0.002-0.018	(0.05-0.45)
KH250	0.002-0.018	(0.05-0.45)
KH400	0.002-0.018	(0.05-0.45)
H1	0.004-0.016	(0.10-0.40)
KH500	0.004-0.016	(0.10-0.40)
H2	0.004-0.016	(0.10-0.40)

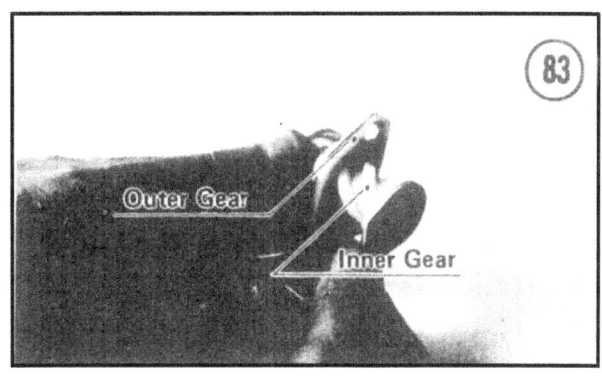

Insert the bushing into the needle bearing in the clutch housing (**Figure 82**). Replace the bushing if there is noticeable play. Excessive play results in gear noise.

To check the clutch release lever and clutch release housing refer to **Figure 83**. Check the assembled parts for wear or play by moving the release lever. Replace both parts if any large scratches or cracks are evident, as these impair clutch action.

Check both pushrods for wear or damage, and straighten or replace them as required.

Clutch Installation

Reverse disassembly procedure to assemble and install the clutch. Note that there are thrust washers in the clutch. Make sure that they are installed correctly to ensure proper clutch operation.

Consider the operating angle of the clutch release lever as it is pulled by the clutch cable. This angle should be about 90 to 100 degrees. Tighten the mounting screws evenly to prevent warpage of the release housing.

On model H2, be sure to install the steel ball into the drive shaft before installing the spring plate pusher. Also be sure to point the arrow on the spring plate toward the mark on the clutch hub.

On other models, be sure that marks on spring plate and clutch hub are aligned (**Figure 84**).

4. Remove the primary gear (**Figure 86**) and distributor pinion (if so equipped), then remove spacer and Woodruff key.

PRIMARY DRIVE GEAR

The primary drive gear is mounted on the right end of the crankshaft. Together with the clutch housing gear the primary gear performs primary reduction.

Removal

1. Remove mounting bolt and lockwasher, then pull off the oil pump pinion and lockwasher (**Figure 85**).
2. Straighten the tab on the lockwasher.
3. Hold clutch, then remove nut and spacer from end of crankshaft.

Inspection

Check the gear teeth for burrs, nicks, or scratches. If any small defects are found, smooth the gear teeth with an oilstone. Replace the gear if the oilstone doesn't clean up the defects.

Installation

Reverse the disassembly procedure to replace the gears. Use new lockwashers upon assembly. Don't forget to bend the tabs on the lockwashers. Be sure to align the primary gear with the key slot before installation. Align the projection on the lockwasher with the hole in the gear (**Figure 87**).

GEARSHIFT MECHANISM

Figure 88 is an exploded view of the H1 shifter mechanism. Shifters for other models are similar. **Figure 89** illustrates shifter operation.

As the rider presses the gearshift pedal, the shaft turns, and moves the change lever. The change lever meshes with pins on the shift drum (part of the transmission assembly). Therefore, as the pedal is moved, the shift drum rotates. Grooves on the shift drum cause shift forks in the transmission to move, and thereby select the various gear ratios.

Set levers are also meshed with the pins on the change drum. They keep the drum in position after each step of rotation of the drum.

Removal

1. Disengage shift lever assembly from shift drum pins (**Figure 90**), then pull out entire assembly.

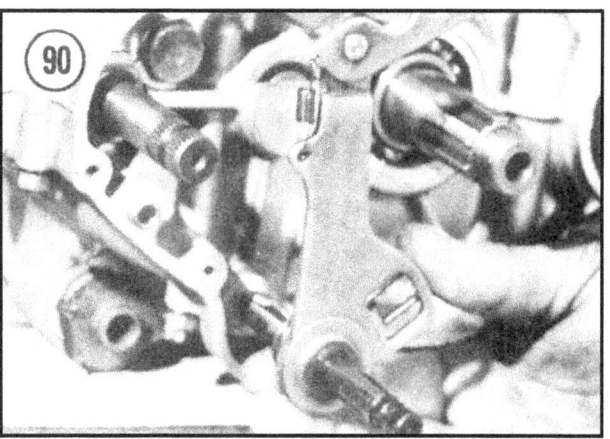

2. Remove hex bolt from set lever (**Figure 91**), then remove set lever and spring.

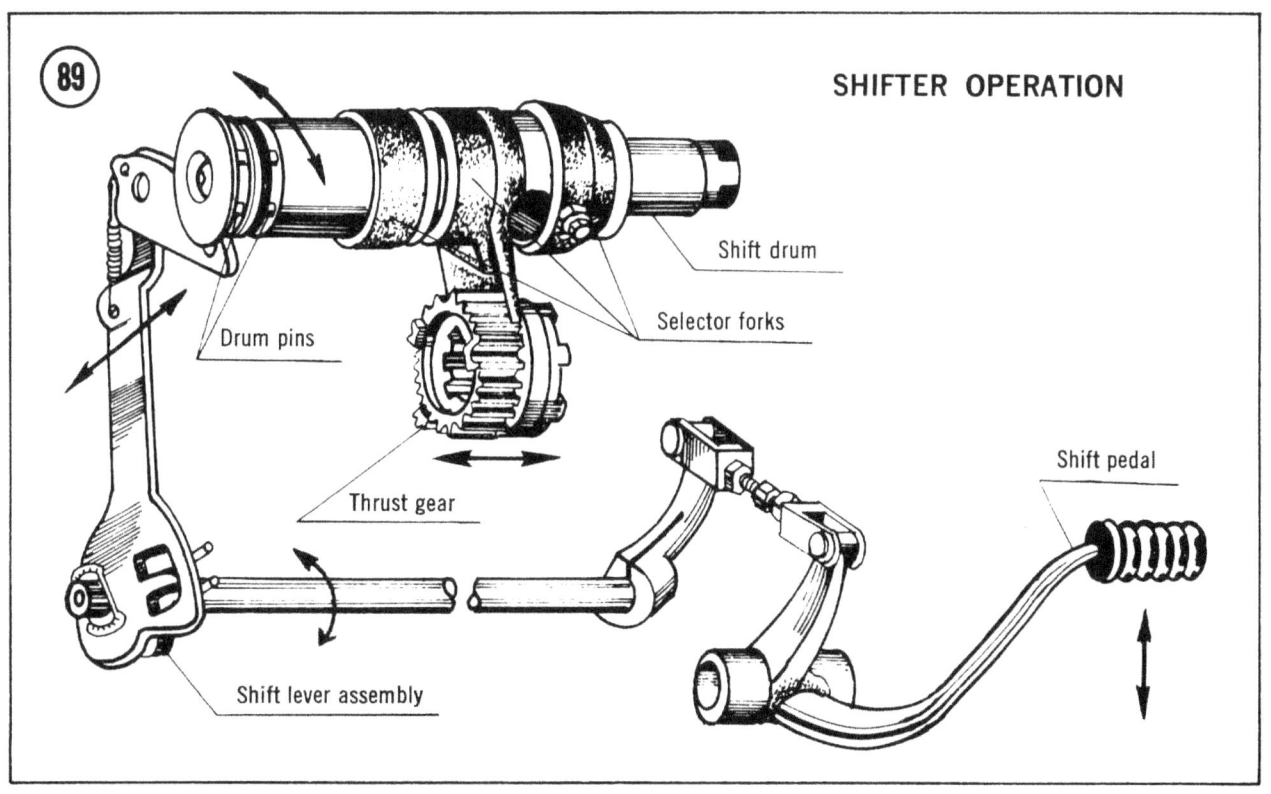

SHIFTER OPERATION

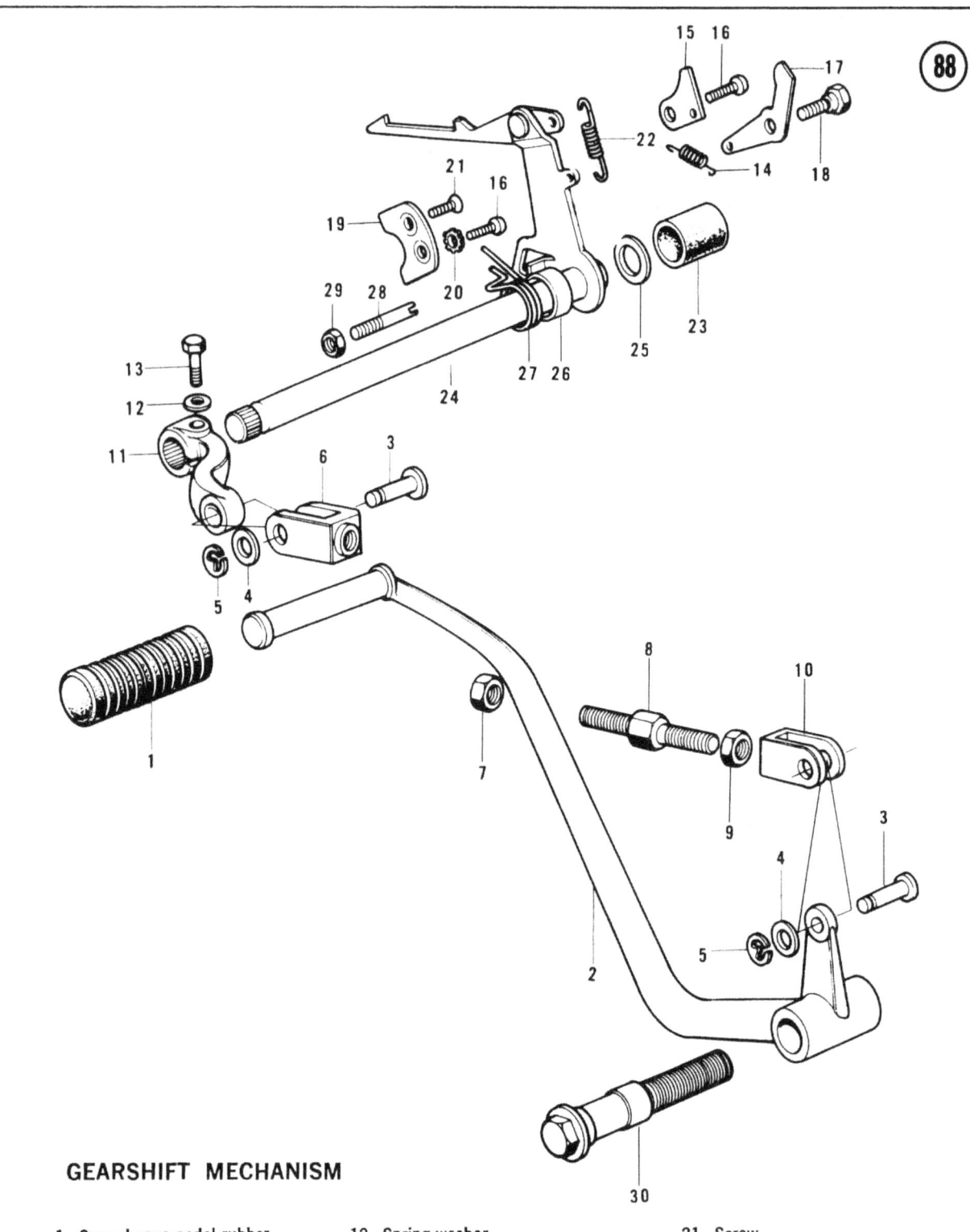

GEARSHIFT MECHANISM

1. Gear change pedal rubber
2. Gear change pedal
3. Pin
4. Washer
5. Snap ring
6. Connector
7. Nut
8. Rod
9. Nut
10. Connector
11. Gear change pedal lever
12. Spring washer
13. Bolt
14. Gear change drum lever spring
15. Gear change drum lever fitting plate
16. Screw
17. Gear change drum lever
18. Gear change drum lever bolt
19. Gear change drum positioning plate
20. Lockwasher
21. Screw
22. Gear change lever spring
23. Rubber cap
24. Shaft assembly
25. Spacer
26. Spacer
27. Gear change pedal return spring
28. Return spring pin
29. Nut
30. Bolt

3. Remove mounting screws, then take off positioning plate (**Figure 92**).

Inspection

Check return spring tension (**Figure 93**). Replace the spring if it is weak or cracked. Inspect set lever spring for cracks or weakness. Be sure that return spring set pin (**Figure 94**) is not loose. If this pin is loose, missed shifts will result. Be sure that the locknut is tight.

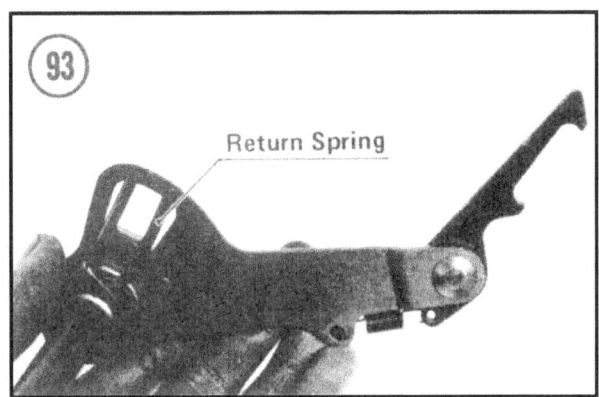

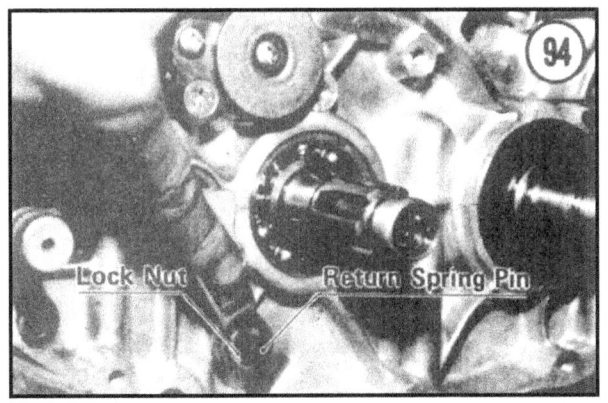

Installation

Reverse the removal procedure to install the shift mechanism. Be sure that each spring is installed correctly. Use a small hammer and center punch to stake the positioning plate screws after they are tightened.

CRANKCASE

Figure 95 is an exploded view of a typical crankcase assembly. The crankcase must be disassembled to permit servicing of the crankshaft, transmission, kickstarter, and internal shifter parts.

Lubricating oil passages are machined in the crankcase. Be very careful that these passages don't become clogged with dirt when you work on the crankcase.

Disassembly

1. Remove oil receiver at the output shaft (**Figure 96**).

2. Remove clutch release mechanism.
3. Loosen kick stopper (**Figure 97**).

4. Invert crankcase, then remove nuts from bottom side.

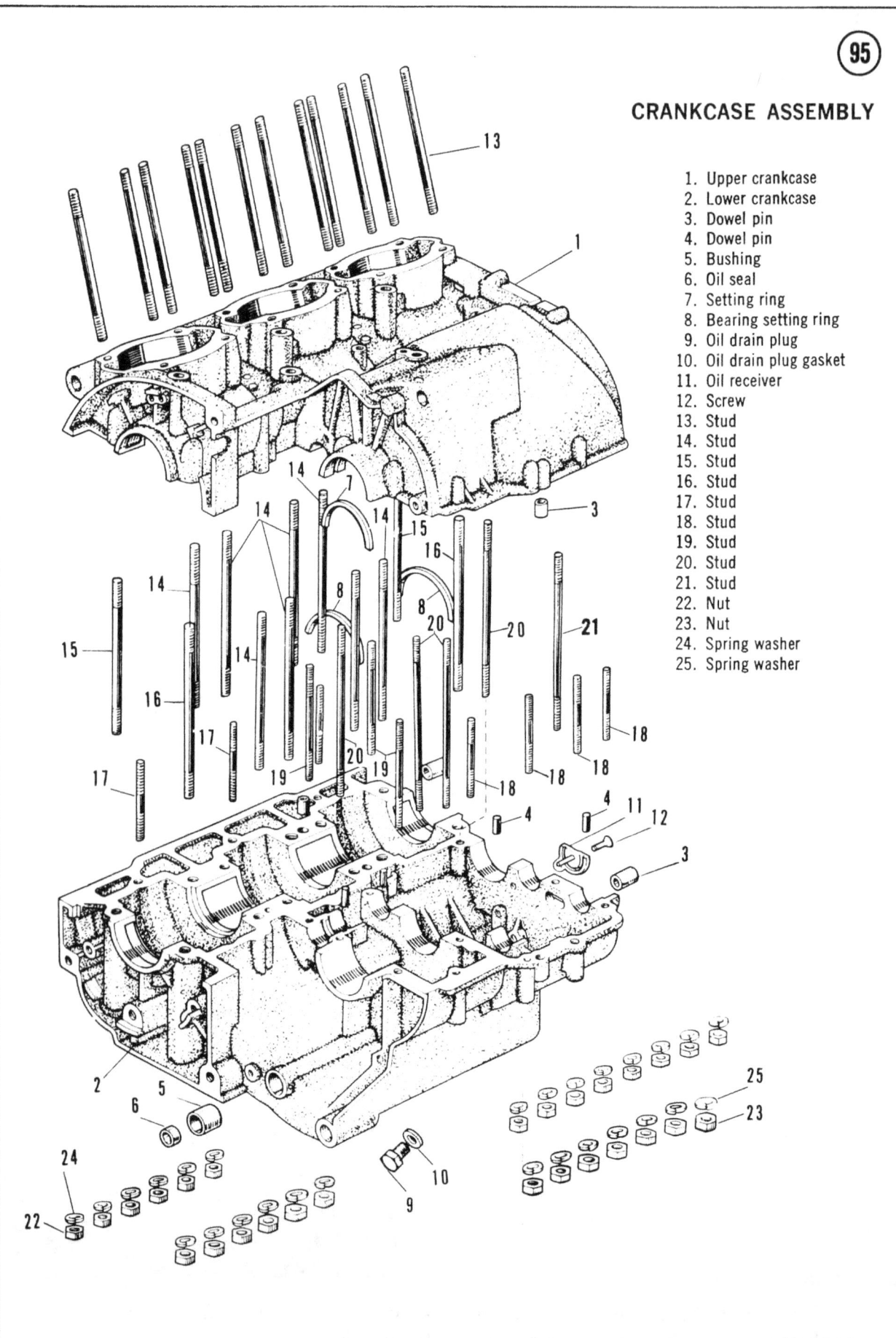

5. With the crankcase still inverted, tap the crankcase and shifter shaft mounting with a plastic mallet to separate the 2 halves (**Figure 98**). Be sure that all parts remain in the upper crankcase half.

6. Remove the crankshaft, transmission, and kickstarter assemblies.

Inspection

Check each lubrication passage (**Figure 99**). If any is found to be clogged, blow it out with compressed air. Check the transmission breather hole. Oil leakage will result if this hole is clogged. Examine the mating surfaces of the crankcase halves. Any nicks or scratches will result in oil leakage.

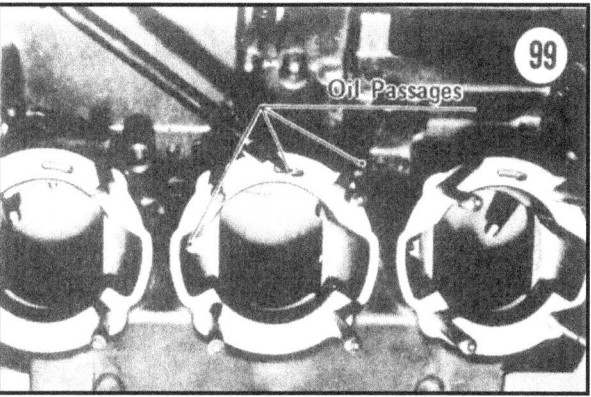

Assembly

1. Install internal parts into upper crankcase. **Figure 100** shows the parts installed.

2. Clean mating surfaces carefully with solvent.

3. Apply a light coat of gasket sealer to the sealing surfaces of both halves. Cover only flat

surfaces, not curved bearing surfaces. Make the coating as thin as possible or the case can shift and hammer out bearings. Join both halves and tap them together lightly with a plastic mallet — do not use a metal hammer as it will damage the cases.

> NOTE: *Use Gasgacinch Gasket Sealer, or equivalent. When selecting an equivalent, avoid thick and hard setting materials.*

4. Place the lower crankcase half into position, then tighten nuts as specified in **Table 11**.

Table 11 CRANKCASE NUT TORQUE VALUES

Model	6mm Nut	8mm Nut
S and KH Series	12–16 ft.-lb. (1.6–2.2 mkg)	19–25 ft.-lb. (2.6–3.5 mkg)
H1 and H2	11–12 ft.-lb. (1.5–1.6 mkg)	16–20 ft.-lb. (2.2–2.7 mkg)

CRANKSHAFT

The crankshaft operates under conditions of high stress. Dimensional tolerances are critical. It is necessary to locate and correct defects in the crankshaft to prevent more serious trouble later. **Figure 101** illustrates a typical crankshaft assembly.

Removal

To remove crankshaft, tap each end lightly with a plastic mallet, then lift it from the crankcase, as shown in **Figure 102**.

Inspection

The crankshaft is serviced as a complete assembly; it cannot be disassembled. If the following checks reveal any defects, the crankshaft must be replaced. The right and left oil seals are replaceable, however.

Mount the crankshaft in a lathe, V-blocks, or other suitable centering device. Rotate the crankshaft through a complete revolution, and measure runout at each of the locations shown in **Figure 103**. The runout limit on a new crankshaft assembly should not exceed 0.0016 in. (0.04mm) at any measurement location. Replace the crankshaft assembly if any measurement exceeds 0.0039 in. (0.10mm).

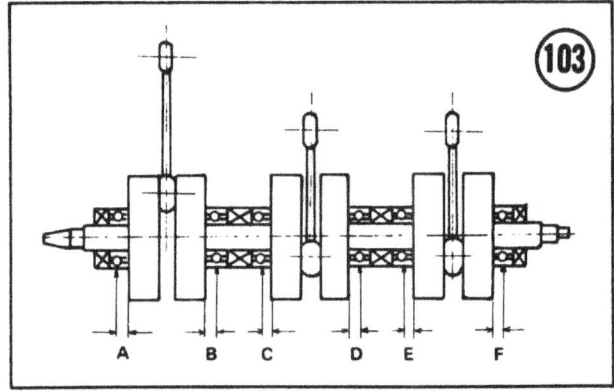

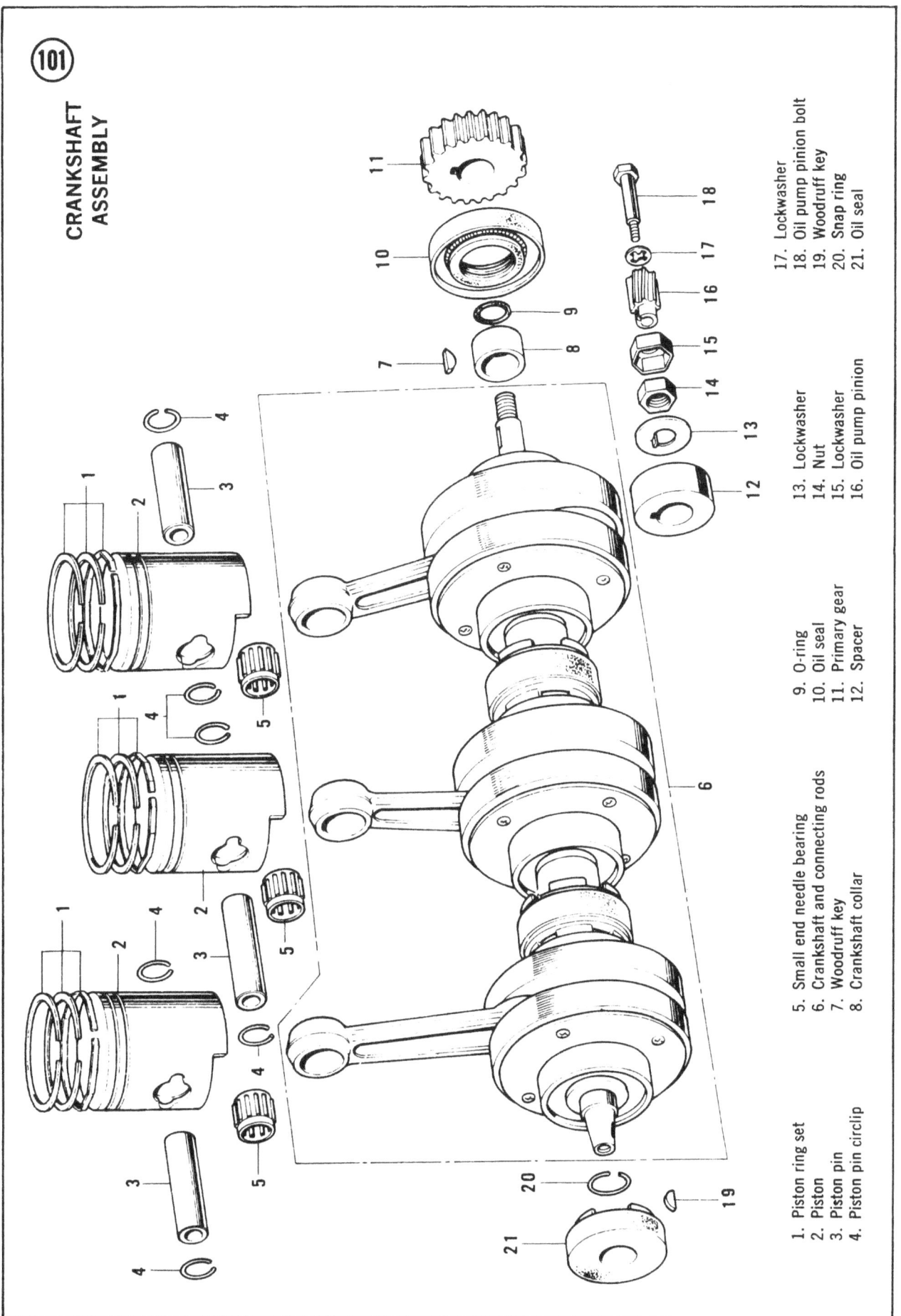

To check bearings, first clean them thoroughly in solvent, dry them, then lubricate them with light oil. Spin each bearing (**Figure 104**), and check for abnormal noise or roughness as it coasts down. Do not spin a dry bearing, *and never spin with compressed air.*

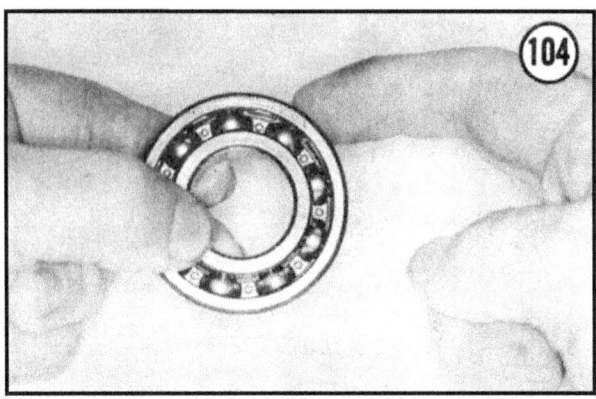

Crankshaft bearings in 2-stroke engines are particularly susceptible to damage resulting from dirt. **Figure 105** shows a bearing which failed after the machine was operated only a short distance without an oil filter.

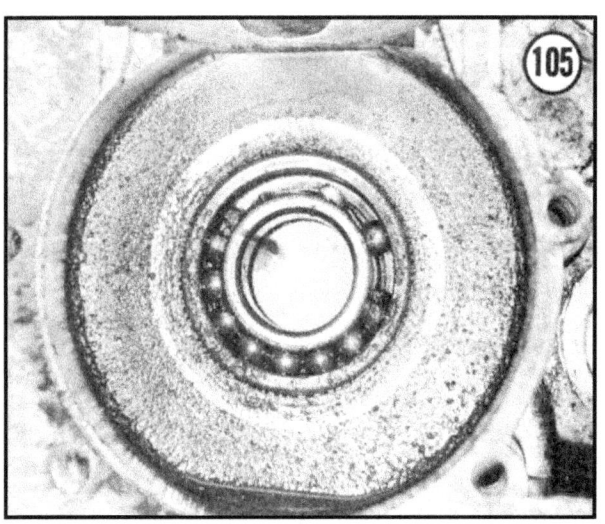

Check oil seals for damage or evidence of leakage. Primary compression leakage will occur if these oil seals leak, thereby causing poor performance. The center oil seal is not replaceable.

Measure radial clearance (**Figure 106**) at the big end of each connecting rod. Standard clearance is 0.00098-0.00138 in. (0.025-0.035mm). Replace the crankshaft assembly if any measurement exceeds 0.0039 in. (0.10mm).

Measure side clearance (**Figure 107**) of each

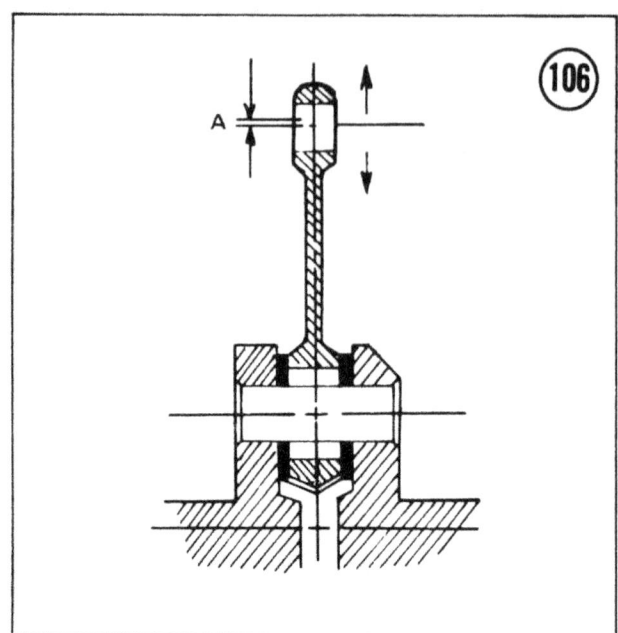

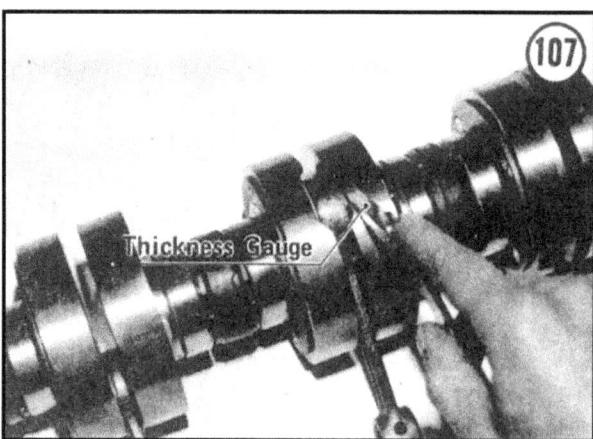

connecting rod, using a feeler gauge. Standard side clearance is 0.016-0.020 in. (0.40-0.50mm). Replace the crankshaft assembly if side clearance exceeds 0.028 in. (0.70mm).

Measure connecting rod alignment as shown in **Figure 108**. Insert a shaft, such as a piston pin, into the small end. Mount the entire assembly on a surface plate. Measure the distance between each end of the shaft and the surface plate. Any difference between the 2 readings is an indication that the connecting rod is bent. Also, check to be sure that the connecting rod is not twisted, by determining that the rod and crankshaft are parallel.

Installation

Install the setting ring (**Figure 109**) into the upper crankcase half. Then tap the crankshaft assembly into position, using a plastic mallet.

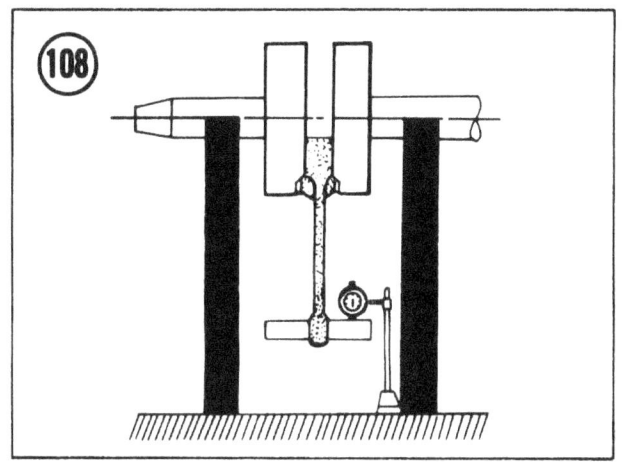

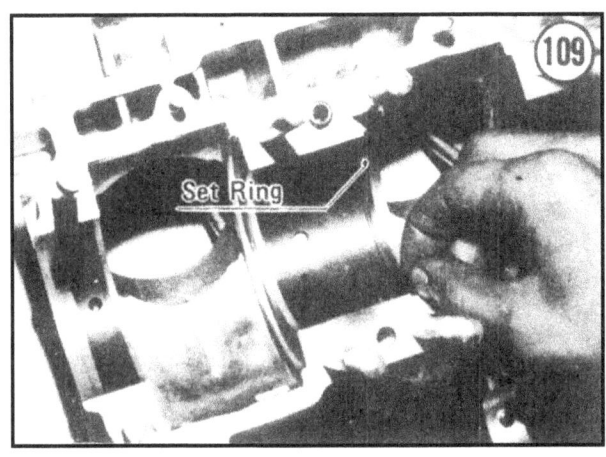

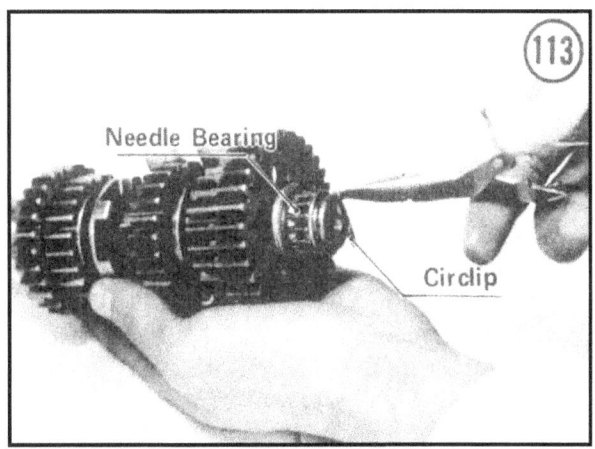

TRANSMISSION

All models are equipped with 5-speed, constant mesh transmissions. **Figures 110 and 111** are exploded views of typical transmissions on these machines. Both transmissions are similar in construction and operation. Differences in service procedures will be pointed out where they exist.

Removal and Disassembly

1. Lift each shaft assembly from the upper crankcase half (**Figure 112**).

2. Remove each bearing, gear, and thrust washer by first removing its associated snap ring (**Figure 113**). Note carefully the order in which the parts are disassembled. Also note the orientation of each part as it is removed.

3. Remove oil seals and bearings (**Figure 114**).

4. On S series and smaller KH models, remove snap ring, then pull out shift rod (**Figure 115**).

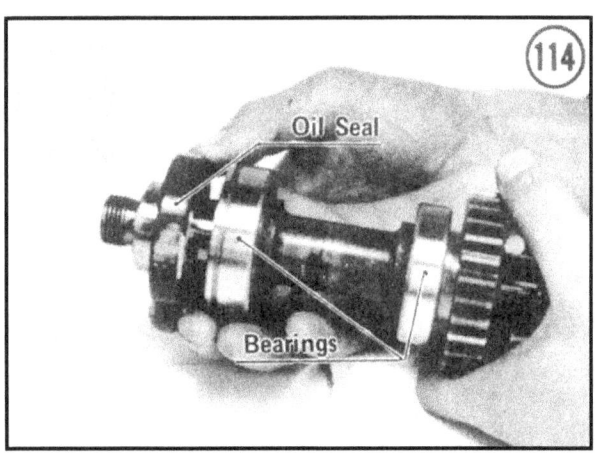

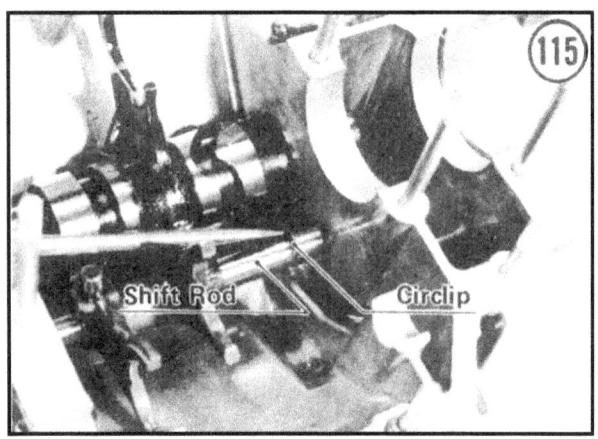

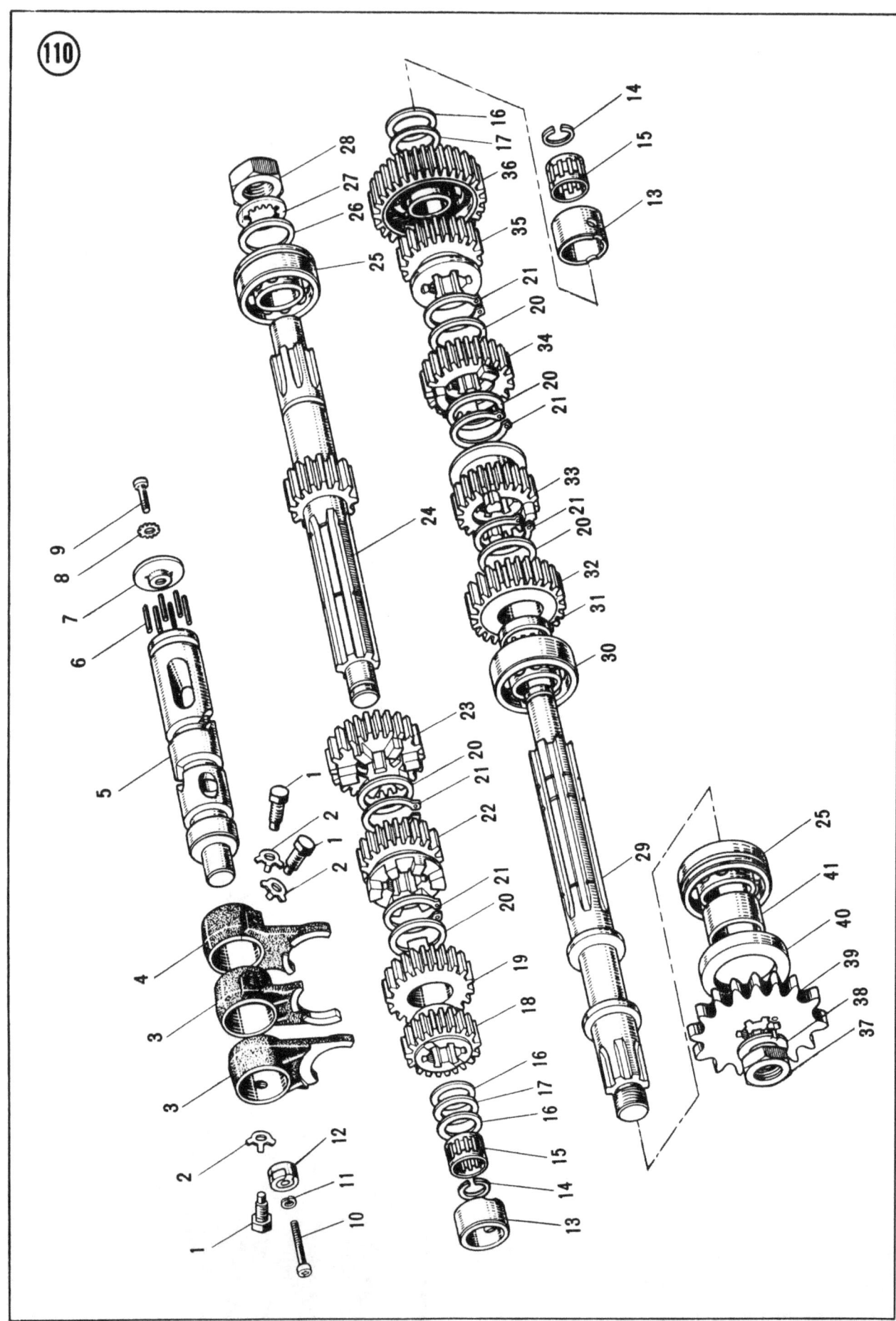

H AND KH500 SERIES TRANSMISSION

1. Selector fork guide pin
2. Lockwasher
3. Selector fork top
4. Selector fork low
5. Gear change drum
6. Gear change drum pin
7. Gear change drum pin plate
8. Toothed lockwasher
9. Screw
10. Screw
11. Spring washer
12. Neutral indicator switch rotor
13. Bushing
14. Snap ring
15. Needle bearing
16. Thrust washer
17. Thrust washer
18. Drive shaft 2nd gear
19. Drive shaft 4th gear
20. Washer
21. Snap ring
22. Drive shaft 3rd gear
23. Drive shaft top gear
24. Drive shaft
25. Ball bearing
26. Thrust washer
27. Lockwasher
28. Nut
29. Output shaft
30. Ball bearing
31. Spacer
32. Output shaft 2nd gear
33. Output shaft 4th gear
34. Output shaft 3rd gear
35. Output shaft top gear
36. Output shaft low gear
37. Nut
38. Lockwasher
39. Engine sprocket
40. Oil seal
41. Engine sprocket spacer

5. On S and smaller KH models, remove the cotter pin, then pull out guide pin (**Figure 116**).

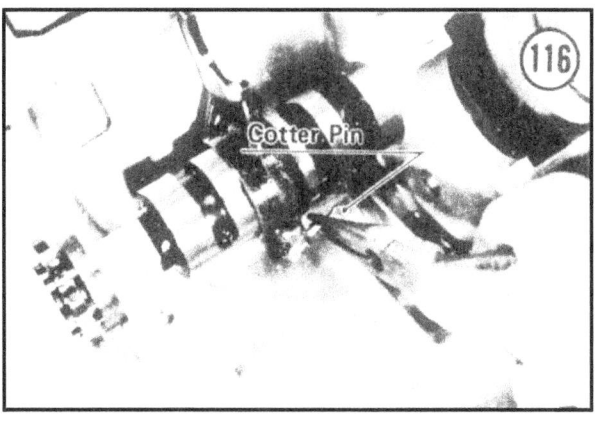

6. On S and smaller KH models, pull out the shift drum (**Figure 117**), then remove the remaining shift selector fork.

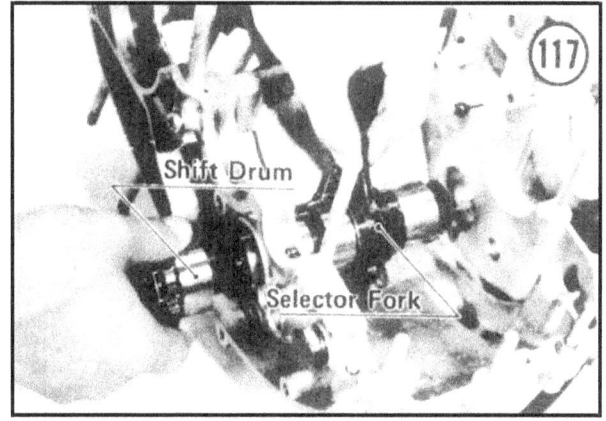

7. On H series and KH500 models, remove the shift drum lever and positioning plate if they have not been removed previously.

8. Straighten the lockwashers, then pull out the guide pins (**Figure 118**).

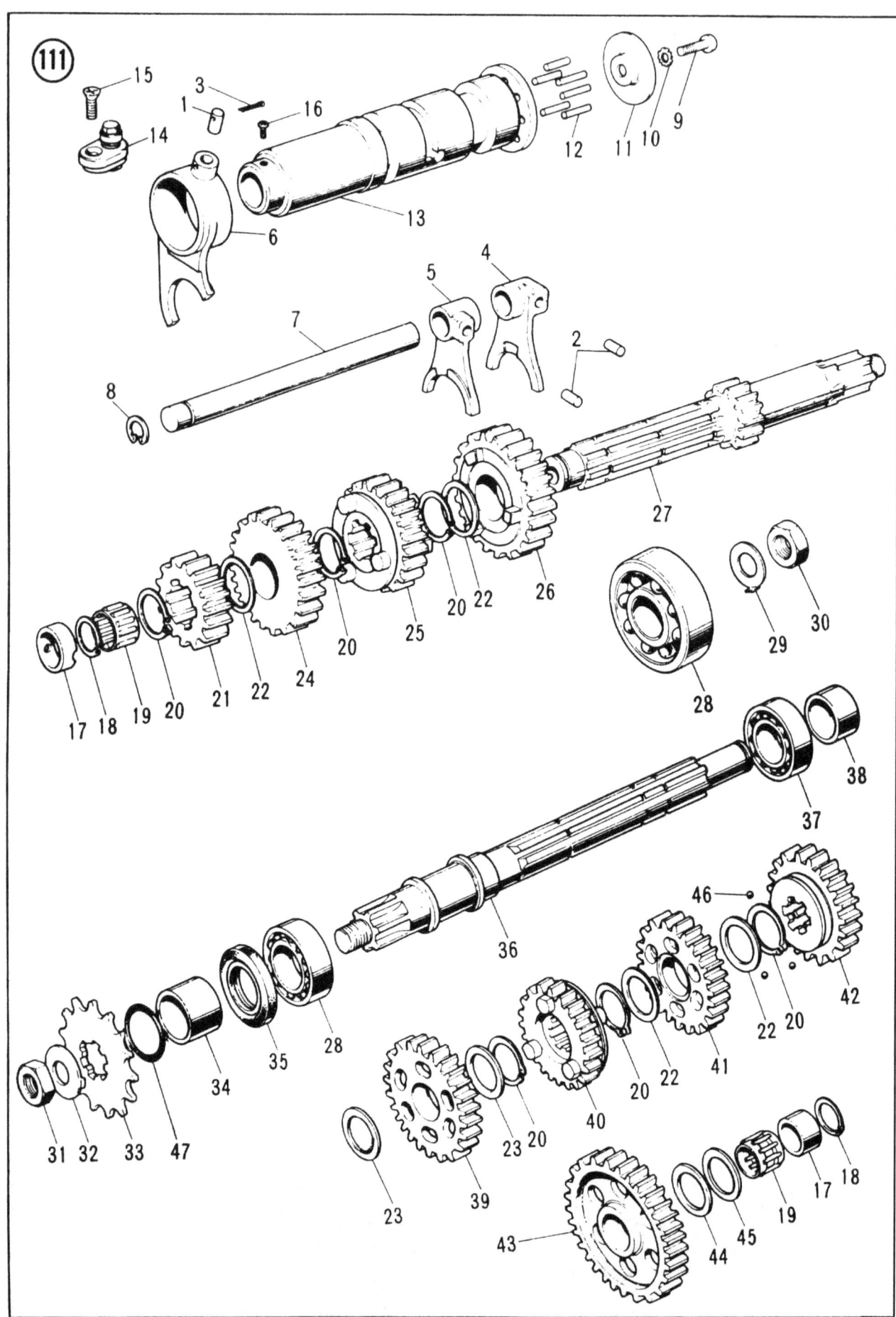

S AND SMALLER KH SERIES TRANSMISSION

1. Selector fork guide pin
2. Selector fork guide pin
3. Cotter pin
4. 1st gear selector fork
5. 2nd and 3rd gear selector fork
6. 4th and 5th gear selector fork
7. Shift rod
8. Snap ring
9. Screw
10. Lockwasher
11. Gear change drum plate
12. Gear change drum pin
13. Gear change drum
14. Neutral indicator switch
15. Screw
16. Screw
17. Bushing
18. Snap ring
19. Needle bearing
20. Snap ring
21. Countershaft 2nd gear
22. Thrust washer
23. Thrust washer
24. Countershaft 1st gear
25. Countershaft 3rd gear
26. Countershaft 4th gear
27. Countershaft
28. Ball bearing
29. Lockwasher
30. Nut
31. Nut
32. Lockwasher
33. Engine sprocket
34. Engine sprocket collar
35. Oil seal
36. Mainshaft
37. Ball bearing
38. Spacer
39. Mainshaft 2nd gear
40. Mainshaft 5th gear
41. Mainshaft 3rd gear
42. Mainshaft 4th gear
43. Mainshaft 1st gear
44. Thrust washer
45. Thrust washer
46. Steel ball
47. Mainshaft O-ring

9. Pull out the shift drum (**Figure 119**), then remove the selector forks.

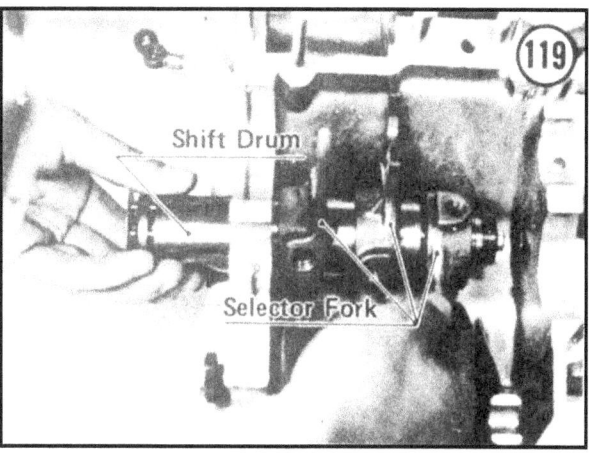

Inspection

1. Measure clearance between each shift fork and the groove on the associated gear (**Figure 120**). Standard clearance is 0.002-0.010 in. (0.05-0.25mm). Replace the gear and/or the fork if clearance exceeds 0.024 in. (0.6mm). Replace the shift fork if there are any burrs or other damage.

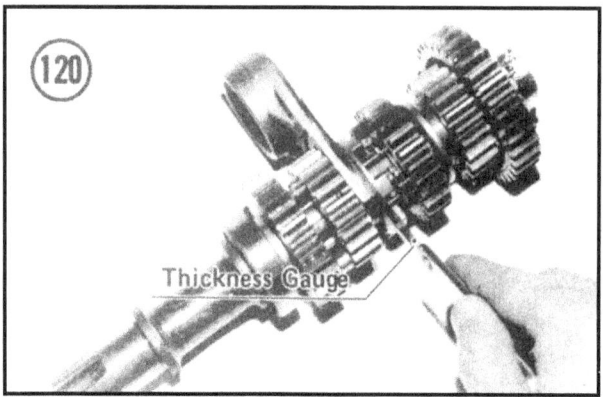

2. Bent shift selector forks can cause shifting difficulties. Replace any bent fork.

3. Any burrs, pits, or roughness on the gear teeth will cause wear on the mating gear. Replace any gear with such defects. Examine its mating gear carefully and replace it if there is any doubt about its condition. It may be possible to smooth minor burrs with an oilstone.

4. Inspect each transmission oil seal for any damage. Replace any that are not in perfect condition. It is good practice to always replace the oil seals whenever the engine is disassembled.

Assembly and Installation

Reverse the disassembly procedure to reassemble and install the transmission. Pay particular attention to the following points.

1. Arrange H series and KH500 selectors forks as shown in **Figure 121**. **Figure 122** shows selector fork arrangement for S series and smaller KH models.

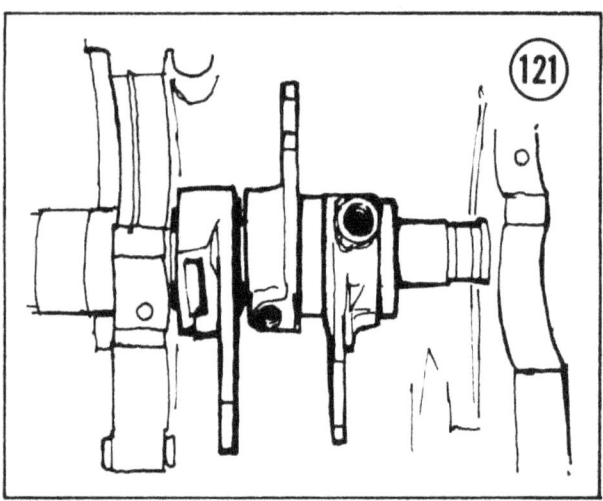

2. Be sure to replace the bearing setting rings.

3. On S series and smaller KH models, when replacing fourth gear on the output shaft, do not use grease to hold the balls in place. If any grease happens to be on the balls, clean it off with solvent.

4. Be sure that the gears are installed correctly on their shafts, and that each snap ring is seated in its groove.

5. Check gear clearance at 3 points:
   a. Between drive shaft second gear and the bearing.
   b. Between the output shaft first gear and the bearing.
   c. Between the output shaft second gear and the fourth gear C-ring.

If the measurement is much over 0.020 in. (0.5mm), insert a 0.5mm shim washer to decrease the clearance.

NOTE: *Do not insert the 0.5mm washer if it makes the shaft hard to turn or if the dogs of any 2 gears touch.*

The 0.5mm shim is Kawasaki part No. 92022-144, and the washer for use between the second gear and fourth gear is Kawasaki part No. 92022-225. Have the parts manager verify that these part numbers apply to your specific model and year prior to purchase.

6. Be sure the lockwasher tabs on the shift fork guide pins are bent over.

Figure 123 shows a typical transmission after installation.

KICKSTARTER

Figures 124 and 125 are exploded and sectional views of the kickstarter. As the rider kicks the pedal, the kickstarter gear slides in the direction of the arrow, and engages with the low driven gear in the transmission. As the kickstarter gear turns, it turns the low driven gear, low drive gear, clutch, and engine.

When the engine starts, rotation of the low gear in the transmission causes the kickstarter gear to rotate, and thereby forces the kickstarter gear to the left along the helical splines on the kickstarter shaft. As the

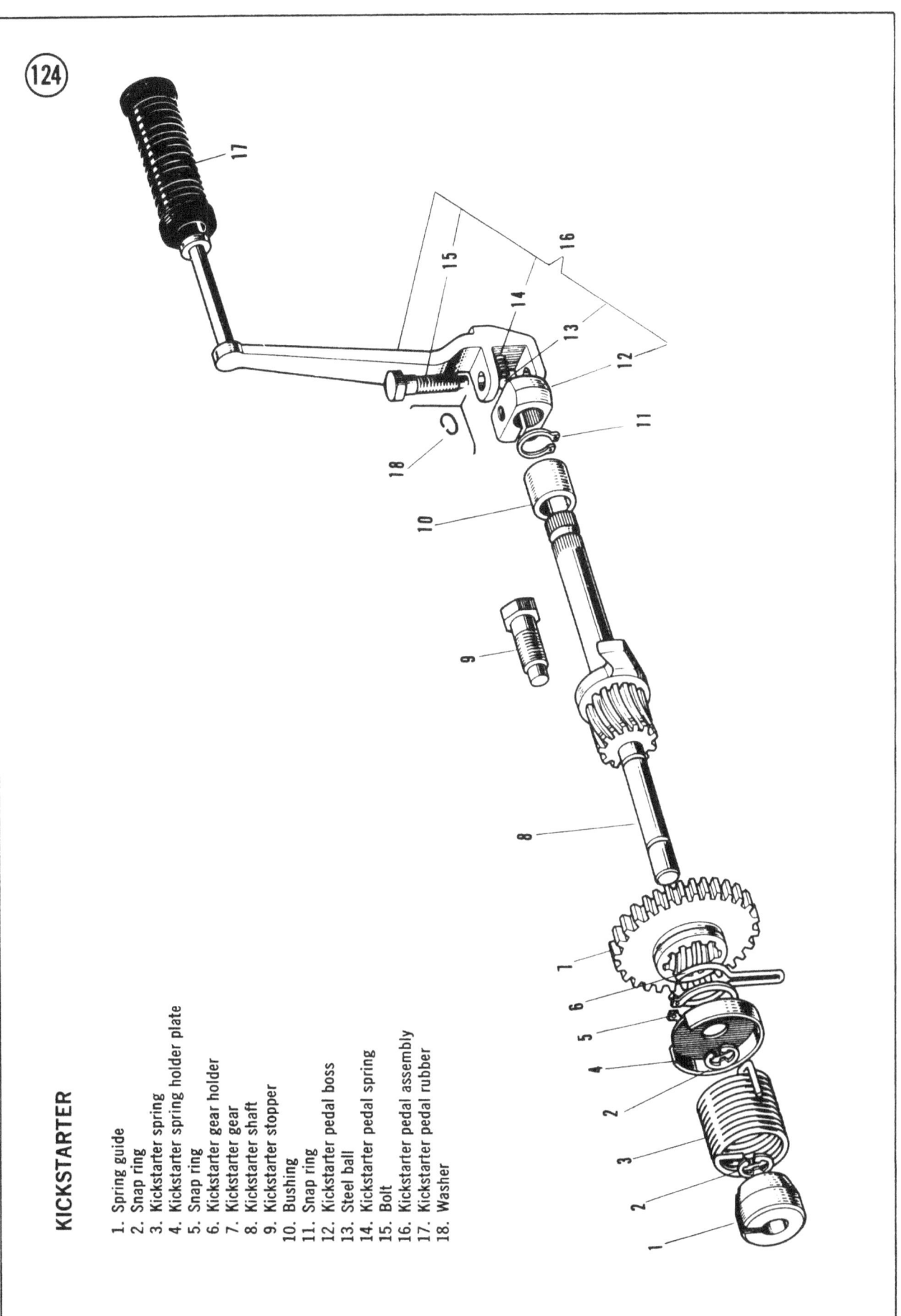

KICKSTARTER

1. Spring guide
2. Snap ring
3. Kickstarter spring
4. Kickstarter spring holder plate
5. Snap ring
6. Kickstarter gear holder
7. Kickstarter gear
8. Kickstarter shaft
9. Kickstarter stopper
10. Bushing
11. Snap ring
12. Kickstarter pedal boss
13. Steel ball
14. Kickstarter pedal spring
15. Bolt
16. Kickstarter pedal assembly
17. Kickstarter pedal rubber
18. Washer

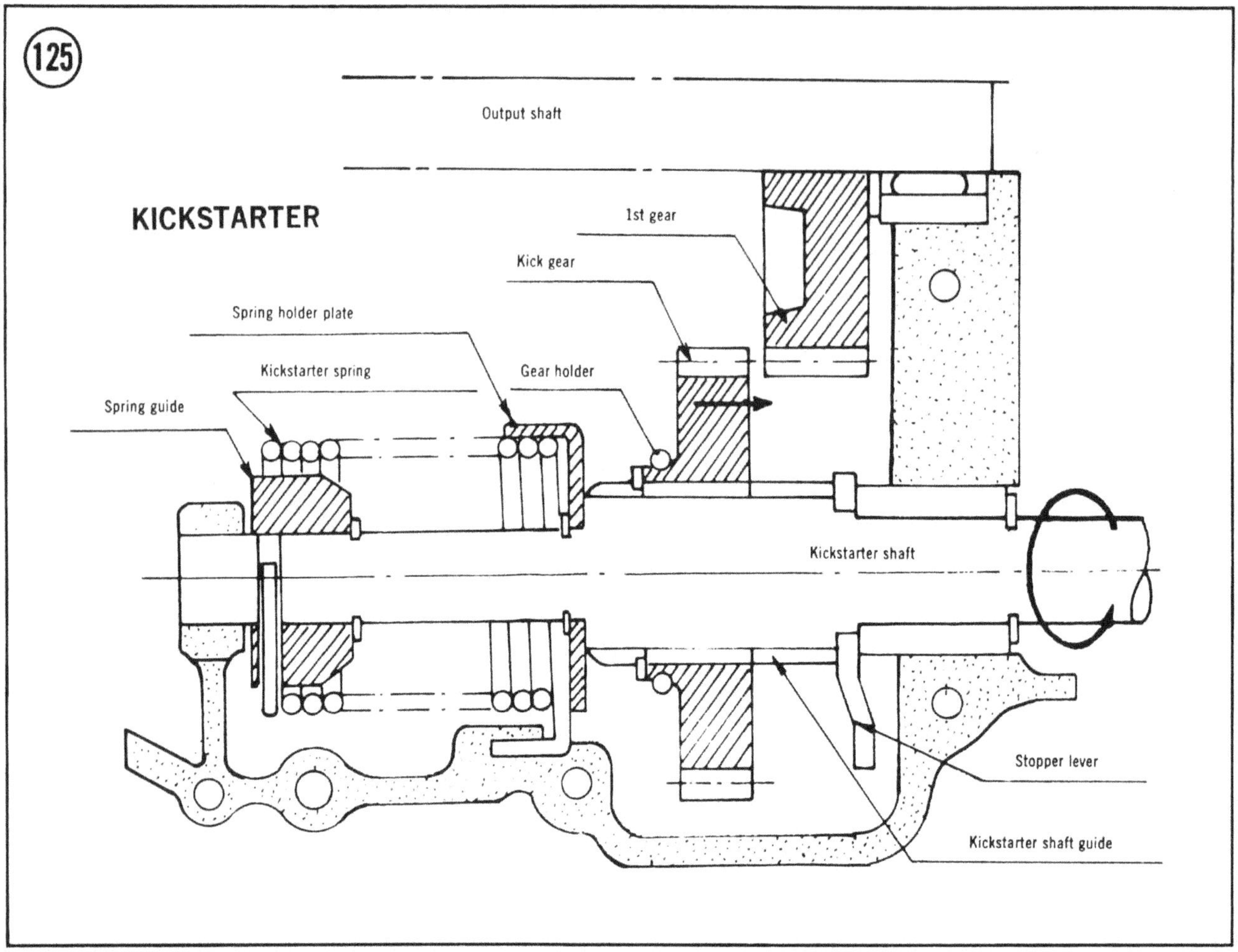

Figure 125 — KICKSTARTER (labels: Output shaft, 1st gear, Kick gear, Spring holder plate, Kickstarter spring, Gear holder, Spring guide, Kickstarter shaft, Stopper lever, Kickstarter shaft guide)

kickstarter gear moves to the left, it disengages itself from the gear in the transmission.

Removal

To remove the kickstarter it is only necessary to lift it from the upper crankcase (**Figure 126**).

Disassembly

1. Remove the spring and spring guide.
2. Remove the snap ring (**Figure 127**) and spring holder plate.

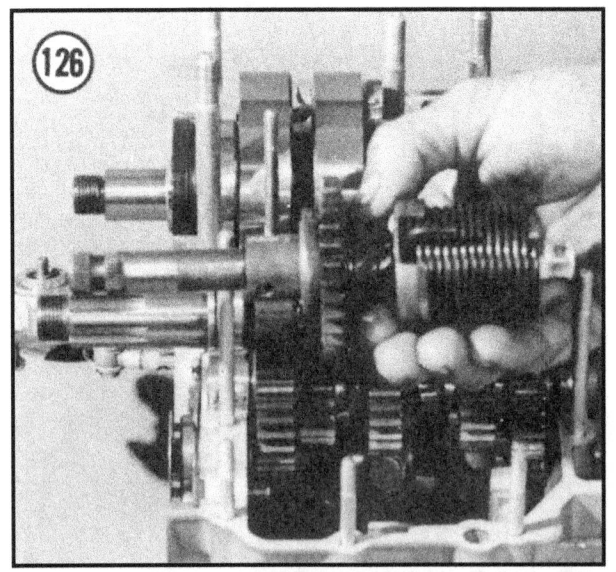

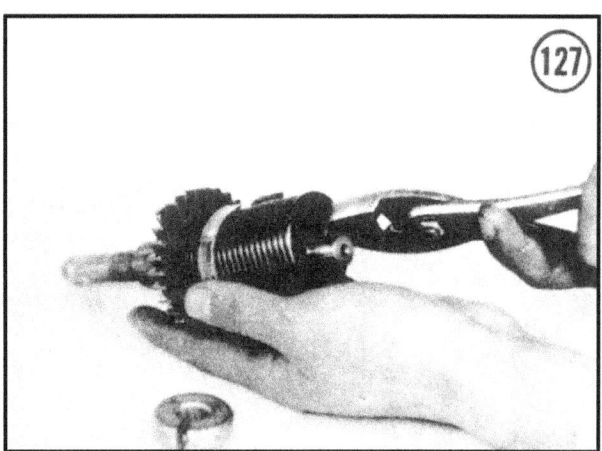

3. Remove the snap rings and kickstarter gear from the kick shaft (**Figure 128**).

Inspection

Slide the kickstarter gear (**Figure 129**) along

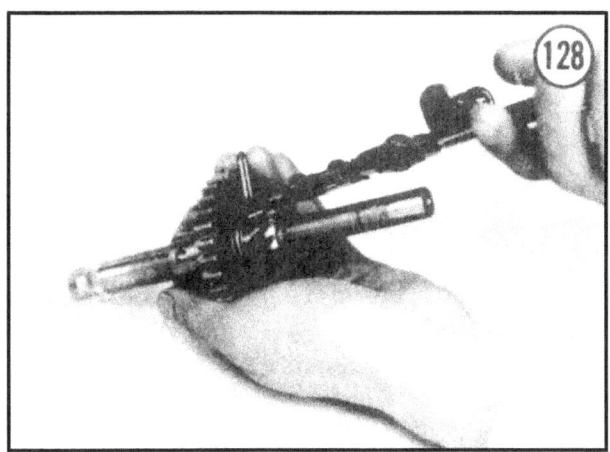

the helical splines on the kick shaft. Check for looseness or binding. Check for weakening of the kickstarter spring. Replace any worn or damaged parts.

Installation

1. Reverse the disassembly procedure to assemble the kickstarter. Be sure that each snap ring is seated in its groove.
2. Consider the angle that the kick spring makes with the kick stopper lever when replacing the kick spring on the kick shaft. Refer to **Figure 130** when assembling these items.
3. Install the kick gear holder properly into the crankcase (**Figure 131**). If it is installed improperly, the kick gear will not slide.

After the crankcase halves are assembled, install the kick stopper. Rotate the kickstarter pedal downward approximately 150 degrees (**Figure 132**), then install the stopper.

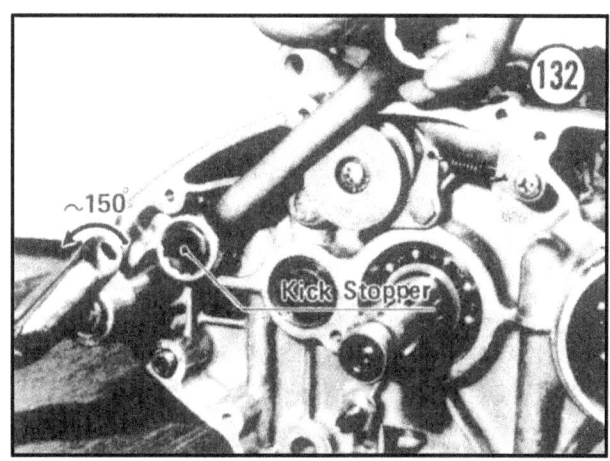

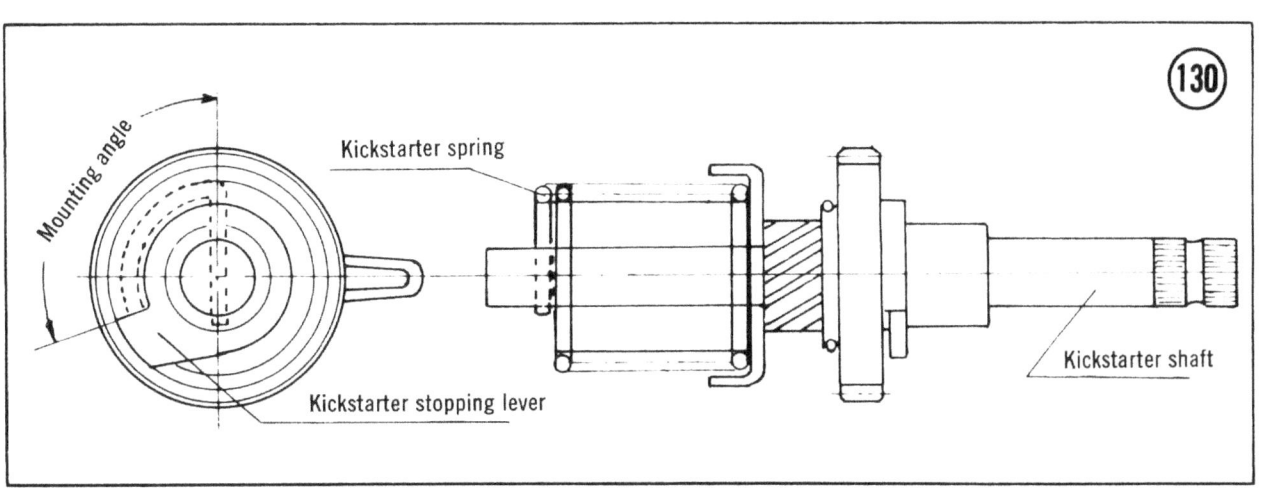

CHAPTER FOUR

ELECTRICAL SYSTEM

This chapter covers operating principles and troubleshooting procedures for the ignition, charging, signal, and lighting systems. Kawasaki triple cylinder machines are equipped with either a conventional battery ignition system or a capacitor discharge system, which uses no breaker points. All models use alternators as the source of electrical system power.

BATTERY IGNITION SYSTEM

A battery ignition system is used on S series and some H1 machines. This system functions in a manner similar to that of an automobile.

Functional Operation

Figure 1 illustrates the battery ignition system used on these machines. Note that the system is shown for a single cylinder only. All components except the battery, fuse, and ignition switch are duplicated for the other two cylinders.

When the breaker points are closed, current flows from the battery through the primary winding of the ignition coil, thereby building a magnetic field around the coil. The breaker cam rotates with the crankshaft and is so adjusted that the breaker points open as the piston reaches firing position.

When the points open, the magnetic field collapses. As the field collapses, a very high voltage (approximately 15,000 volts) is induced in the secondary winding of the ignition coil. This high voltage is sufficient to jump the gap at the spark plug.

The condenser serves primarily to protect the points. Inductance of the ignition coil primary tends to keep a surge of current flowing through the circuit even after the points have started to open. The condenser stores this surge and thus prevents arcing at the points.

Point adjustment and ignition timing are discussed in Chapter Two.

Battery Ignition Troubleshooting

Ignition system problems can be classified as no spark, weak spark, or improperly timed spark. These conditions can affect any or all cylinders of a three cylinder engine. **Table 1** lists common causes and remedies for ignition system malfunctions.

If the problem is no spark at any cylinder, it is almost certainly because current is not reaching the coils. Since the only current path is through the battery connections and the main switch, the defect will be easy to locate.

Ignition failures confined to one cylinder are also easy to isolate.

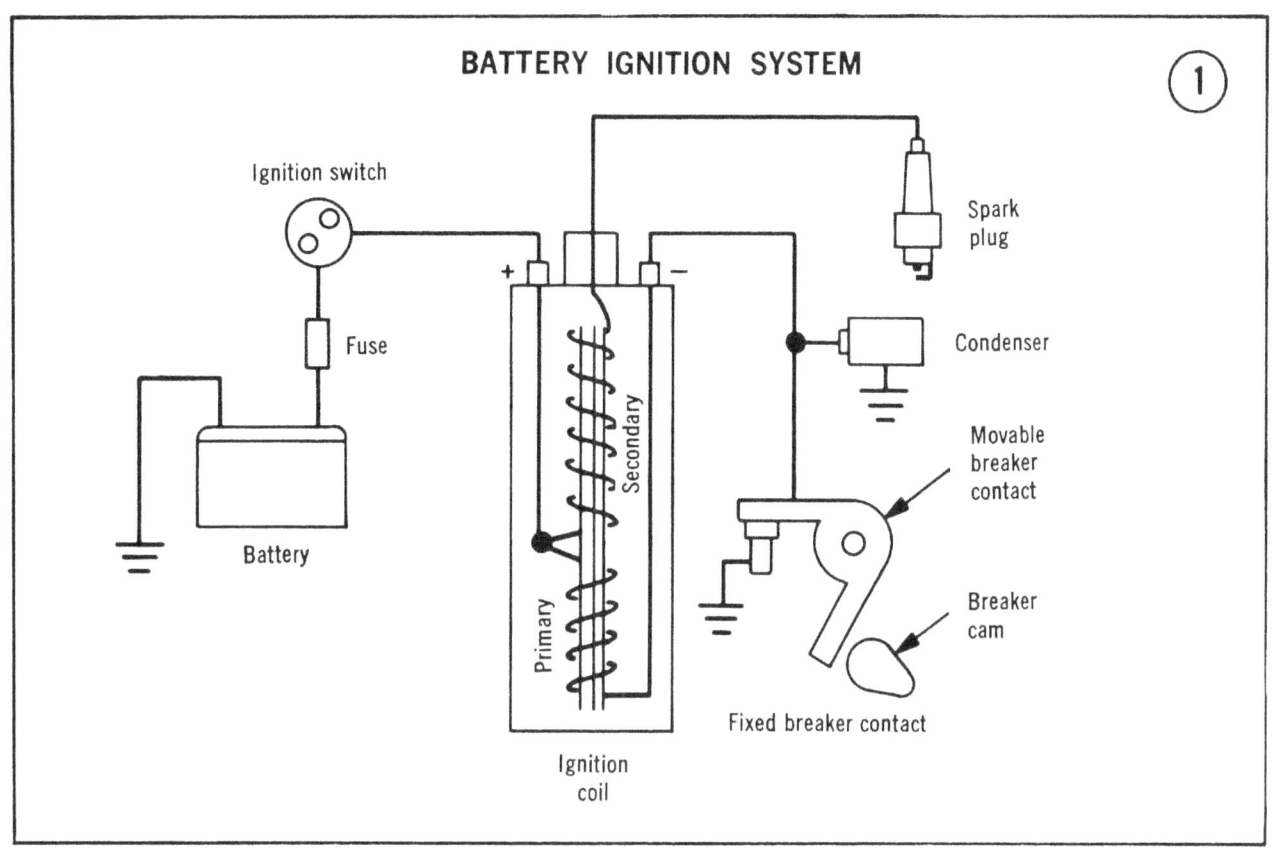

Table 1 BATTERY IGNITION TROUBLESHOOTING

Symptom	Probable Cause	Remedy
No spark or weak spark, all cylinders	Discharged battery	Charge battery
	Defective fuse	Replace
	Defective main switch	Replace
	Loose or corroded connections	Clean & tighten
	Broken wire	Repair
No spark or weak spark, one cylinder only	Incorrect point gap	Reset points. Be sure to readjust timing
	Dirty or oily points	Clean points
	Spark plug lead damaged	Replace wire
	Broken primary wire	Repair wire
	Open winding in coil	Replace coil
	Shorted winding in coil	Replace coil
	Defective condenser	Replace condenser
Misfires	Dirty spark plug	Clean or replace plug
	Spark plug is too hot	Replace with colder plug
	Spark plug is too cold	Replace with hotter plug
	Spring on ignition points is weak	Replace points, reset timing
	Incorrect timing	Adjust timing

1. Rotate the engine until the points associated with the affected cylinder are closed.

2. Disconnect the high voltage lead from the affected spark plug and hold it one-quarter inch away from the cylinder head. Turn on the ignition. With an insulated tool, such as a piece of wood, open the points. A fat, blue-white spark should jump from the spark plug lead to the cylinder head. If the spark is good, clean or replace the spark plug. If there is no spark, or if it is thin, yellowish, or weak, continue with Step 3.

3. Connect the leads of a voltmeter to the wire on the points and to a good ground. Turn on the ignition switch. If the meter indicates more than 1/8 volt, the problem is defective points. Replace them.

4. Open the points with an insulated tool, such as a piece of wood. The voltmeter should indicate battery voltage. If not, there are three possibilities.

   a. Shorted points
   b. Shorted condenser
   c. Open coil primary circuit

5. Disconnect the condenser and the wire from the points. Connect the underground (positive) voltmeter lead to the wire which was connected to the points. If the voltmeter does not indicate battery voltage, the problem is an open coil primary circuit. Replace the suspected coil with a known good one. You may borrow one from another cylinder. If that coil doesn't work, the problem is in the primary wiring.

6. If the voltmeter indicated battery voltage in Step 5, the coil primary circuit is OK. Connect the positive voltmeter lead to the wire which goes from the coil to the points. Block the points open with a calling card or similar piece of cardboard. Connect the negative voltmeter lead to the movable point. If the voltmeter indicates any voltage, the points are shorted and must be replaced.

7. If the foregoing checks are satisfactory, the problem is in the coil or condenser. Substitute each of these separately with a known good one from another cylinder to determine which is defective.

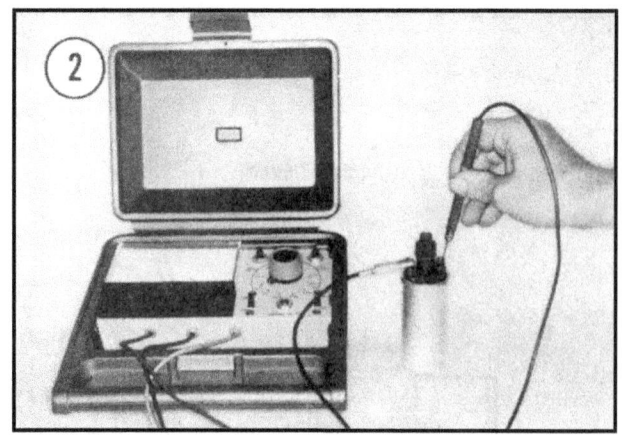

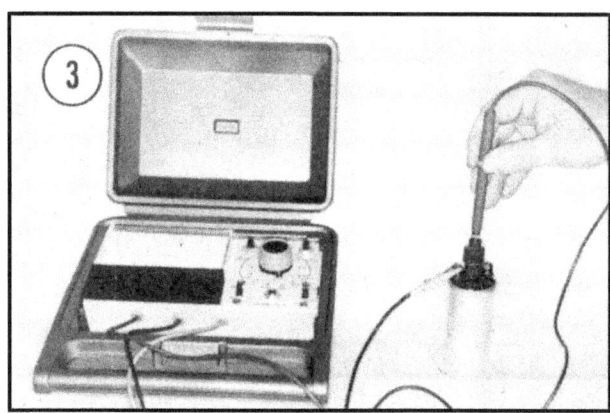

Ignition Coil

The ignition coil is a form of transformer which develops the high voltage required to jump the spark plug gap. The only maintenance required is keeping the electrical connections clean and tight, and occasionally checking to see that the coil is mounted securely.

If coil condition is doubtful, there are several checks which should be made.

1. Measure the resistance with an ohmmeter between the positive and negative primary terminals (**Figure 2**). Resistance should measure approximately five ohms. Some coils, however, have a primary resistance of less than one ohm. Compare the measurement with that of a known good coil from one of the other cylinders.

2. Measure the resistance between either primary terminal and the secondary high voltage terminal (**Figure 3**). Resistance should be in the range of 5,000 to 11,000 ohms.

3. Scrape the paint from the coil housing down to bare metal. Set the ohmmeter to its highest range, then measure insulation resistance between this bare spot and the high voltage term-

inal (**Figure 4**). Insulation resistance must be at least 3 megohms (3 million ohms).

4. If these checks don't reveal any defects, but coil condition is still doubtful, substitute a known good one.

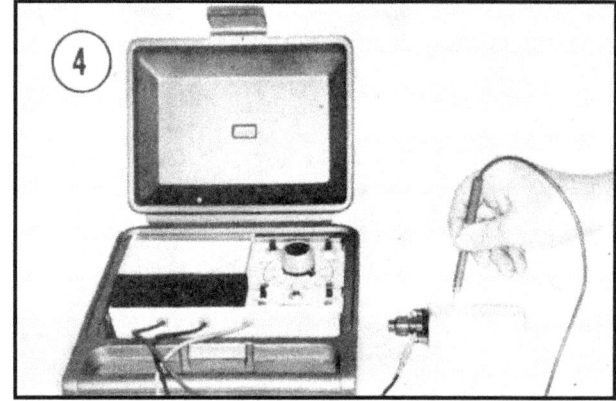

Be sure to connect the primary wires correctly when replacing the coil.

Condenser

The condenser is a sealed unit that requires no maintenance. Be sure that both connections are clean and tight.

Two tests can be made on the condenser. Measure condenser capacity with a condenser tester. Capacity should be 0.18 to 0.25 microfarad. The other test is insulation resistance, which should not be less than 5 megohms, measured between the condenser pigtail and case.

In the event that no test equipment is available, a quick test of the condenser may be made by connecting the condenser case to the negative terminal of a 12-volt battery, and the positive lead to the positive battery terminal. Allow the condenser to charge for a few seconds, then quickly disconnect the battery and touch the condenser pigtail to the condenser case. If you observe a spark as the pigtail touches the case, you may assume that the condenser is OK.

Arcing between the breaker points is a common symptom of condenser failure.

KH500 AND H1 CAPACITOR DISCHARGE IGNITION SYSTEM

KH500 and some H1 models are equipped with a capacitor discharge ignition system (CDI). This system, unlike battery or magneto ignition systems, uses no breaker points or other moving parts. Because of the extremely fast rise time of the high voltage, effects of spark plug fouling are minimized.

Since there are no components to wear, ignition timing should not change for the life of the bike. If timing is required, as after engine disassembly, refer to Chapter Two.

CDI Operation

Figure 5 is a functional diagram of the capacitor discharge system. Battery voltage is converted to alternating current, then stepped up, and rectified into high voltage direct current in a DC-to-DC converter which is part of the "B" unit. This current charges the capacitor (condenser) in the capacitor discharge circuit.

A small magnet attached to and rotating with the alternator shaft generates a pulse in the signal pickup coil in the alternator. This pulse is amplified, then shaped, and used to trigger the thyristor. When the thyristor is triggered, it conducts, and thereby provides a discharge path for the capacitor.

The capacitor discharges very quickly into the primary circuit of the ignition coil, where it is stepped up to as much as 30,000 volts.

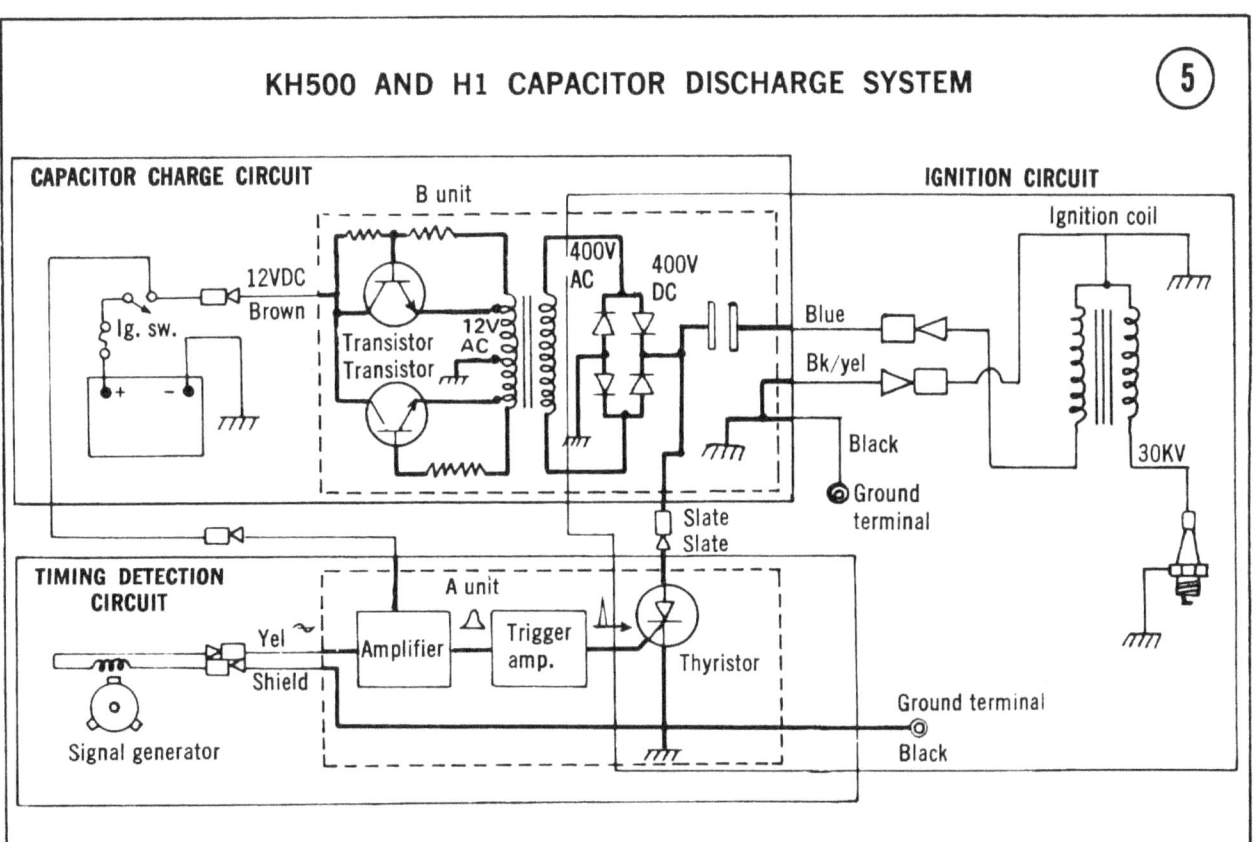

H Series Distributor

The distributor is a form of switch which directs the high voltage developed by the coil to the proper spark plug. The distributor rotor is driven by the crankshaft.

To install and adjust the distributor, proceed as follows.

1. Position the piston of the right-hand cylinder at top dead center.

2. Refer to **Figure 6**. Press the rotor onto the shaft by hand, so that the line on the rotor aligns with the center of the timing mark. It may happen that the line on the rotor does not align exactly with the center of the mark. In such a case, its position is satisfactory as long as the line on the rotor falls within the tolerance "T" marks on either side of the center.

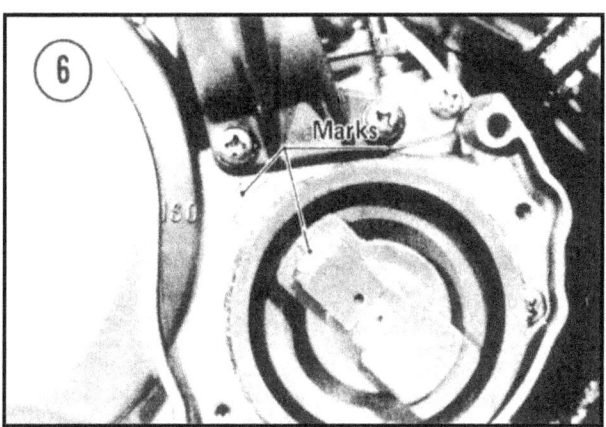

CDI Cautions

Certain measures must be taken to protect the capacitor discharge system. Instantaneous damage to the semiconductors in the system will occur if the following precautions are not observed.

1. Never connect the battery backward. If battery polarity is wrong, damage will occur to the rectifier, alternator, and CDI system.

2. Do not disconnect the battery when the engine is running. A voltage surge will occur which will damage the rectifier and possibly burn out the lights.

3. Keep all connections between the various units clean and tight. Be sure that the wiring connectors are pushed together firmly.

4. Do not substitute another type of ignition coil or battery.

5. Each unit is mounted with a rubber vibration isolator. Always be sure that the isolators are in place when replacing any units.

CDI Troubleshooting

Problems with the capacitor discharge system fall into one of the following categories. See **Table 2**.

a. Weak spark
b. No spark
c. Sparks occur at random

Table 2 CDI TROUBLESHOOTING

Symptom	Probable Cause	Remedy
Weak spark	Low battery	Charge battery
	Poor connections	Clean and tighten connections
	High voltage leakage	Replace defective wire
	Defective coil	Replace coil
	Unit "B" defective	Replace
No spark	Discharged battery	Charge battery
	Fuse burned out	Replace fuse
	Wiring broken	Repair wire
	Defective coil	Replace coil
	Unit "A" or "B" defective	Replace defective unit
	Defective signal generator coil	Replace signal generator coil
Random sparks	Unit "A" or "B" defective	Replace defective unit

Unit Tests

Although the most conclusive test can be made by substituting a known good unit for a suspected one, some tests may be made with a voltmeter, ammeter, and ohmmeter.

1. Refer to **Figure 7**. Measure the resistance between the black wire and gray wire on unit "A". The ohmmeter must indicate infinite resistance.

2. Reverse the meter connections. The meter must again indicate infinite resistance.

> **CAUTION**
> *Unit "B" develops high voltage. Follow the procedure exactly to avoid shock hazard.*

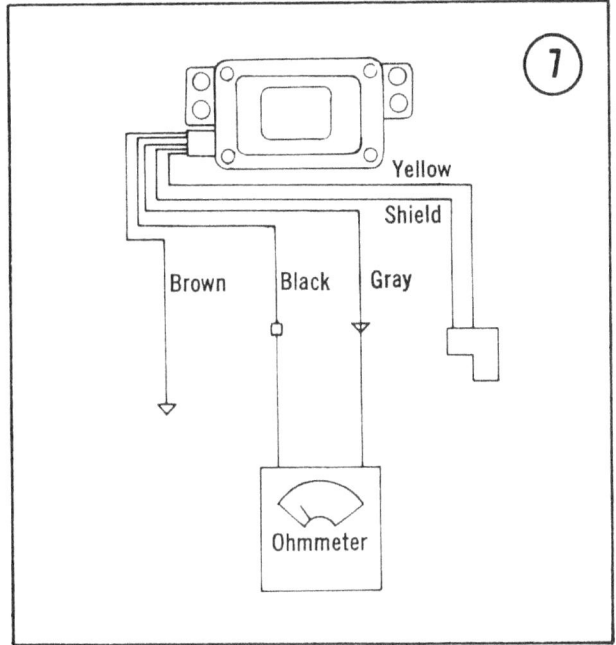

3. Connect unit "B" as shown in **Figure 8**. Connect the brown wire to the negative terminal of the ammeter. Connect the positive terminal of the 12-volt battery to the positive terminal of the ammeter. Connect the black wire to the negative battery terminal.

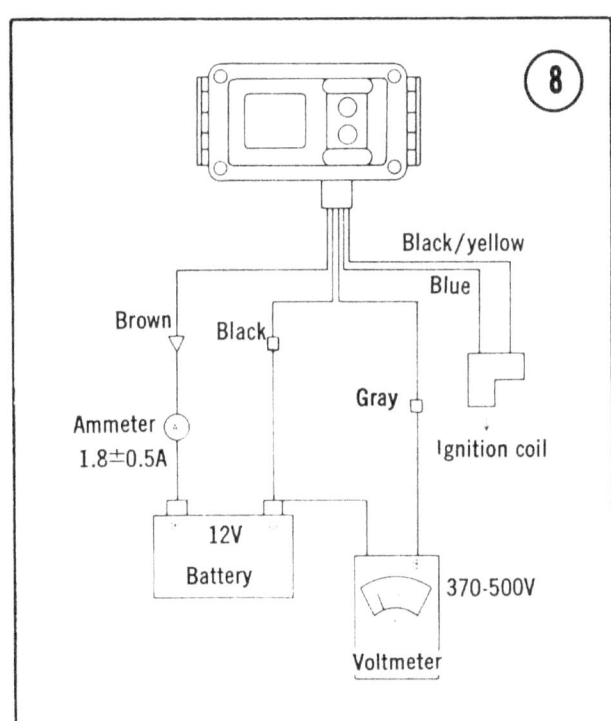

4. The ammeter must indicate 1.8 ± 0.5 amperes, and not fluctuate.

5. Disconnect the brown wire from the battery. Connect the negative lead of the voltmeter to the negative battery terminal. Connect the positive voltmeter lead to the gray wire.

6. Reconnect the brown wire to the battery. The voltmeter must indicate 370 to 500 volts.

7. It is normal that the unit emits a tone.

8. Disconnect the battery, then the voltmeter.

9. Connect both units together, as shown in **Figure 9** (next page), but do not connect the battery.

10. Connect the voltmeter to the gray wire. It may be necessary to fabricate some suitable wires to connect the plugs and the voltmeter.

11. Connect the battery as in Step 3.

12. If unit "B" checked OK earlier, but the ammeter does not indicate 2.0 plus or minus 0.5 amperes, or the voltmeter does not indicate 370 to 500 volts, unit "A" is defective.

H2 IGNITION SYSTEM

Model H2 machines are equipped with a magneto CDI system. **Figures 10 and 11** compare battery and magneto CDI systems. Unlike the H1 CDI system, which charges the ignition capacitor through a DC-to-DC converter, the H2 system obtains the necessary power directly from the magneto. Another major difference is that pulses from the signal generator are of sufficient amplitude to trigger the spark without amplification.

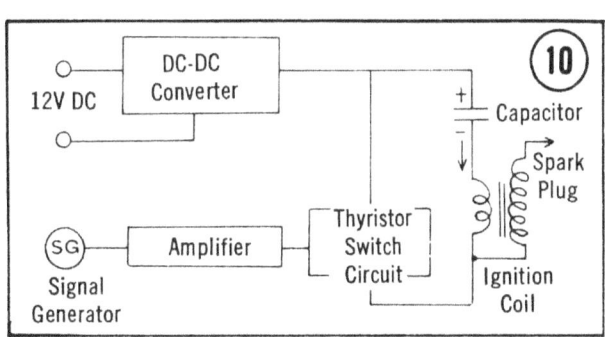

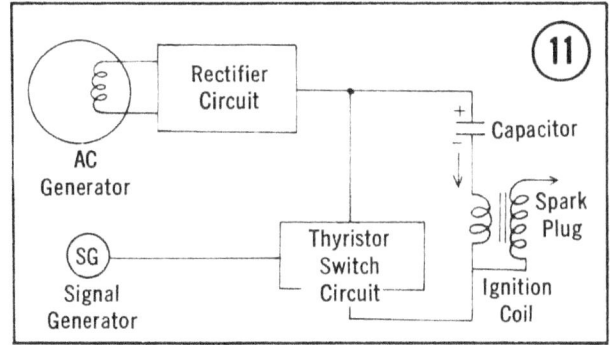

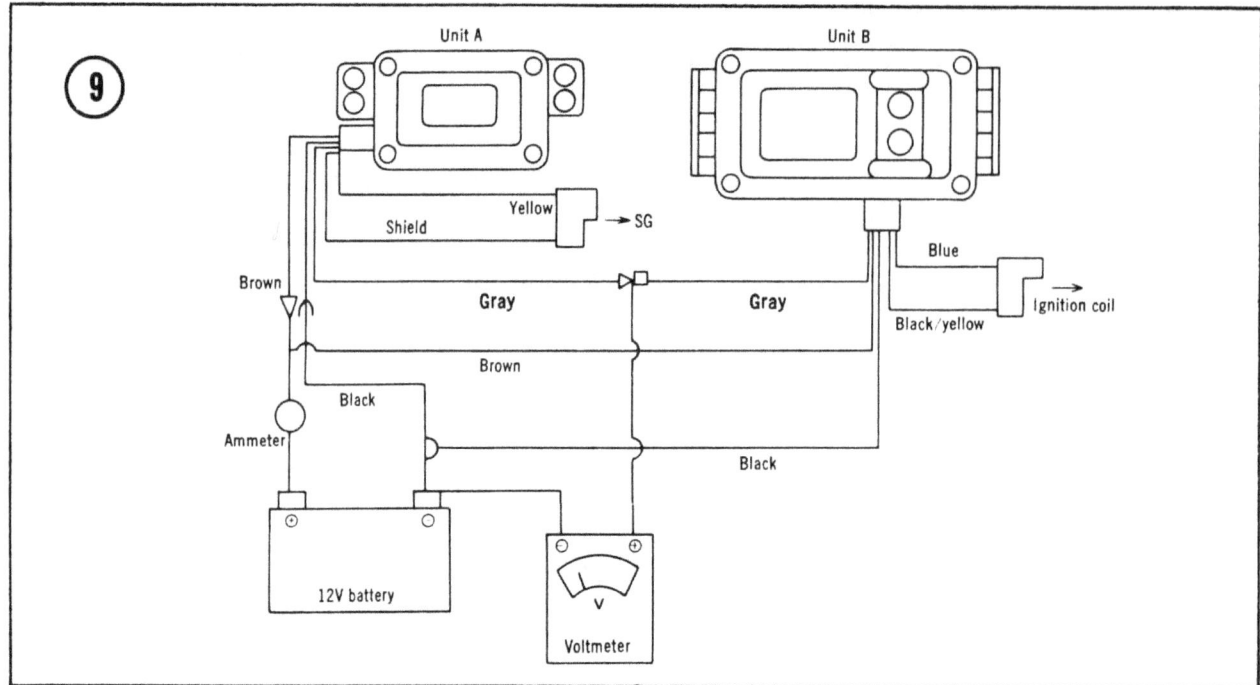

The alternator contains two high voltage windings (**Figure 12**). One winding is used at low speeds; the other at high speeds.

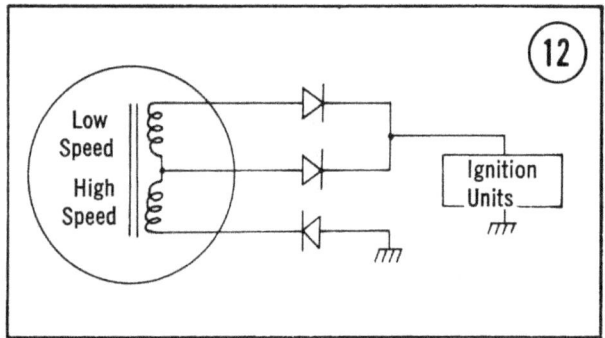

The low speed windings have a large number of turns so that high voltage can be generated at relatively low engine speeds. As engine speed rises, however, these windings cannot supply sufficient current to charge the capacitor, so the high speed winding takes over.

At the point where low speed winding voltage begins to fall off, the voltage from the high speed winding rises sufficiently to supply charging current for the capacitor. The high speed windings have fewer turns and much lower resistance, and consequently do not become loaded down so much at high speeds.

Figure 13 is a schematic diagram of one channel of the H2 ignition system. The capacitor (C) charges through diodes D2, D3, and D4. The positive pulse from the signal generator coil turns on the thyristor (Th), which completes the discharge path for the capacitor through the primary winding of the ignition coil. The resistor (R) bleeds the charge from the capacitor when the machine is not running.

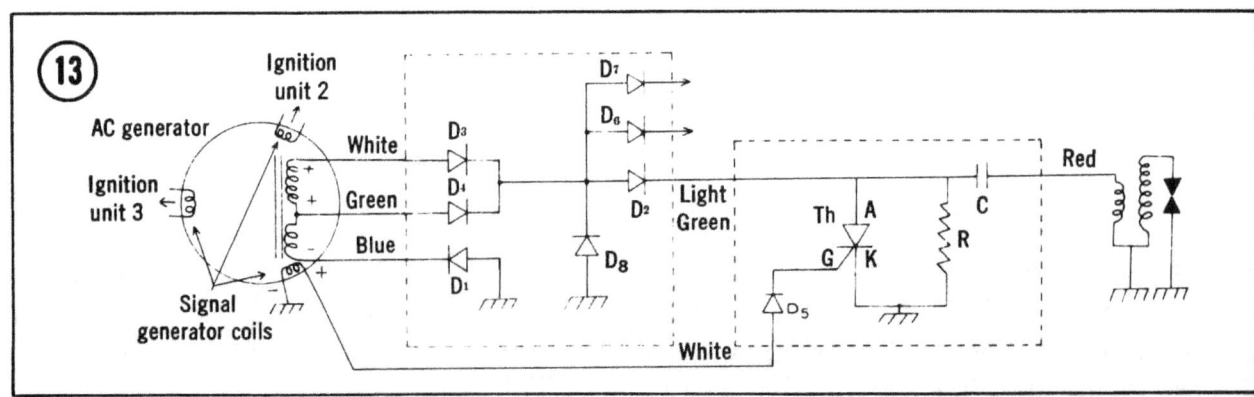

The ignition units for the two remaining cylinders operate in the same manner. They are supplied through diodes D6 and D7.

H2 Ignition Troubleshooting

The first step in troubleshooting this system is to narrow down the failure to the smallest possible area. Testing of individual CDI components is frequently possible without elaborate equipment. **Table 3** lists symptoms and possible causes.

If the engine will not start at all, first pull off the spark plug wires and test for a good spark at each cylinder, using known good spark plugs. Connect each spark plug to its cable and observe each spark plug as the engine is cranked briskly.

> CAUTION
> *Battery failure is not listed as a possible ignition trouble source because the motorcycle will start and run without the battery. Prolonged operation without battery connected will result in eventual failure of ignition unit.*

Unit Tests

Some tests may be performed without test equipment. The following paragraphs describe such tests.

To check the spark, pull off a plug wire and connect it to a plug known to be good. Lay the plug against the engine where you can observe it and crank the engine. If a strong blue-white spark jumps the gap, the ignition spark is good.

If you suspect a bad spark plug, check the spark as described in the foregoing paragraph, then substitute the suspected plug. If the spark is then weak or nonexistent with the suspected plug, you can be sure that the plug was faulty.

The engine will not start if the spark plug wires are not connected to the proper plugs, or if one of the ignition unit red or white wires is transposed with another of the same color. These wires are clearly marked as to left, center, or right cylinder connection.

If the spark appears to be grounding out, examine the high voltage wiring and replace any that show broken or cracked insulation. If no cracks are visible, run the engine in a dark place to see where the spark is jumping.

Table 3   H2 IGNITION TROUBLESHOOTING

Strong spark, all cylinders	Problem not in ignition system Plugs firing in wrong order because of improper wiring Original plugs defective
Weak spark, all cylinders	Defective alternator Defective ignition rectifier unit
No spark at any cylinder	Defective alternator Defective ignition unit Defective ignition rectifier Defective wiring

If the engine is hard to start or lacks power at low speeds.

Strong spark, all cylinders	Trouble is not in ignition system Defective or dirty plugs Timing incorrect
Weak spark, all cylinders	Defective alternator (especially low speed windings) Defective ignition rectifier unit
Weak spark, one cylinder	High voltage insulation leak Defective ignition coil Defective signal generator coil
No spark, one cylinder	Faulty wiring Insulation leak Defective coil Defective ignition unit Defective ignition rectifier Defective signal generator

If the machine misses or lacks power at high speeds.

Strong spark, all cylinders	Problem not in ignition system Defective or dirty plugs Timing misadjusted Defective alternator (high speed windings)
Weak or no spark, one cylinder	Defective alternator Defective ignition unit Defective ignition coil Defective wiring Defective signal generator

> WARNING
> *Do not run the engine inside a closed area. Carbon monoxide gas is generated whenever the engine runs. This gas is deadly.*

When there is no spark at any cylinder, the trouble can sometimes be caused by failure of a single ignition unit. In this case, the trouble can be isolated without test equipment.

1. Disconnect the three light green wires from the ignition rectifier unit to the ignition units.

2. Reconnect one light green wire at a time to its associated ignition unit and check for spark at that cylinder.

3. If two of the cylinders will spark when connected alone, the ignition unit for the remaining cylinder is defective.

If there is no spark, or a weak spark, at one cylinder, check the spark plug and wiring. If those are not at fault, there are only four possibilities: coil, ignition unit, ignition rectifier unit, or signal generator. To isolate the unit proceed as follows.

1. There are three light green wires which go from the ignition rectifier unit to each ignition unit. Take the light green wire which goes to the bad cylinder ignition unit and transpose it with the light green wire which goes to either remaining good cylinder ignition unit. If the trouble has now shifted to the previously good cylinder, the ignition rectifier unit is defective. If the trouble remains in the previously bad cylinder, go on to Step 2.

2. Transpose the spark plug wires between the bad cylinder and either good cylinder. There are three red wires, one from each ignition unit to its associated coil. Transpose the red wires for the bad cylinder and the good cylinder. If the trouble has not shifted from the bad cylinder to the previously good cylinder, replace the coil for the bad cylinder. If the trouble still remains in the bad cylinder, go on to Step 3.

3. Return the spark plug wires to normal but leave the red wires transposed. Each ignition unit has a white wire coming from it. Transpose the white wire from the bad cylinder ignition unit and the white wire from another ignition unit. If the trouble is now in the previously good cylinder, the ignition unit for the bad cylinder is defective. If the trouble remains in the bad cylinder, the bad cylinder signal generator coil is defective.

SPARK PLUGS

The spark plugs recommended by the factory are usually the most suitable for your machine. Refer to the specifications in the Appendix for the recommended spark plugs for each machine. If riding conditions are mild, it may be advisable to go to spark plugs one step hotter than normal. Unusually severe riding conditions may require slightly colder plugs.

The proper heat range for the spark plugs is determined by whether the plugs operate hot enough to burn off unwanted deposits, but not so hot that they burn themselves or cause pre-ignition. A spark plug of the correct heat range will show a light tan color on the portion of the insulator within the cylinder after the plug has been in service.

If the insulator appears to be burned or white, the plug is too hot. Possibly the insulator and center electrode will even show evidence of melting. Such plugs should be replaced with colder ones.

Unburned residue such as fluffy black carbon or grimy oil deposits indicate a spark plug that is too cold. The insulator color may range from dark brown to black. Try using hotter plugs if these conditions are found.

Spark plug service is discussed in Chapter Two.

ALTERNATORS

An alternator is a form of electrical generator in which a magnetized field called a rotor revolves within a set of stationary coils called a stator. As the rotor revolves, alternating current is induced in the stator. The current is then rectified and used to operate the electrical accessories on the motorcycle and for charging the battery. The rotor may be either permanently magnetized, or magnetized by a separate winding in the rotor. Kawasaki machines use both types.

Alternators with permanently magnetized rotors are controlled by a solid state regulator. Alternators with externally excited field windings require a regulator similar to that in an automobile. **Figure 14** illustrates a typical rotor used on Kawasaki machines. Rotors on some models are permanently magnetized; others require separate excitation.

Exploded views of typical alternators, together with their associated electrical equipment, are shown in **Figures 15, 16, and 17**.

Figure 15 shows the KH400, KH250, and S series (without CDI); **Figure 16** shows H1 (with CDI) and **Figure 17** shows H2.

If alternator or regulator problems are suspected, as in the case of a chronically undercharged battery or dim headlights, first check the alternator output voltage.

1. Connect a 0-20 DC voltmeter across the battery terminals **(Figure 18)**. Be sure that you connect the positive voltmeter lead to the positive battery terminal, and the negative voltmeter lead to the negative battery terminal.

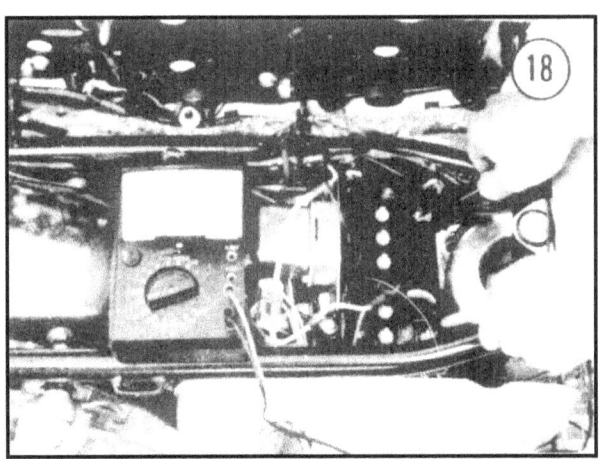

2. Start the engine and run it at 5,000 rpm. If the voltmeter indicates 14 to 15 volts, you may assume that the alternator and regulator are OK.

3. If the voltmeter does not indicate 14 to 15 volts, further checking will be required. Trouble may lie in the alternator, regulator, or wiring.

KH250, KH400, and S Series (Without CDI) Alternator Troubleshooting

1. There are 3 stator leads from the alternator.

Check for continuity between the following leads, as shown in **Figure 19A**.

   a. Pink to yellow
   b. Pink to white
   c. Yellow to white

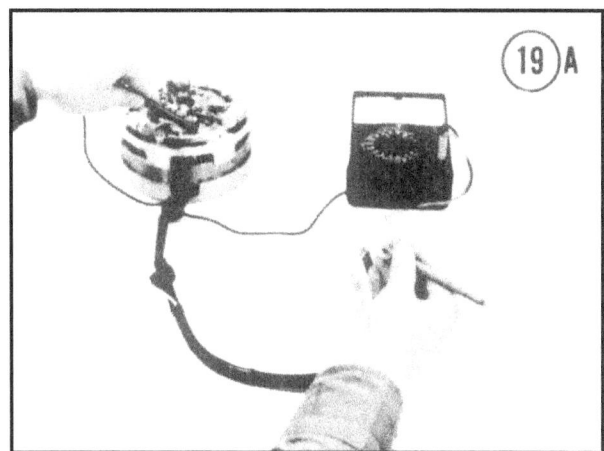

2. Set the ohmmeter to its highest range. Connect one lead to any stator wire, and the other to the alternator housing **(Figure 19B)**. The meter should indicate infinite resistance.

3. Replace the stator if the unit fails either of the preceding tests.

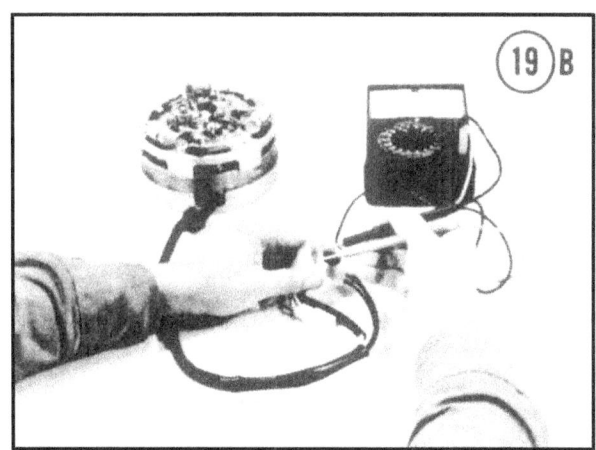

KH400 Alternator (with CDI) Troubleshooting

1. There are 3 leads from the alternator to the voltage regulator.

2. Set the ohmmeter to the R x 1 range. Measure the resistance between the 2 yellow leads **(Figure 20)**; it should be 0.45-0.7 ohms. If the reading is less, the coils are probably shorted. A higher reading or no reading at all indicates the coils are open.

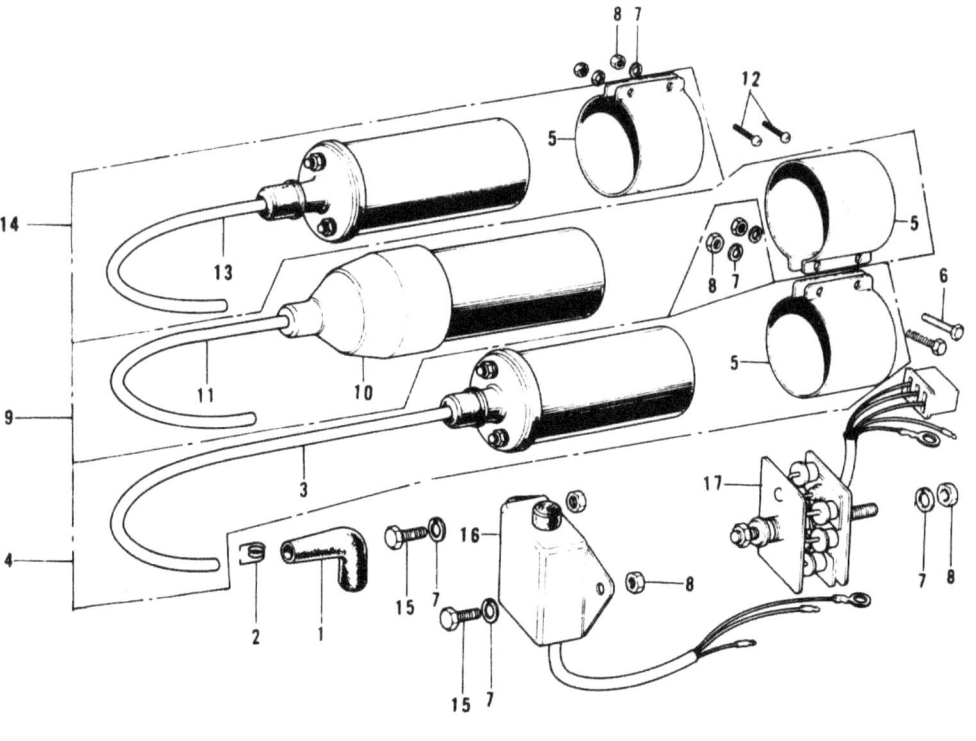
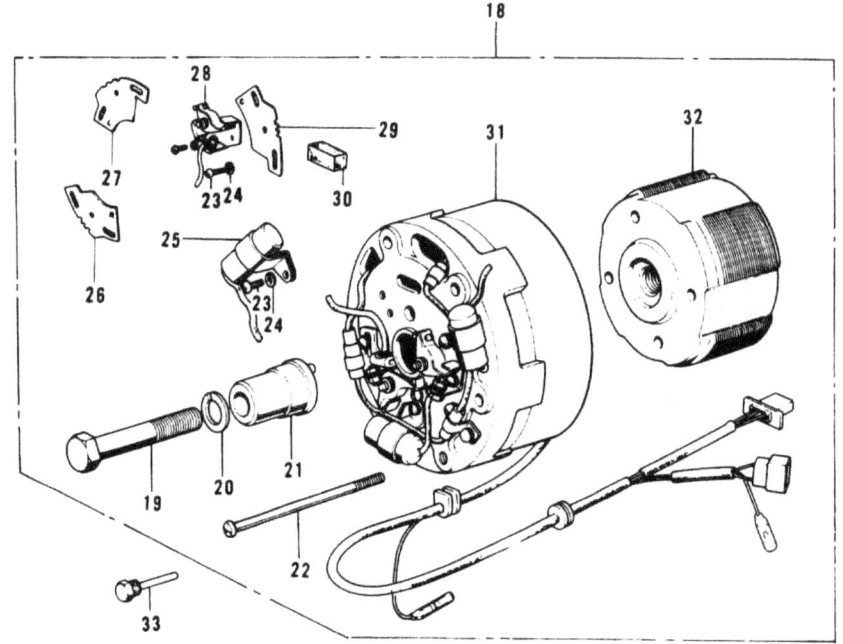

KH250, KH400, AND S SERIES ALTERNATOR (WITHOUT CDI)

1. Spark plug cap
2. Spark plug cap spring
3. Left high tension cable
4. Ignition coil
5. Ignition coil holder
6. Hex bolt
7. Lockwasher
8. Nut
9. Ignition coil
10. Ignition coil cap
11. Center high tension cable
12. Pan head screw
13. Right high tension cable
14. Ignition coil
15. Hex bolt
16. Regulator
17. Rectifier
18. Alternator
19. Hex bolt
20. Lockwasher
21. Cam
22. Pan head screw
23. Pan head screw
24. Lockwasher
25. Condenser
26. Right contact breaker plate
27. Left contact breaker plate
28. Breaker points
29. Center contact breaker plate
30. Felt oiling block
31. Stator assembly
32. Rotor
33. Puller

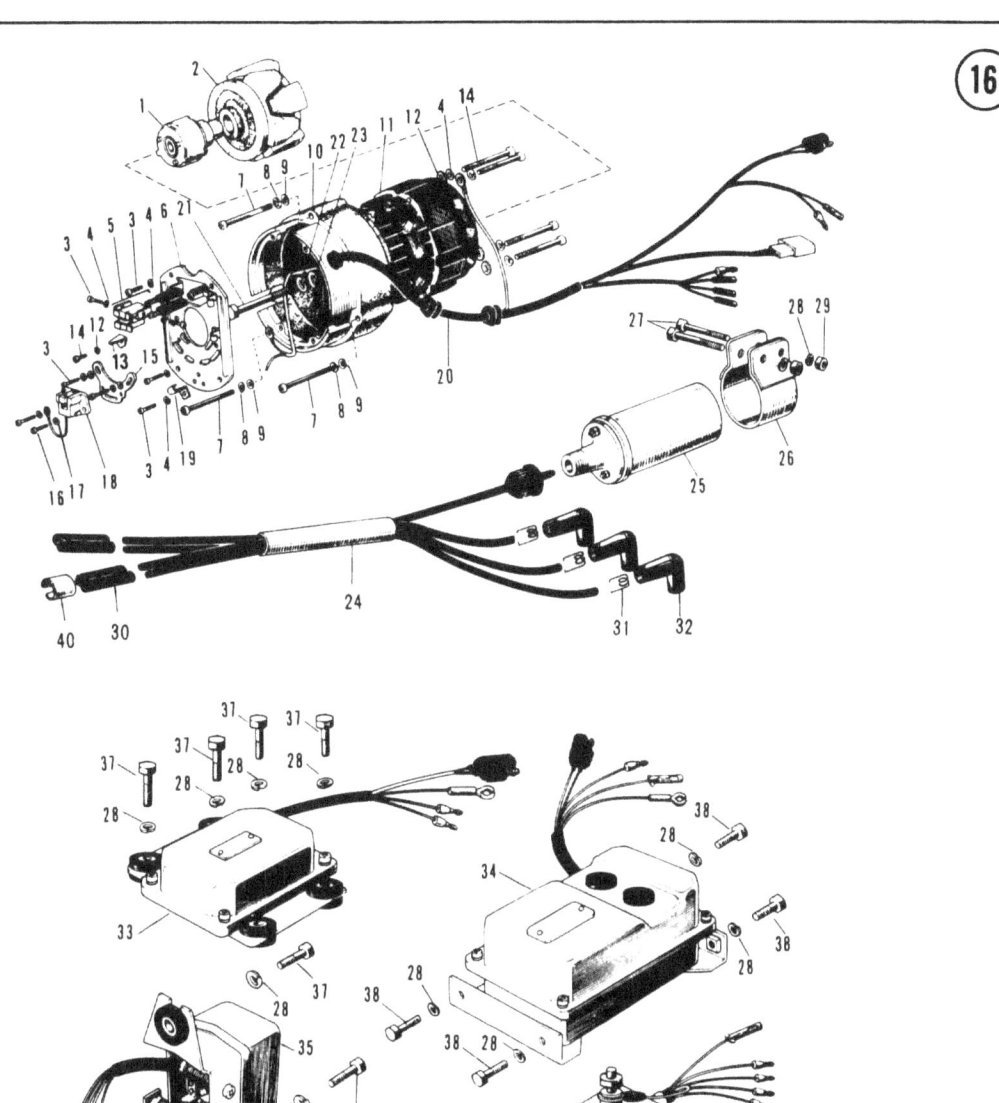

H1 ALTERNATOR (WITH CDI)

1. Starter rotor
2. Rotor

3-20. Yoke assembly
3. Screw
4. Spring washer
5. Carbon brush and holder
6. Yoke plate
7. Screw
8. Spring washer
9. Plain washer
10. Alternator housing
11. Stator
12. Plain washer
13. Ignition timing pointer
14. Screw
15. Pick-up plate
16. Screw
17. Washer
18. Pick-up
19. Lead wire clamp
20. Wiring harness complete
21. Hex head bolt
22. Spring washer
23. Plain washer
24. High tension cord assembly
25-26. Ignition coil
26. Ignition coil band
27. Bolt
28. Spring washer
29. Nut
30. High tension cord protector
31. Spark plug cap spring
32. Spark plug cap
33. Ignition unit (A)
34. Ignition unit (B)
35. Voltage regulator
36. Rectifier
37. Bolt
38. Bolt
39. Washer
40. Cord protector

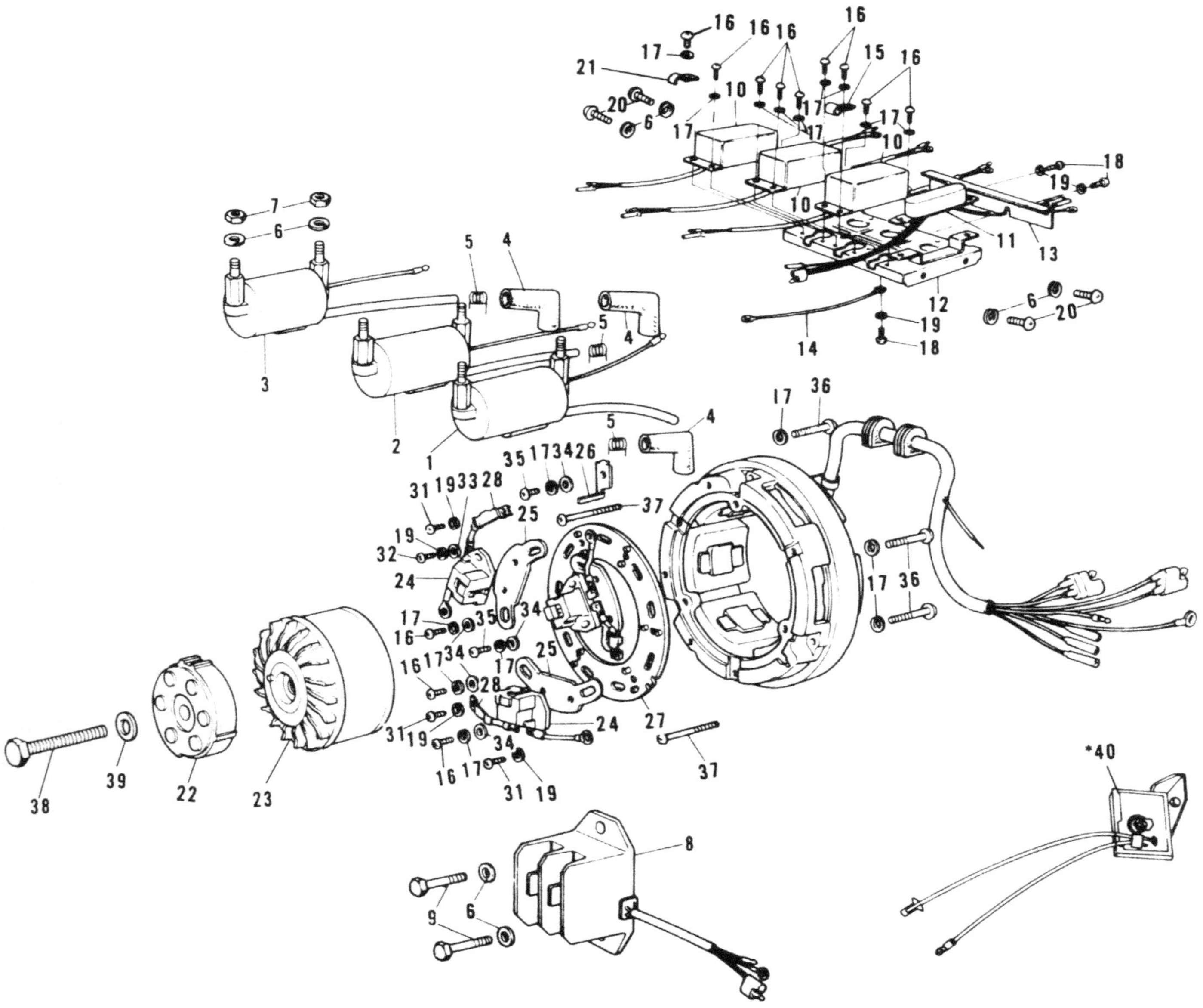

H2 ALTERNATOR

1. Ignition coil
2. Ignition coil
3. Ignition coil
4. Spark plug cap
5. Spark plug cap spring
6. Lockwasher
7. Hex nut
8. Regulator
9. Hex bolt
10. Ignition unit A
11. Ignition unit B
12. Ignition unit plate
13. Plate
14. Lead wire
15. Clamp
16. Pan head screw
17. Lockwasher
18. Pan head screw
19. Lockwasher
20. Pan head screw
21. Oil breather clamp
22. Rotor cover
23. Rotor
24. Pickup
25. Pickup plate
26. Ignition timing pointer
27. Yoke plate
28. Lead wire clamp
31. Pan head screw
32. Pan head screw
33. Flat washer
34. Flat washer
35. Pan head screw
36. Pan head screw
37. Pan head screw
38. Hex bolt
39. Lockwasher
40. Rectifier

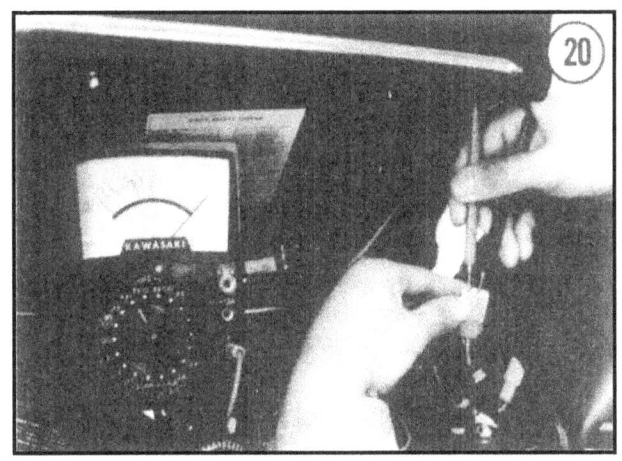

3. Set the ohmmeter to the highest range. Connect one lead to a yellow lead and one to the chassis (frame, engine, etc.); repeat for the other yellow lead. The meter should indicate infinity. If there is any meter reading, it indicates a short.

4. If the windings indicate normal resistance, but voltage and current tests indicate that the alternator is defective, then the magnets in the rotor are probably weak and must be replaced.

5. Replace the stator if the unit fails any of the preceding tests.

KH500 and H1
Alternator Troubleshooting

1. Measure field winding resistance between the slip rings, as shown in **Figure 21**. If the resistance is not 3.5 to 5.5 ohms, replace the rotor.

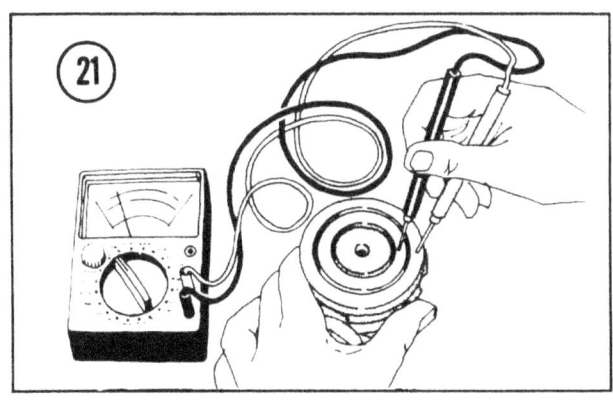

2. Measure insulation resistance of the field winding. Set the ohmmeter to its highest range, then measure resistance between either slip ring and the rotor shaft. Insulation resistance must be essentially infinite.

3. Inspect the brushes. Replace them if they are worn to ⅜ inch (9.3 millimeters). Standard length for new brushes is 9/16 inch (14 millimeters).

4. Check for continuity between each pair of yellow wires coming from the alternator stator.

5. Set the ohmmeter to its highest range, then measure insulation resistance between the stator housing and the three yellow leads. Insulation resistance must be essentially infinite.

H2 Alternator Troubleshooting

1. Measure resistance between both yellow leads. Resistance should be approximately 0.4 ohm.

2. With the ohmmeter set to its highest range, measure insulation resistance between either yellow lead and ground. Insulation resistance must be essentially infinite.

3. Measure resistance between the blue and the green leads. Resistance should be approximately 5 ohms.

4. Measure resistance between the black lead and each white lead. Resistance should be approximately 200 ohms.

5. Measure resistance between the white and green leads. Resistance should be approximately 200 ohms.

RECTIFIER

The rectifier assembly serves two purposes. It converts alternating current produced by the alternator into direct current which is used to charge the battery. It also prevents discharge of the battery through the alternator when the engine isn't running, or at other times when the output voltage of the alternator is less than battery voltage.

KH250, KH400, and S Series
Rectifer Troubleshooting

The rectifier assembly has 3 yellow leads, one red lead and one black lead.

1. Measure resistance between each yellow lead and the red lead (**Figure 22**). Record each ohmmeter reading.

2. Reverse the ohmmeter leads and repeat Step 1.

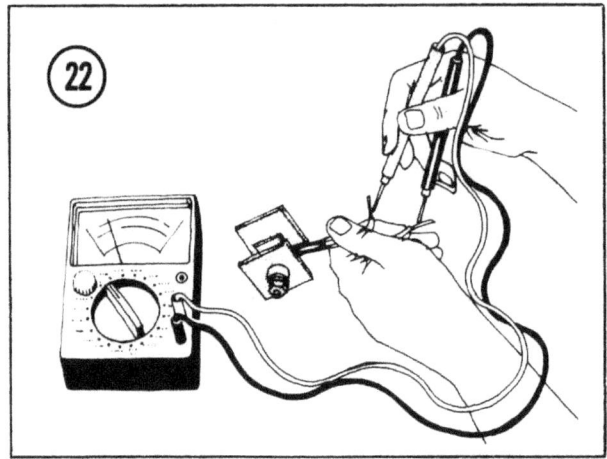

3. If each pair of measurements was essentially infinite in one direction and low in the reverse direction, proceed with Step 4. If any pair of measurements was either high or low in both directions, replace the rectifier assembly.

4. Measure resistance between each yellow lead and the black lead. Record the meter readings.

5. Reverse the meter connections and repeat Step 4. If any pair of measurements was either high or low in both directions, replace the rectifier assembly.

KH500 and H1 Rectifier Troubleshooting

The H1 rectifier is similar to that for S series models, except that it has one additional blue lead to be checked. Proceed as follows.

1. Measure resistance between each yellow wire to the red wire. Record the meter indications.

2. Reverse the meter leads and repeat the measurements.

3. If each pair of measurements was essentially infinite in one direction and low in the reverse direction, proceed with Step 4. If any pair of measurements was either high or low in both directions, replace the rectifier.

4. Measure the resistance between each yellow wire and the black wire. Record the meter indications.

5. Reverse the meter leads and repeat the measurements. If any pair of measurements was either high or low in both directions, replace the rectifier. If OK, proceed with Step 6.

6. Measure resistance between the black and blue wires, then reverse the meter leads and repeat the measurement. If the meter indicates low resistance in one direction and high resistance with the leads reversed, the rectifier is OK. If both measurements are either high or low, replace the rectifier.

H2 Voltage Regulator/Rectifier Troubleshooting

The H2 rectifier unit performs the dual functions of current rectification and voltage regulation. To check the unit, proceed as follows.

1. Refer to **Figure 23**. Measure resistance between the black and red leads, then repeat the measurement with the ohmmeter leads reversed. The meter should indicate approximately 70 ohms in one direction and 1,000 ohms in the other. If OK, proceed to Step 2.

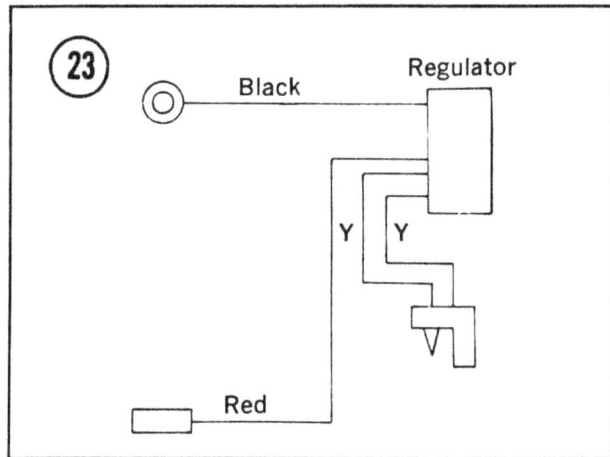

2. Measure resistance between the black lead and each yellow lead, then repeat the measurements with the meter leads reversed. Resistance should be approximately 25 ohms in one direction and 1,000 ohms in the other.

3. Measure resistance between each yellow lead and the red lead, then reverse the meter leads and repeat the measurements. Both sets of readings should be approximately 25 ohms in one direction. In the reverse direction, one reading should be approximately 1,000 ohms and the other should be approximately 4,000 ohms.

4. Connect the circuit shown in **Figure 24** using a suitable power supply. Then measure resistance between the two yellow leads. Resistance should be essentially infinite in one direction and approximately 500 ohms with the ohmmeter leads reversed.

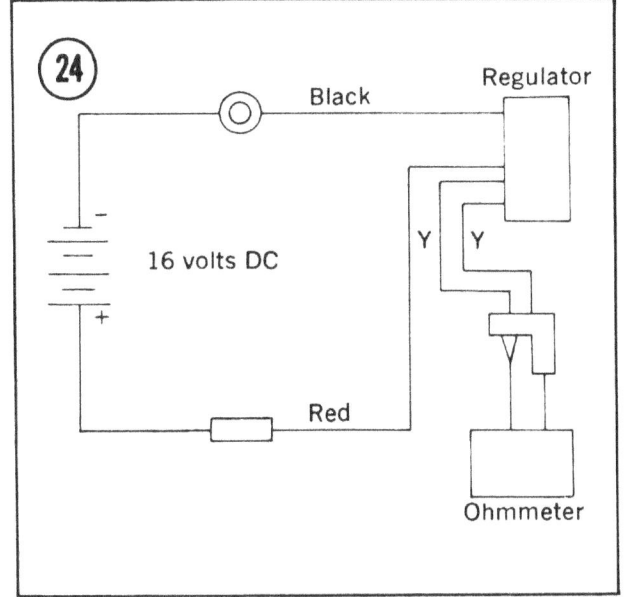

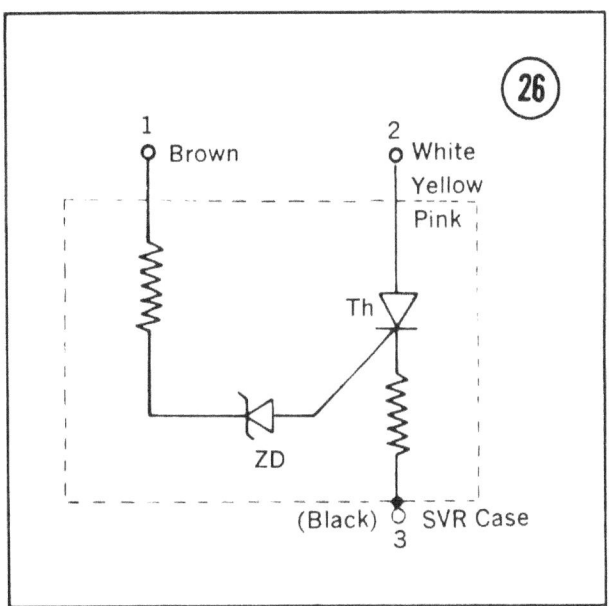

5. Reverse the power supply polarity, and lower its output voltage, as shown in **Figure 25**. Measure resistance between both yellow leads. Resistance should be essentially infinite in both directions.

6. Replace the rectifier unit if it fails any of the foregoing tests.

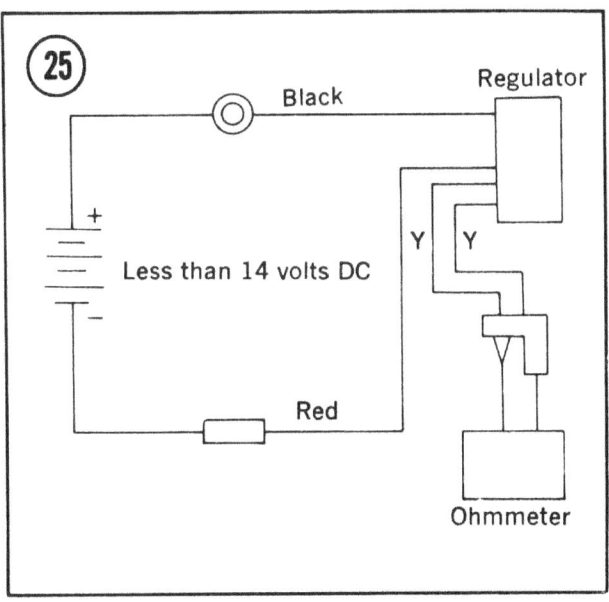

SOLID STATE VOLTAGE REGULATOR

Models KH400, KH250, and S series are equipped with a solid state voltage regulator (SVR). This unit consists of a zener diode (ZD), a thyristor (Th), and two resistors, as shown in **Figure 26**.

KH250 and S Series Troubleshooting

If a malfunction of the solid state voltage regulator is suspected, it may be checked by the following tests. However, bear in mind that if the battery is low, the regulator will not work properly even though it may be in good condition. Therefore, be sure that the battery is in good condition and at or near full charge before attempting to troubleshooting a suspected malfunction.

1. Measure resistance between the brown wire and the case. Resistance must be greater than 1,000 ohms.

2. Measure resistance in both directions between terminals 2 and 3. Resistance should be essentially infinite in both directions.

3. Connect the motorcycle battery to the regulator as shown in **Figure 27**. Be careful to observe proper polarity. No current should flow in the circuit between terminals 1 and 3. Measure resistance between terminals 2 and 3. Resistance should be essentially infinite.

4. Connect an additional 4 to 6 volt battery in series with the first battery to make a total of over 16 volts across terminals 1 and 3. If current does not flow, either the zener diode or the first thyristor is defective.

5. Replace the regulator if it fails any of the foregoing checks. If its condition is still doubtful, check it by trial replacement with a known good unit.

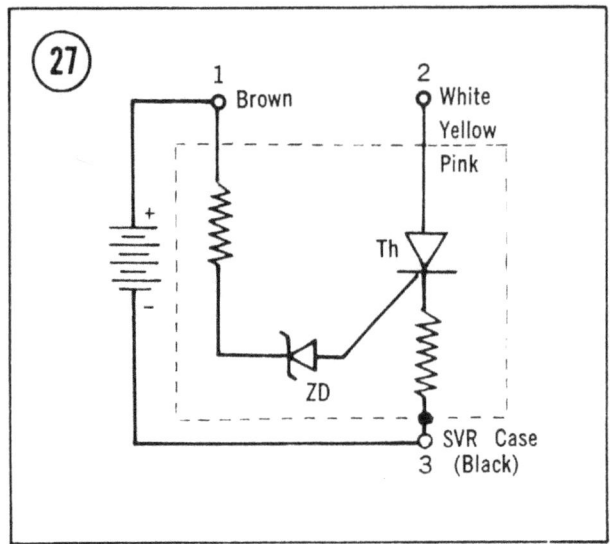

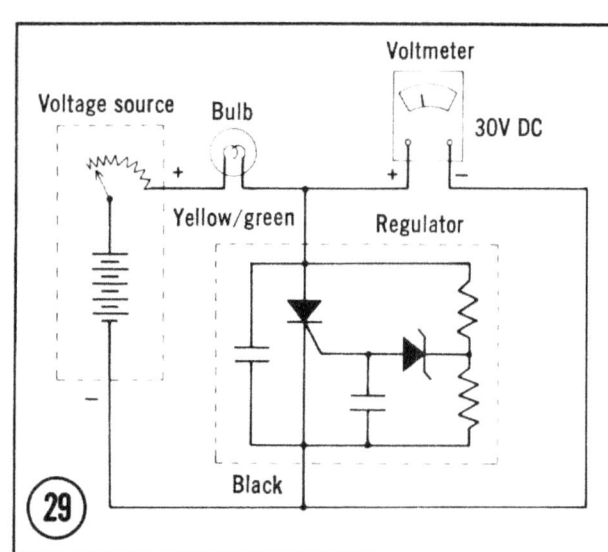

KH400 Troubleshooting

1. Check the resistance between the black and yellow/green leads (**Figure 28**). Resistance should be between 1,000-1,200 ohms.

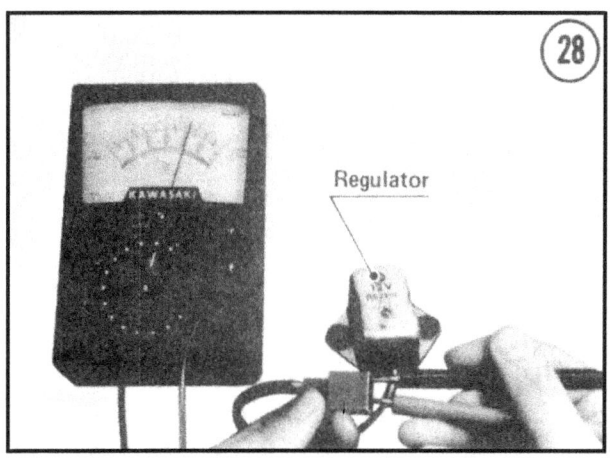

2. Connect the circuit shown in **Figure 29** using a suitable power supply. Set the voltmeter to the 30V DC range. Turn on the power supply; the light should be off. Gradually increase the voltage from 8 to 14 volts; if the regulator is good, the bulb will light between 10-12 volts.

3. Replace the voltage regulator if it fails either of these tests. If its condition is still doubtful, check it by trial replacement with a known good one.

Handling Precautions

Certain precautions must be observed when you handle or service the solid state regulator. Failure to observe these may result in damage to the unit.

1. Be sure that the mounting screws are tight.

2. Always be sure that the main switch is off before connecting or disconnecting the unit.

3. Be sure that the unit is mounted securely.

4. Be sure that the wires are connected properly. Improper wiring will result in damage to the battery and regulator.

5. The battery must be charged to near full capacity for the regulator to work properly. If the battery is very low, charge it before installation.

ELECTROMAGNETIC VOLTAGE REGULATOR—H1

Operation

Some alternators use separately excited field windings. Such alternators require a more complex regulator. As engine speed increases, alternator output tends to increase. It is possible, however, to control alternator output by controlling its field current, which is used for excitation.

Figure 30 illustrates the situation at low engine speeds. The rectified alternator output is applied to coil B. However, since the output is low, the magnetic field developed by coil B is too low to open contacts C_1 and C_0. Under these conditions, field current is supplied by the battery through the ignition switch, and is at its maximum value.

As alternator output voltage tends to increase, coil B develops more magnetic force, which breaks contacts C_1 and C_0. Field current

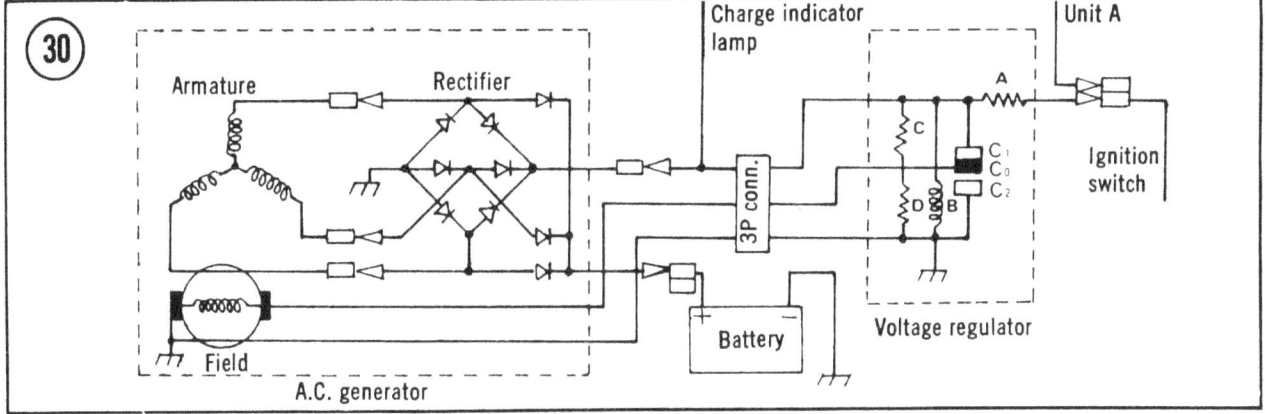

is then supplied from the alternator output through resistor C. Resistor C limits the field current, and thereby reduces alternator output so that contacts C_1 and C_0 again close, repeating the cycle.

At high engine speeds and light electrical loads, the action of the upper and center contacts is insufficient to control alternator output. As output voltage continues to rise, coil B pulls the movable contact C_0 down to the lower contact C_2. Under this condition the field is grounded, and alternator output drops to zero. As it drops, the movable and lower contacts separate, and the cycle repeats.

Regulator Testing

The most common causes of voltage regulator trouble are open wires or short circuits. To check the regulator, proceed as follows.

1. Remove the regulator.
2. Measure resistance between the brown and black leads (**Figure 31**). Resistance should be approximately 55 ohms.

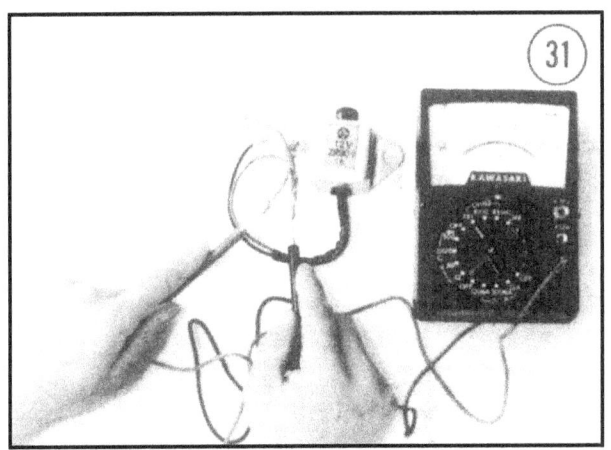

3. Connect a voltmeter across the battery terminals. Reconnect the regulator.
4. Start the engine and run it at 5,000 rpm. If the measured voltage is 14.5 plus or minus 0.5, the regulator is OK.

BATTERY

Kawasaki triple cylinder motorcycles are equipped with lead-acid storage batteries, smaller in size but similar in construction to batteries used in automobiles.

WARNING
Read and thoroughly understand the section on safety precautions before doing any battery service.

Safety Precautions

When working with batteries, use extreme care to avoid spilling or splashing the electrolyte. This electrolyte is sulfuric acid, which can destroy clothing and cause serious chemical burns. If any electrolyte is spilled or splashed on clothing or body, it should immediately be neutralized with a solution of baking soda and water, then flushed with plenty of clean water.

Electrolyte splashed into the eyes is extremely dangerous. Safety glasses should always be worn when working with batteries. If electrolyte is splashed into the eye, call a physician immediately, force the eye open, and flood with cool clean water for about 5 minutes.

If electrolyte is spilled or splashed onto painted or unpainted surfaces, it should be neutralized immediately with baking soda solution and then rinsed with clean water.

When batteries are being charged, highly explosive hydrogen gas forms in each cell. Some of this gas escapes through the filler openings and may form an explosive atmosphere around the battery. *This explosive atmosphere may exist for several hours.* Sparks, open flame, or a lighted cigarette can ignite this gas, causing an internal explosion and possible serious personal injury. The following precautions should be taken to prevent an explosion.

1. Do not smoke or permit any open flame near any battery being charged or which has been recently charged.

2. Do not disconnect live circuits at battery terminals, because a spark usually occurs where a live circuit is broken. Care must always be taken when connecting or disconnecting any battery charger; be sure its power switch is off before making or breaking connections. Poor connections are a common cause of electrical arcs which cause explosions.

Electrolyte Level

Battery electrolyte level should be checked regularly, particularly during hot weather. Most batteries are marked with electrolyte level limit lines (**Figure 32**). Always maintain the fluid level between the two lines, using distilled water as required for replenishment. Distilled water is available at almost every supermarket. It is sold for use in steam irons and is quite inexpensive.

Overfilling leads to loss of electrolyte, resulting in poor battery performance, short life, and excessive corrosion. Never allow the electrolyte level to drop below the top of the plates. That portion of the plates exposed to air may be permanently damaged, resulting in loss of battery performance and shortened life.

Excessive use of water is an indication that the battery is being overcharged. The two most common causes of overcharging are high battery temperature or high voltage regulator setting. It is advisable to check the voltage regulator, on machines so equipped, if this situation exists.

Cleaning

Check the battery occasionally for presence of dirt or corrosion. The top of the battery, in particular, should be kept clean. Acid film and dirt permit current to flow between terminals, which will slowly discharge the battery.

For best results when cleaning, wash first with diluted ammonia or baking soda solution, then flush with plenty of clean water. Take care to keep filler plugs tight so that no cleaning solution enters the cells.

Battery Cables

To ensure good electrical contact, cables must be clean and tight on battery terminals. If the battery or cable terminals are corroded, the cables should be disconnected and cleaned separately with a wire brush and baking soda solution. After cleaning, apply a very thin coating of petroleum jelly to the battery terminals before installing the cables (**Figure 33**). After connecting the cables, apply a light coating to the connection. This procedure will help to prevent future corrosion.

Battery Charging

> WARNING
> *Do not smoke or permit any open flame in any area where batteries are being charged, or immediately after charging. Highly explosive hydrogen gas is formed during the charging process. Be sure to reread* Safety Precautions *in the beginning of this section.*

Motorcycle batteries are not designed for high charge or discharge rates. For this reason, it is recommended that a motorcycle battery be charged at a rate not exceeding ten percent of its ampere-hour capacity. That is, do not exceed 0.5 ampere charging rate for a 5 ampere-hour battery, or 1.5 amperes for a 15 ampere-hour battery. This charge rate should continue for ten hours if the battery is completely discharged, or until specific gravity of each cell is up to 1.260-1.280, corrected for temperature. If after prolonged charging, specific gravity of one or more cells does not come up to at least 1.230, the battery will not perform as well as it should, but it may continue to provide satisfactory service for a time.

Some temperature rise is normal as a battery is being charged. do not allow the electrolyte temperature to exceed 110 degrees F. Should temperature reach that figure, discontinue charging until the battery cools, then resume charging at a lower rate.

Testing State of Charge

Although sophisticated battery testing devices are on the market, they are not available to the average motorcycle owner, and their use is beyond the scope of this book. A hydrometer, however, is an inexpensive tool, and will tell much about battery condition.

To use a hydrometer, place the suction tube into the filler opening and draw in just enough electrolyte to lift the float (**Figure 34**). Hold the instrument in a vertical position and read specific gravity on the scale, where the float stem emerges from the electrolyte.

Specific gravity of the electrolyte varies with temperature, so it is necessary to apply a temperature correction to the reading so obtained. For each 10 degrees that battery temperature exceeds 80 degrees F, add 0.004 to the indicated value. Subtract 0.004 for each 10 degrees that battery temperature is below 80 degrees F.

Repeat this measurement for each battery cell. If there is more than 0.050 difference (50 points) between cells, battery condition is questionable.

State of charge may be determined from **Table 4**.

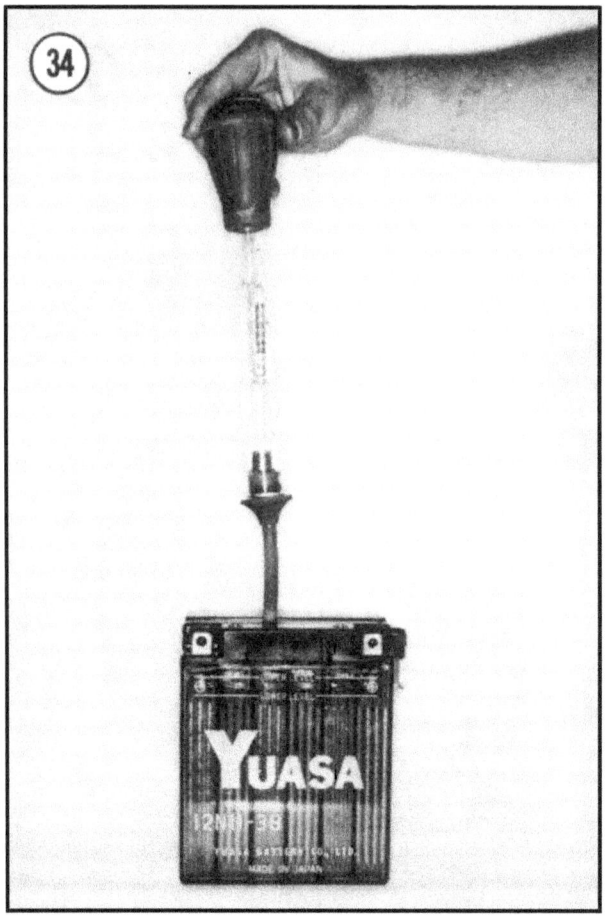

Table 4   STATE OF CHARGE

Specific Gravity	State of Charge
1.110 - 1.130	Discharged
1.140 - 1.160	Almost discharged
1.170 - 1.190	One-quarter charged
1.200 - 1.220	One-half charged
1.230 - 1.250	Three-quarters charged
1.260 - 1.280	Fully charged

Don't measure specific gravity immediately after adding water. Ride the machine a few miles to ensure thorough mixing of the electrolyte.

It is most important to maintain batteries fully charged during cold weather. A fully charged battery freezes at a much lower temperature than does one which is partially discharged. Freezing temperature depends on specific gravity, as shown in **Table 5**.

Battery life should normally be two to three years. This period will be shortened by any of the following conditions.

1. Overcharging.
2. Leaving the battery in a discharged state.

Table 5   BATTERY FREEZING TEMPERATURES

Specific Gravity	Freezing Temperature Degrees F.
1.100	18
1.120	13
1.140	8
1.160	1
1.180	—6
1.200	—17
1.220	—31
1.240	—50
1.260	—75
1.280	—92

3. Freezing — a fully charged batter will freeze at a much lower temperature than one that is discharged. If the machine is exposed to cold weather, be sure to keep the battery fully charged.

4. Allowing the electrolyte level to drop below the tops of the plates.

5. Adding anything to the electrolyte except distilled water.

If the motorcycle is not to be used for an extended period, charge the battery fully, remove it from the machine, and store it in a cool, dry place. Recharge the battery every two months while it is in storage, and again before it is put back into service.

Be very careful when installing the battery to connect it properly. If the battery is installed backward, the rectifier and alternator will be damaged. It is also possible that the CDI will be damaged.

LIGHTS

Machines which are intended to be ridden on public streets are equipped with lights. Check them periodically to be sure that they are working properly.

Headlight

The headlight unit consists primarily of a lamp body, a dual-filament bulb, a lens and reflector unit, a rim, and a socket. To adjust the headlight, loosen the two mounting bolts and remove the assembly as required.

Brake Light

The switch is actuated by the brake pedal. Adjust the switch so that the stoplight goes on just before braking action occurs. Move the switch body up or down as required for adjustment. Tighten the clamp nut after adjustment.

Turn Signals

Kawasaki machines are equipped with two different types of turn signal flasher relays. If replacement becomes necessary, be sure to replace with the proper type.

If any turn signal bulb burns out, be sure to replace it with the same type. Improper action of the flasher relay, or even failure to operate, may result from use of the wrong bulbs.

HORN

Current for the horn is supplied by the battery. One horn terminal is connected to the battery through the main switch. The other terminal is connected to the horn button, current flows through the horn.

CHAPTER FIVE

CARBURETORS

For proper operation, a gasoline engine must be supplied with fuel and air, mixed in the proper proportions by weight. A mixture in which there is an excess of fuel is said to be rich. A lean mixture is one which contains insufficient fuel. It is the function of the carburetors to supply the proper mixture to the engine under all operating conditions.

Kawasaki triple cylinder machines are equipped with Mikuni slide valve carburetors. Service procedures are similar for the various models. Differences are pointed out where they exist.

CARBURETOR OPERATION

The essential functional parts of Kawasaki carburetors are: a float and float valve mechanism for maintaining a constant fuel level in the float bowl, a pilot system for supplying fuel at low speeds, a main fuel system which supplies the engine at medium and high speeds, and a starter system which supplies the very rich mixture needed to start a cold engine. The operation of each system is discussed in the following paragraphs.

Float Mechanism

Figure 1 illustrates a typical float mechanism. Proper operation of the carburetor is dependent on a constant fuel level in the carburetor float

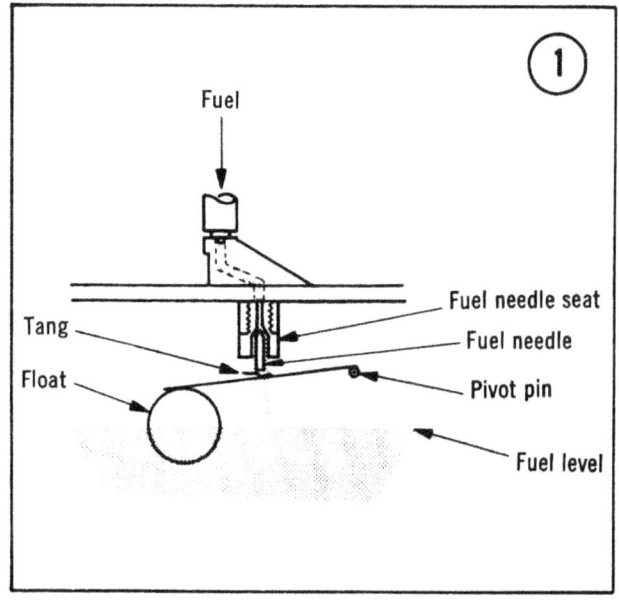

bowl. As fuel is drawn from the float bowl, the float level drops. When the float drops, the float needle valve moves away from its seat and allows fuel to flow past the valve and seat into the float bowl. As this occurs, the float is then raised, pressing the needle valve against its seat, thereby shutting off fuel flow. It can be seen from this discussion that a small piece of dirt can be trapped between the valve and seat, preventing the valve from closing and allowing fuel to rise beyond the normal level, resulting in flooding. **Figure 2** illustrates this condition.

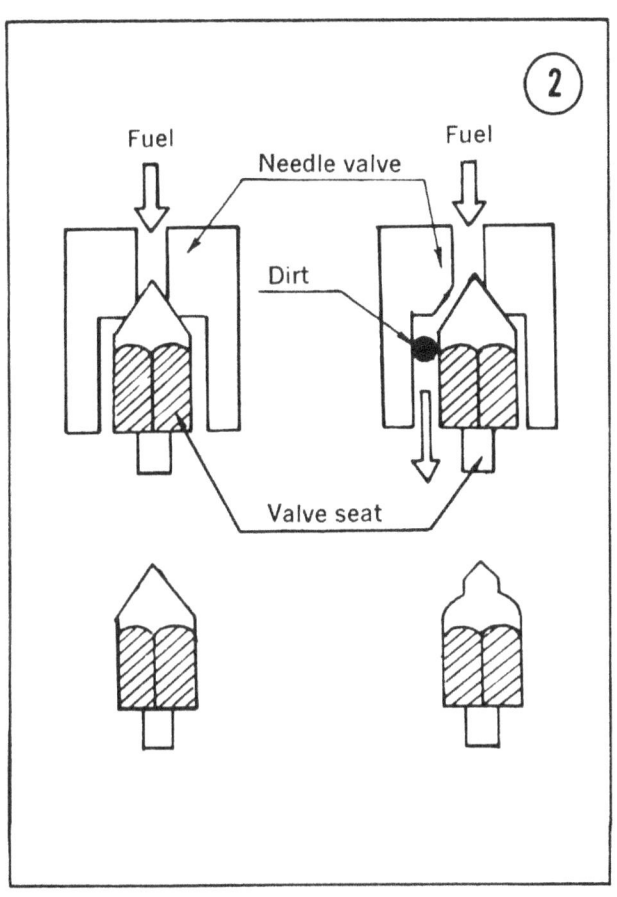

Pilot System

Under idle or low speed conditions, at less than one-eighth throttle, the engine doesn't require much fuel or air, and the throttle valve is almost closed. A separate pilot system is required for operation under such conditions. **Figure 3** illustrates operation of the pilot system. Air is drawn through the pilot air inlet and controlled by the pilot air screw. This air is then mixed with fuel drawn through the pilot jet. The fuel/air mixture then travels from the pilot outlet into the main air passage, where it is further mixed with air prior to being drawn into the engine. The pilot air screw controls the idle mixture.

If proper idle and low speed mixture cannot be obtained within the normal adjustment range of the idle mixture screw, refer to **Table 1** for possible causes.

Main Fuel System

As the throttle is opened still more (up to about one-quarter open) the pilot circuit begins

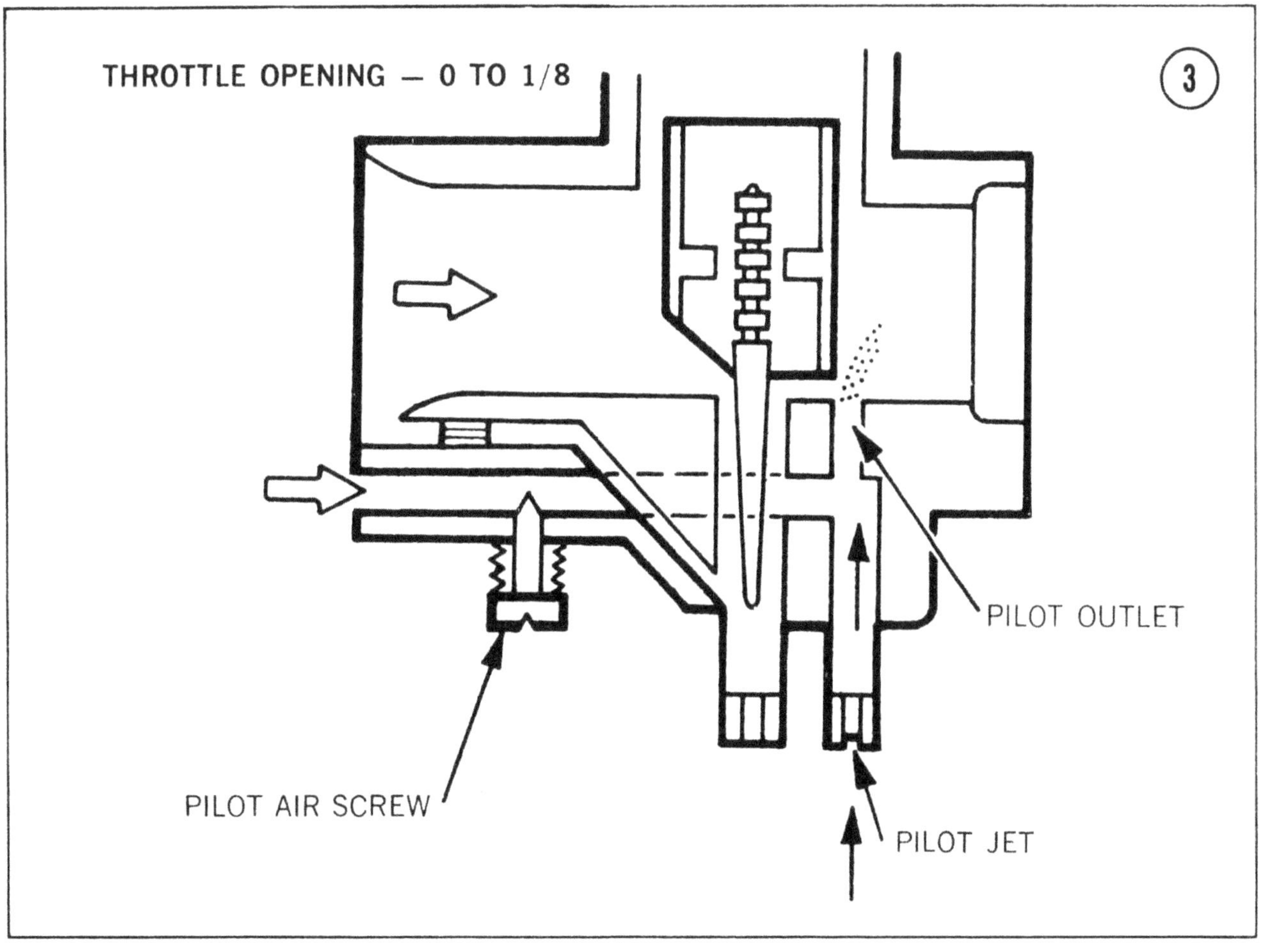

Table 1　IDLE MIXTURE TROUBLESHOOTING

Too rich
Clogged pilot air intake
Clogged air passage
Clogged air bleed opening
Pilot jet loose

Too lean
Obstructed pilot jet
Obstructed jet outlet
Worn throttle valve
Carburetor mounting loose

to supply less of the mixture to the engine, as the main fuel system, illustrated in **Figure 4**, begins to function. The main jet, the needle jet, the jet needle, and the air jet make up the main fuel circuit. As the throttle valve opens more than about one-eighth of its travel, air is drawn through the main port, and passes under the throttle valve in the main bore. The velocity of the air stream results in reduced pressure around the jet needle. Fuel then passes through the main jet, past the needle jet and jet needle, and into the air stream where it is atomized and sent to the engine. As the throttle valve opens, more air flows through the carburetor, and the jet needle, which is attached to the throttle slide, rises to permit more fuel to flow.

A portion of the air bled past the air jet passes through the needle jet bleed air inlet into the needle jet, where the air is mixed with the main air stream and atomized.

Air flow at small throttle openings is controlled primarily by the cutaway on the throttle slide.

As the throttle is opened wider (up to about three-quarters open) the circuit draws air from two sources, as shown in **Figure 5**. The first source is air passing through the venturi; the second source is through the air jet. Air passing through the venturi draws fuel through the needle jet. The jet needle is tapered, and therefore allows more fuel to pass. Air passing through the air jet passes to the needle jet to aid atomization of the fuel there.

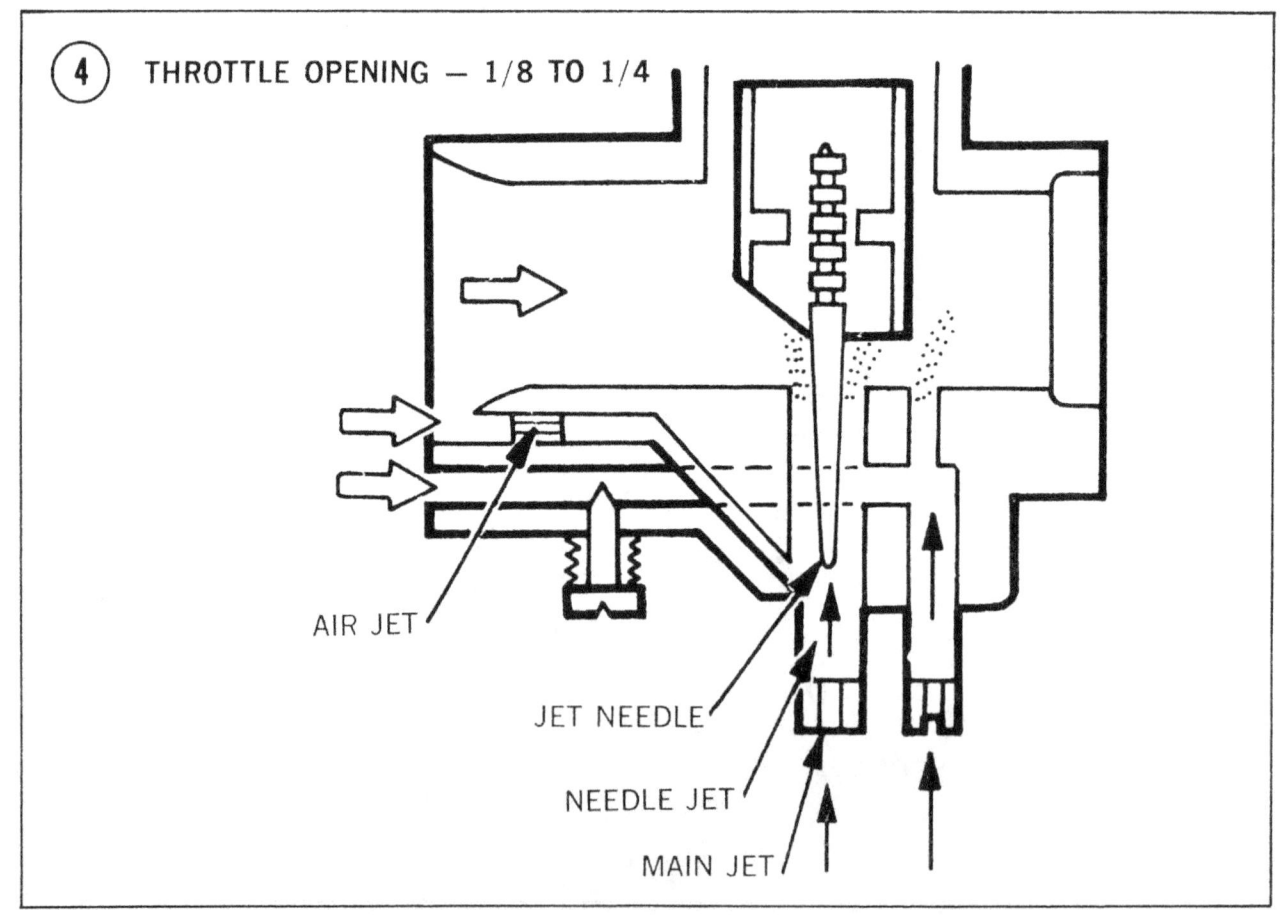

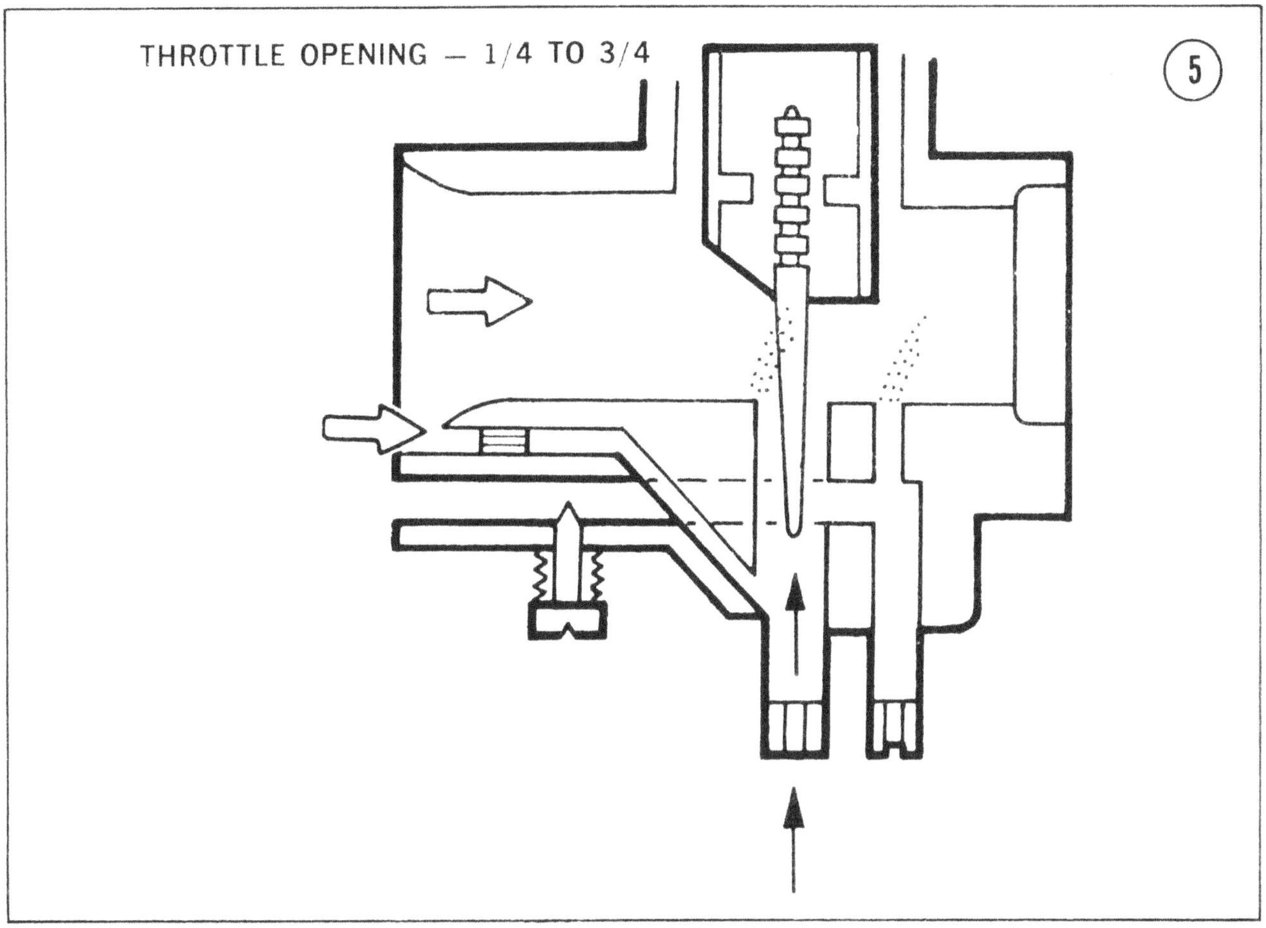

THROTTLE OPENING — 1/4 TO 3/4

⑤

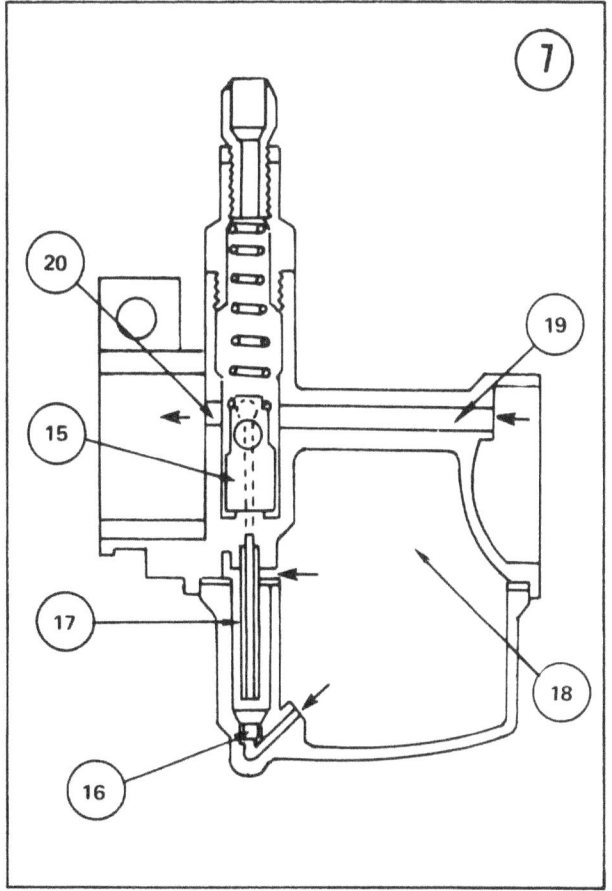

⑦

Figure 6 (next page) illustrates the circuit at high speeds. The jet needle is withdrawn almost completely from the needle jet. Fuel flow is then controlled by the main jet. Air passing through the air jet continues to aid atomization of the fuel as described in the foregoing paragraphs.

Any dirt which collects in the main jet or in the needle jet obstructs fuel flow and causes a lean mixture. Any clogged air passage, such as the air bleed opening or air jet, may result in an overrich mixture. Other causes of a rich mixture are a worn needle jet, loose needle jet, or loose main jet. If the jet needle is worn, it should be replaced; however, it may be possible to effect a temporary repair by placing the jet needle clip in a higher groove.

Starter System

A cold engine requires a mixture which is far richer than normal. Figure 7 illustrates the starter system. When the rider operates the lever, the starter plunger (15) is pulled upward. As the engine is cranked, suction from the engine draws fuel through the starter jet (16). This fuel is

6 THROTTLE OPENING — 3/4 TO FULL

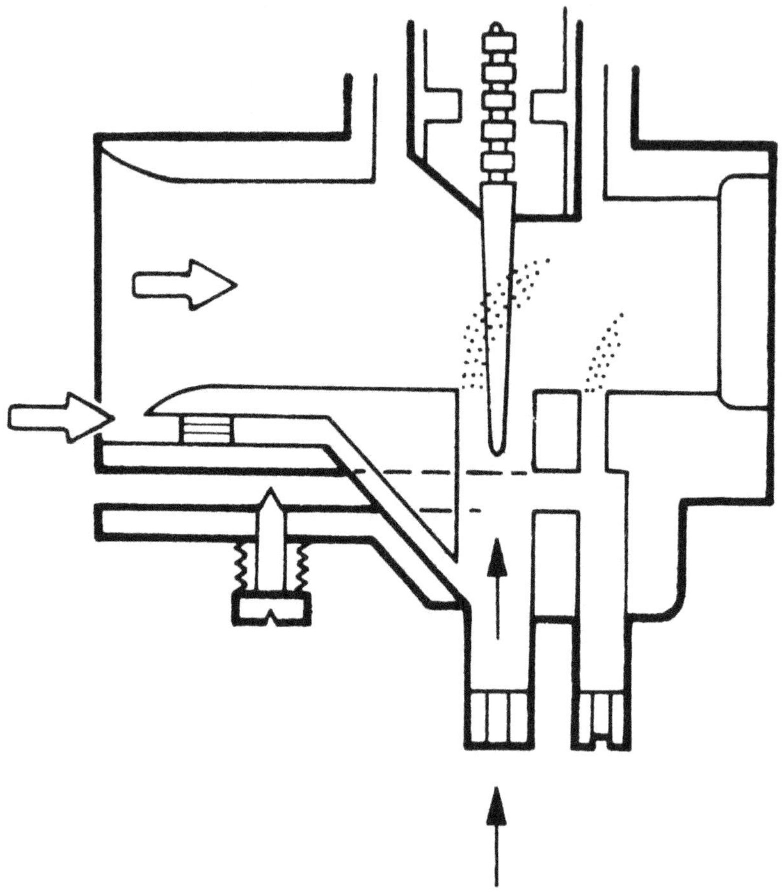

then mixed with air from the bleed air port (17) in the float chamber (18). This mixture is further mixed with primary air coming through the air passage (19), and is then delivered to the engine through the port (20) behind the throttle valve. Note that the mixture from the starter system is mixed with that from the pilot system.

CARBURETOR OVERHAUL

There is no set rule regarding frequency of carburetor overhaul. The carburetor on a machine used primarily for street riding may go 5,000 miles without attention. If the machine is used in dirt, the carburetor might need an overhaul in less than 1,000 miles. Poor engine performance, hesitation, and little response to idle mixture adjustment are all symptoms of possible carburetor malfunctions. As a general rule, it is good practice to overhaul the carburetor each time you perform a routine decarbonization of the engine.

Carburetor Disassembly

Figure 8 is an exploded view of a typical carburetor. Refer to this illustration during disassembly.

1. Remove the ring nut from the mixing chamber (**Figure 9**) if this step was not done previously.

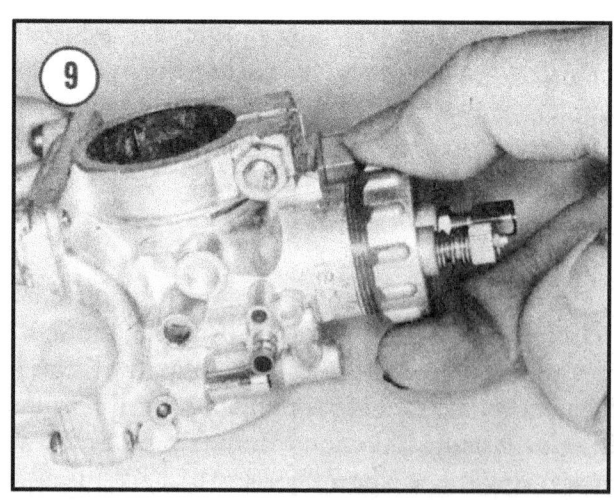

98

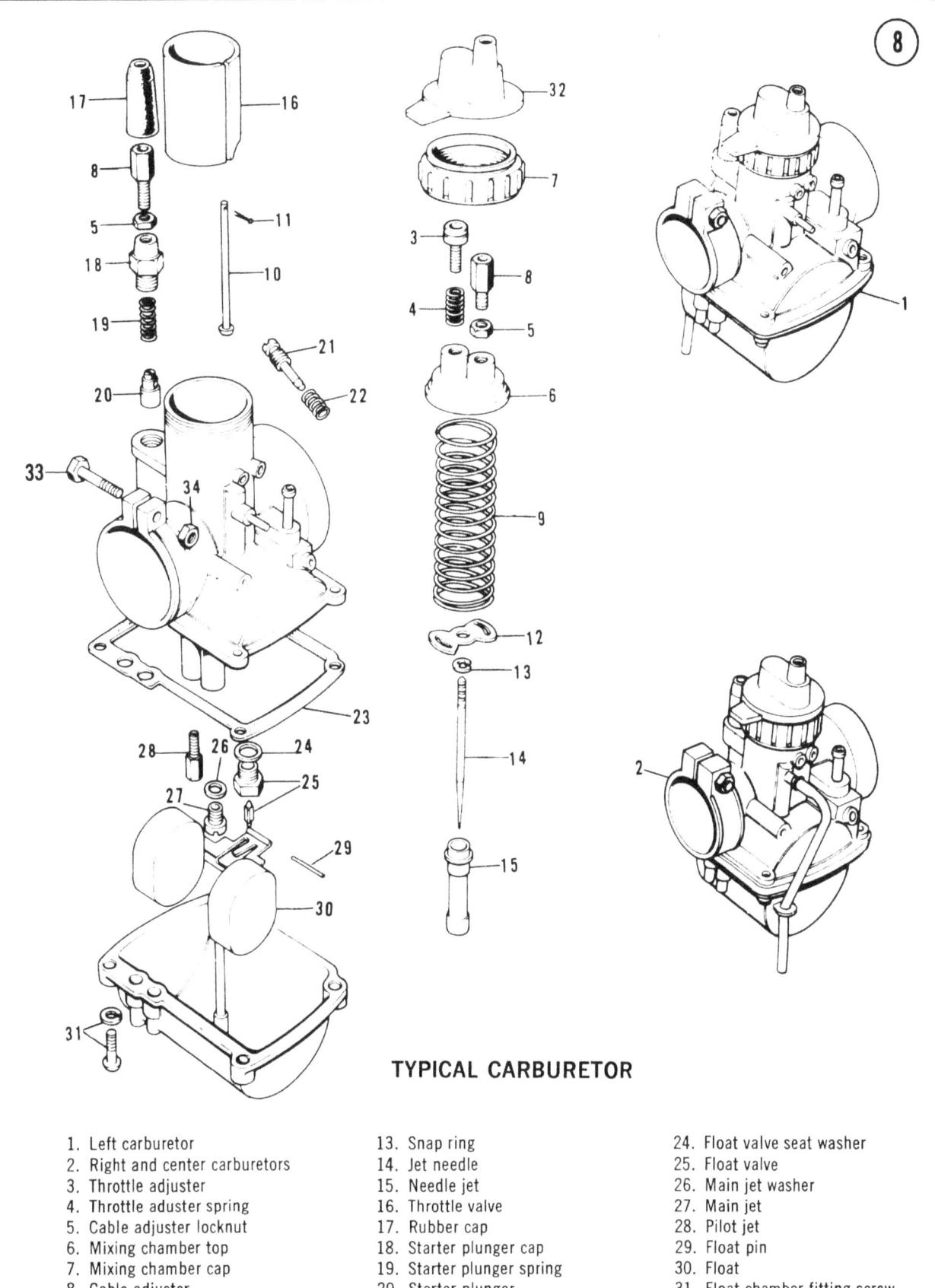

TYPICAL CARBURETOR

1. Left carburetor
2. Right and center carburetors
3. Throttle adjuster
4. Throttle aduster spring
5. Cable adjuster locknut
6. Mixing chamber top
7. Mixing chamber cap
8. Cable adjuster
9. Throttle valve spring
10. Throttle valve stop rod
11. Cotter pin
12. Throttle valve spring seat
13. Snap ring
14. Jet needle
15. Needle jet
16. Throttle valve
17. Rubber cap
18. Starter plunger cap
19. Starter plunger spring
20. Starter plunger
21. Pilot air adjustment screw
22. Pilot air adjustment screw spring
23. Float chamber gasket
24. Float valve seat washer
25. Float valve
26. Main jet washer
27. Main jet
28. Pilot jet
29. Float pin
30. Float
31. Float chamber fitting screw
32. Carburetor cap
33. Clamp screw
34. Hex nut

2. Remove the throttle slide (**Figure 10**).

3. Remove four retaining screws, then pull off the float bowl (**Figure 11**).

5. Remove the main jet and needle jet as a unit (**Figure 13**), by unscrewing the needle jet from the carburetor body.

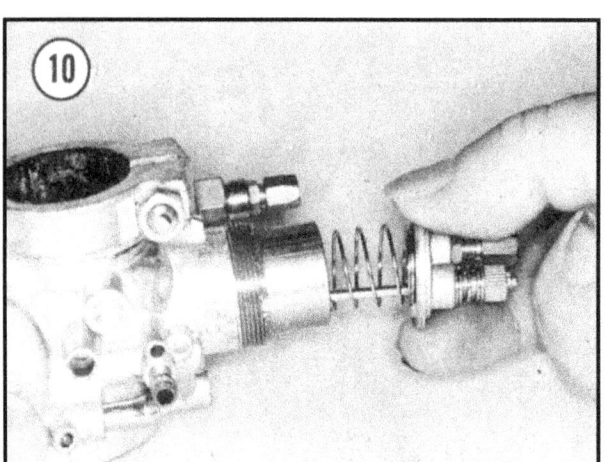

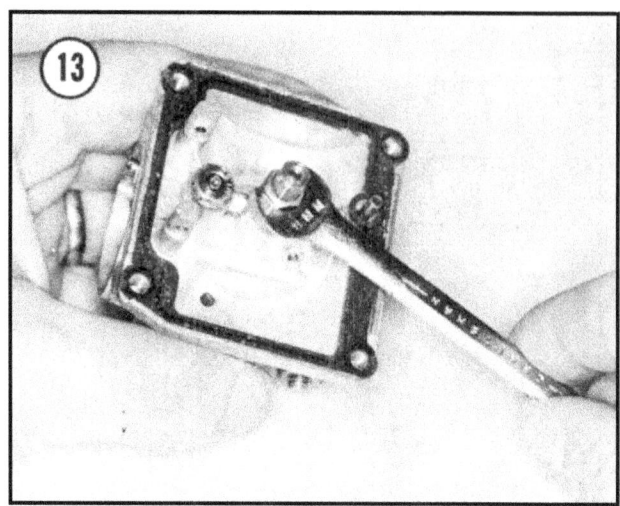

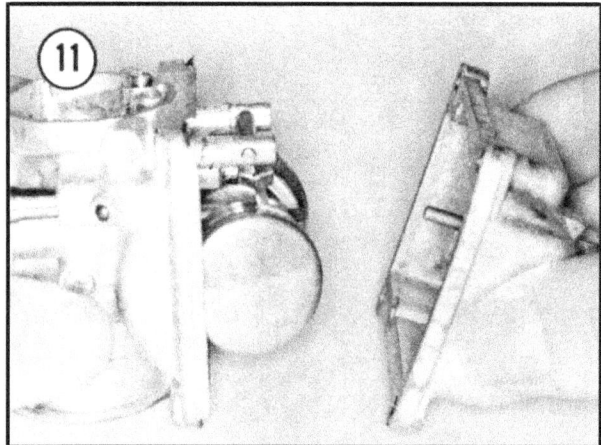

6. Separate the main jet from the needle jet (**Figure 14**).

7. Remove the pilot jet (**Figure 15**).

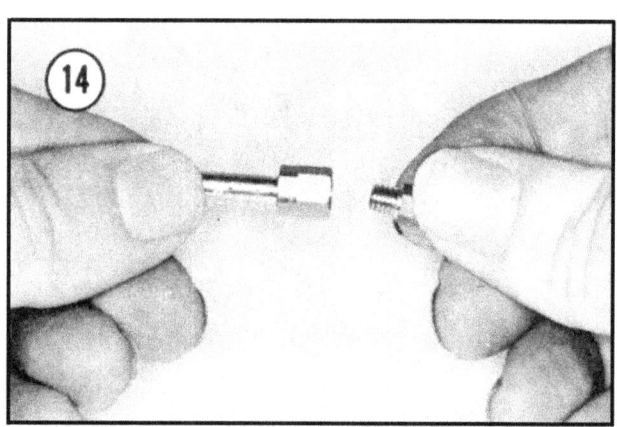

4. Pull out the float pivot shaft (**Figure 12**) to remove the float assembly. Handle this float gently to prevent bending.

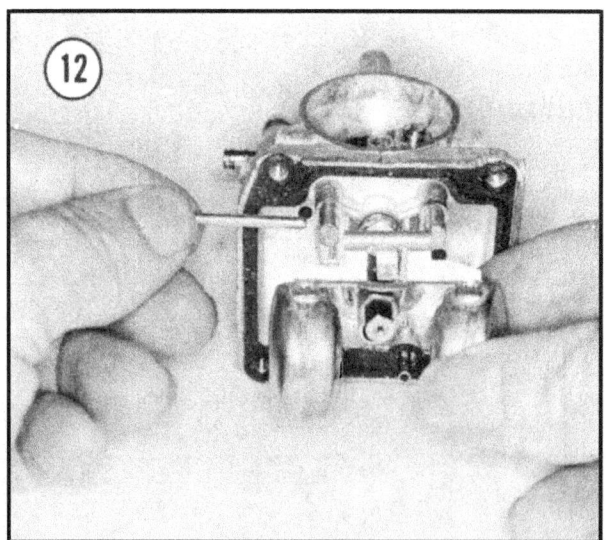

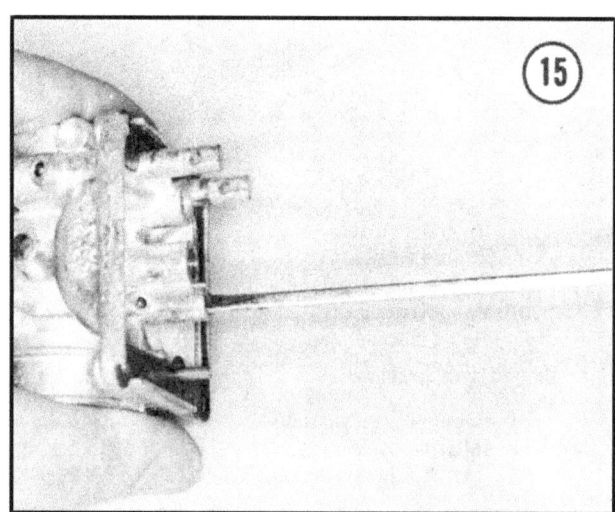

8. Remove the starter plunger assembly by loosening its spring cover (**Figure 16**). Be careful, since the spring is under compression.

9. Remove the pilot air screw (**Figure 17**).

10. Remove the float needle valve assembly. Refer to **Figure 18**.

11. To disassemble the throttle slide assembly, remove the cotter pin (**Figure 19**).

12. Push the jet needle out from the throttle slide (**Figure 20**).

13. Reverse Steps 1 through 12 for reassembly.

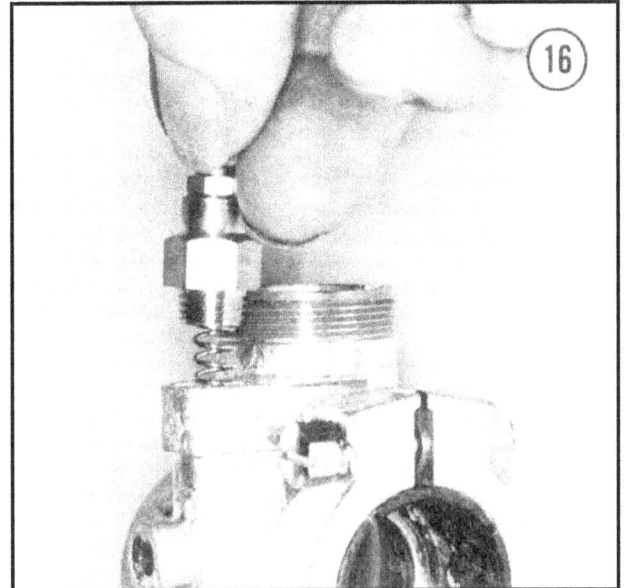

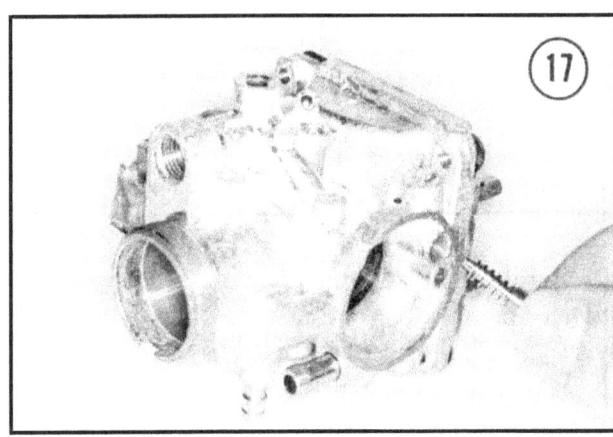

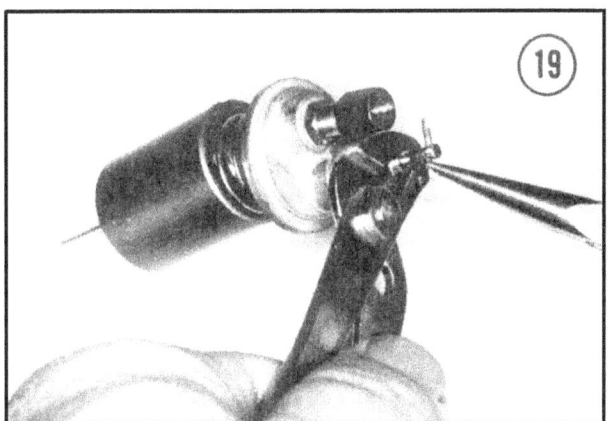

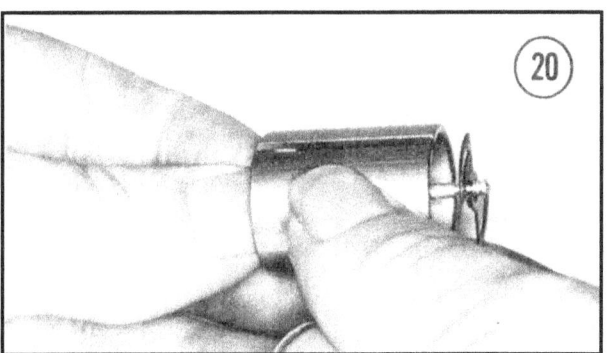

Inspection

Shake the float to check for gasoline inside (**Figure 21**). If fuel leaks into the float, the float chamber fuel level will rise, resulting in an over-rich mixture. Replace the float if it is deformed or leaking.

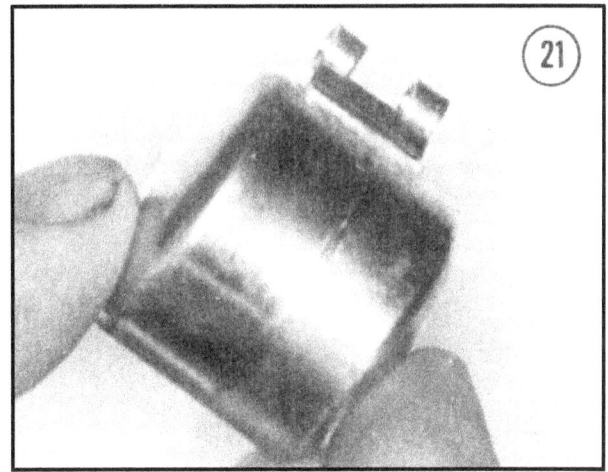

Replace the float valve if its seating end is scratched or worn. Press the float valve down gently with your finger and make sure that the valve seats properly. If the float valve spring is weak, fuel will overflow, causing an overrich mixture and flooding the float chamber whenever the fuel petcock is open.

Clean all parts in carburetor cleaning solvent. Dry the parts with compressed air. Clean the jets and other delicate parts with compressed air after the float bowl has been removed. Use new gaskets upon reassembly.

Never use compressed air to clean an assembled carburetor, since the float and float valve can be damaged.

CARBURETOR ADJUSTMENT

Carburetor adjustment is not normally required except for an occasional adjustment of idling speed, or at the time of carburetor overhaul. The adjustments described here should only be undertaken if the rider has definite reason to believe they are required.

Float Level Check/Adjustment

The machine was delivered with the float level adjusted correctly. Rough riding, a bent float arm, or a worn float needle and seat can cause the float level to change.

A special tool is needed for this procedure; it is available from a Kawasaki dealer.

1. Remove the carburetor from the intake manifold. Leave the fuel hose attached to the carburetor.

2. Attach the fuel level gauge to the float bowl.

3. Hold the clear tube of the tool up against the carburetor body. Hold the carburetor vertical and turn the fuel tap to the ON position.

4. Check fuel level in the clear tube (**Figure 22**). On S series, KH250, and KH400 models, it should be about 0.125-0.187 in. (3-5mm) from the top of the float bowl. On models KH500, H1, and H2 it should be about 0.08-0.16 in. (2-4mm).

5. If the fuel level is not within this area, turn the fuel tap to the OFF position.

6. Remove the float bowl, float pin, and float. Catch the float needle as the float is removed.

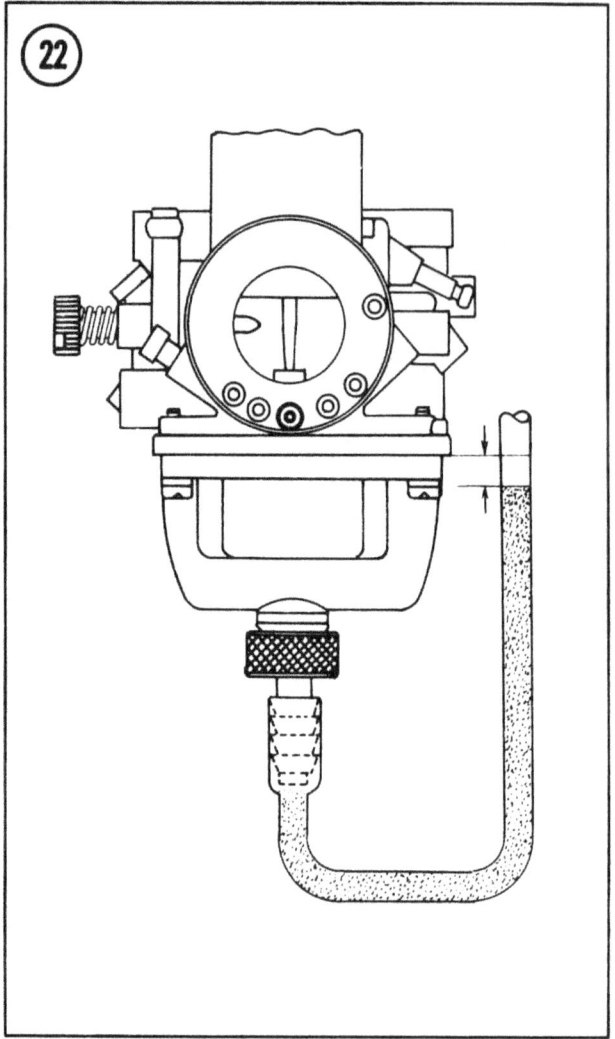

7. Bend the tang (**Figure 23**) upward slightly to lower the fuel level; bend the tang downward very slightly to raise the fuel level.

8. Reassemble the carburetor and recheck the fuel level; readjust if necessary.

9. Repeat for the 2 remaining carburetors.

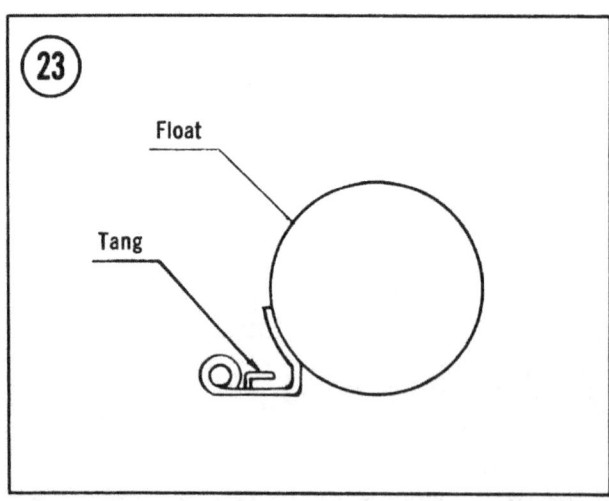

Speed Range Adjustments

The carburetors on your machine were designed to provide the proper mixture under all operating conditions. Little or no benefit will result from experimenting. However, unusual operating conditions (such as sustained operation at high altitudes or unusually high or low temperatures) may make modifications to the standard specifications desirable. The adjustments described in the following paragraphs should only be undertaken if the rider has definite reason to believe they are required. Make the test and adjustments in the order specified.

Figure 24 illustrates typical carburetor components which may be changed to meet individual operating conditions. Shown left to right are the main jet, needle jet, jet needle and clip, and throttle valve.

Make a road test at full throttle for final determination of main jet size. To make such a test, operate the motorcycle at full throttle for at least two minutes, then shut the engine off, release the clutch, and bring the machine to a stop.

If at full throttle the engine runs "heavily," the main jets are too large. If the engine runs better by closing the throttle slightly, the main jets are too small. The engine will run at full throttle evenly and regularly if the main jets are of the correct size.

After each such test, remove and examine the spark plug. The insulators should have a light tan color. If the insulators have black sooty deposits, the mixture is too rich. If there are signs of intense heat, such as a blistered white appearance, the mixture is too lean.

As a general rule, main jet size should be reduced approximately five percent for each 3,000 feet (1,000 meters) above sea level.

Table 2 lists symptoms caused by rich and lean mixtures.

Adjust the pilot air screw as follows.

1. Turn the pilot air screw in until it seats lightly, then back it out about one and one-half turns.

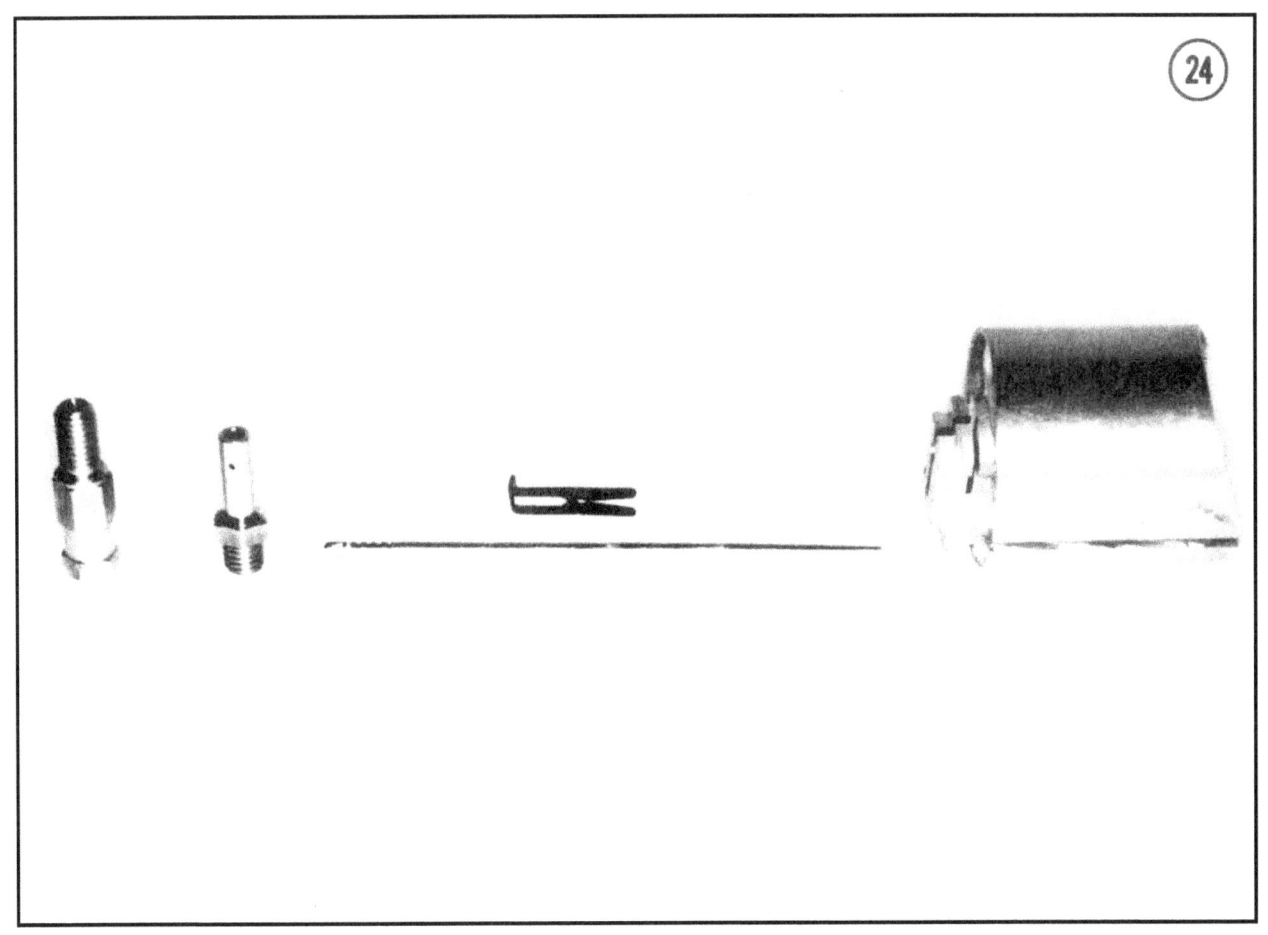

Table 2   IDLE MIXTURE SYMPTOMS

Condition	Symptom
Rich mixture	Rough idle Black exhaust smoke Hard starting, especially when hot "Blubbering" under acceleration Black deposits in exhaust pipe Gas-fouled spark plugs Poor gas mileage Engine performs worse as it warms up
Lean mixture	Backfiring Rough idle Overheating Hesitation upon acceleration Engine speed varies at fixed throttle Loss of power White color on spark plug insulators Poor acceleration

2. Start the engine and warm it to normal operating temperature.

3. Turn the idle speed screw until the engine runs slower and begins to falter.

4. Adjust the pilot air screw as required to make the engine run smoothly.

5. Repeat Steps 3 and 4 to achieve the lowest stable idle speed.

6. Hold your hands behind the mufflers to check for equal exhaust pressures. Make fine adjustments with the idle speed screw and/or the pilot air screw to achieve even exhaust pressures on all 3 cylinders.

Next, determine the proper throttle valve cutaway size. With the engine running at idle, open the throttle. If the engine does not accelerate smoothly from idle, turn the pilot air screw in (clockwise) slightly to richen the mixture. If the condition still exists, return the air screw to its original position and replace the throttle valve with one having a smaller cutaway. If engine operation is worsened by turning the air screw, replace the throttle valve with one having a larger cutaway.

For operation at one- to three-quarters throttle opening, adjustment is made with the jet needle. Operate the engine at half throttle in a manner similar to that for full throttle tests described earlier. To enrich the mixture, place the jet needle clip in a lower groove. Conversely, placing the clip in a higher groove leans the mixture.

A summary of carburetor adjustments is given in **Table 3**.

Table 3   CARBURETOR ADJUSTMENTS

Throttle Opening	Adjustment	If too rich	If too lean
0 - 1/8	Air screw	Turn out	Turn in
1/8 - 1/4	Throttle valve cutaway	Use larger cutaway	Use smaller cutaway
1/4 - 3/4	Jet needle	Raise clip	Lower clip
3/4 - full	Main jet	Use smaller number	Use larger number

CARBURETOR COMPONENTS

The following paragraphs describe the various components of the carburetor which may be changed to vary the performance characteristics.

Refer to **Table 4** for carburetor specifications.

Throttle Valve

The throttle valve cutaway (**Figure 25**) controls air flow at small throttle openings. Cutaway sizes are numbered. Larger numbers permit more air to flow at a given throttle opening and result in a leaner mixture. Conversely, smaller numbers result in a richer mixture.

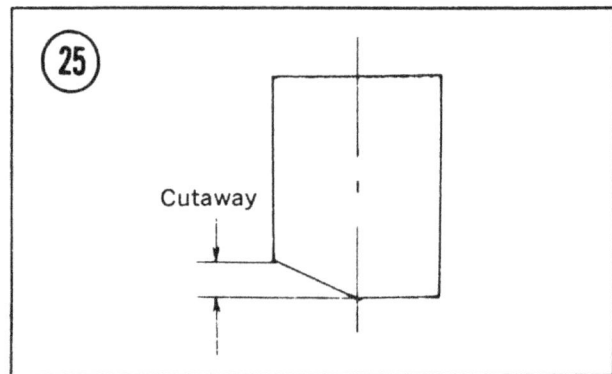

Jet Needle

The jet needle (**Figure 26**) with the needle jet, controls the mixture at medium speeds. As the throttle valve rises to increase air flow through

Table 4 CARBURETOR SPECIFICATIONS

Model	Type	Main Jet	Air Jet	Needle Jet	Jet Needle	Pilot Jet	Cut-away	Air Screw (Turns Out)	Fuel Level
S1	VM22SC	75*	—	0-0/4	4EJ8-3	20	2.0	1¾	1.06-1.14 in. (27-29mm)
S1A and S1B	VM22SC	75*	—	0-2/4	4EJ9-3	17.5	2.5	1¼	1.06-1.14 in. (27-29mm)
S1C and KH250-A5	VM22SC	75*	—	0-2/4	4EJ9-3	20	2.5	1½	1.06-1.14 in. (27-29mm)
KH250-B1	VM22SC	67.5*	—	0-2/4	4EJ9-3	20	2.5	1½	1.06-1.14 in. (27-29mm)
S2 and S2A	VM24SC	85*	—	0-2/4	4EJ4-3	25	2.0	1½	1.02-1.10 in. (26-28mm)
S3 and S3A	VM26SC	85*	—	0-2/4	4EJ4-3	22.5	2.0	1¾	1.02-1.10 in. (26-28mm)
KH400-A3	VM26SC	77.5*	—	0-6/4	4EJ4-3	20	2.5	1¼	1.02-1.10 in. (26-28mm)
KH500 (CDI)	VM28SC	100	0.5	0-2	5GL3-3	30	3.0	1¼	1.18 ± 0.04 in. (30 ± 1mm)
KH500	VM28SC	90	0.5	0-2	5EH7-3	30	2.5	1½	1.18 ± 0.04 in. (30 ± 1mm)
H1-B	VM28SC	95	0.5	0-4/8 0-4**	5DJ19-4	30	2.0 2.5**	1½ 1¼**	1.18 ± 0.04 in. (30 ± 1mm)
H1-C	VM28SC	100	0.5	0-2	5GL3-3	30	3.0	1¼	1.18 ± 0.04 in. (30 ± 1mm)
H1-D and H1-E	VM28SC	92.5	0.5	0-4/8	5DJ19-4	30	2.5	1¼	1.18 ± 0.04 in. (30 ± 1mm)
H2/H2-A	VM30SC	97.5	0.5	0-6/8	5EJ15-3	35	2.5	1½	1.18 ± 0.04 in. (30 ± 1mm)
H2-B	VM30SC	102.5	0.5	0-6/8	5EJ15-4	40	2.5	1¾	1.18 ± 0.04 in. (30 ± 1mm)

* Reverse type.
** European model only.

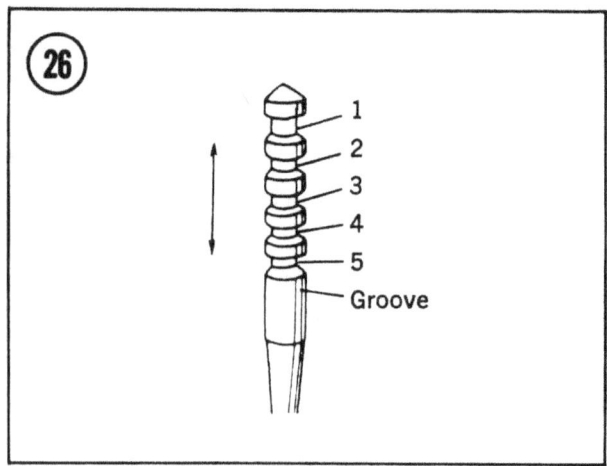

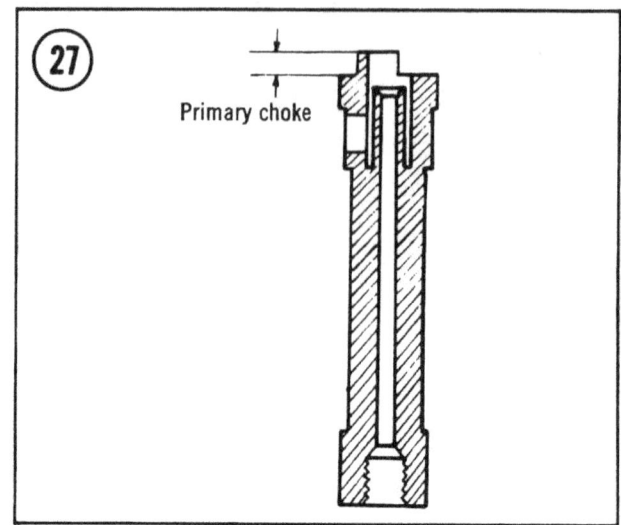

the carburetor, the jet needle rises with it. The tapered portion of the jet needle rises from the needle jet and allows more fuel to flow, thereby providing the engine with the proper mixture at up to about three-quarters throttle opening. The grooves at the top of the jet needle permit adjustment of the mixture ratio in the medium speed range.

Main Jet

The main jet controls the mixture at full throttle, and has some effect at lesser throttle openings. Each main jet is stamped with a number. Fuel flow is approximately proportional to the number. Larger numbers provide a richer mixture.

Needle Jet

The needle jet (**Figure 27**) operates with the jet needle. Several holes are drilled through the side of the needle jet. These holes meter the airflow from the air jet. Air from the air jet is bled into the needle jet to assist in atomization of the fuel.

MISCELLANEOUS CARBURETOR PROBLEMS

Water in the carburetor float bowl and sticking carburetor slide valves can result from careless washing of the motorcycle. To remedy the problem, remove and clean the carburetor bowl, main jet, and any other affected parts. Be sure to cover the air intake when washing the machine.

Be sure that the ring nut on the top of the carburetor is secure. Also be sure that the carburetor mounting bolts are tight.

If gasoline leaks past the float bowl gasket, high speed fuel starvation may occur. Varnish deposits on the outside of the float bowl are evidence of this condition.

Dirt in the fuel may lodge in the float valve and cause an overrich mixture. As a temporary measure, tap the carburetor lightly with any convenient tool to dislodge the dirt. Should this occur, clean the fuel tank, petcock, fuel line, and carburetor at the first opportunity.

CHAPTER SIX

CHASSIS, SUSPENSION, AND STEERING

FRAME

Frames on these machines are of welded steel tubing. **Figure 1** illustrates a typical frame. The double loop construction of the frame results in light weight and rigidity. H series frames are so designed that the rider may select either right or left braking and shifting.

Service on the frame is limited to inspection for bending of the frame members, or cracked welds. Examine the frame carefully in the event that the machine has been subjected to a collision or hard spill. See end of chapter for *Frame Repair*.

HANDLEBAR

The handlebar (**Figure 2**) is made from solid drawn steel tubing. Most of the manual controls are mounted on the handlebar assembly. Wiring from the switches on the handlebar

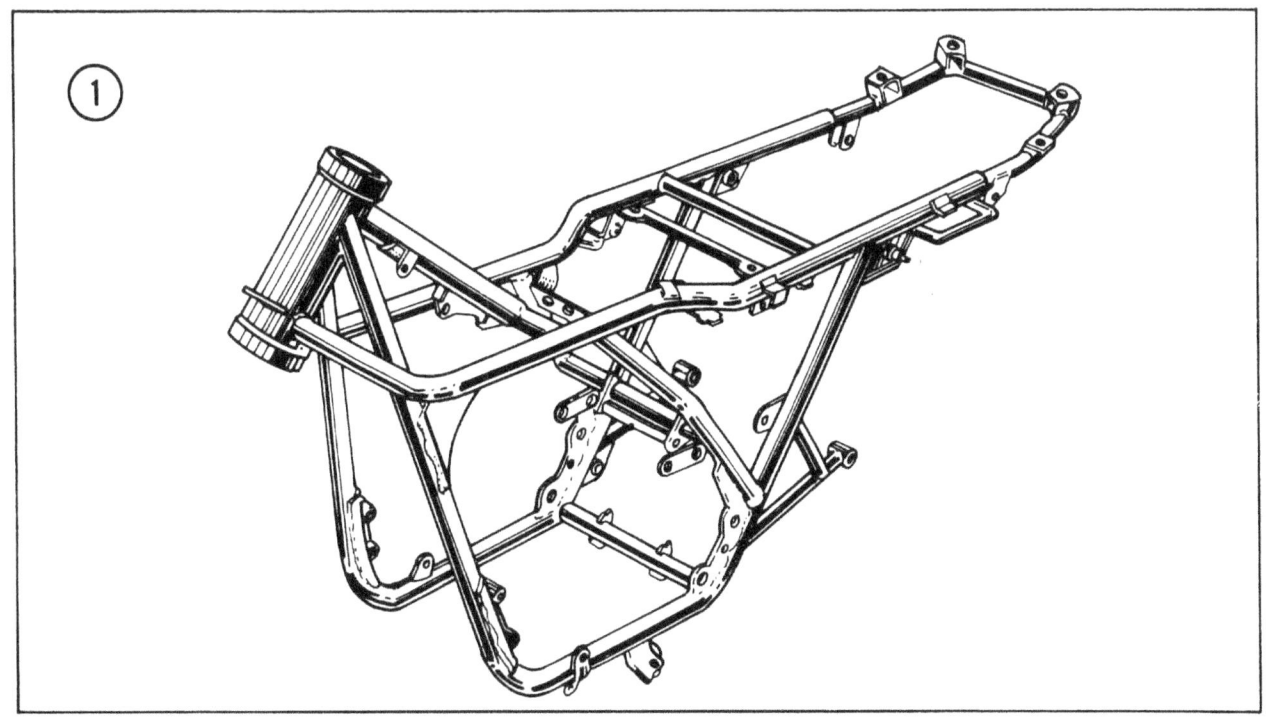

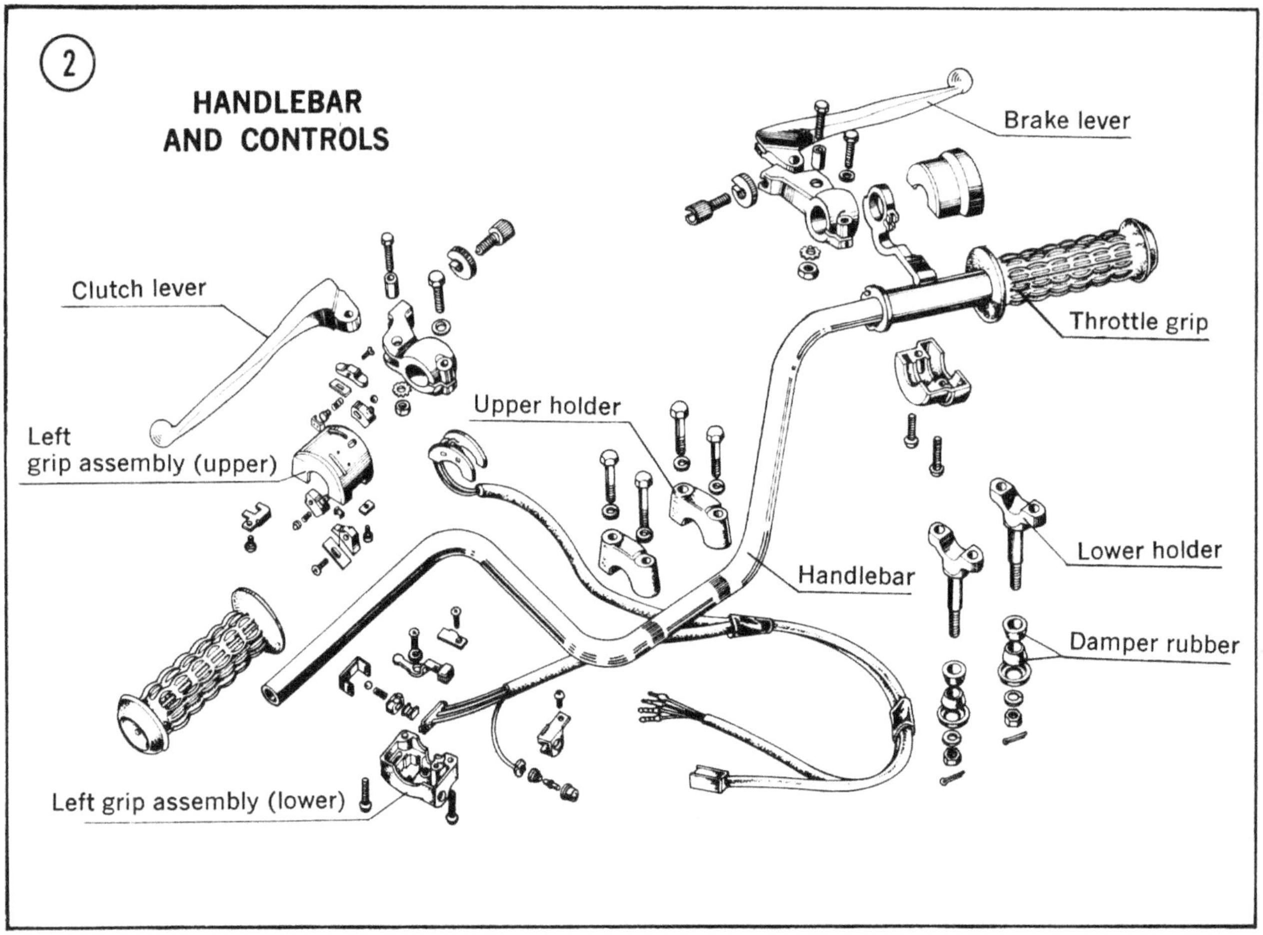

HANDLEBAR AND CONTROLS (2)

assembly is routed to the headlight assembly, where it is connected to the main wiring harness.

Disassembly

1. Loosen the clutch cable locknut (**Figure 3**), then rotate the adjustment nut to provide the inner clutch cable with sufficient slack to remove the clutch cable from the lever.

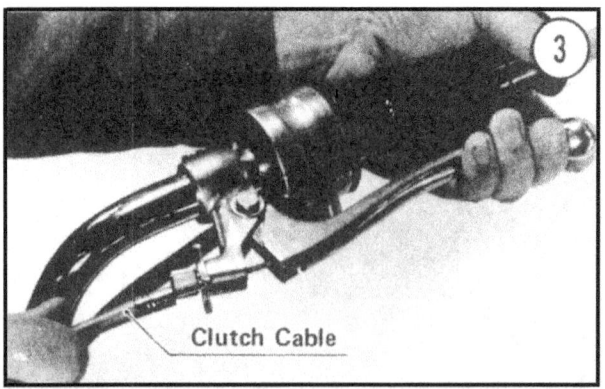

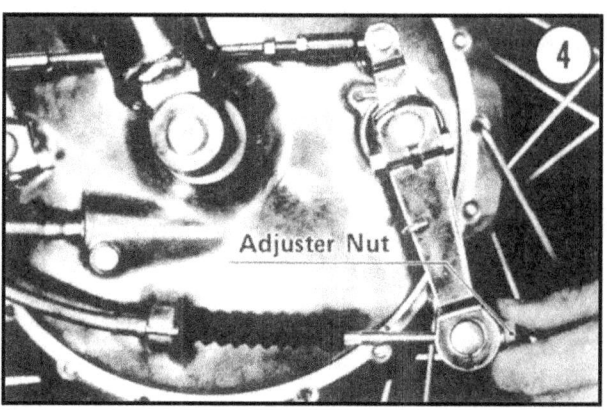

2. Loosen the front brake adjustment nut (**Figure 4**), then remove the brake cable from the brake lever on the handlebar. On some machines, the front brake stoplight switch is built into the front brake cable. Disconnect the switch lead from the main wire harness before you remove the cable.

3. On disc brake models, remove the master cylinder (**Figure 5**).

> CAUTION
> *Cover the fuel tank and instrument cluster with a heavy cloth or plastic tarp to protect it from accidental spilling of brake fluid. Wash any brake fluid off any painted or plated surface im-*

mediately, as it will destroy the finish. Use soapy water and rinse completely.

4. Loosen handlebar holder clamps **(Figure 6)**, remove the right upper mount, slide the handlebar assembly to the left, then retighten the left mount.

5. Loosen the throttle and starter cable adjusters **(Figure 7)**.

6. Disassemble the throttle grip assembly **(Figure 8)** then remove the control cables.

7. Remove the horn, turn signal, and headlight leads from the wire harness inside the headlight assembly, then disassemble the left-hand grip assembly **(Figure 9)**.

8. Remove the clamp bolts, then remove the handlebar from the bracket **(Figure 10)**.

Inspection

Examine the handlebar for cracking or bending. Minor bends may be straightened. Replace the handlebar if any cracks exist, or in the event of major bending.

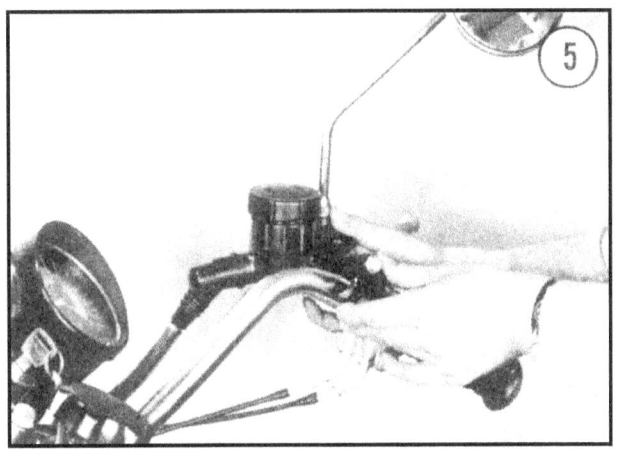

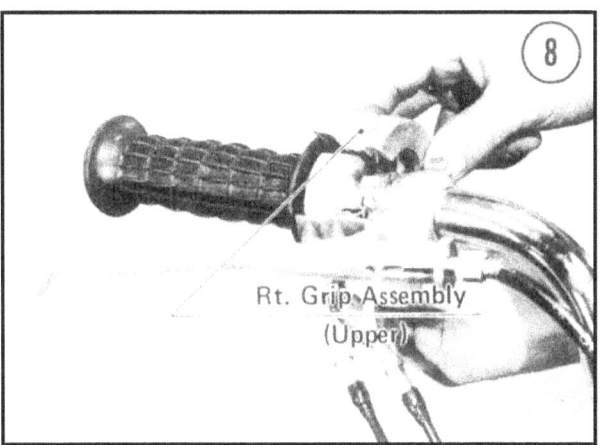

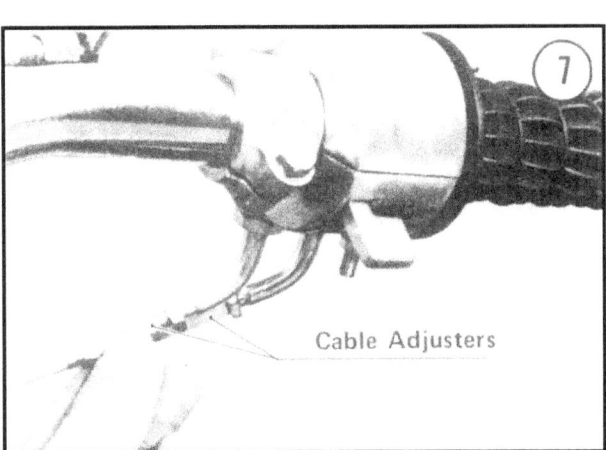

Installation

Reverse the removal procedure to install the handlebar. Pass the wiring through the handlebar tubing and through the cord protector in the headlight. After installation, adjust the play in the throttle, clutch, and starter lever cables. Adjust the play in the front brake lever to ¼-⅜ in. (7-10mm) by means of the brake adjusting nut on the brake. Adjust the throttle grip with the adjustment screw (**Figure 11**), as desired.

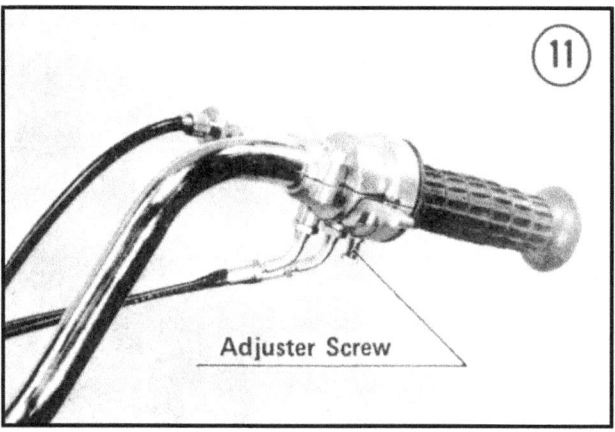

WHEELS AND TIRES

Tires

Figure 12 is a cutaway view of a typical wheel and tire assembly. **Figure 13** is a sectional view of a tire mounted on its rim. Various tire sizes are fitted to Kawasaki machines. Refer to the specifications for tire sizes for your machine. Tires are available in different tread types to suit the different requirements of the rider. **Table 1** lists the normal tire pressures for the various models, measured with the tires cold. It is normal for tire pressure to increase after prolonged operation. Do not bleed air from a hot tire to decrease pressure.

Check the tires periodically for wear, bruises, cuts, or other damage. Remove any small stones which may lodge in the tread, using a small screwdriver or similar tool.

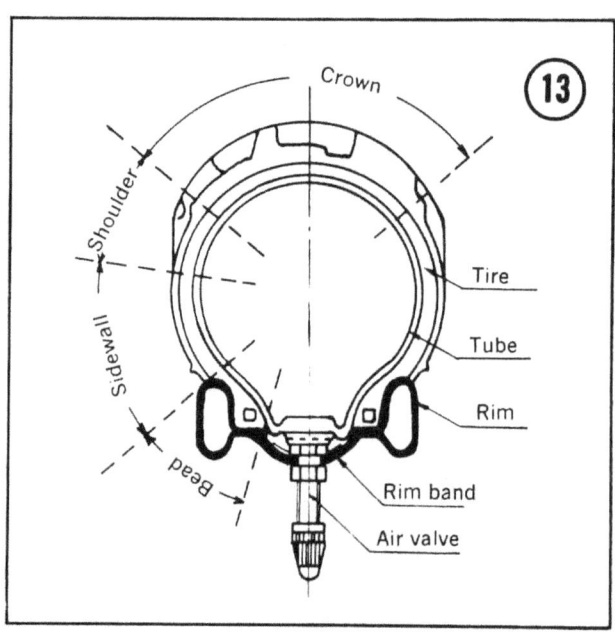

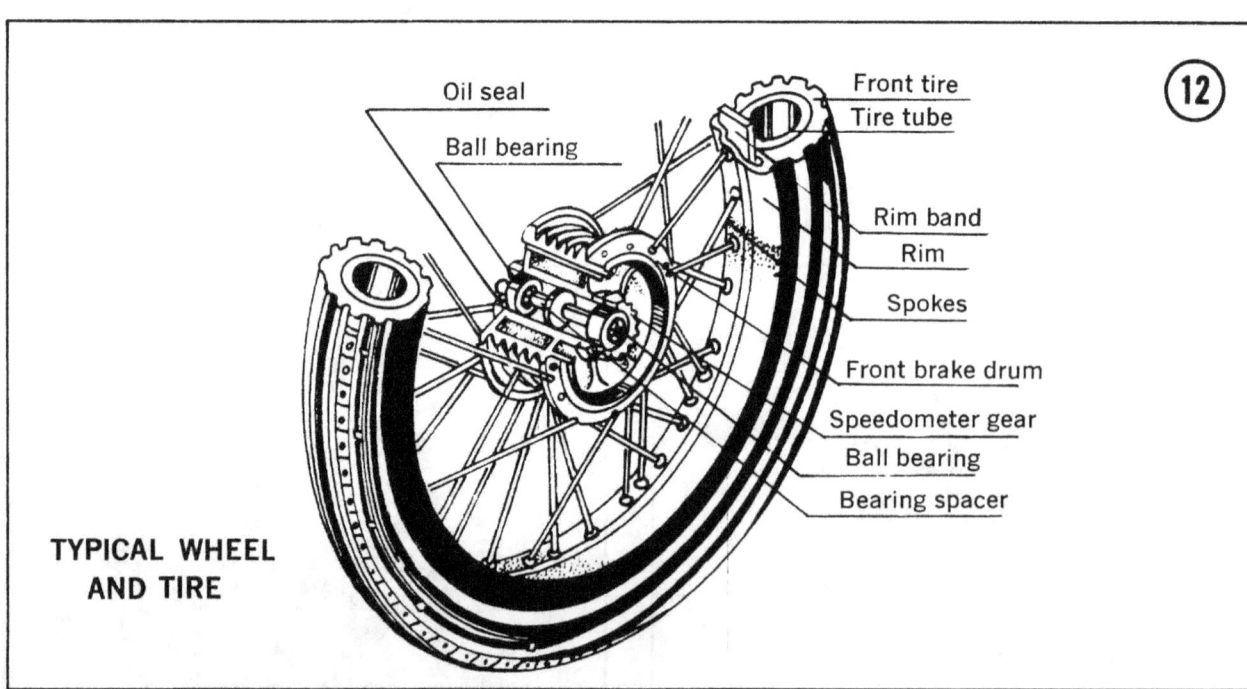

Table 1 TIRE PRESSURE

Model	Front	Rear
KH250	25 psi	28 psi
KH400	25 psi	28 psi
KH500	28 psi	32 psi
S series	24 psi	31 psi
H series	26 psi	31 psi

Rims

The rim supports the tire and provides rigidity to the wheel assembly. A rim band protects the inner tube from abrasion.

Spokes

The spokes support the weight of the motorcycle and rider, and transmit tractive and braking forces, as shown in **Figure 14**. Diagram A illustrates action of the spokes as they support the machine. Diagram B shows tractive forces. Braking forces are shown in Diagram C.

Check the spokes periodically for looseness or binding. A bent or otherwise faulty spoke will adversely affect neighboring spokes, and should therefore be replaced immediately. To remove the spoke, completely unscrew the threaded portion, then remove the bent end from the hub.

Spokes tend to loosen as the machine is used. Retighten each spoke one turn, beginning with those on one side of the hub, then those on the other side. Tighten the spokes on a new machine after the first 50 miles of operation, then at 50-mile intervals until they no longer loosen.

If the machine is subjected to particularly severe service, as in off-road or competition riding, check the spokes frequently.

Bead Protector

H series machines are equipped with a bead protector (**Figure 15**) on each wheel. The bead protector prevents the tire from slipping on the rim, especially during maximum effort braking at high speed, and thereby prevents damage to the valve stem.

Wheel Balance

An unbalanced wheel results in unsafe riding

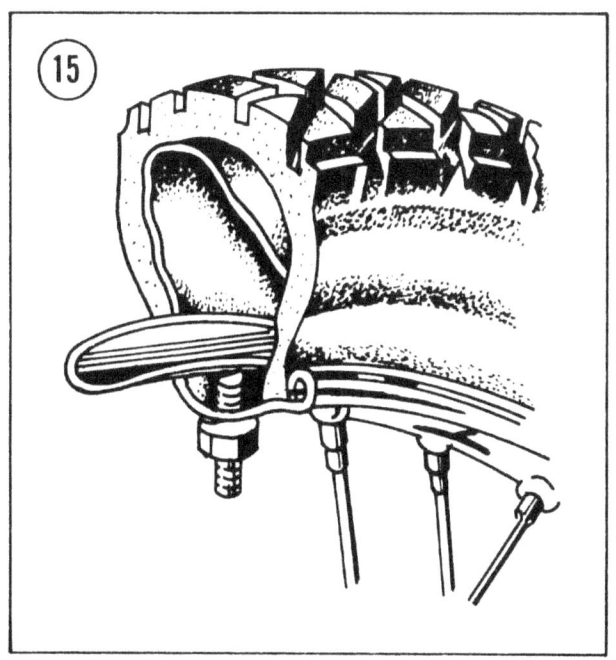

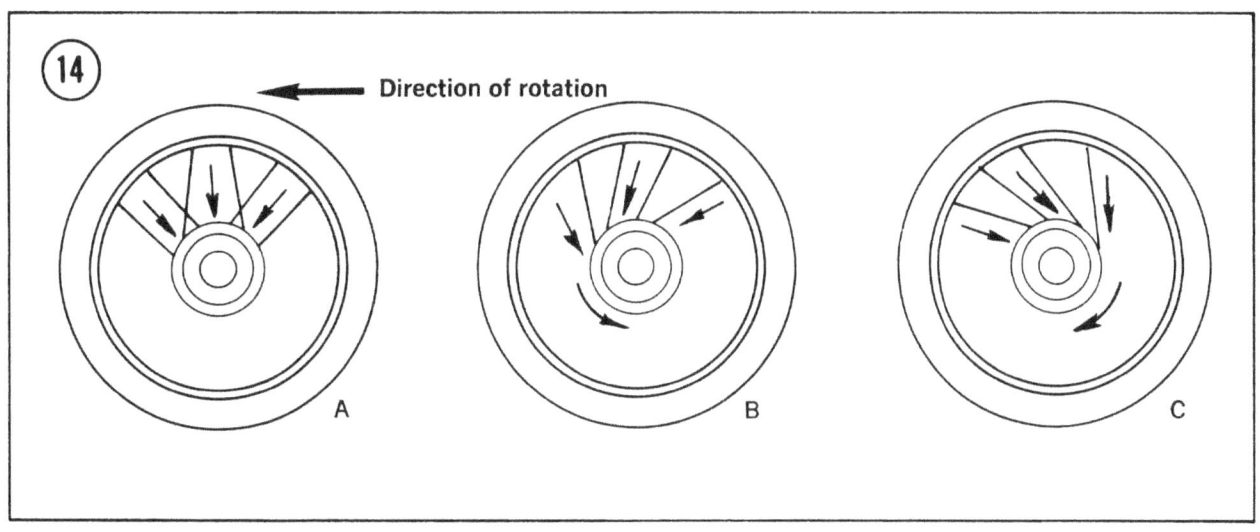

conditions. Depending on the degree of unbalance and the speed of the motorcycle, the rider may experience anything from a mild vibration to a violent shimmy which may even result in loss of control. Balance weights **(Figure 16)** are applied to the spokes on the light side of the wheel to correct this condition.

Before you attempt to balance the wheel, check to be sure that the wheel bearings are in good condition and properly lubricated, and that the brakes do not drag, so that the wheel rotates freely. With the wheel free of the ground, spin it slowly and allow it to come to rest by itself. Add balance weights to the spokes on the light side as required, so that the wheel comes to rest at a different position each time it is spun. Balance weights are available in weights of ⅓, ⅔, and 1 ounce (10, 20, and 30 grams). Remove the drive chain when you balance the rear wheel.

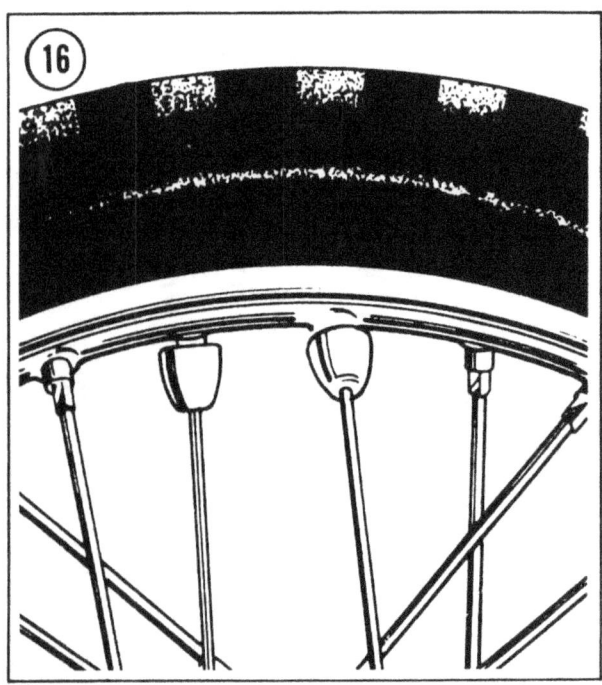

Front Hub

Figure 17 (models H1 and H2) and **Figure 18** (models KH250, KH400, and S series) show the front hub assembly used with drum brakes. **Figure 19** shows all components of the front hub on disc brake models. The entire hub assembly rotates on two ball bearings. The speedometer gears transmit the front wheel rotation to the speedometer. The brake panel supports the brake assembly.

Rear Hub

Figure 20 (models H1 and H2) and **Figure 21** (models KH250, KH400, and S series) show the rear hub assembly.

The rear hub consists of four major parts: the brake drum, the brake panel, the sprocket coupling, and the rear sprocket. The rear wheel bearings are mounted in the brake drum. The brake panel supports the brake mechanism, except for the brake drum. The sprocket coupling absorbs shocks throughout the entire drive train. The sprocket transmits engine power to the rear wheel through the sprocket coupling. Some rear hubs are equipped with an adjustable ventilator for brake cooling.

Front Wheel Removal (Drum Brake)

Front wheel removal is similar for all models without disc brakes. Proceed as follows.

1. Loosen the front brake adjustment nut, then remove the brake cable at the front hub **(Figure 22)**.

2. Remove speedometer cable bolt **(Figure 23)**, then pull out the speedometer cable.

3. Raise the front of the motorcycle and support it on a box or stand under the engine.

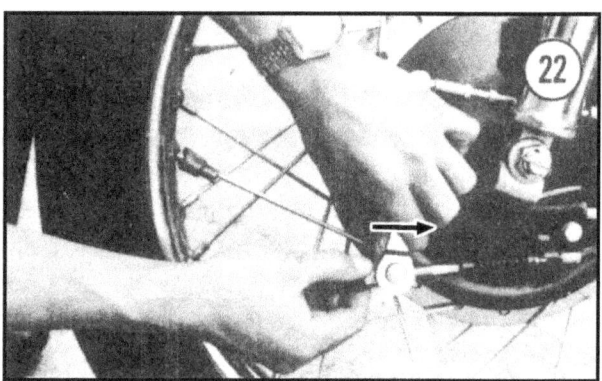

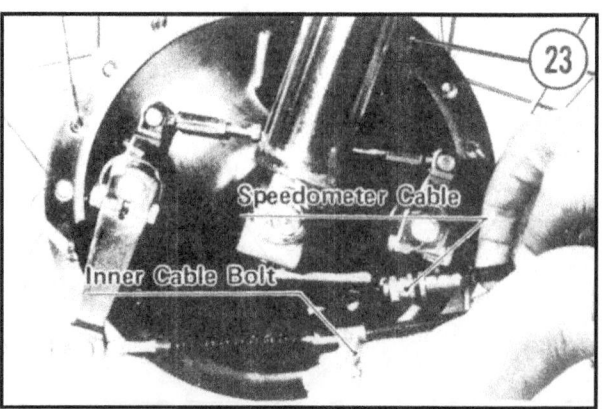

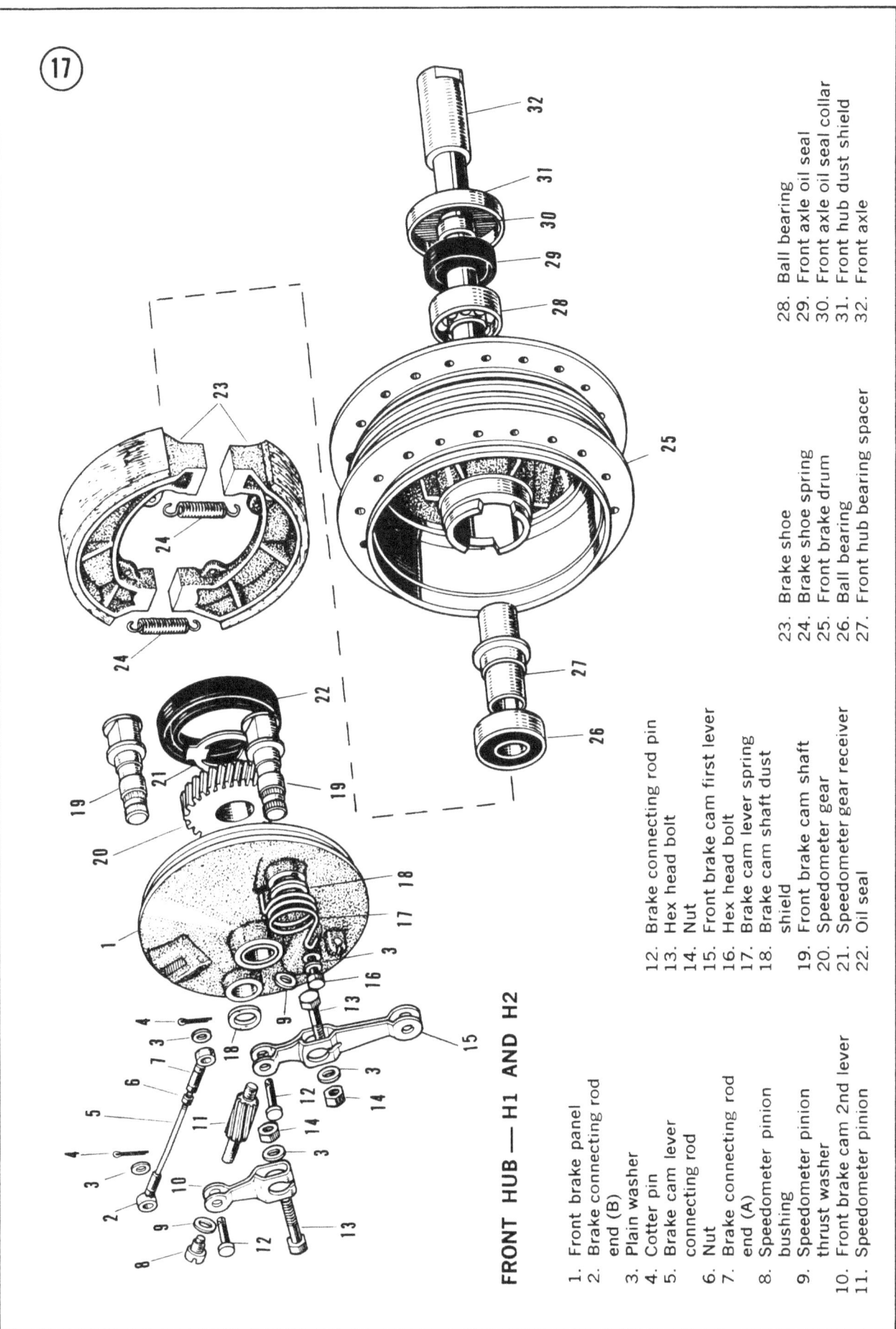

FRONT HUB — H1 AND H2

1. Front brake panel
2. Brake connecting rod end (B)
3. Plain washer
4. Cotter pin
5. Brake cam lever connecting rod
6. Nut
7. Brake connecting rod end (A)
8. Speedometer pinion bushing
9. Speedometer pinion thrust washer
10. Front brake cam 2nd lever
11. Speedometer pinion
12. Brake connecting rod pin
13. Hex head bolt
14. Nut
15. Front brake cam first lever
16. Hex head bolt
17. Brake cam lever spring
18. Brake cam shaft dust shield
19. Front brake cam shaft
20. Speedometer gear
21. Speedometer gear receiver
22. Oil seal
23. Brake shoe
24. Brake shoe spring
25. Front brake drum
26. Ball bearing
27. Front hub bearing spacer
28. Ball bearing
29. Front axle oil seal
30. Front axle oil seal collar
31. Front hub dust shield
32. Front axle

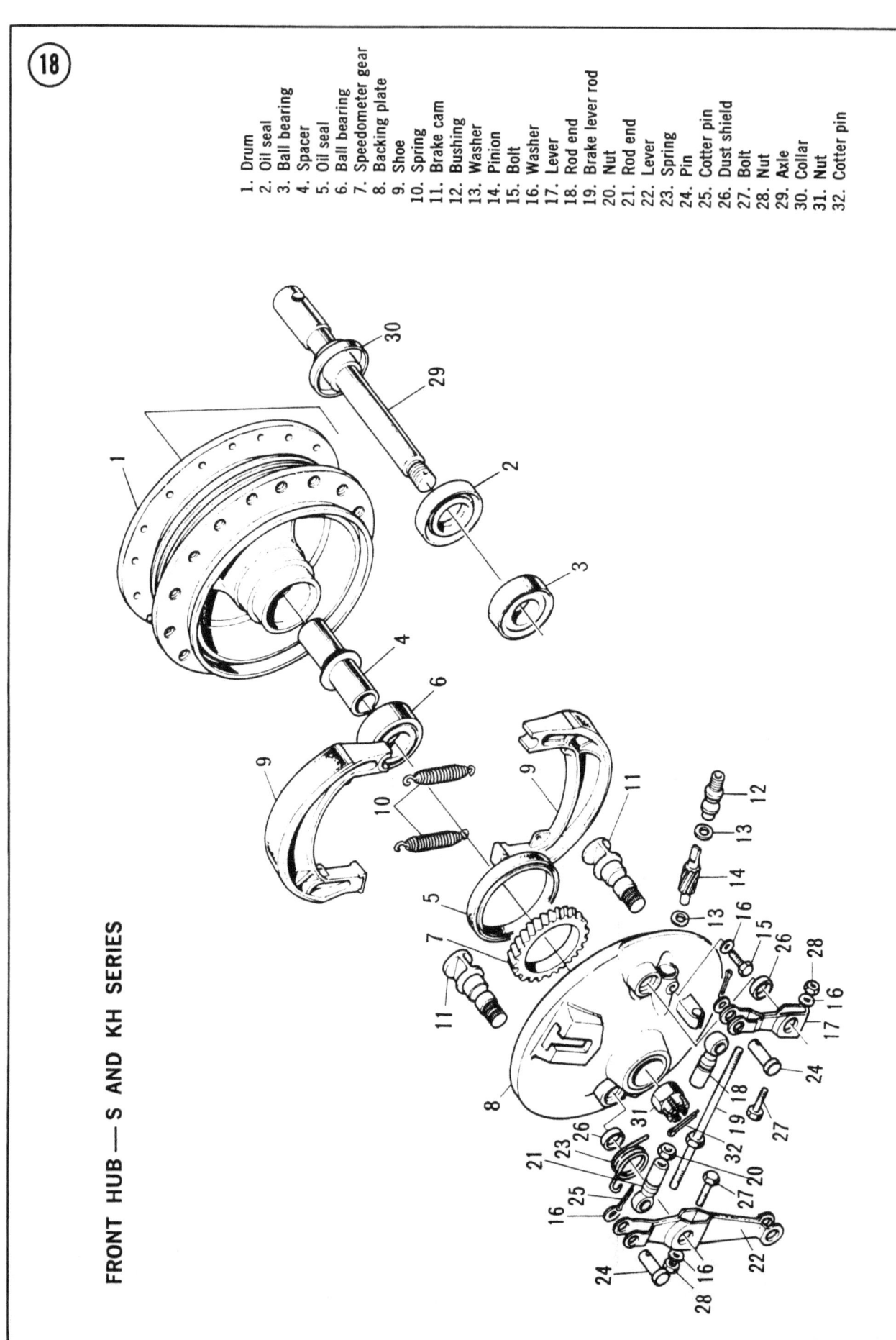

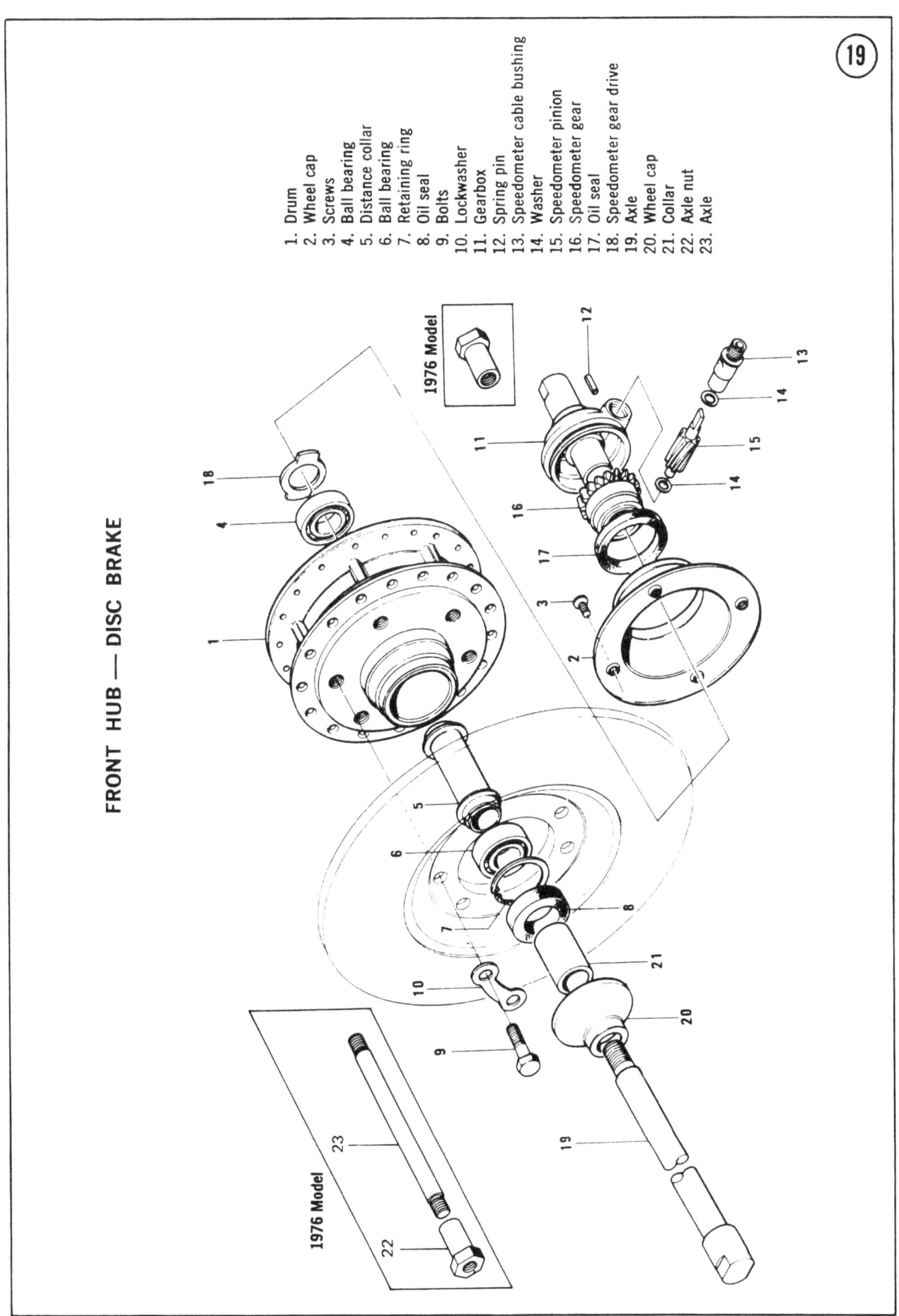

REAR HUB — H1 AND H2

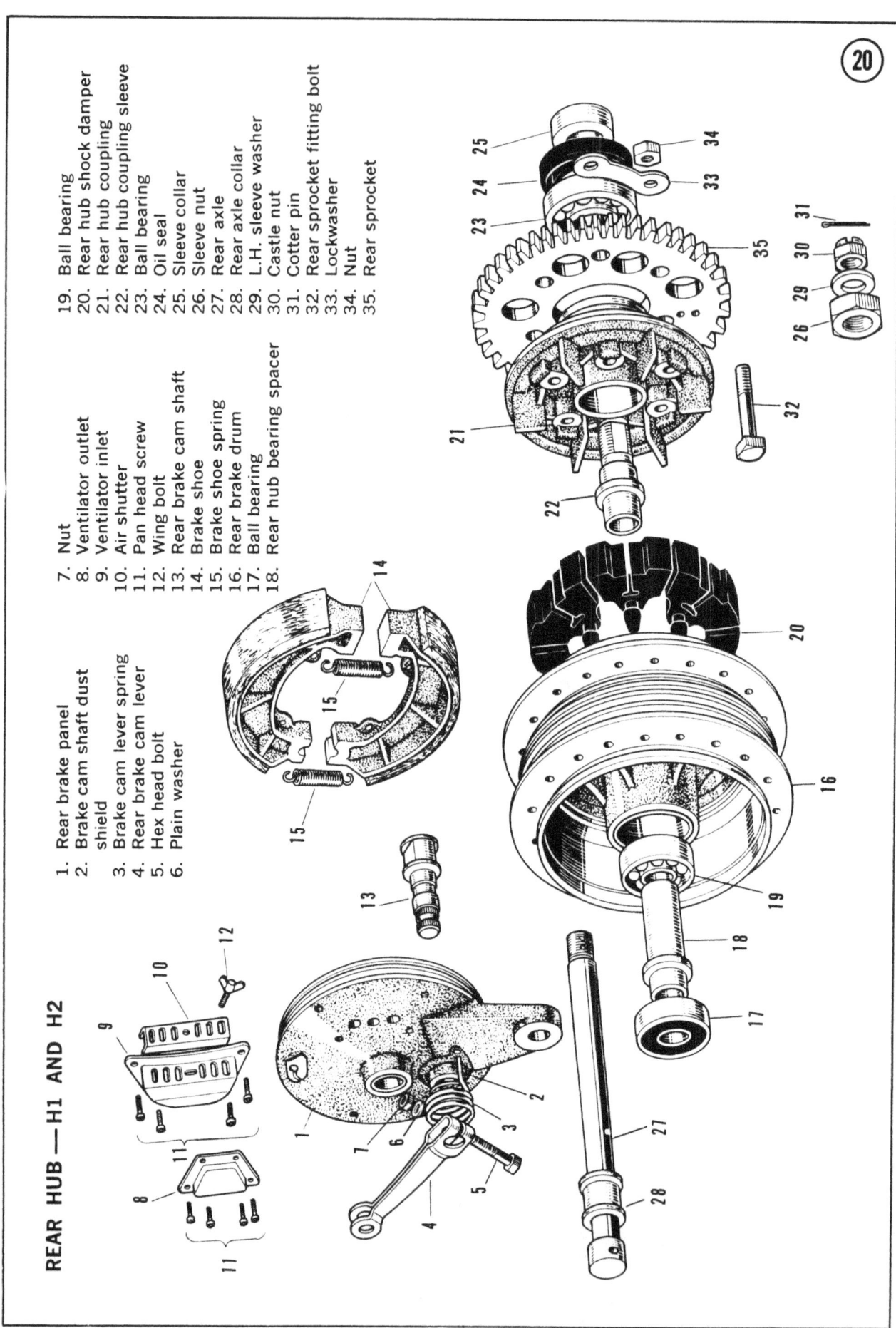

1. Rear brake panel
2. Brake cam shaft dust shield
3. Brake cam lever spring
4. Rear brake cam lever
5. Hex head bolt
6. Plain washer
7. Nut
8. Ventilator outlet
9. Ventilator inlet
10. Air shutter
11. Pan head screw
12. Wing bolt
13. Rear brake cam shaft
14. Brake shoe
15. Brake shoe spring
16. Rear brake drum
17. Ball bearing
18. Rear hub bearing spacer
19. Ball bearing
20. Rear hub shock damper
21. Rear hub coupling
22. Rear hub coupling sleeve
23. Ball bearing
24. Oil seal
25. Sleeve collar
26. Sleeve nut
27. Rear axle
28. Rear axle collar
29. L.H. sleeve washer
30. Castle nut
31. Cotter pin
32. Rear sprocket fitting bolt
33. Lockwasher
34. Nut
35. Rear sprocket

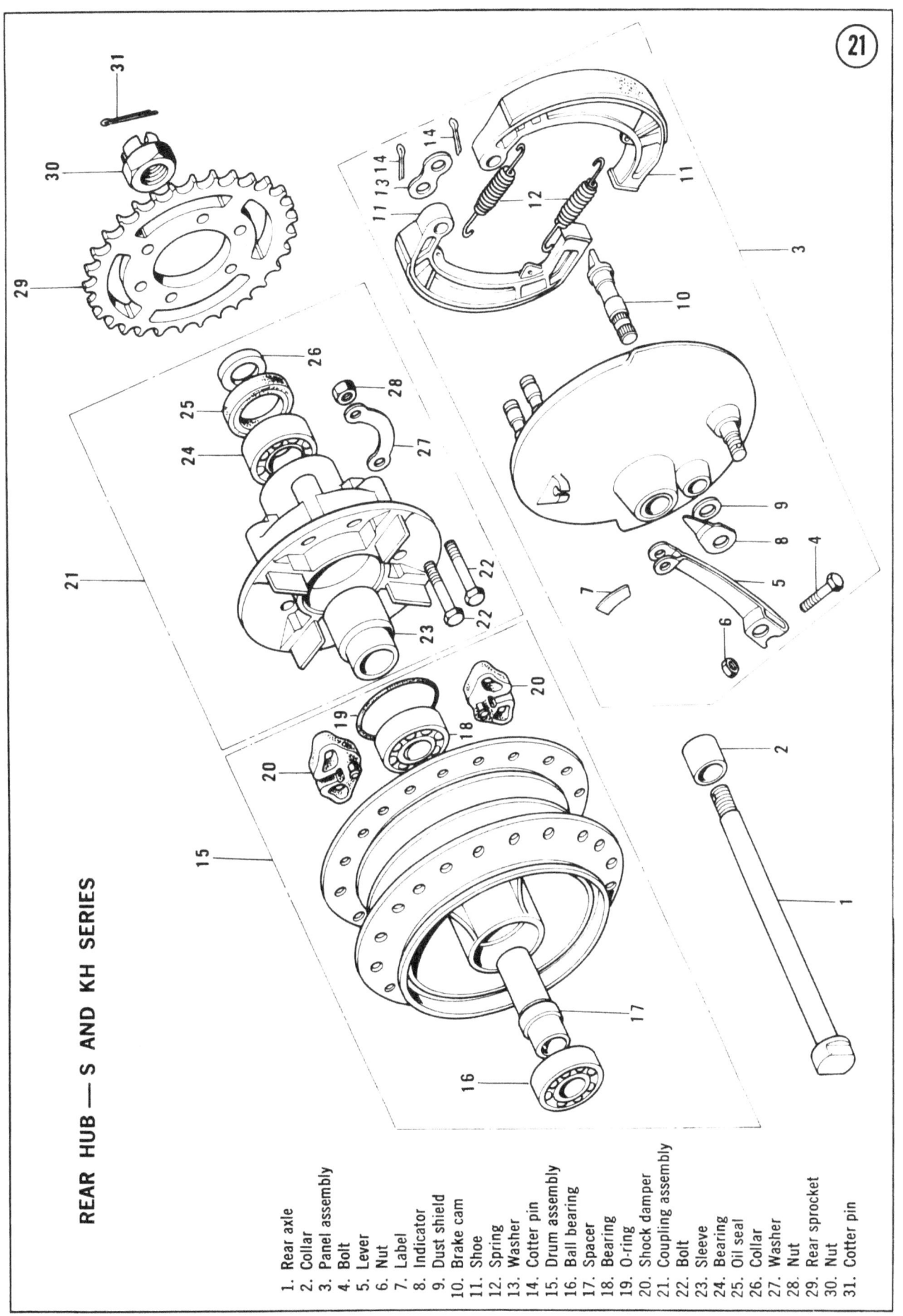

4. Remove the shaft pinch bolt (**Figure 24**).

5. Unscrew the axle on KH500 and H series models (**Figure 25**). Remove the axle nut on other models, then pull out the axle shaft (**Figure 26**).

Front Wheel Removal (Disc Brake)

To remove the front wheel on these machines, first remove the speedometer cable, then remove the four mounting bolts, as shown in **Figure 27**.

> NOTE: *On disc brake models, insert a piece of wood in the caliper in place of the disc. That way, if the brake lever is inadvertently squeezed, the piston will not be forced out of the cylinder. If this does happen, the caliper might have to be disassembled to reseat the piston, and the system will have to be bled. By using the wood, bleeding the brake is not necessary when installing the wheel.*

Rear Wheel Removal (KH, S, and H1 Series)

1. Support the machine on a suitable stand, so the rear wheel is free.

2. Remove right footpeg and position mufflers out of the way.

3. Remove rear brake cable or rod (**Figure 28**).

4. Disconnect the torque link (**Figure 29**).

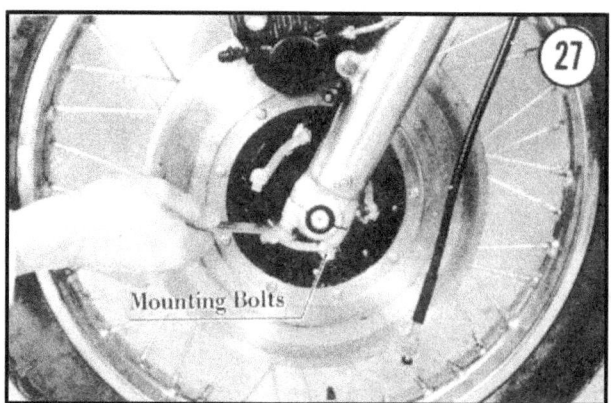

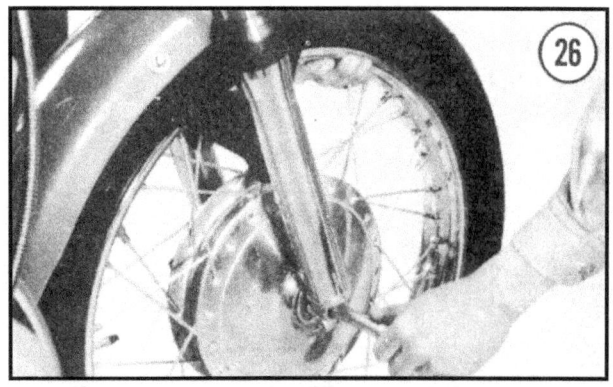

5. Loosen chain adjuster locknuts (**Figure 30**) and back off each chain adjuster 2-3 turns. Push wheel forward and remove chain from sprocket.

6. Remove the cotter pin, then the axle shaft nut (**Figure 31**).

> NOTE: *On 1973 and later models, fully loosen both chain adjusters. Remove the adjuster bolts and the chain adjuster stopper bolts (**Figure 30**). Push the wheel forward and slip off the drive chain. Pull the wheel to the rear and remove it.*

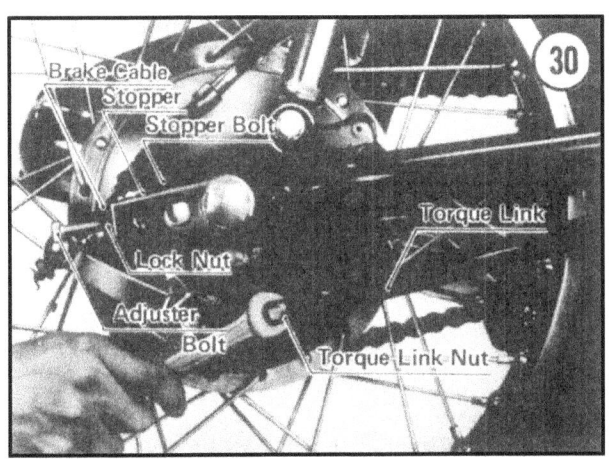

7. Pull out the axle shaft (**Figure 32**), then remove the wheel assembly. Install the footpeg and the mufflers.

8. Installation is the reverse of these removal steps.

Rear Wheel Removal (Model H2)

1. Remove the cotter pin and nut, then disconnect the torque link (**Figure 33**).

2. Loosen the axle shaft nut, then chain adjusters.

3. Push the rear wheel forward enough so that you can pull the chain from the sprocket and up over the chain guard (**Figure 34**).

4. Withdraw the axle shaft.

5. Remove the wheel and sprocket assembly.

6. Installation is the reverse of these steps.

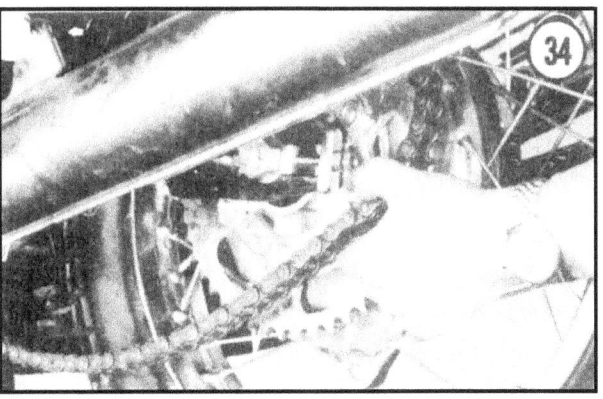

Front and Rear Wheel Disassembly (Drum Brake)

1. Pull the brake assembly straight up and out of the drum/hub.

2. Insert a long drift punch (**Figure 35**) from the inner side of the brake drum, with its end against the inner race of the wheel bearing on the opposite side. Drive out the bearing and oil seal together. Be sure to reposition the drift punch after each hammer blow so that the bearing is not cocked in its bore.

3. Insert the drift punch from the other side of the brake drum, then repeat Step 2 to drive out the other bearing.

Align the speedometer drive when assembling.

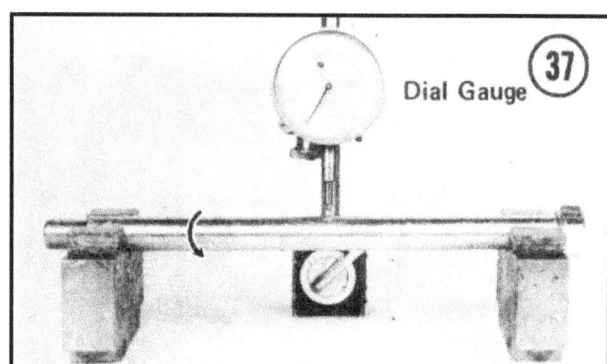

Dial Gauge

Front Wheel Disassembly/Assembly (Disc Brake)

1. Hold the speedometer gearcase stationary and unscrew the front axle.

CAUTION
Do not unscrew the speedometer gearcase from the axle as the drive gear will be damaged.

2. Remove the wheel cap and collar.

3. Insert a long drift punch from the left side, with its end against the inner race of the right-hand bearing. Tap out the bearing.

4. Remove the distance collar.

5. Remove the oil seal on the left side.

6. Remove the retaining ring.

7. Insert a long drift punch from the right side and repeat Step 3 to drive out the other bearing.

8. Assemble by reversing the disassembly steps.

9. Be sure to align the speedometer drive gear (**Figure 36**) when assembling.

CAUTION
To avoid damage to the speedometer drive gear, hold the speedometer gear housing stationary and screw the axle into it.

Inspection

1. Support each wheel shaft in a lathe, V-blocks, or other suitable centering device as shown in **Figure 37**. Rotate the shaft through a complete revolution. Straighten or replace the shaft if it is bent more than 0.028 in. (0.7mm).

2. Check the inner and outer races of the wheel bearings for cracks, galling, or pitting. Rotate the bearings by hand and check for roughness. Replace the bearings if they are worn or damaged.

3. Inspect the main and auxiliary lips of the oil seal for wear or damage. Replace the oil seal if there is any doubt about its condition.

4. Inspect the rubber shock dampers in the rear hub. Replace the dampers if they are worn or damaged.

Wheel Reassembly

Reverse the disassembly procedure to reassemble the wheels. Observe the following steps as you reassemble the wheel.

1. Clean the wheel bearings carefully, then lubricate them before installation.

2. Use an arbor press to install the bearings and oil seals. Be sure that the bearings and seals are seated squarely in their bores. Grease the oil seal lips upon assembly.

3. Be sure that there are no scratches, oil, or grease on the inner surface of the brake drum, or on the friction surfaces of the brake shoes. Clean the contact surfaces thoroughly with lacquer thinner before assembly.

4. Be sure that the rubber shock dampers are not reversed when they are installed. Shock dampers on H1 and KH500 models have a projection in the center. Insert this projection into the hole in the brake drum (**Figure 38**).

5. Check the wheels for runout after assembly.

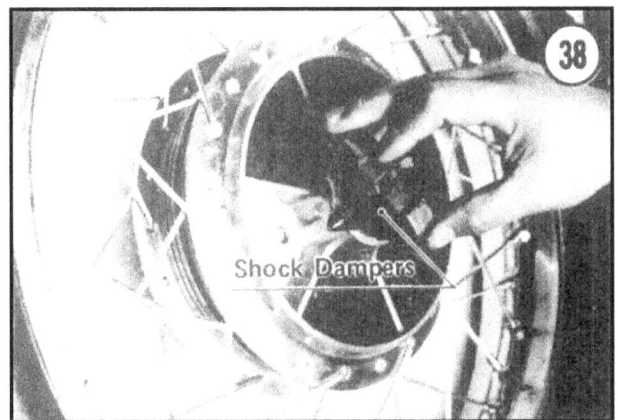

Wheel Runout Inspection

To measure runout of the wheel rim, support the wheel so that it is free to rotate. Position a dial indicator as shown in **Figure 39**. Observe the dial indicator as you rotate the wheel through a complete revolution. The runout limit for all models is 0.12 in. (3.0mm). Excessive runout may be caused by a bent rim or loose spokes. Repair or replace them as required.

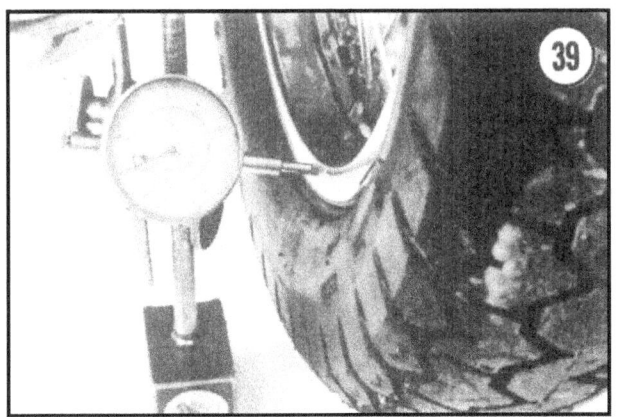

FRONT DISC BRAKES
(Models KH250-B1, KH400, SA2, H1, and H2)

Some machines are equipped with front wheel disc brakes. The major components of the disc brake are the brake lever, master cylinder, pressure switch, brake liner, caliper assembly, and disc.

When the rider pulls the brake lever, a piston in the master cylinder pressurizes the brake fluid. Fluid pressure is then transmitted through the brake line to the caliper assembly. The caliper assembly grips the disc attached to the front wheel and thereby slows or stops it.

Special Tools

Certain special tools are required for disc brake service. Be sure to have them on hand. They are available from Kawasaki dealers.

1. Tool A (**Figure 40**) is a seal hook. This tool is required for seal service.

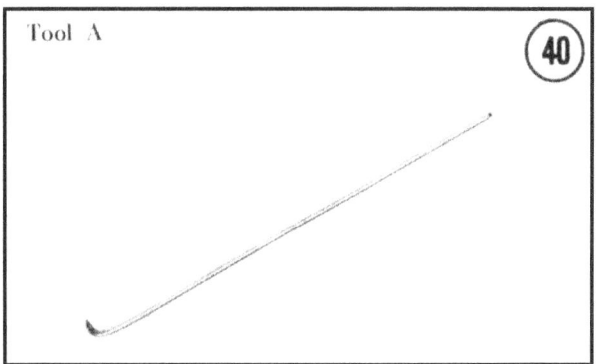

2. Tool B (**Figure 41**) is a pair of snap ring pliers. They are required for removing and replacing snap rings.

3. Tool C (**Figure 42**) is a seal installing tool.

> **WARNING**
> *Your life depends on your brakes. Failure to observe certain precautions when you service hydraulic brakes may result in brake failure. Pay particular attention to the following points:*
> *1. Do not use gasoline or any other mineral base solvent for cleaning any parts in contact with brake fluid.* **Use only brake fluid, ethyl alcohol, or isopropyl alcohol for cleaning purposes.**
> *2. Do not allow any rubber part to remain in contact with alcohol for longer than 30 seconds.*

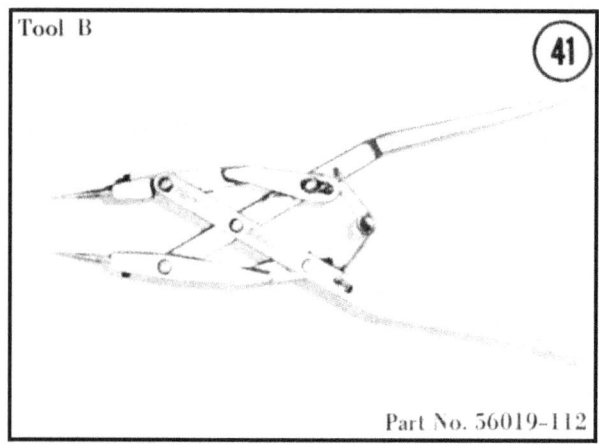

Part No. 56019-112

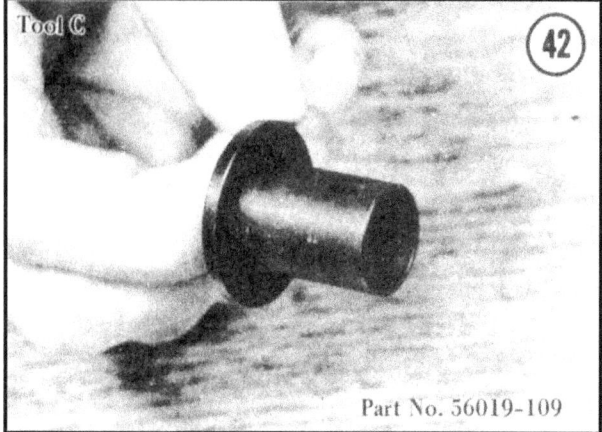

Part No. 56019-109

Refer to **Table 2** for disc brake assembly torque specifications.

Table 2 DISC BRAKE ASSEMBLY TORQUE SPECIFICATIONS

Item	Torque	
Brake lever	43-61 in.-lb.	(0.5-0.7 mkg)
Brake lever adjuster	13.0-16.5 ft.-lb.	(1.8-2.3 mkg)
Master cylinder clamp	52-78 in.-lb.	(0.6-0.9 mkg)
Fitting (banjo) bolts	21-22 ft.-lb.	(2.9-3.1 mkg)
Brake pipe nipple	12.0-13.5 ft.-lb.	1.7-1.9 mkg)
3-way fitting mounting	61-78 in.-lb.	(0.7-0.9 mkg)
Front brake light switch	19-22 ft.-lb.	(2.6-3.0 mkg)
Caliper shafts	17.5-20 ft.-lb.	(2.4-2.8 mkg)
Caliper mounting	25-33 ft.-lb.	(3.4-4.6 mkg)
Bleeder valve	61-87 in.-lb.	(0.7-1.0 mkg)
Disc mounting bolts	25-33 ft.-lb.	(3.4-4.6 mkg)

Master Cylinder Disassembly

Figure 43 is an exploded view of the master cylinder and related components. Refer to this illustration as you service the master cylinder.

1. Remove the brake line **(Figure 44)**.
2. Remove the master cylinder from the handlebar **(Figure 45)**.

> **CAUTION**
> *Cover the fuel tank with a heavy cloth or plastic tarp to protect it from accidental spilling of brake fluid. Wash any brake fluid off any painted or plated surface immediately, as it will destroy the finish. Use soapy water and rinse thoroughly.*

3. Remove the reservoir cap, cap seal, and plate. Discard the brake fluid.
4. Remove the brake lever **(Figure 46)**.

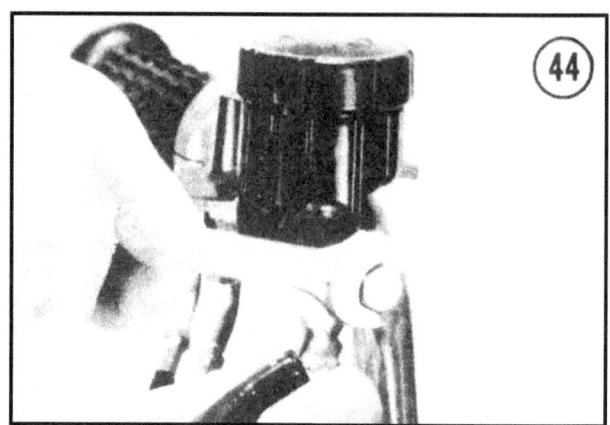

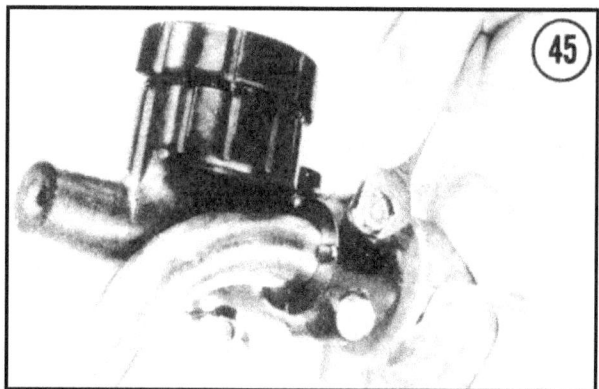

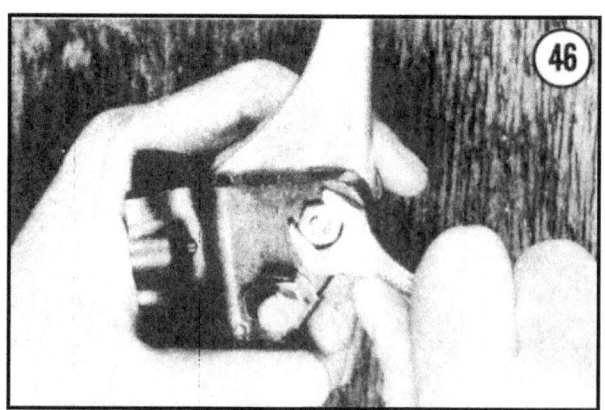

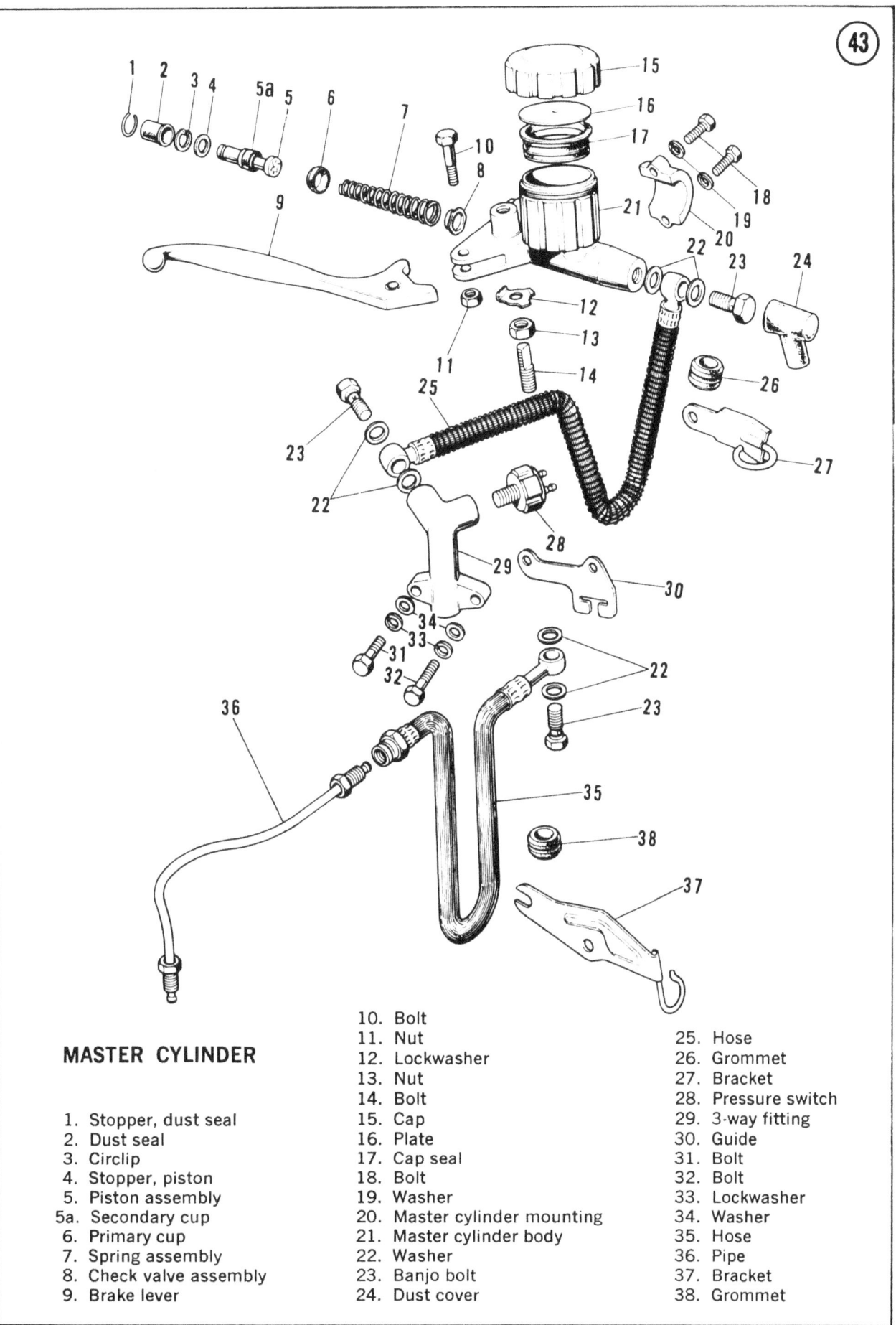

MASTER CYLINDER

1. Stopper, dust seal
2. Dust seal
3. Circlip
4. Stopper, piston
5. Piston assembly
5a. Secondary cup
6. Primary cup
7. Spring assembly
8. Check valve assembly
9. Brake lever
10. Bolt
11. Nut
12. Lockwasher
13. Nut
14. Bolt
15. Cap
16. Plate
17. Cap seal
18. Bolt
19. Washer
20. Master cylinder mounting
21. Master cylinder body
22. Washer
23. Banjo bolt
24. Dust cover
25. Hose
26. Grommet
27. Bracket
28. Pressure switch
29. 3-way fitting
30. Guide
31. Bolt
32. Bolt
33. Lockwasher
34. Washer
35. Hose
36. Pipe
37. Bracket
38. Grommet

5. Use the seal hook (Tool A) to remove the ring and dust seal (**Figure 47**). Take care not to damage the seal.

6. Remove the snap ring (**Figure 48**). Then remove the stopper plate, piston assembly, and check valve. If these parts do not come out easily, blow lightly into the brake line that fits into the cylinder.

> NOTE: *If the secondary cup is undamaged, do not remove it from the piston. Do not remove the spring seal from the spring. Do not clamp the master cylinder too tightly in a vise.*

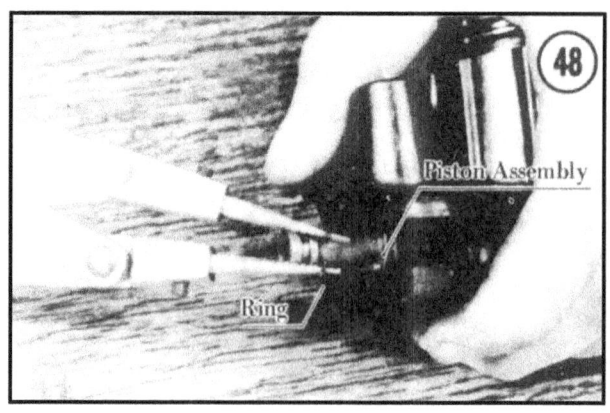

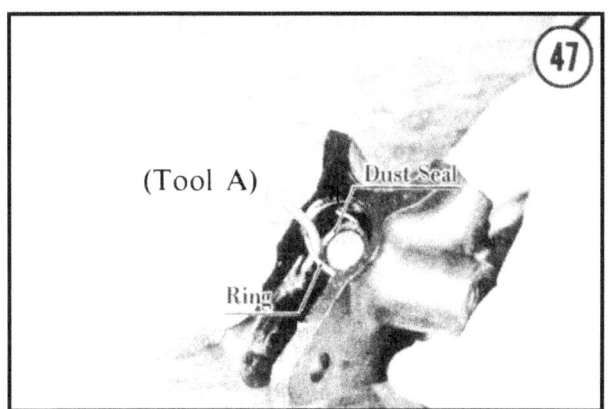

Inspect all parts for wear or damage. Remove any corrosion from the cylinder bore with a brake hone. If honing won't clean up the cylinder, replace it. Replace all rubber parts. Service limits for the various parts are listed in **Table 3**.

Master Cylinder Assembly

To reassemble the master cylinder, refer to **Figure 49**, then proceed as follows.

1. Dip the piston assembly, primary cup, and check valve in brake fluid before assembly. Also lubricate the cylinder bore with brake fluid.

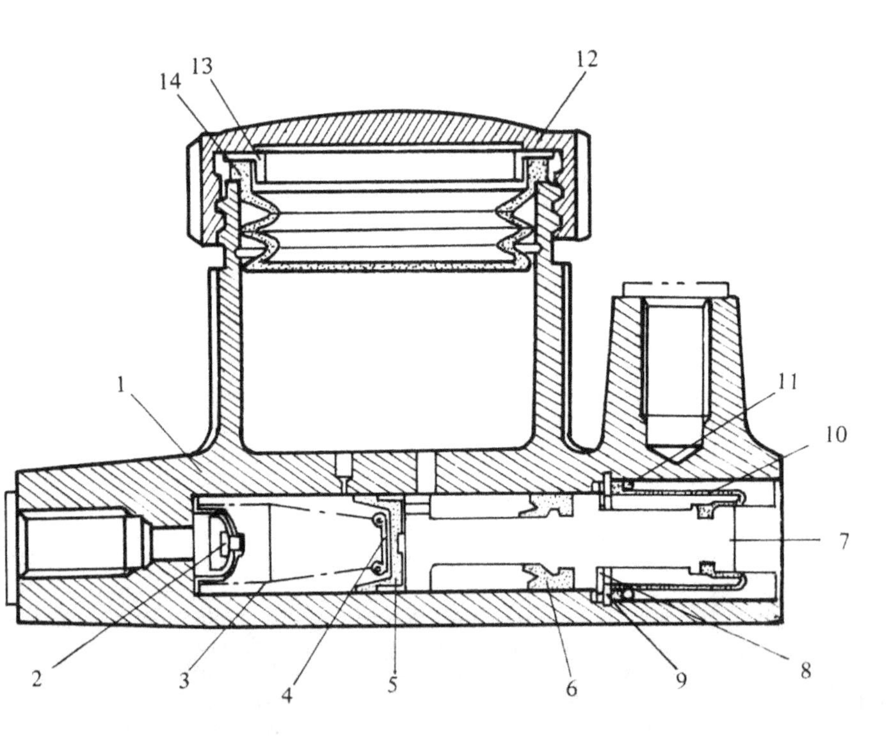

MASTER CYLINDER

1. Master cylinder body
2. Check valve
3. Spring
4. Spring seat
5. Primary cup
6. Secondary cup
7. Piston
8. Piston stopper
9. Circlip
10. Dust seal
11. Dust seal stopper
12. Cap
13. Plate
14. Cap seal

Table 3 MASTER CYLINDER SPECIFICATIONS

Measurement	Standard Inches (Millimeters)	Service Limit Inches (Millimeters)
Cylinder bore	0.5512-0.5529 (14.000-14.043)	0.5543 (14.080)
Piston diameter	0.5495-0.5506 (13.957-13.984)	0.5496 (13.960)
Cup diameter	0.577-0596 (14.65-15.15)	0.571 (14.50)
Spring length	2.01 (51)	1.89 (48)

2. Insert the primary cup, then the piston assembly.

CAUTION
During assembly, be sure that the check valve and primary cup do not turn sideways or backwards.

3. Insert the stopper, then install the snap ring into its groove. Be sure that the snap ring is in place. To do so, slide it around in its groove. If the snap ring is distorted or bent, replace it.

4. Use Tool A to install the dust seal flange into the piston groove.

5. Push the dust seal stopper in as far as it will go, using Tool C.

6. Install the brake lever.

7. Hold the cylinder, then check for smooth operation of the lever. Put your finger over the brake line connection and check for suction when the lever is released.

CAUTION
To avoid damage to the secondary cup, do not squeeze the lever as far as it will go.

8. Fill the reservoir with fresh brake fluid, then screw on the cap. Squeeze and release the lever several times to be sure fluid is pumped from the outlet.

WARNING
Use brake fluid clearly marked DOT 3 and/or SAE J1703 only. Others may vaporize and cause brake failure. Always use the same brand name; do not intermix as many brands are not compatible.

9. Squeeze the lever, then cover the outlet with your finger. Release the lever suddenly. The lever should return quickly and smoothly.

10. Install the assembly on the handlebar. Tighten the top bolt first.

11. Loosen the locknut, then turn the adjuster so that free play, measured at the tip of the lever, is less than 3/16 inch (5 millimeters), as shown in **Figure 50**. Tighten the locknut.

12. Attach the brake line, fill the reservoir with fresh brake fluid, and bleed the line.

WARNING
*Do not ride the motorcycle until you are sure that the brake is operating correctly with full hydraulic advantage. If necessary, bleed the brakes as described under **Bleeding the Brake** in this chapter.*

Brake Pads

Brake pads wear from normal use of the front brake. Wear rate depends on riding conditions and the rider's habits, so no definite replacement schedule can be specified. Replace both pads when either is worn to the red line. When service is required, refer to **Figure 51**, then proceed as follows.

1. Remove the front wheel.

2. Remove the attaching screw **(Figure 52)**, then remove Pad B.

3. Squeeze the brake lever gently to push out Pad A.

4. Wipe off the new pads with alcohol before installation.

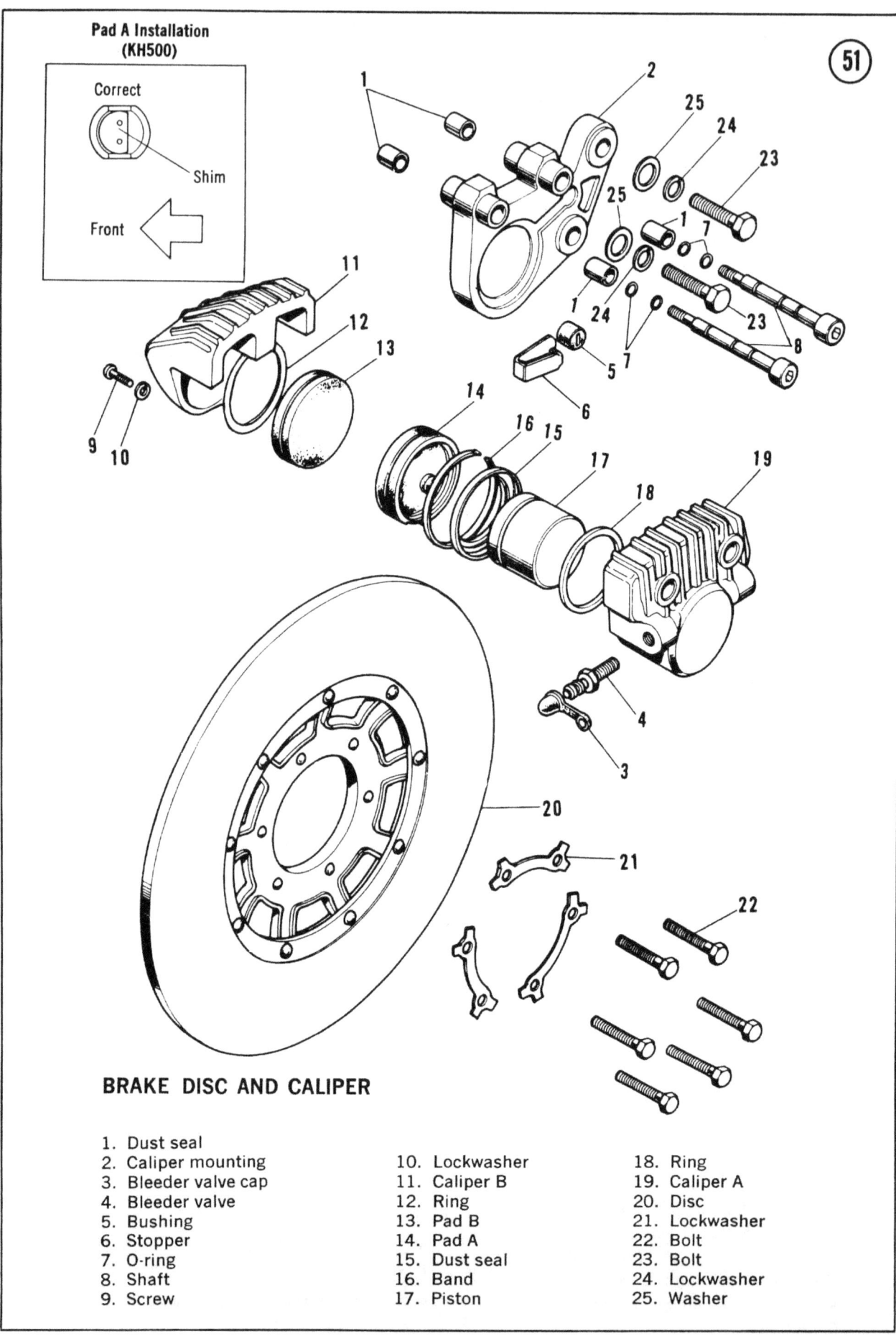

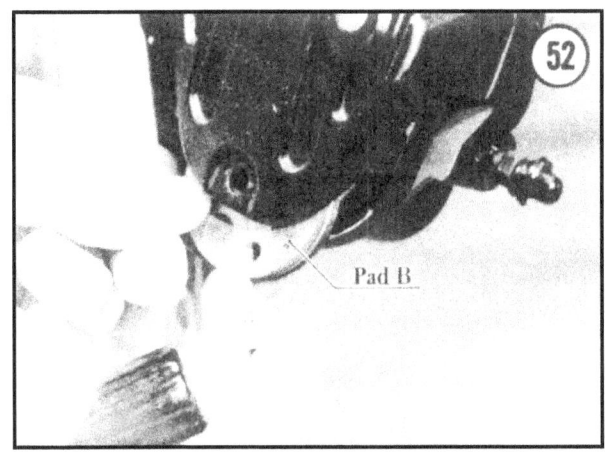

5. Open the bleeder valve (**Figure 53**) slightly, then push in the piston fully, and close the valve.

6. Insert Pad A. Align its groove with the positioning pin. Be sure that the pad moves in and out easily.

> NOTE: *On some KH500 models, Pad A is equipped with a shim. Install the pad and shim with the shim positioned toward the front of the bike. Refer to Figure 51.*

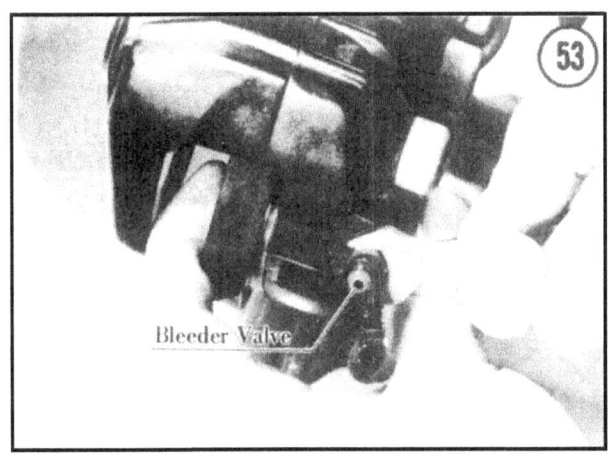

7. Install Pad B. Apply Loctite Lock 'N' Seal to the threads of the screw prior to installation.

8. Install the front wheel.

9. Since the bleeder valve was open, check for air in the brake system by squeezing the lever. If the lever pulls in too easily, bleed the brake as described in the next section.

10. Spin the front wheel lightly to be sure that the pads do not rub against the disc. If the rubbing occurs, check for the following:

   a. Pad A not fully seated

   b. Piston oil seal damaged or mispositioned

   c. Warped disc

Bleeding the Brake

The brake must be bled any time air enters the system. Air may enter any time that the bleeder valve is open or if the reservoir fluid level becomes too low.

1. Fill the reservoir with fresh fluid. Check the level frequently during the bleeding procedure, as some fluid will be lost.

2. Remove the rubber cap from the bleeder valve, then connect a length of clear plastic tubing to the bleeder valve (**Figure 54**). Push the other end of the tubing into a vessel containing brake fluid. Be sure that the end of the tubing remains submerged in brake fluid during the entire procedure.

3. Open the bleeder valve, squeeze the lever slowly, close the valve, and release the lever. Repeat this sequence several times until the tube is full of fluid.

4. Open the bleeder valve. With the bleeder valve open, continue to slowly squeeze and release the lever until no bubbles appear in either the brake fluid reservoir or in the fluid flowing from the bleeder valve. Add brake fluid to the reservoir as necessary to maintain the proper level.

5. Close the bleeder valve, replace the rubber cap, and fill the reservoir to the line.

Caliper Assembly

1. Remove the brake line at the caliper

assembly. Cap the end of the line with rubber bleeder valve cap (**Figure 55**).

2. Loosen the 2 socket head shafts (**Figure 56**). Then remove the 2 mounting bolts and take off the caliper assembly.

3. Remove both pads.

4. Completely unscrew both socket head shafts (**Figure 57**), then remove one side of the caliper assembly.

> CAUTION
> *Unscrew both shafts alternately, a little at a time, to avoid damage to the seals and O-rings.*

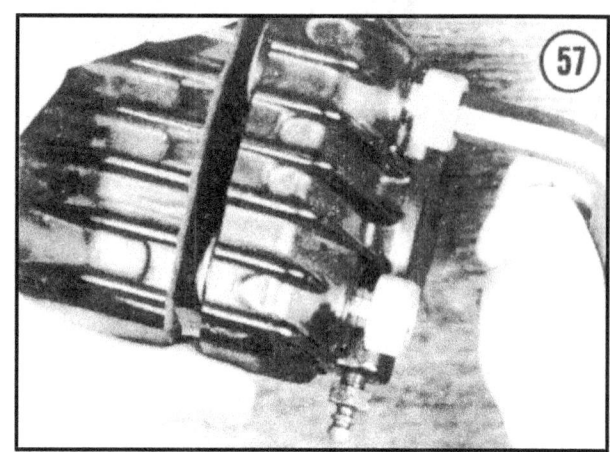

5. Pull the caliper mounting off the shafts (**Figure 58**). Be careful that you don't damage the shafts, O-rings, or seals. Then remove both shafts.

6. Remove the band and dust seal from the piston. Blow compressed air into the caliper inlet fitting to remove the piston. If compressed air is not available, reconnect the brake line and pump the piston out with the brake lever.

7. Remove the oil seal from the cylinder.

8. Examine the piston and cylinder for wear, scoring, or corrosion. Service limits are listed in **Table 4**.

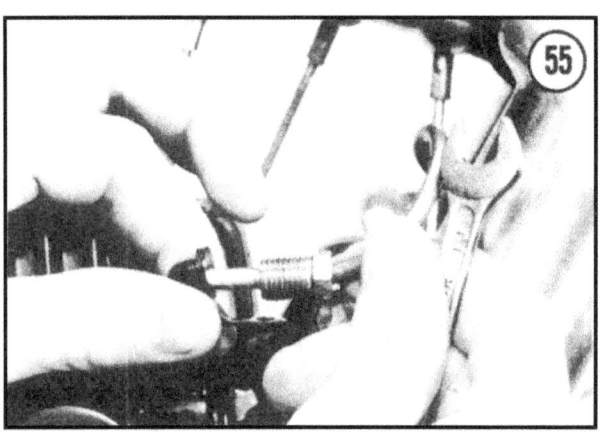

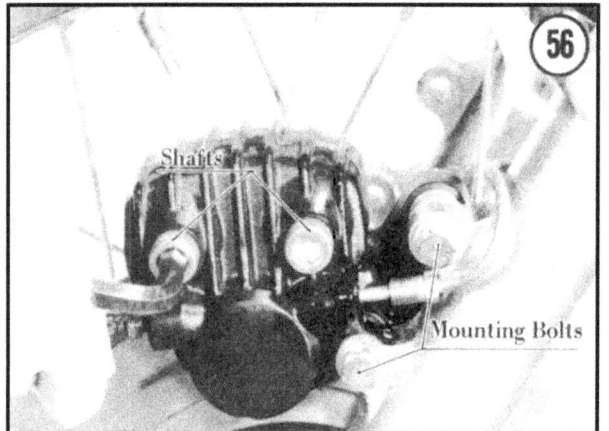

Table 4 CALIPER SPECIFICATIONS

Model	Item	Standard	Service Limit
S2A, S3, S3A, H1 and H2	Cylinder inside diameter	1.5031-1.5039 in. (38.180-38.200mm)	1.5045 in. (38.215mm)
	Piston outside diameter	1.5006-1.5019 in. (38.180-38.200mm)	1.5002 in. (38.105mm)
KH400-A3, KH250-B1, and KH500	Cylinder inside diameter	1.6870-1.6890 in. (42.850-42.900mm)	1.690 in. (42.92mm)
	Piston outside diameter	1.6846-1.6858 in. (42.788-42.820mm)	1.683 in. (42.75mm)

The piston oil seal maintains the proper pad/disc clearance. If this seal is bad, the pads will wear unevenly. Replace the oil seal under any of the following conditions:

a. Brake fluid leakage near the pads
b. Overheating brakes
c. Large difference in pad wear rate
d. Oil seal is stuck to the piston
e. Every other pad replacement

Brake Line

High pressure within the brake line may result in leakage and loss of braking power if the line is not maintained properly. Replace the line if any cracks or bulges appear when you bend or twist the line. Examine the fittings for cracks or leakage.

Brake Disc

Measure disc thickness and replace it if it is worn beyond the service limit. See **Table 5**. Measure runout with a dial gauge in a manner similar to that for measuring wheel runout. Brake drag, wear, and overheating will occur if the disc is warped. Remove any oil from the disc with trichloroethylene.

Table 5 DISC SPECIFICATIONS

Measurement	Standard		Service Limit	
	Inch	(Millimeters)	Inch	(Millimeters)
Thickness	0.276	(7.0)	0.217	(5.5)
Runout	0.004	(0.1)	0.012	(0.3)

DRUM BRAKES

Each brake consists of a brake pedal or lever, cable, brake panel assembly, and brake drum. The brake panel assembly consists of the cam lever, camshaft, brake shoes, retracting springs, and brake panel body. Front brakes are of the dual leading shoe type. The rear brakes have one leading and one trailing shoe. Both brakes are equipped with stoplight switches.

Front Brake

The front brake mechanism is shown in **Figure 59**. Two camshafts are used, one for each brake shoe. As each camshaft turns, it forces its associated shoe into contact with the brake drum. Notice that as the brake drum turns counterclockwise, the movement of the brake drum tends to increase the pressure of the brake shoe against the drum, thereby increasing the braking power. Because of the self-energizing action of both brake shoes, this brake arrangement is sometimes called a dual leading shoe type.

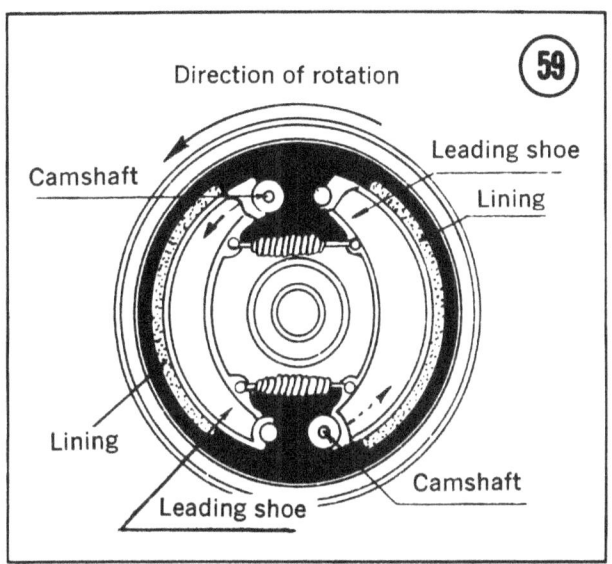

Rear Brake

Figure 60 illustrates the rear brake. There is only one camshaft which operates both brake shoes. When the camshaft turns, it forces both shoes against the brake drum. The movement of the brake drum tends to increase the pressure of the forward shoe against the drum; therefore the forward shoe is a leading shoe because of the self-energizing effect. The rear shoe, however, makes contact in the direction of drum rotation, and the self-energizing effect does not occur. Therefore, the rear brake shoe is a trailing shoe.

Rear Brake Ventilator (H1 and H2)

The rear brake on some models is equipped with a ventilator (**Figure 61**). The ventilator allows air to circulate within the brake mechanism, and thereby carry away the heat generated by the use of the brake. In wet weather, however, water may enter the brake and impair braking efficiency. Under wet riding conditions the ventilator inlet should be closed.

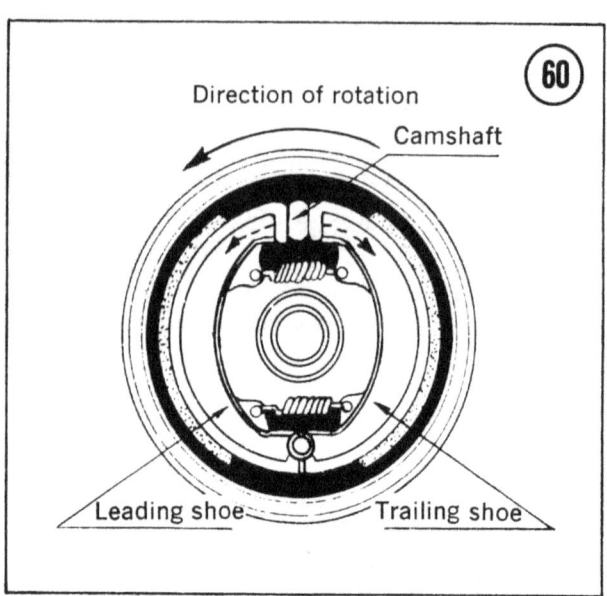

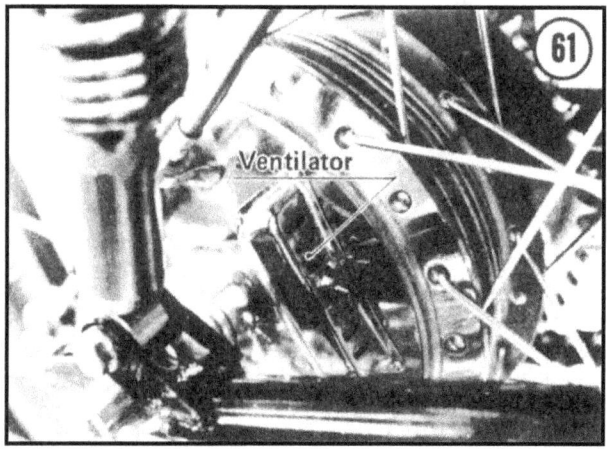

Inspection

1. Thoroughly clean and dry all the parts *except the linings*.

2. Check the contact surface of the drum for scoring. If there are deep grooves, deep enough to snag a fingernail, the drum should be reground.

3. Measure the inside diameter of the brake drum with a vernier caliper (**Figure 63**). Check against dimensions given in **Table 6**. If the dimension is greater than the wear limit, the drum must be replaced.

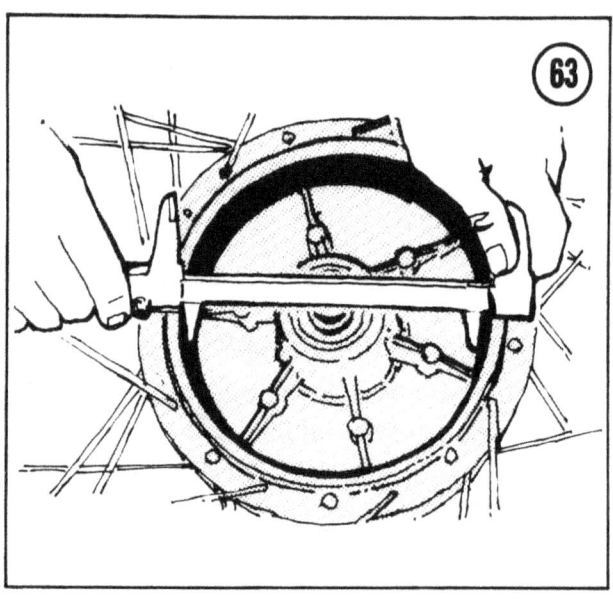

4. If the brake drum is turned, the linings will have to be replaced and the new ones arced to the new drum contour.

5. Check the brake linings. They should be replaced if worn within 0.118 in. (0.3mm) of the metal shoe table (**Figure 64**).

and impair braking efficiency. Under wet riding conditions the ventilator inlet should be closed.

Brake Disassembly (Front and Rear)

1. Remove the wheel as described earlier.

2. Pull the brake assembly straight up and out of the brake drum.

3. On the front brake, pull up on one shoe first, at right angles to the brake panel (**Figure 62**). Remove both shoe assemblies.

4. On rear brake, pull both shoe assemblies straight up and off the pivot studs and remove them.

5. Remove the bolts and nuts on the brake levers.

6. Remove the locknut on the link rod (front brake only) and remove the link rod.

7. Remove the levers from the camshafts and pull the cams out of the brake panel.

Table 6 BRAKE DRUM SPECIFICATIONS

Model	Standard Value				Wear Limit			
	Front		Rear		Front		Rear	
	Inches	(mm)	Inches	(mm)	Inches	(mm)	Inches	(mm)
S series	7.087	(180)	7.087	(180)	7.116	(180.75)	7.116	(180.75)
KH250	7.087	(180)	7.087	(180)	7.116	(180.75)	7.116	(180.75)
KH400	—		7.087	(180)	—		7.116	(180.75)
KH500	—		7.087	(180)	—		7.116	(180.75)
H1	7.874	(200)	7.087	(180)	7.904	(200.75)	7.116	(180.75)
H2	—		7.874	(200)	—		7.904	(200.75)

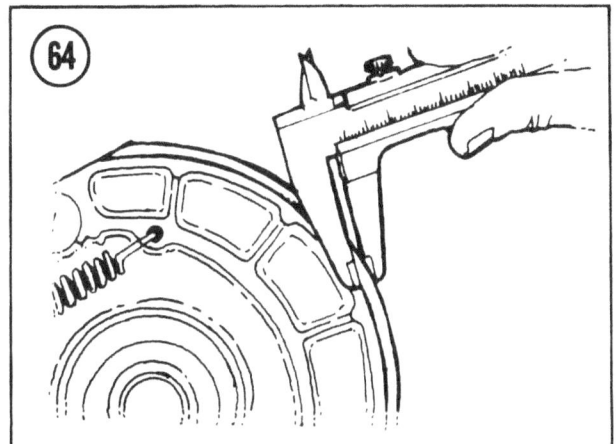

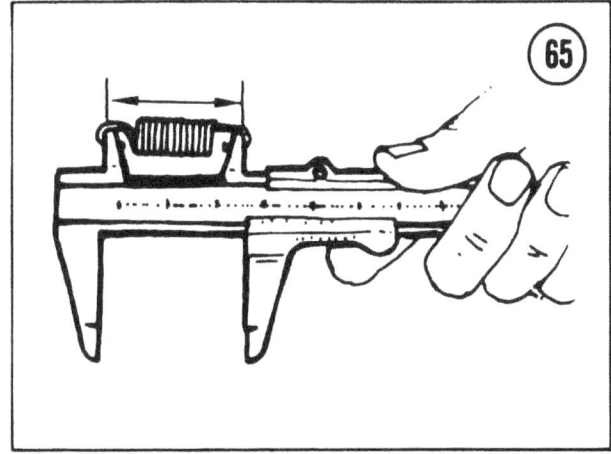

6. Inspect the linings for imbedded foreign material. Dirt can be removed with a stiff wire brush. Check for any traces of oil or grease; if they are contaminated, they must be replaced.

7. Inspect the cam lobes and the pivot pin area of the shaft for wear and corrosion. Minor roughness can be removed with fine emery cloth.

8. Inspect the brake shoe return springs (**Figure 65**) for wear. If they are stretched, they will not fully retract the brake shoes and they will drag and wear out prematurely. Replace if necessary. Check against dimensions given in **Table 7**.

Measure the clearance between the brake camshaft and the bushing in the brake panel. Standard clearance for all models is 0.0008 to 0.0028 in. (0.02-0.07mm). Replace the camshaft and the brake panel as a set if the clearance exceeds 0.02 in. (0.5mm).

Table 7 RETURN SPRING SPECIFICATIONS

Model	Standard Value				Repair Limit			
	Front		Rear		Front		Rear	
	Inches	(mm)	Inches	(mm)	Inches	(mm)	Inches	(mm)
S series	1.85	(47.0)	2.20	(56.0)	1.97	(50.0)	2.32	(59.0)
KH250	1.85	(47.0)	2.20	(56.0)	1.97	(50.0)	2.32	(59.0)
KH400	—		2.20	(56.0)	—		2.32	(59.0)
KH500	—		2.62	(66.5)	—		2.74	(69.5)
H1/H1-E	2.36	(60.0)	2.62	(66.5)	2.48	(63.0)	2.74	(69.5)
H2/H2-B	—		2.62	(66.5)	—		2.74	(69.5)

Assembly

1. Assemble the brake by reversing the disassembly steps.

2. Grease the shafts, cams, and pivot posts with a light coat of molybdenum disulphide grease; avoid getting any grease on the brake panel where the linings may come in contact with it.

3. On the front brake, be sure to install the brake cable approximately perpendicular to the brake cam lever (**Figure 66**).

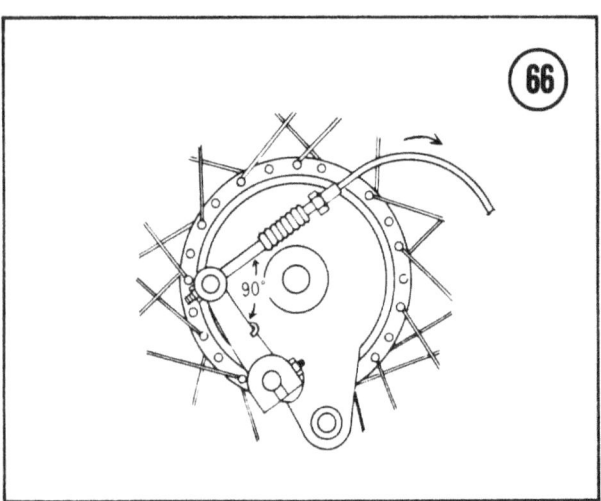

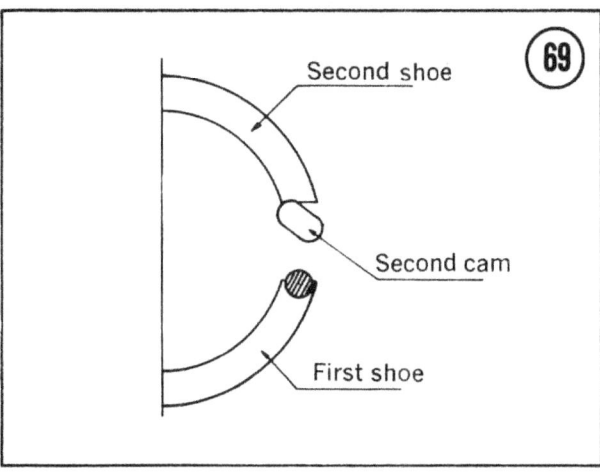

Front Brake Adjustment (At Drum)

Adjust the front brake by turning the adjustment nut at the front brake cam lever. The adjustment is correct when braking action begins when the front brake lever is pulled approximately 1 in. (25mm). Since the front brake stoplight switch is built into the cable, no adjustment is required.

Adjustment of the front brake lever connecting rod is normally not required, except after replacement of the brake shoes. To adjust the lever, proceed as follows.

1. Align the first cam lever with the serrations on the camshaft so that it is 90 degrees to the brake cable when the brake first starts to take effect (**Figure 67**). Install the second cam lever parallel to the first.

2. Loosen the connecting rod so that it turns easily, then turn it about one turn in direction A as shown in **Figure 68**. This procedure backs off the second shoe so that it will not operate when the first shoe is adjusted (**Figure 69**).

3. Support the machine so that the front wheel is clear of the ground.

4. Spin the front wheel, then tighten the adjustment nut (**Figure 70**) until the front brake drags very slightly.

5. Turn the connecting rod in direction C as shown in **Figure 71** so that the second brake shoe makes light contact with the drum. Brake drag will increase slightly at this point. Tighten the locknut.

6. Readjust front brake lever play.

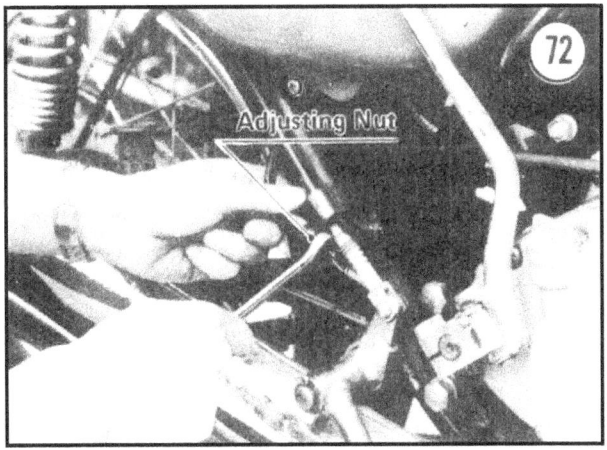

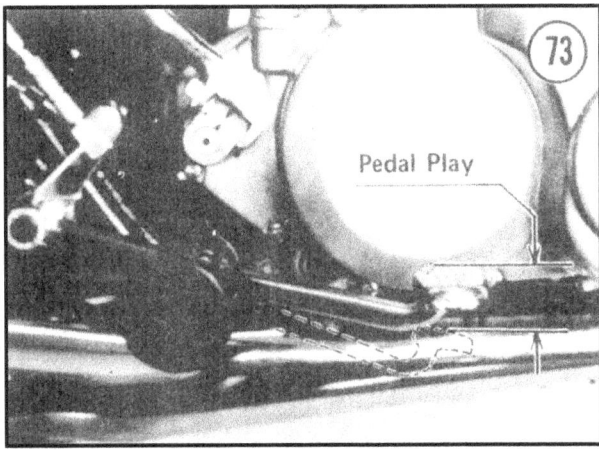

Rear Brake Adjustment

Adjust the rear brake by turning the adjustment nut (**Figure 72**) until braking action begins as follows:

a. Model H2 — ½-⅝ in. (12-15mm) of brake pedal travel.

b. All other models — ¾-1¼ in. (20-30mm) of brake pedal travel. Refer to **Figure 73**.

Adjust the rear brake stoplight switch nut so that the stoplight lights when the brake pedal has traveled as follows:

a. Model H2 — ⅜ in. (10mm)

b. All other models — ⅝-¾ in. (15-20mm)

CAUTION
Do not rotate the switch body for adjustment as the electrical wires will be damaged.

Front Brake Lever Adjustment (Drum Brake)

The front brake cable should be adjusted so that there is ¼-⅜ in. (7-10mm) clearance at the

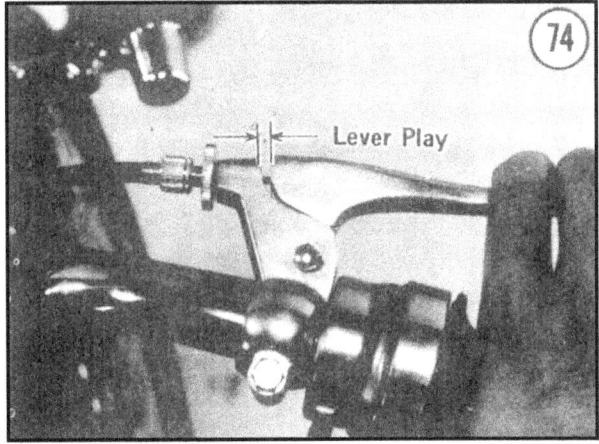

brake lever as shown in **Figure 74**. It must not be adjusted so closely that the brake shoes contact the drum with the lever relaxed. Loosen the locknut and turn the adjusting barrel in order to achieve the correct amount of free play. Tighten the locknut.

Front Brake Lever Adjustment (Disc Brake)

The front brake is self-adjusting as the pads wear. If there is a lot of play in the lever, check the brake fluid level and condition of the brake pads. A small amount of adjustment can be made to keep the lever from vibrating — keep a small amount of play to ensure a full stroke when applying the brake. Adjust by loosening the locknut (**Figure 75**) and turn the adjusting bolt a fraction of a turn so the lever has less than 3/16 in. (5mm) free play (**Figure 75**). Tighten the locknut.

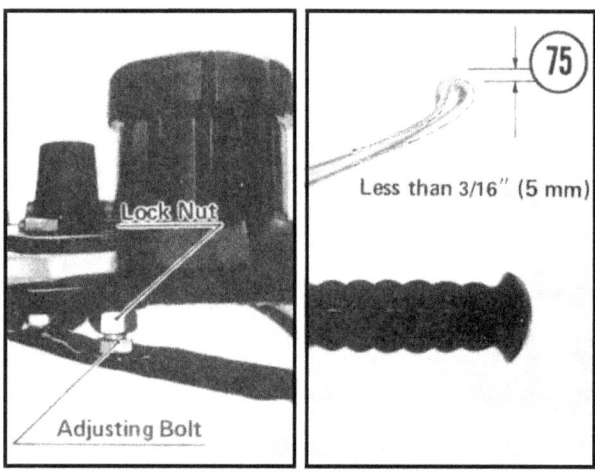

FRONT FORKS

The front fork assembly serves as a shock absorber for the front wheel. The forks consist of 2 telescoping tubes mounted to the steering stem.

Figure 76 is a sectional view of a typical fork tube. Major components include inner and outer tubes, spring, and spring holder. Damping action is provided by spring tension and oil within the tubes.

Fork Removal

The initial steps for fork removal are similar for all models. Proceed as follows.

1. Remove all connectors in headlight assembly from main wire harness (**Figure 77**).

2. Remove the headlight assembly.

3. Remove the handlebar assembly (**Figure 78**).

4. On S2 and disc brake models, the left grip wiring is connected under the fuel tank. Remove the tank to disconnect it (**Figure 79**). At the same time, separate the ignition switch wiring connector.

5. Remove the speedometer and tachometer

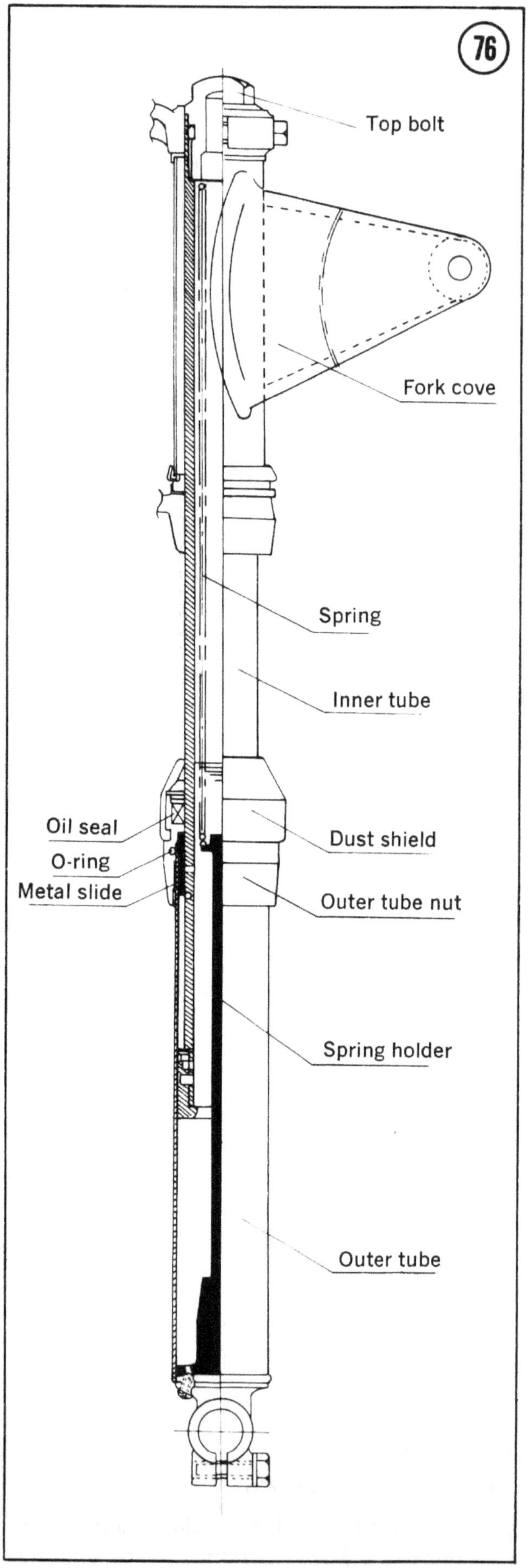

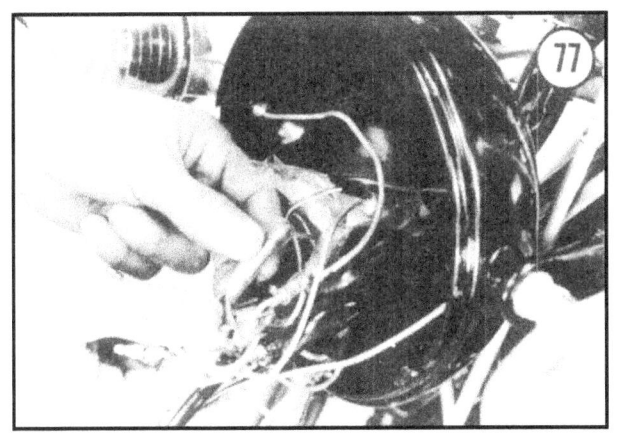

cables, as shown in **Figure 80**. Then remove both instruments (**Figure 81**).

6. Remove the cotter pin and nut at the lower end of the steering damper rod (**Figure 82**). Then loosen steering damper knob (**Figure 83**) and remove the steering damper.

7. Remove the steering stem nut with the special spanner wrench (**Figure 84**) provided in the Kawasaki owner's tool box.

8. Remove the top bolts (**Figure 85**) on models with drum brakes.

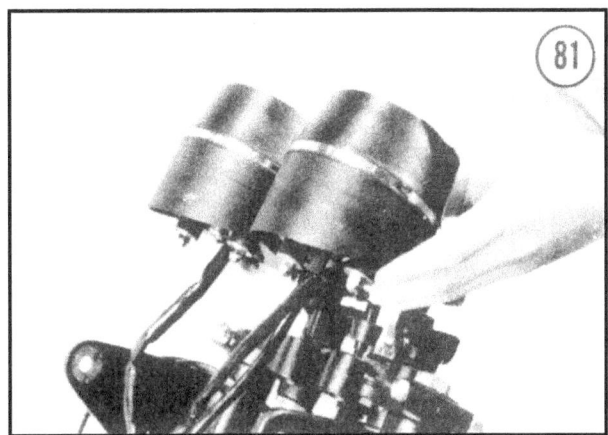

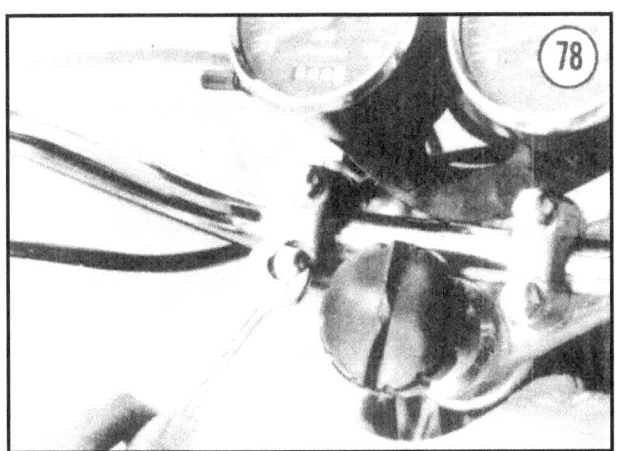

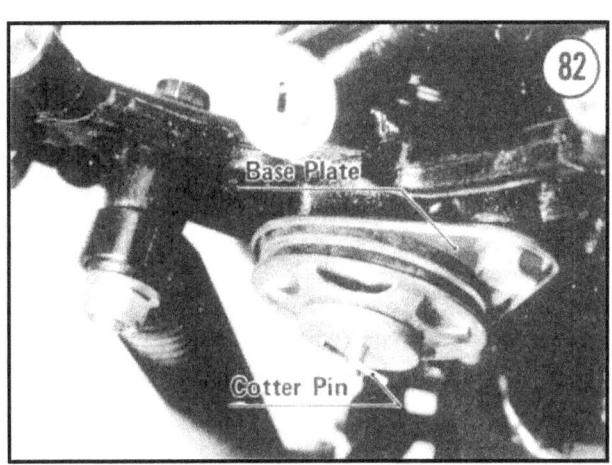

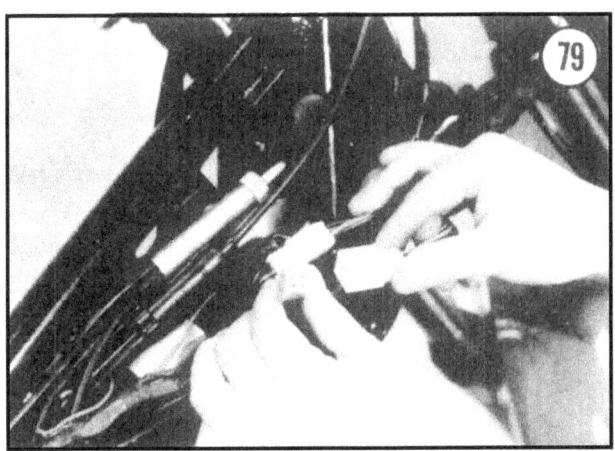

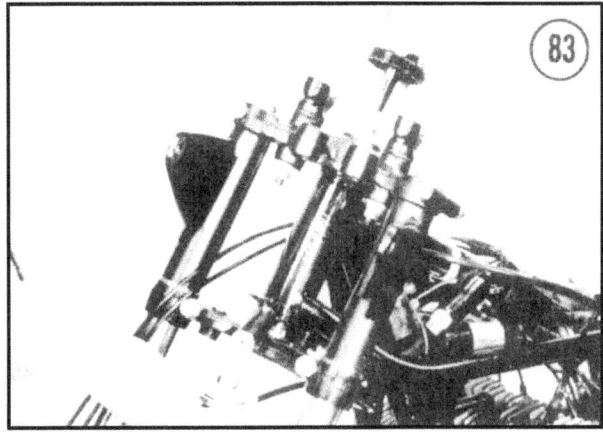

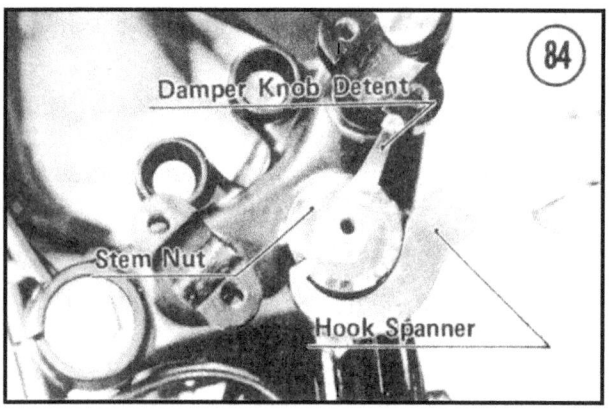

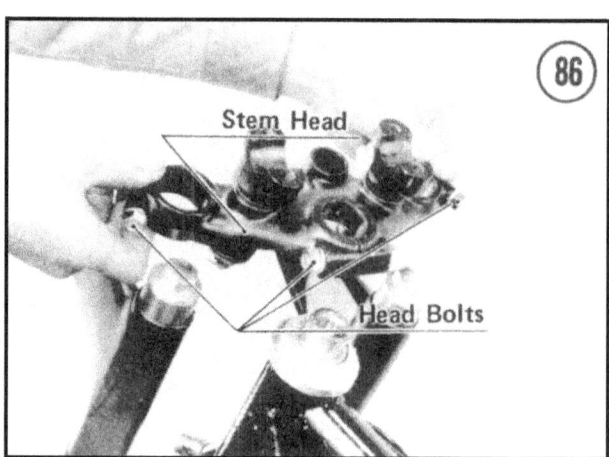

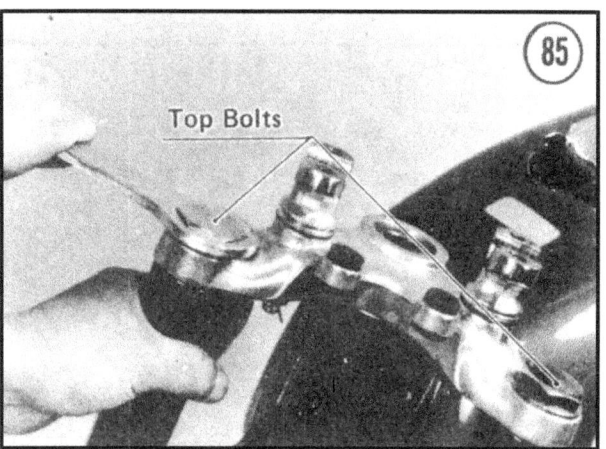

9. On models with disc brakes, remove the steering stem head bolts (**Figure 86**), then remove the stem head.

10. Remove the stem bolts (**Figure 87**), then pull out the fork legs (**Figure 88**).

Fork Disassembly (Except H1-E and H2-B)

1. Invert the fork and drain the oil, as shown in **Figure 89**. Alternatively, oil may be drained from the drain fittings (**Figure 90**) prior to removal.

2. Wrap a piece of rubber sheeting or section of inner tube around the lower end of the tube, then clamp it in a vise. Be careful that you do not deform the tube by clamping the vise too tightly.

3. Turn the outer tube nut counterclockwise, using a chain wrench to separate the tubes (**Figure 91**).

Fork Disassembly (H1-E and H2-B)

> NOTE: *Disassembly and reassembly of the forks on these models requires special tools. It may be possible to order these tools through your Kawasaki dealer, or to devise substitutes. It may be more economical to have the forks repaired by your Kawasaki dealer.*

1. Remove the top bolt (2, **Figure 92**) and tilt the assembly to remove the spring (20) and the fork oil.

3. Remove the dust seal (25) from the outer tube (29).

4. Use a special tool (**Figure 93**) to hold the assembly and remove the Allen bolt (33, Figure 93) from the bottom of the tube. Pull the inner tube (21) out of the outer tube (29).

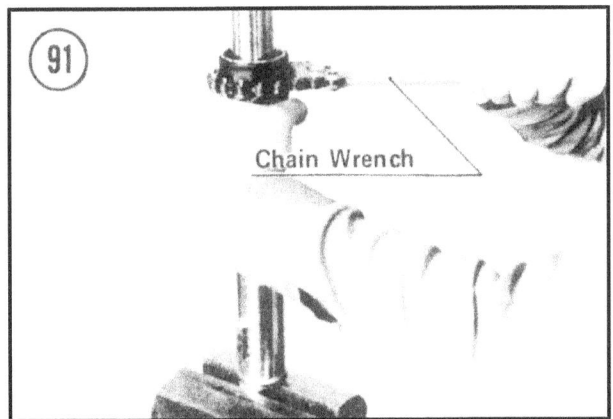

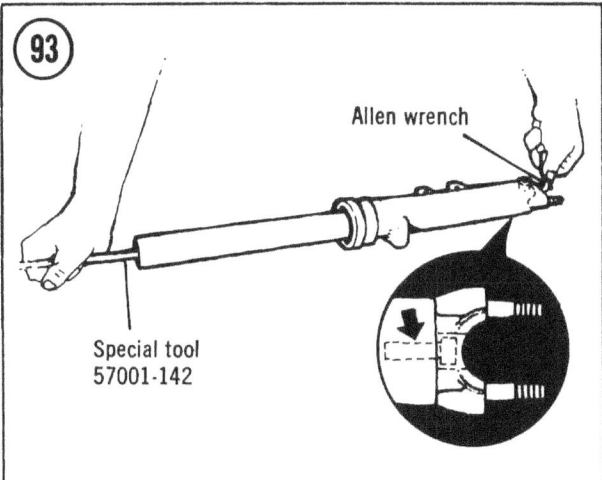

5. Remove the circlip (24) from the inside of the inner tube, then remove the cylinder assembly (22).

6. Remove the circlip (26) from the outer tube and remove the washer (27) and seal (28). Seal removal can be done easily with a seal hook.

Inspection

1. Assemble the inner and outer tubes (**Figure 94**), then slide them together. Check for looseness, noise, or binding. Replace defective parts.

2. Any scratches or roughness on the inner tube in the area where it passes through the oil seal will damage the oil seal. Examine this area carefully.

3. Inspect the dust seal carefully. If this seal is damaged, foreign material will enter the fork.

4. Measure the free length of each fork spring (**Figure 95**). Replace any spring which is shorter than the repair limit, as specified in **Table 8**.

Fork Reassembly (Except H1-E and H2-B)

Reverse the disassembly procedure to reassemble the fork. Be sure to replace the oil seal and O-ring which are attached to the outer tube nut.

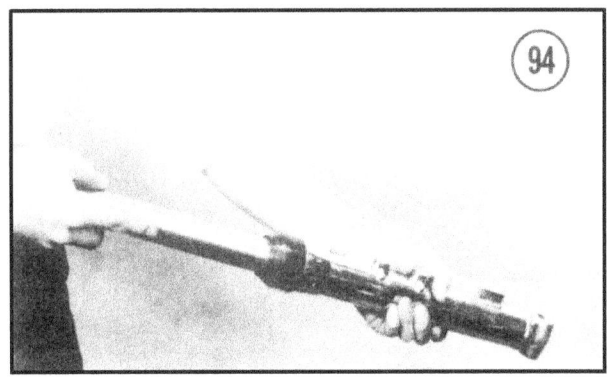

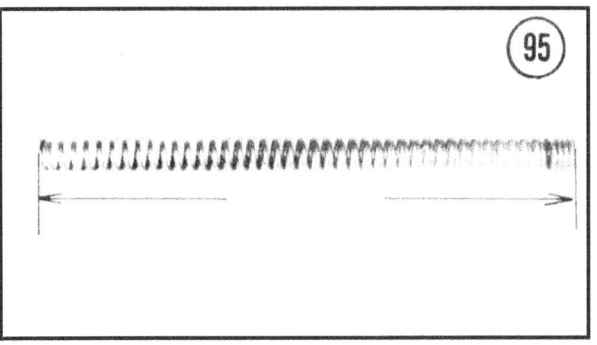

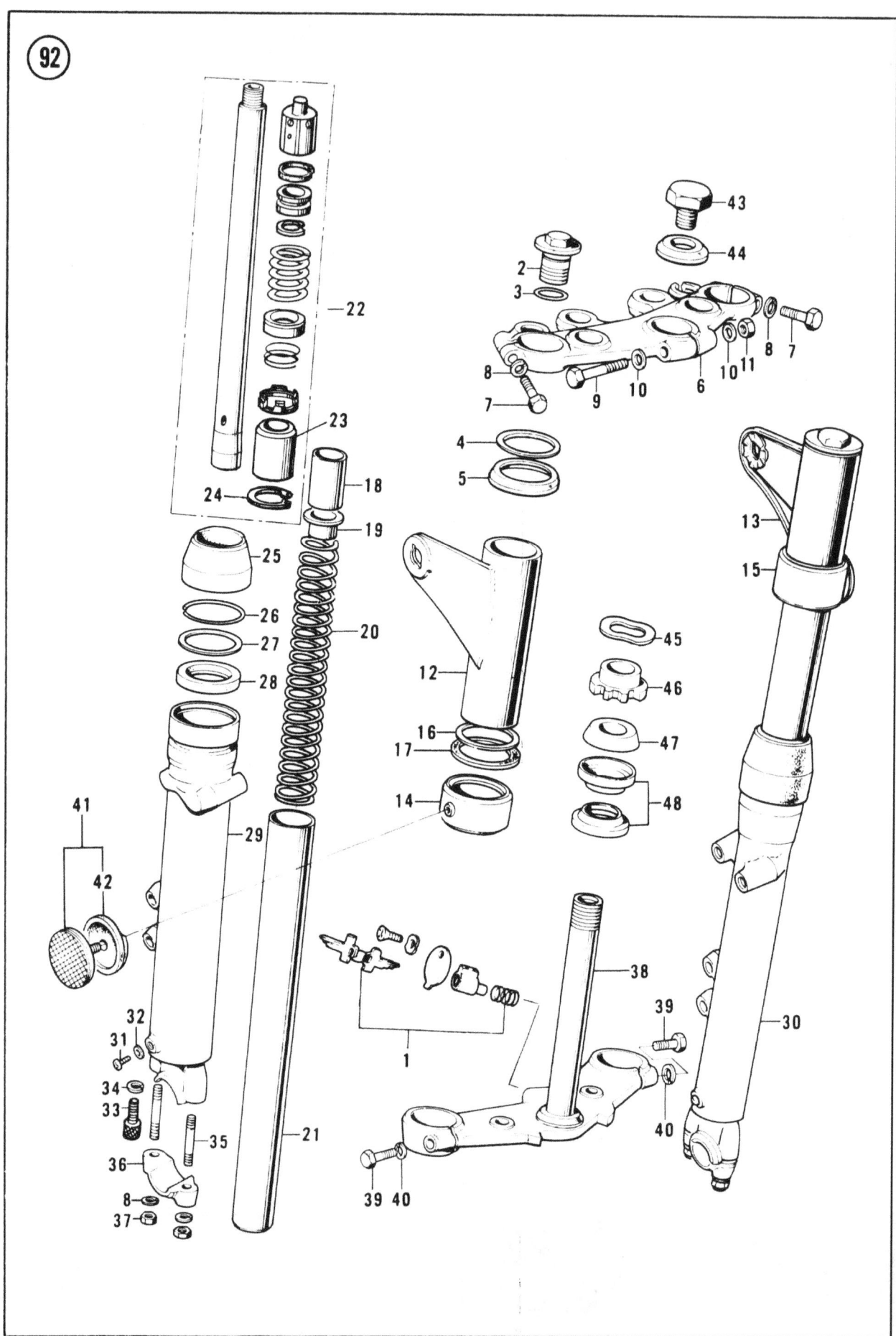

FRONT FORK (H1E AND H2B MODELS)

1. Lock assembly
2. Top bolt
3. O-ring
4. Gasket
5. Washer
6. Stem head
7. Clamp bolt
8. Lockwasher
9. Stem head clamp bolt
10. Lockwasher
11. Nut
12. Headlight stay
13. Headlight stay
14. Stay guide
15. Stay guide
16. Washer
17. Gasket
18. Spacer
19. Spring guide
20. Spring
21. Inner tube
22. Cylinder assembly
23. Piston
24. Circlip
25. Dust seal
26. Circlip
27. Washer
28. Oil seal
29. Outer tube
30. Outer tube
31. Drain plug
32. Gasket
33. Allen bolt
34. Lockwasher
35. Stud
36. Axle
37. Nut
38. Steering stem
39. Clamp bolt
40. Lockwasher
41. Reflector
42. Dumper rubber
43. Stem head bolt
44. Washer
45. Washer
46. Stem locknut
47. Stem cap
48. Bearing race

Table 8   FORK SPRING SPECIFICATIONS

Model	Standard Value Inches	(mm)	Service Limit Inches	(mm)
S series	14.21	(361)	13.78	(350)
KH250	14.21	(361)	13.78	(350)
KH400	14.21	(361)	13.78	(350)
KH500	13.58	(345)	13.19	(335)
H1/H1-E	13.58	(345)	13.19	(335)
H2/H2-B	13.58	(345)	13.19	(335)

Fork Reassembly (H1-E and H2-B)

NOTE: *Fork disassembly and reassembly requires the use of special tools. It may be possible to order these tools from your Kawasaki dealer, or to devise substitutes. It may be more economical to have the forks repaired by your Kawasaki dealer.*

1. Use a special tool, as shown in **Figure 96** and **Figure 97**, to install the cylinder assembly into the inner tube. See Figure 92 for the proper arrangement of cylinder assembly parts.

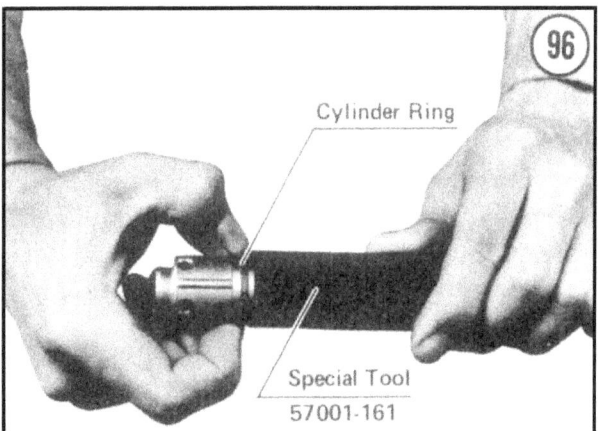

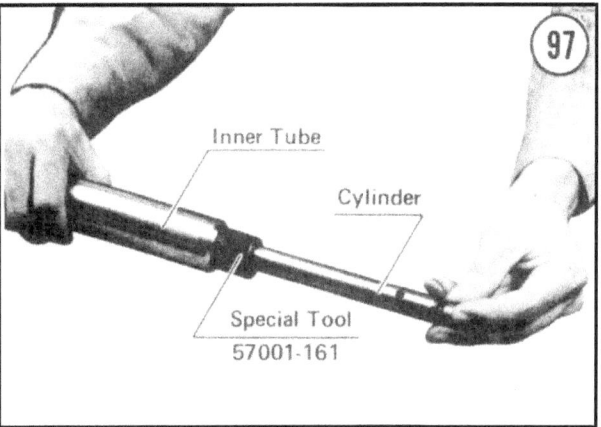

2. Install the circlip (24, Figure 92) to retain the cylinder assembly in the inner tube.

3. Using a special tool, as shown in **Figure 98**, install a new oil seal in the outer tube. Install the washer and circlip.

4. Insert the inner tube assembly into the outer tube assembly. Using a special tool (Figure 93) to hold the cylinder, install the Allen bolt.

5. Install the spring, and fill the fork with the proper amount and type of oil (see *Front Fork Oil*, this chapter).

6. Install the top bolt, using a new O-ring.

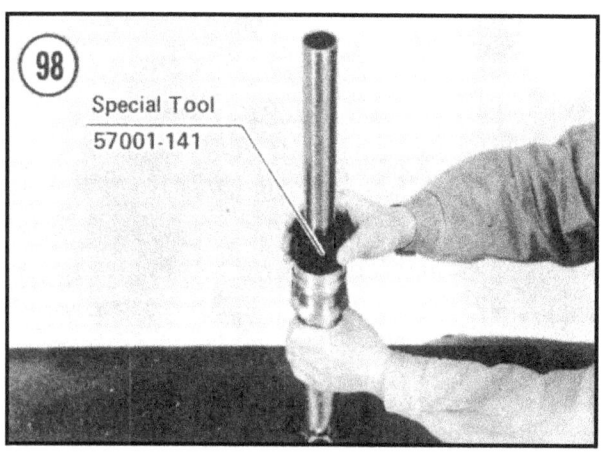

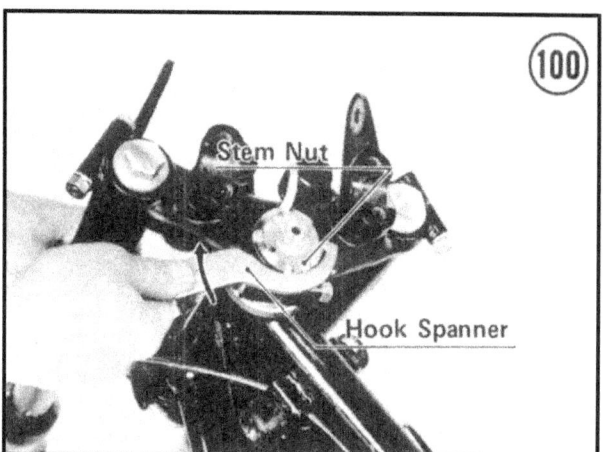

Fork Installation
(H1 Models Without Disc Brakes)

1. Install the fork covers, then insert each fork leg through the bottom of the steering stem.

2. Screw in the top bolt loosely (**Figure 99**).

3. Tighten the steering stem nut (**Figure 100**).

4. Push the fork leg inner tube into the steering stem hole until the top of the tube hits the step in the hole, then tighten the top bolts (**Figure 101**).

5. Tighten the steering stem lower bolts. See **Figure 102**.

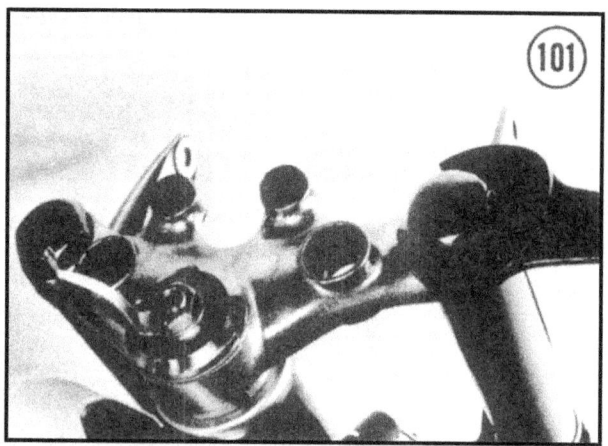

Fork Installation
(Disc Brake Models and S2)

1. Install the fork covers, then install the fork leg up through the steering stem until it is even with the steering stem upper surface. Then temporarily tighten the steering stem lower bolts (**Figure 103**).

2. Tighten the steering stem nut.

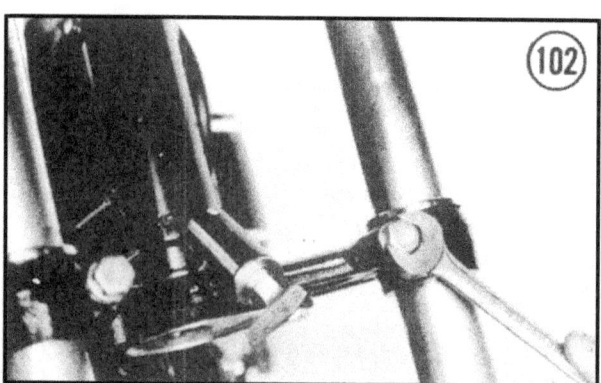

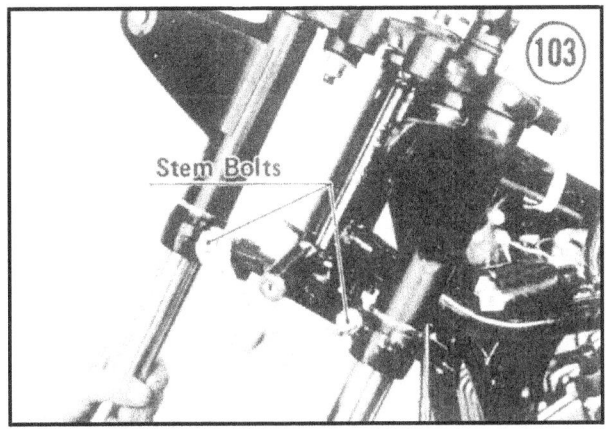

3. Align the tops of the fork legs with the upper surface of the steering stem head (**Figure 104**), then tighten the stem bolts.

4. Tighten the steering head bolts (**Figure 105**).

Front Fork Oil

The forks must be filled with the correct quantity of clear SAE 10 weight oil to ensure proper operation. If the oil level is low, the fork will be noisy. Too much oil results in harsh riding.

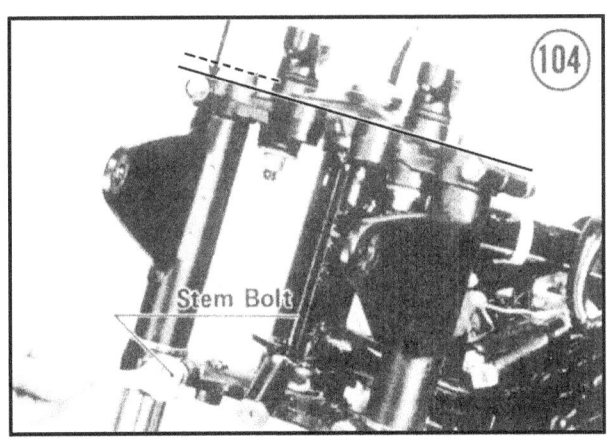

Measure the oil level with the front wheel raised completely from the ground. Unscrew the top bolt, insert a rod into the inner tube (**Figure 106**), then measure oil level. The proper distance from the top of the fork, together with the proper refill quantity for an empty fork, is specified in **Table 9**.

STEERING SYSTEM

Figure 107 is a sectional view of a typical steering stem. The frame head pipe and the under-bracket are provided with ball bearings for smooth action. A friction damper adjusts the steering action to suit the rider.

Disassembly

1. Remove the handlebar, tachometer, speedometer, and front fork.
2. Remove the steering stem head.
3. Remove the locknut (**Figure 108**).
4. Have an assistant hold a large pan under the steering stem to catch the loose ball bearings and carefully lower steering stem (**Figure 109**).

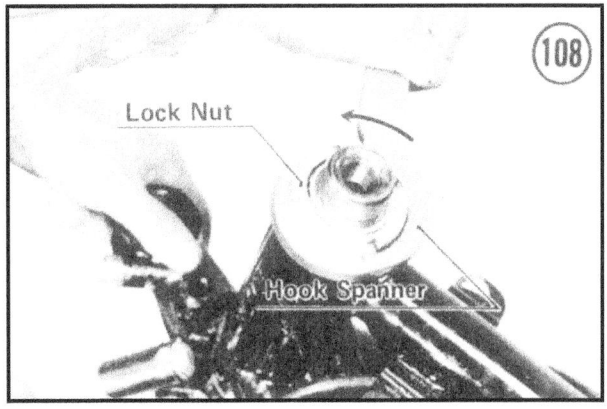

Table 9 FORK OIL QUANTITY*

Model	Quantity Ounces	(Milliliters)	Distance Inches	(Millimeters)
S1	6.8	(200)	$14\frac{3}{4}$	(375)
KH250	7.1	(212)	14	(355)
S2	5.24	(155)	14	(355)
S3	5.24	(155)	14	(355)
KH400	4.9	(145)	$13\frac{5}{8}$	(345)
KH500	5.9	(175)	$16\frac{1}{4}$	(412)
H1 (drum brake)	7.8	(230)	15	(380)
H1 (disc brake, except H1-E)	5.4	(160)	$17\frac{5}{8}$	(448)
H1-E	5.7	(170)	$15\frac{1}{4}$	(385)
H2-A	5.4	(160)	$17\frac{5}{8}$	(448)
H2-B	5.9	(175)	15	(379)

*All models use SAE 10 oil.

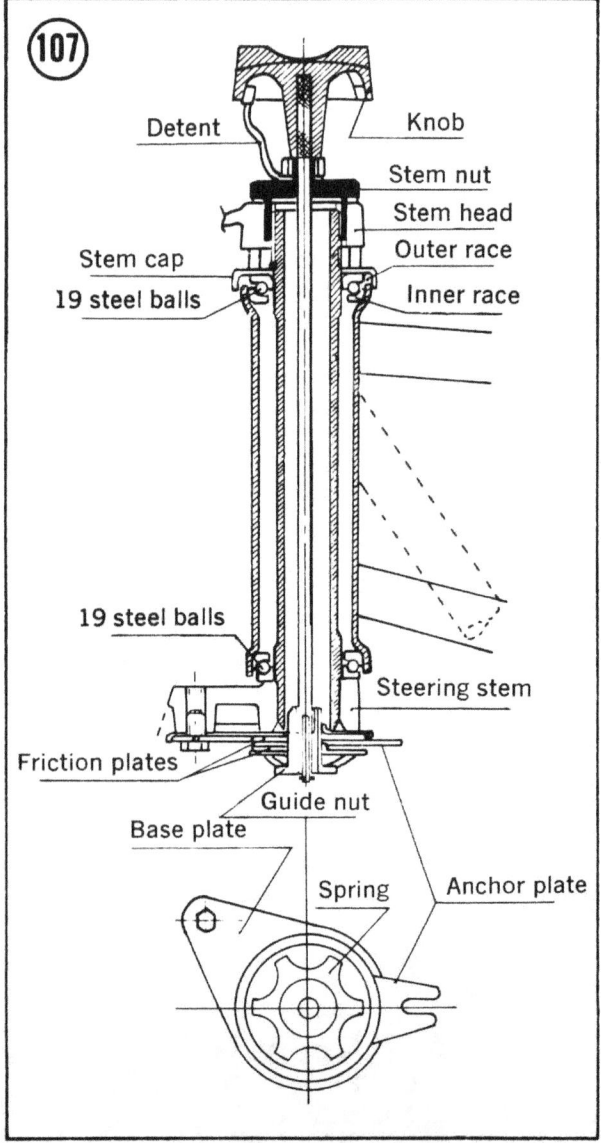

NOTE: *There are 38 balls total — 19 on the top and 19 on the bottom.*

5. Remove the lower race from the steering stem with a hammer and chisel (**Figure 110**).

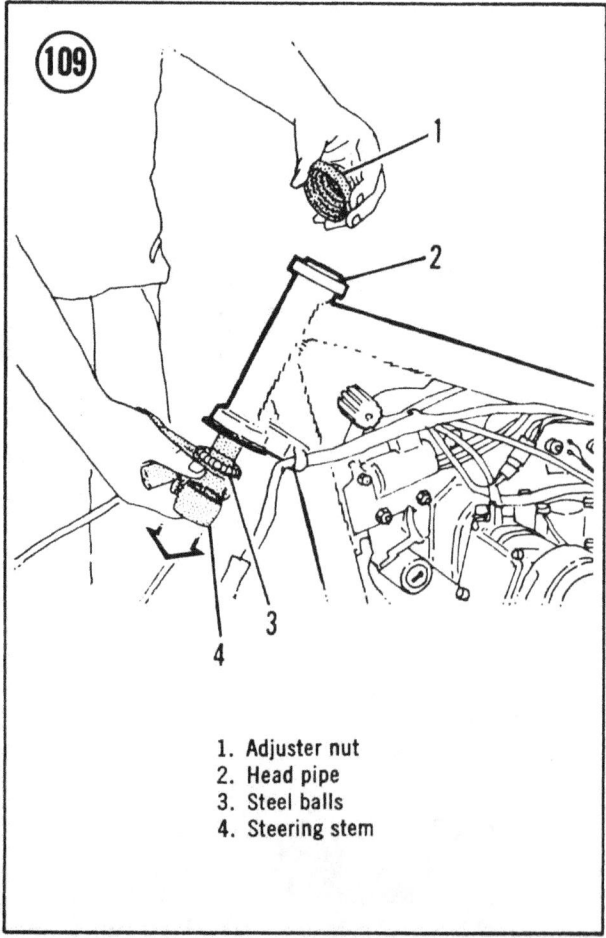

1. Adjuster nut
2. Head pipe
3. Steel balls
4. Steering stem

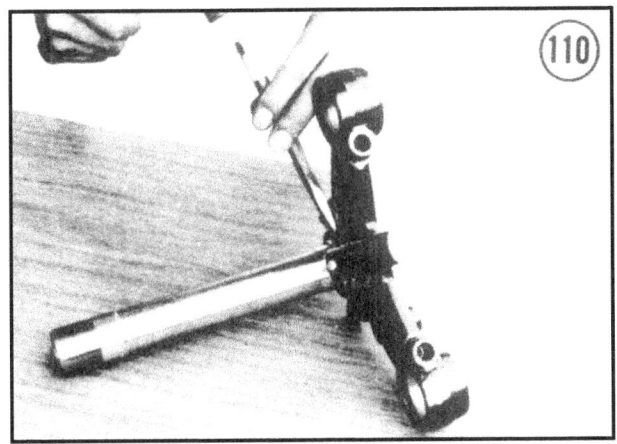

Inspection

1. Clean the bearing races in the steering head, the steering stem races, and all the ball bearings with solvent.

2. Check for broken welds on the frame around the steering head.

3. Check each of the balls for pitting, scratches, or discoloration indicating wear or corrosion. Replace them in sets if any are bad.

4. Check upper and lower races in the steering head. See *Bearing Race Replacement* if races are pitted, scratched, or badly worn.

5. Check steering stem for cracks. Check bearing race on stem for pitting, scratches, or excessive wear.

6. Check inside of steering head adjuster (top ball race) for pitting, scratches, or excessive wear.

Bearing Race Replacement

The headset and steering stem bearing races are pressed into place. Because they are easily bent, do not remove them unless they are worn and require replacement. Take old races to the dealer to ensure exact replacement.

To remove a headset race, insert a hardwood stick into the head tube and carefully tap the race out from the inside (**Figure 111**). Tap all around the race so that neither the race nor the head tube are bent. To install a race, fit it into the end of the head tube. Tap it slowly and squarely with a block of wood (**Figure 112**).

> NOTE: *The upper and lower races are different. Be sure that you install them at the proper ends of the head tube.*

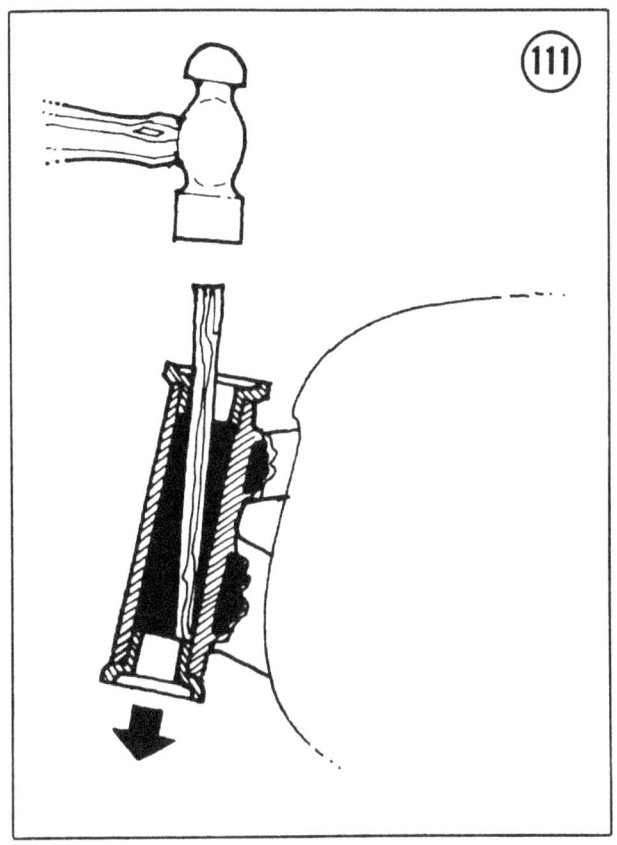

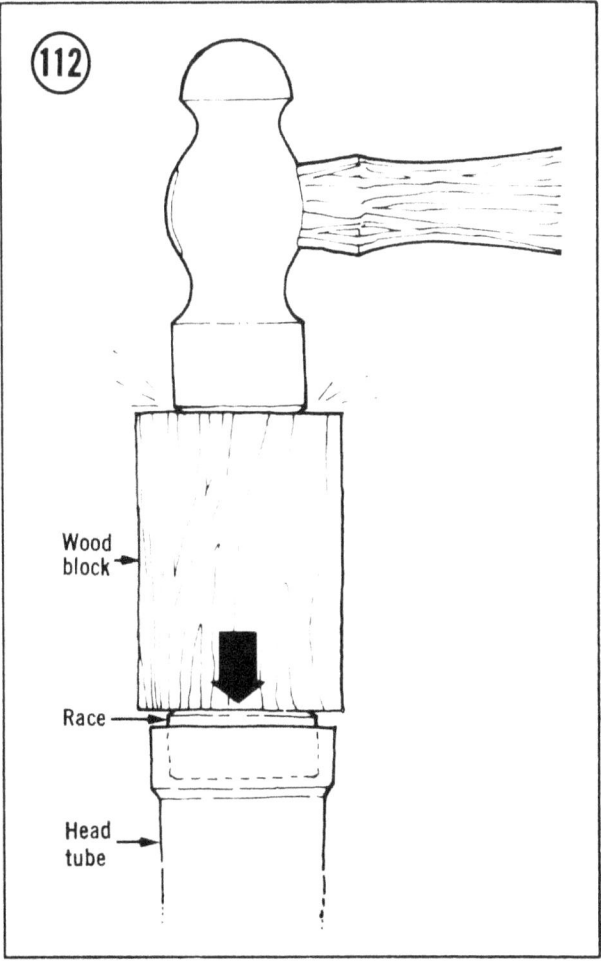

Assembly

Refer to **Figure 109** for this procedure.

1. Make sure the steering head and stem races are properly seated.

2. Install bottom bearing race cone over steering stem. Slide it down as far as possible.

3. Apply a coat of grease to bottom race cone and fit 19 ball bearings around it (**Figure 113**). The grease will hold them in place.

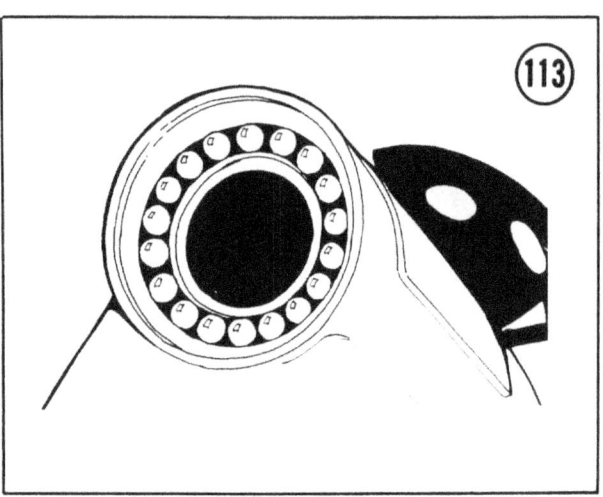

4. Fit 19 ball bearings into top race (**Figure 114**) in head tube. Grease will hold them in place.

5. Insert steering stem into head tube. Hold it firmly in place.

6. Install top bearing race cone.

7. Screw steering stem adjuster nut onto stem.

8. Tighten adjuster firmly to seat bearings. Use the pin spanner or tool shown in **Figure 115**.

9. Loosen adjuster until there is noticeable play in stem.

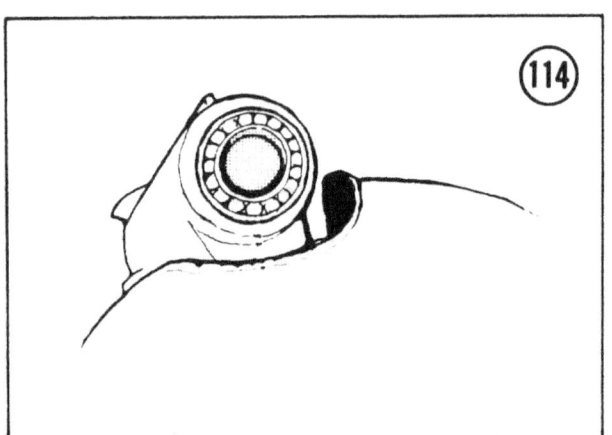

10. Tighten adjuster tight enough to remove all play, both horizontal and vertical (**Figure 116**), yet loose enough so that the assembly will turn to the locks under its own weight after an initial assist.

11. Install the steering stem head.

12. Install the front forks and front wheel.

13. Recheck the adjustment of the locknut by grasping the tips of the forks and checking for any play (**Figure 117**).

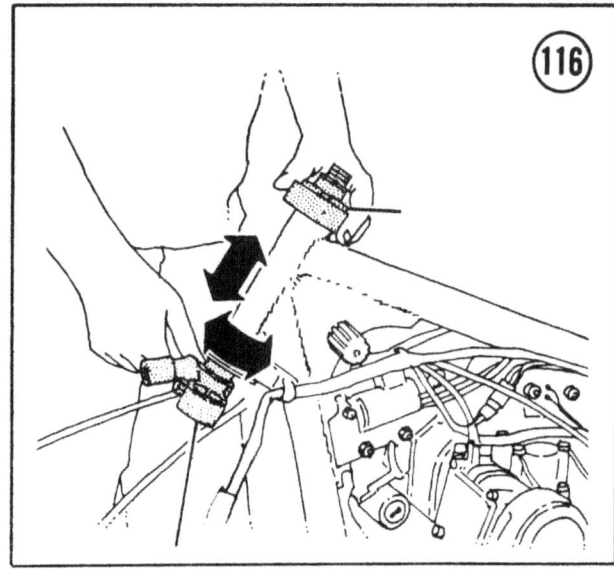

SHOCK ABSORBERS

Figure 118 is a sectional view of a typical rear shock absorber. The major parts of the shock absorber are a spring, and a hydraulic damping mechanism encased within the inner and outer shells. The shock absorbers may be adjusted to suit various riding conditions, as shown in **Figure 119**. Adjust both sides equally.

To remove the shock absorbers, remove the mounting bolts (**Figure 120**). Do not damage the rubber bushings as you remove and replace the bolts.

Check the damping force by attempting to compress and extend the units quickly. If there is no marked difference between the effort required to operate the unit quickly or slowly, or if there are any oil leaks, replace the shock absorber.

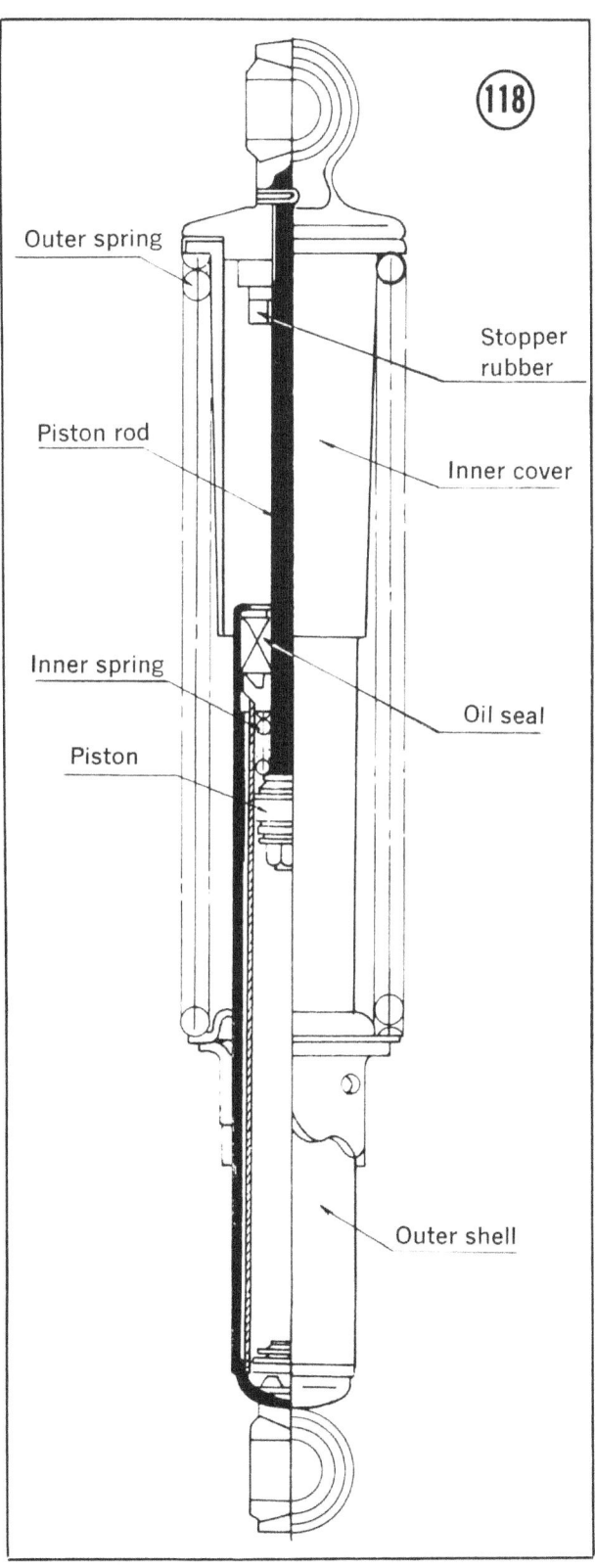

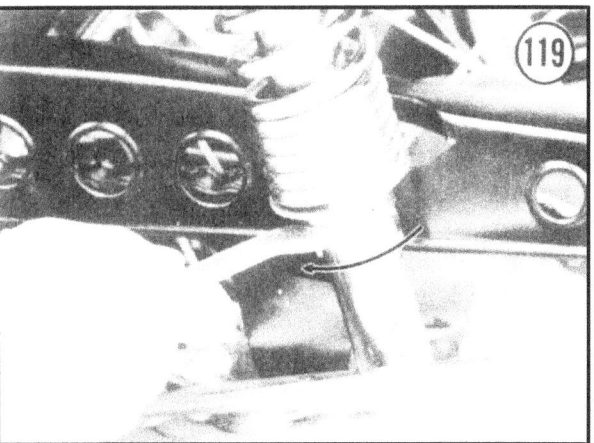

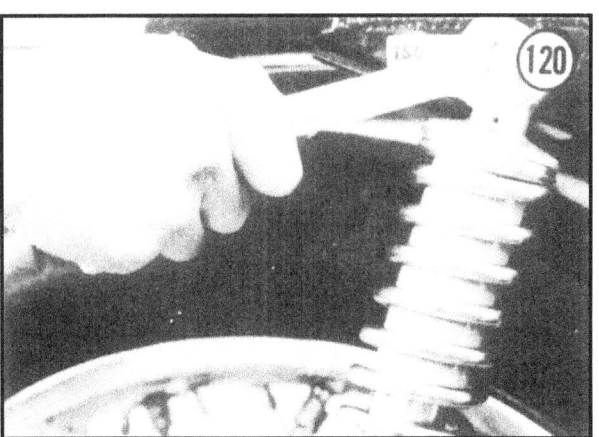

SWINGING ARM

Figure 121 illustrates a typical swinging arm assembly. The entire assembly pivots up and down on the pivot shaft. The rear part of the swinging arm is attached to the motorcycle frame through the shock absorbers.

1. Remove rear wheel and sprocket coupling.

2. Remove the left muffler, then the chain cover (**Figure 122**).

3. Remove the right mufflers, and then the rear shock absorbers (**Figure 123**).

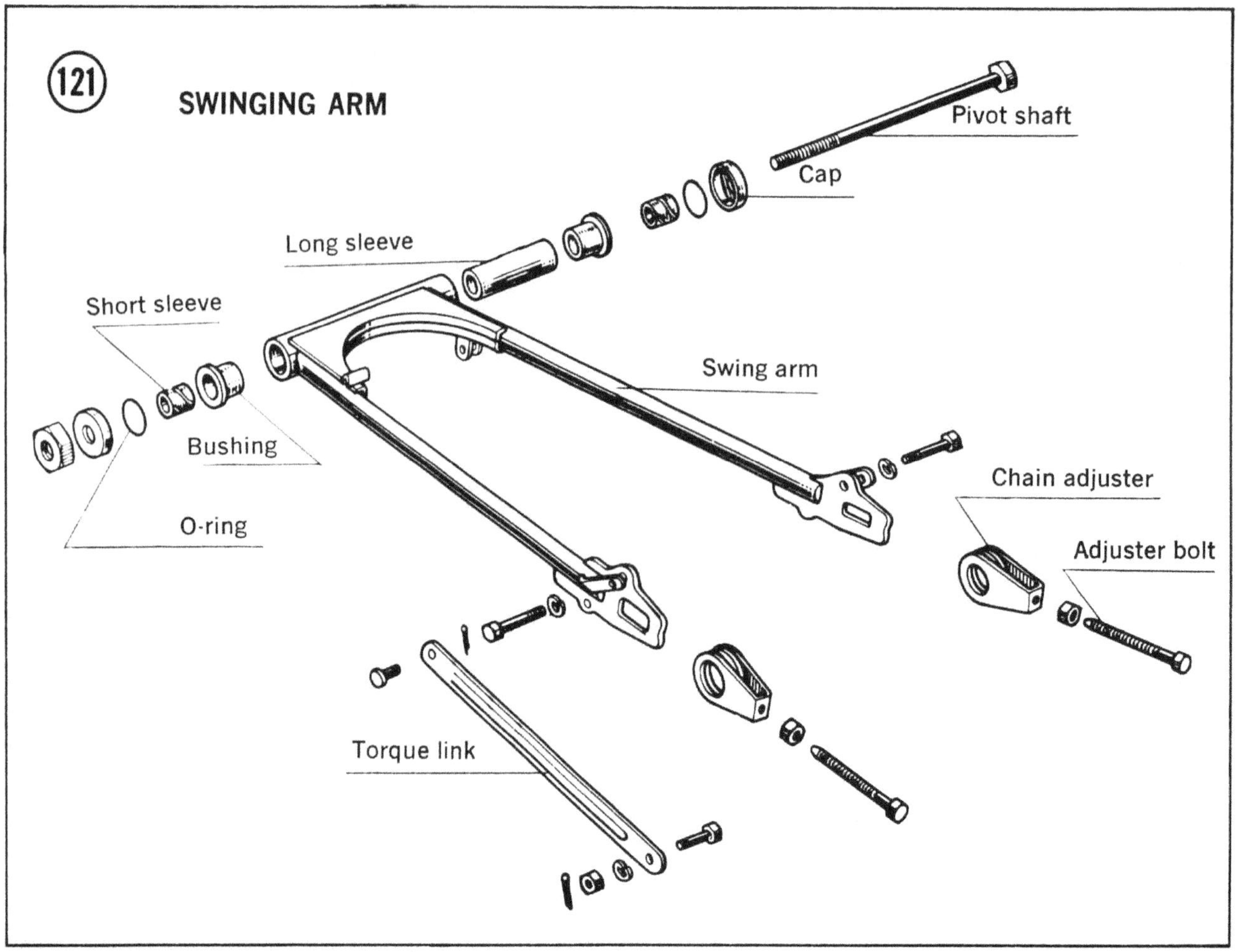

121 SWINGING ARM

(Exploded view showing: Pivot shaft, Cap, Long sleeve, Short sleeve, Bushing, O-ring, Swing arm, Chain adjuster, Adjuster bolt, Torque link)

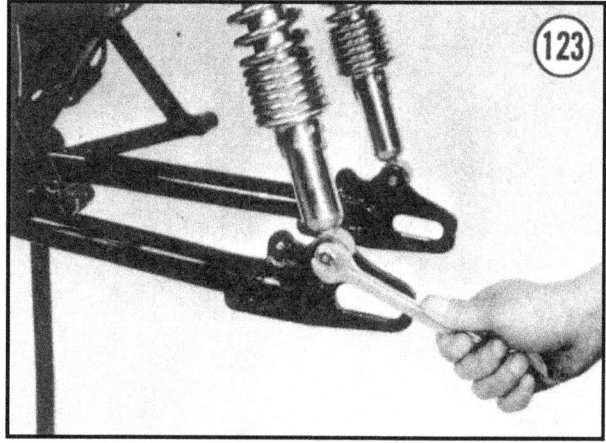

4. Remove the locknut, then pull out the pivot shaft (**Figure 124**).

Removal (H Series)

1. On H1 models, remove the lower shock absorber mounting. Remove the upper mounting on H2 models (**Figure 125**).

2. Disconnect the brake lamp switch spring. Also remove the rear brake cable on model H1 (**Figure 126**).

3. Remove locknut, then pull out pivot shaft.

Disassembly

1. Remove both short sleeves as shown in **Figure 127**. Insert a long punch into the pivot, then tap out the sleeve.

2. Remove the long sleeve, which pushes out easily.

3. Do not remove the bushings unless they are worn so much as to require replacement. The

146

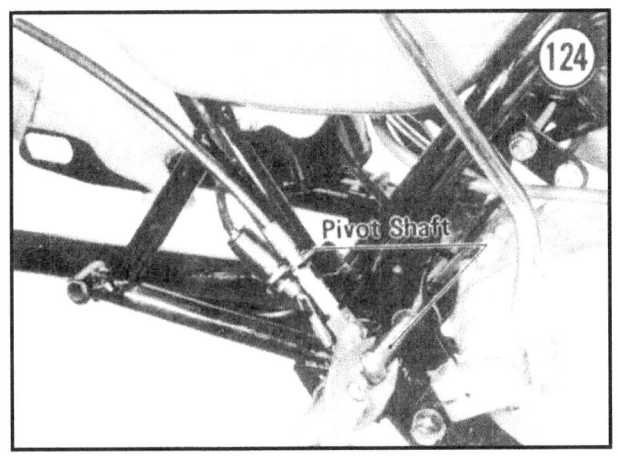

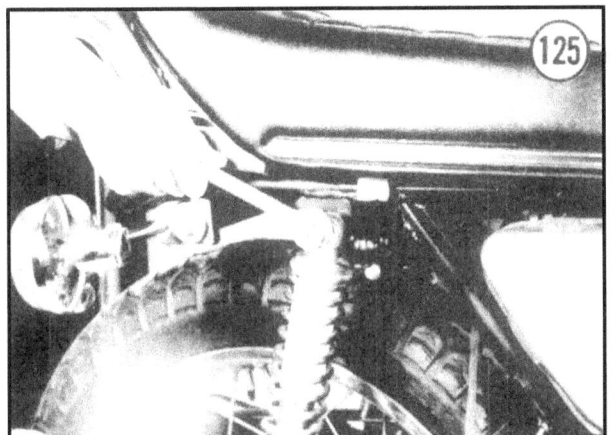

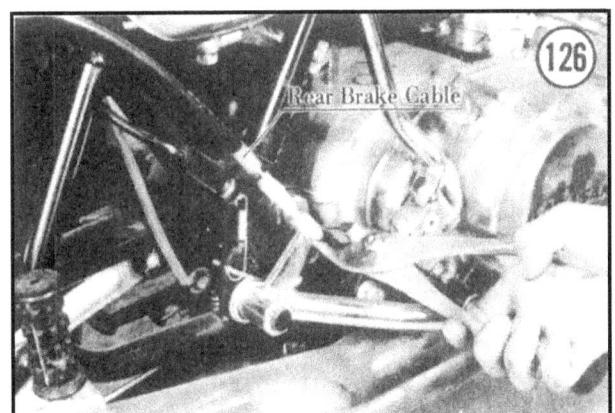

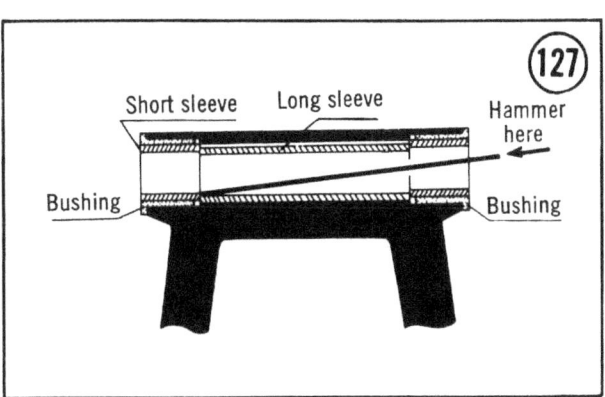

bushings cannot be reused once they are removed.

Inspection

Measure the outer diameter of the sleeves (**Figure 128**) and inner diameter of the bushings (**Figure 129**). Service limits are listed in **Table 10**. Replace the sleeves and/or the bushings if clearance exceeds specifications in **Table 10**. Shimmy, wander, and wheel hop are common symptoms of worn swinging arm bushings.

Measure pivot shaft runout as shown in **Figure 130**. Replace the pivot shaft if it is bent more than 0.006 in. (0.14mm).

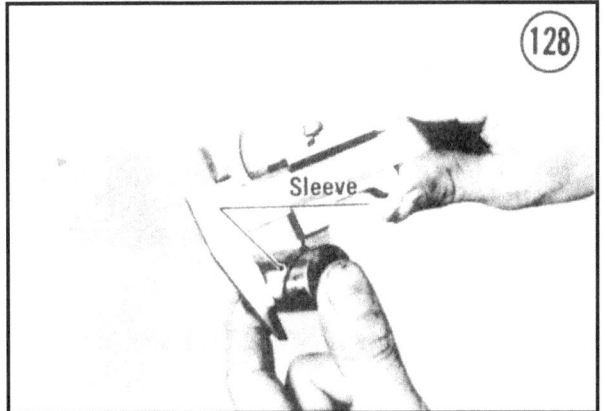

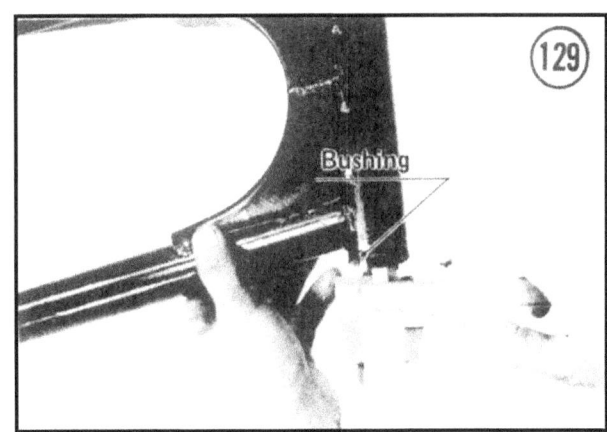

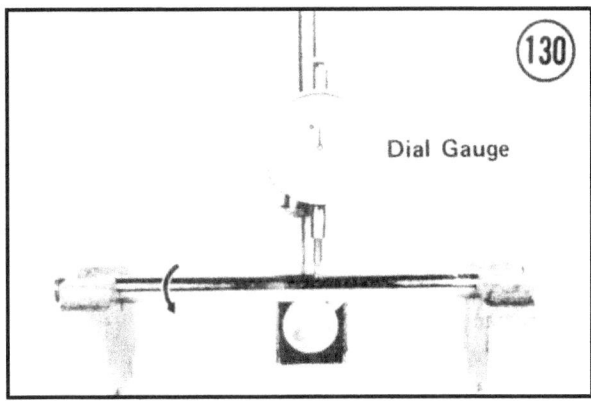

Table 10 SLEEVE AND BUSHING SPECIFICATIONS

Model	Item	Standard	Service Limit
S1, S2, S3, KH250, and KH400	Sleeve outer diameter	0.8653-0.8661 in. (21.979-22.000mm)	0.8641 in. (21.95mm)
S1 and KH250	Bushing inner diameter	0.8712-0.8719 in. (22.128-22.171mm)	0.8807 in. (22.37mm)
S2, S3, and KH400	Bushing inner diameter	0.8673-0.8686 in. (22.030-22.063mm)	0.8780 in. (22.30mm)
S1 and KH250	Sleeve/bushing clearance	0.0051-0.0076 in. (0.128-0.192mm)	0.0165 in. (0.42mm)
S2, S3, and KH400	Sleeve/bushing clearance	0.0012-0.0033 in. (0.030-0.084mm)	0.0139 in. (0.35mm)
H1, H2, and KH500	Sleeve outer diameter	0.866 in. (22.00mm)	0.860 in. (21.85mm)
H1, H2, and KH500	Bushing inner diameter	0.872 in. (22.15mm)	0.882 in. (22.40mm)
H1, H2, and KH500	Sleeve/bushing clearance	0.0059 in. (0.15mm)	0.0217 in. (0.55mm)

If either of the arms is bent, the rear wheel will be out of alignment. Examine the weld carefully. Replace the entire swinging arm assembly if the weld is cracked.

Assembly

Reverse the disassembly procedure to reassemble the swinging arm. Pay particular attention to the following points:

1. To prevent seizure from overheating, lubricate the outside of the sleeve with grease before installation (**Figure 131**).
2. Tighten the locknut as specified in **Table 11**.

Table 11 SWING ARM LOCKNUT TORQUE SPECIFICATIONS

Model	Ft.-Lb.	(Mkg)
S1, S2, S3, KH250 and KH400	43-72	(6-10)
H1, H2 and KH500	58-87	(8-12)

REAR SPROCKET

To remove the rear sprocket, use a hammer and chisel (**Figure 132**) to straighten the lockwashers, then remove the nuts which attach the sprocket to the sprocket coupling.

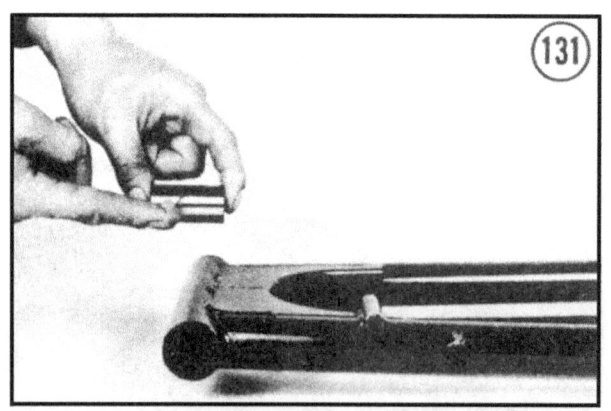

Any bending of the sprocket will make drive chain adjustment difficult, and may result in chain breakage. To check for bending, place the sprocket on a flat surface, then check the gap between the surface and the sprocket. Replace the sprocket if the gap exceeds 0.02 inch (0.5 millimeter) at any point.

The drive chain may slip from the sprocket if the sprocket is worn. Measure the diameter (**Figure 133**) of the sprocket at the base of the teeth. Replace any sprocket worn beyond the repair limit, as specified in **Table 12**.

FUEL AND OIL TANKS

Figure 134 illustrates a typical fuel tank. The tank is made from corrosion resistant steel. A fuel tap is attached to the lower portion of the tank so that the fuel may be shut off when the machine is not running. Some models are equipped with an automatic fuel tap.

Fuel Tank Removal

WARNING
Before attempting any service on the fuel tank be sure to have a fire extinguisher rated for gasoline or chemical fires within reach. Do not smoke or work where there are any open flames. The work areas must be well ventilated.

1. Turn the fuel tap to "S" (STOP). On models with automatic cocks, turn the cock to ON or RES.

2. Remove the 2 bolts from the front of the tank (**Figure 135**). There is one on each side.

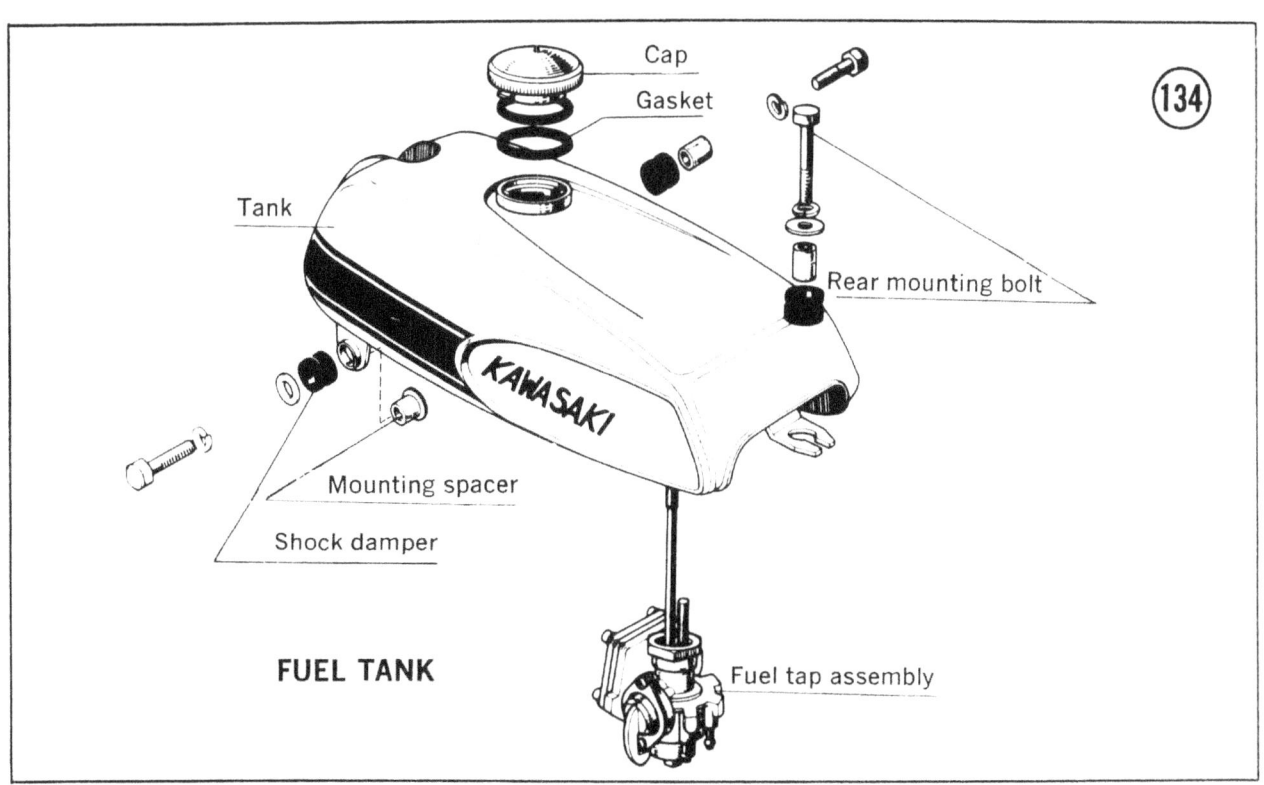

FUEL TANK

Table 12 SPROCKET SPECIFICATIONS

Model	Number of Teeth	Standard Value Inches	(Millimeters)	Repair Limit Inches	(Millimeters)
S1	48	9.16	(232.6)	9.07	(230.5)
KH250	48	9.16	(232.6)	9.07	(230.5)
S2	42	8.16	(207.3)	8.09	(205.5)
KH400	41	7.76	(197.2)	7.70	(195.5)
S3 and KH400*	37	6.97	(177.0)	6.91	(175.5)
S3	41	7.76	(197.2)	7.70	(195.5)
KH500	45	8.56	(217.4)	8.48	(215.5)
H1	45	8.56	(217.4)	8.48	(215.5)
H2	47	8.96	(227.5)	8.88	(225.5)

*U.K. Model

3. Remove the bolt from the rear of the tank (**Figure 136**).

4. Disconnect the fuel line from the fuel cock.

5. Lift the tank from the machine (**Figure 137**). Be sure that the wire harness does not interfere as you remove the tank.

Fuel Tap

All models are equipped with a fuel tap. During normal running, fuel is drawn from the main standpipe within the fuel tank, which permits fuel to flow only as long as the fuel level remains above the top of the standpipe.

Inspect the fuel tap for leakage. Remove and clean the sediment bowl occasionally. Clean the fuel tap by blowing compressed air through it.

Automatic Fuel Tap

Some models are equipped with an automatic fuel tap (**Figure 138**). Negative pressure developed in the carburetor when the engine is running is transmitted through a tube to a diaphragm-actuated valve within the assembly.

If the fuel tap leaks, remove the diaphragm cover and diaphragm, then clean the valve and seat. Be sure to assemble the valve correctly (**Figure 139**) with the vent holes aligned. Also, be sure that there are no leaks in the signal tube from the carburetor to the fuel tap. Air leaks will result in poor fuel flow.

Oil Tank

The oil tank (**Figure 140**) is below the seat, on

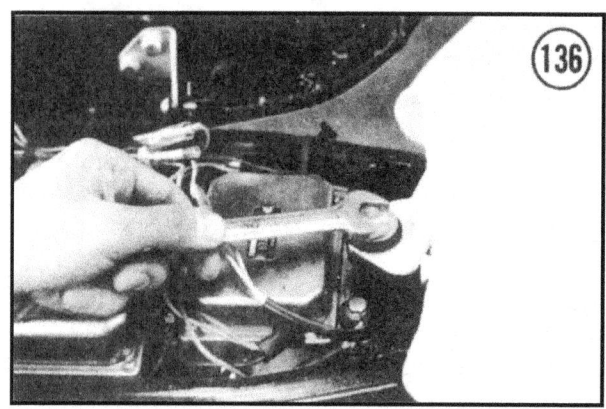

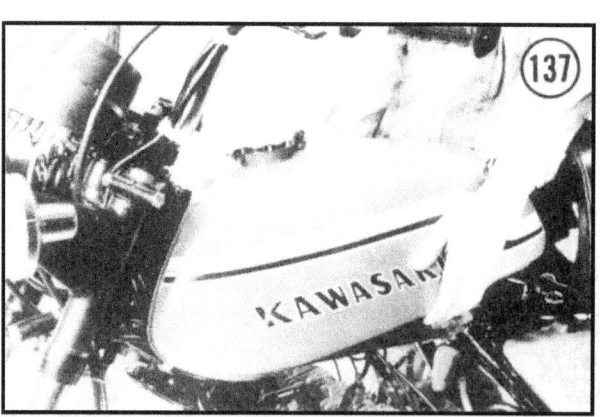

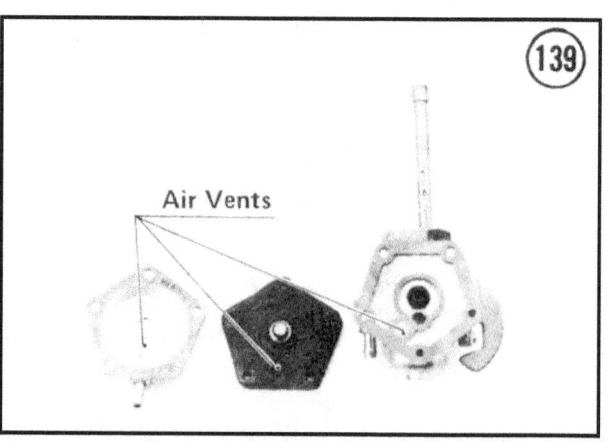

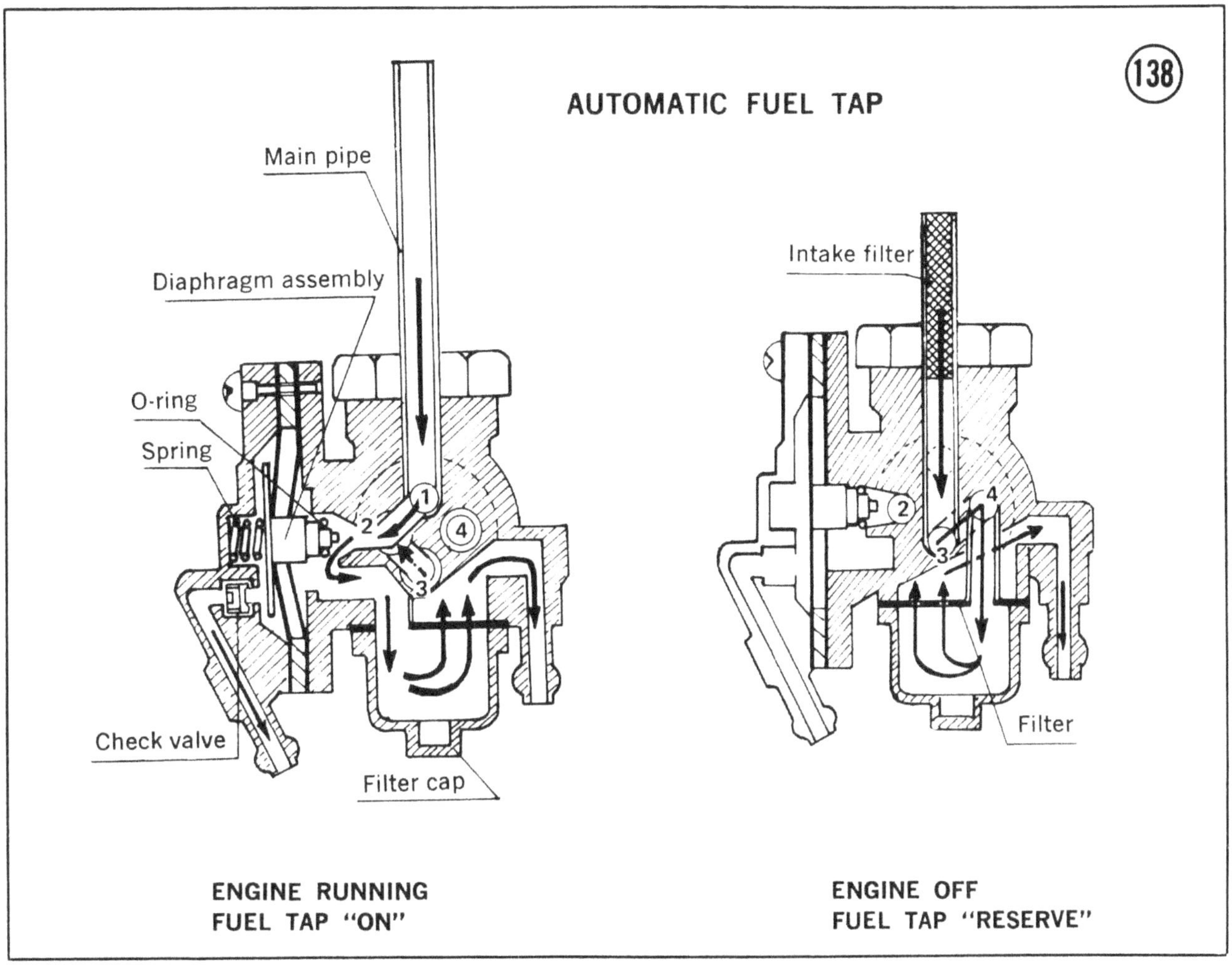

(138) AUTOMATIC FUEL TAP

Engine running — Fuel tap "ON"
- Main pipe
- Diaphragm assembly
- O-ring
- Spring
- Check valve
- Filter cap

Engine off — Fuel tap "RESERVE"
- Intake filter
- Filter

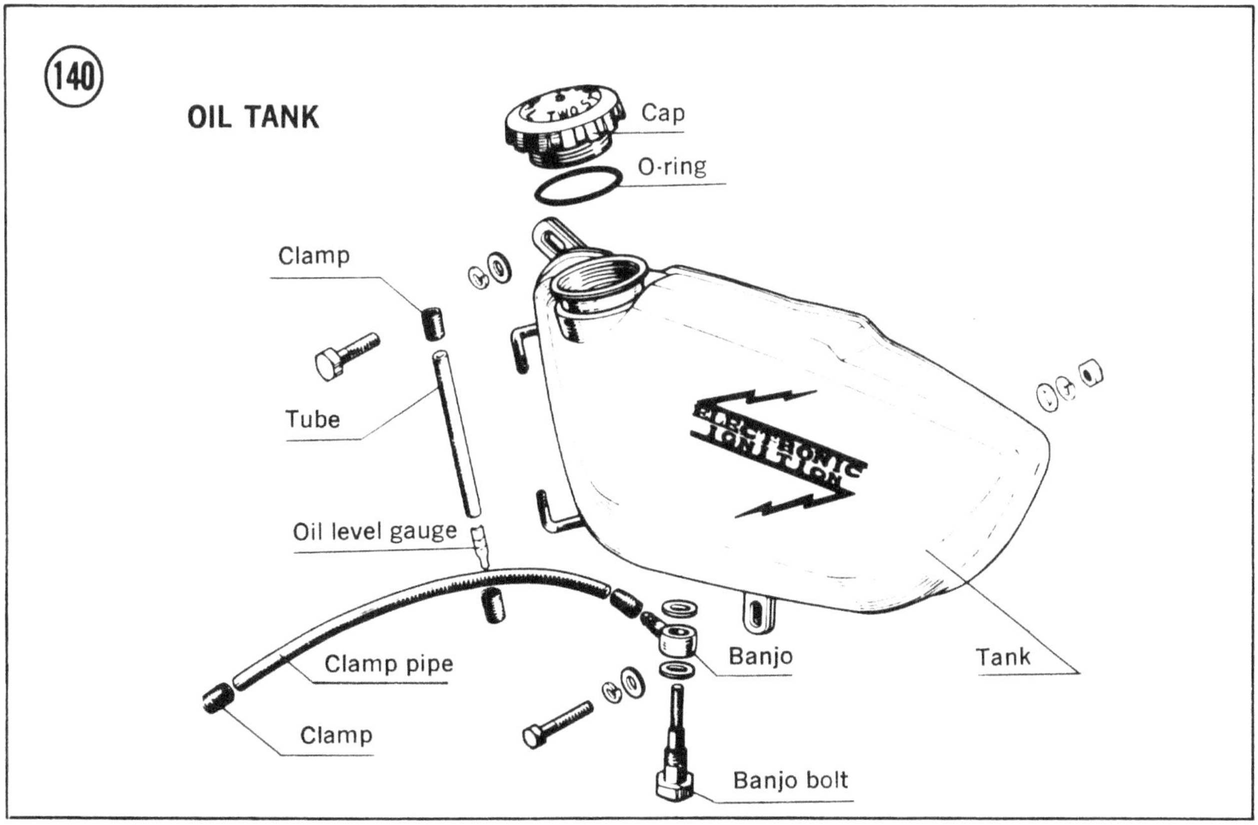

(140) OIL TANK

- Cap
- O-ring
- Clamp
- Tube
- Oil level gauge
- Clamp pipe
- Clamp
- Banjo
- Tank
- Banjo bolt

the right-hand side. Service to the oil tank is limited to occasional cleaning. Remember to bleed the oil pump after you clean the tank.

KICKSTAND

Raise the kickstand to release return spring pressure. Remove the spring from the frame with Vise Grips. Remove the mounting bolt and nut (**Figure 141**) and remove the stand.

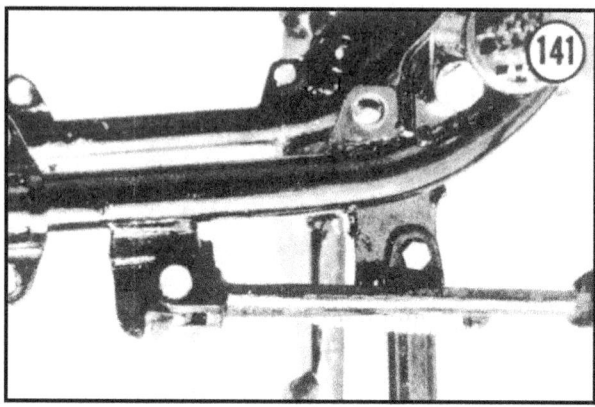

CENTERSTAND

Raise the centerstand to release return spring pressure. Remove the spring from the stand with Vise Grips. Remove the cotter pins and joint pins (**Figure 142**) and remove the stand. Apply grease to all pivoting parts prior to installation.

EXHAUST PIPES AND MUFFLERS

Removal

To remove the exhaust pipes and mufflers, first loosen the muffler attachment hardware and remove the exhaust pipes at the cylinders,

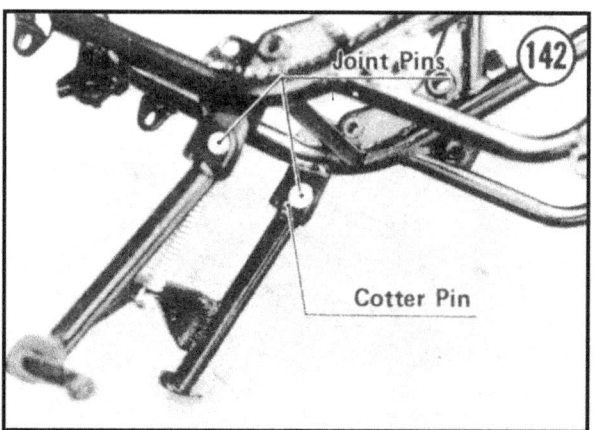

as shown in **Figure 143**. Then remove the front and rear attachment bolts from the mufflers (**Figures 144 and 145**) and remove the mufflers.

To remove the baffle tube, remove the bolt at the back of the muffler (**Figure 146**), then pull out the baffle tube (**Figure 147**).

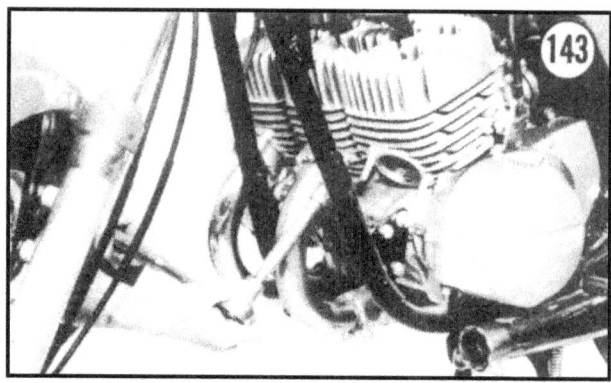
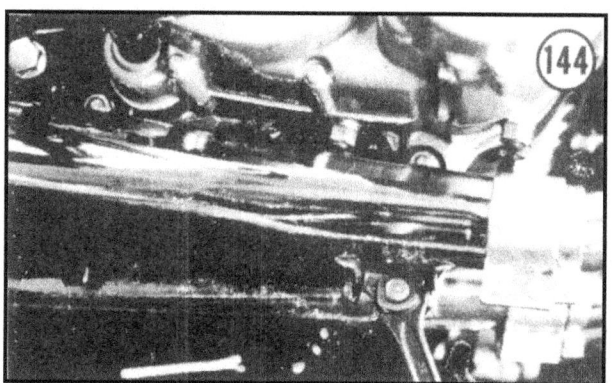

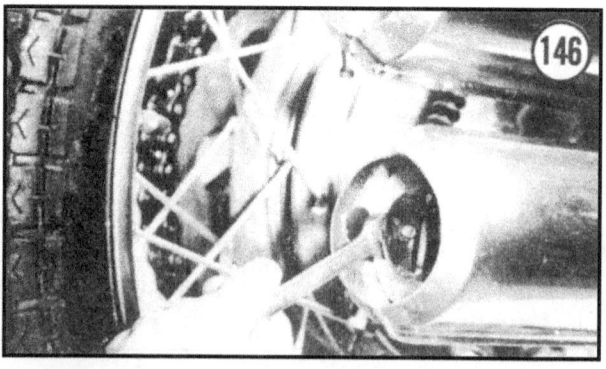

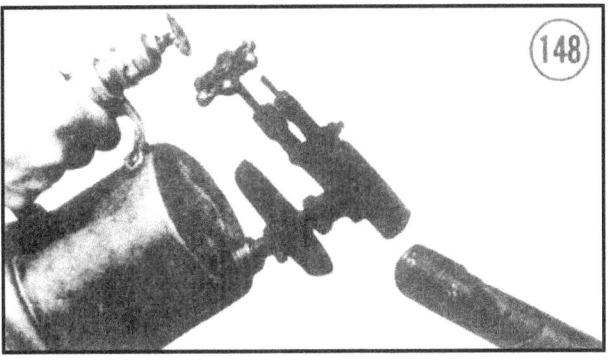

Inspection

Carbon deposits within the exhaust pipe and muffler cause the engine to lose power. Clean the carbon from the baffle tube with a wire brush. If the deposits are too heavy to remove with a brush, heat the baffle tube with a torch (**Figure 148**) and tap the tube lightly. Clean the carbon from the exhaust pipe by running a used drive chain through the pipe.

As the machine ages, the joint between the exhaust pipe and muffler may leak. Replace the rubber connector if leakage occurs.

Always use new gaskets at the cylinder head upon reassembly.

DRIVE CHAIN

The drive chain (**Figure 149**) becomes worn after prolonged use. Wear in the pins, bushings, and rollers causes the chain to stretch. Sliding between the roller surface and sprocket teeth also contributes to wear.

Inspection

Inspect and lubricate the drive chain periodically. Pay particular attention to cracks in the rollers and link plates, and replace the chain if there is any doubt about its condition.

Adjust the free play in the chain so that there is ¾ in. (20mm) vertical play (**Figure 150**) in the center of the chain run with the machine on the ground. **Figure 151** illustrates the adjustment procedure. Be sure to adjust each side equally. The rear brake is affected by any chain adjustment. Be sure to adjust the rear brake after you adjust the chain.

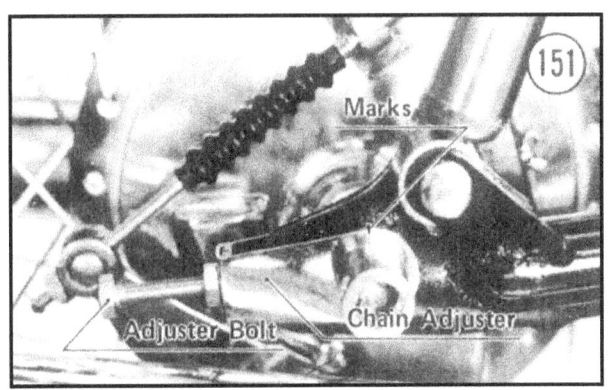

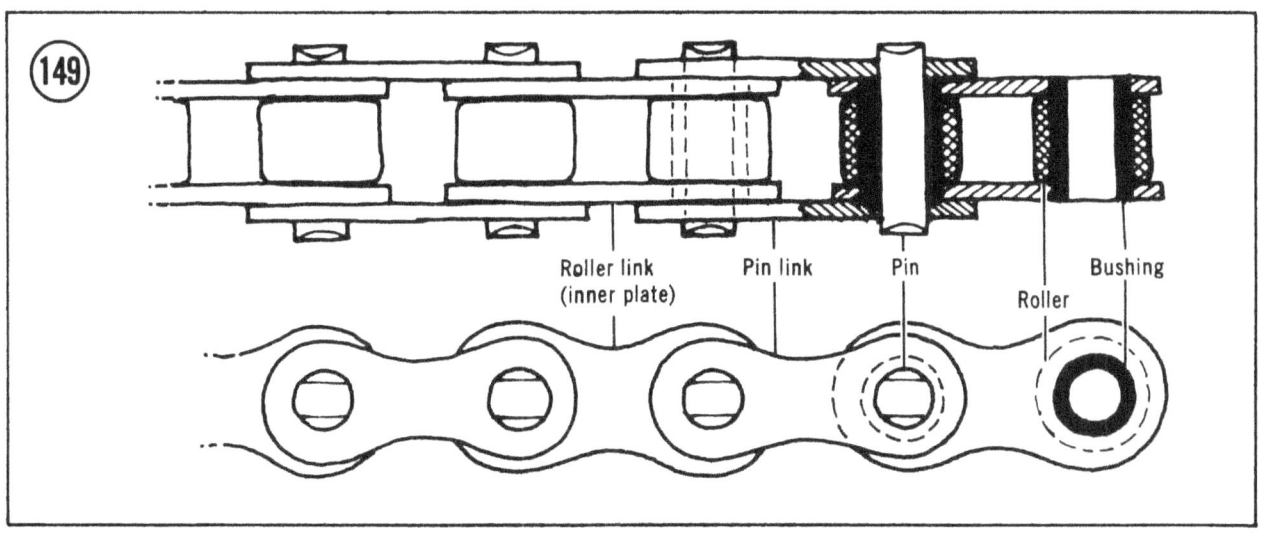

153

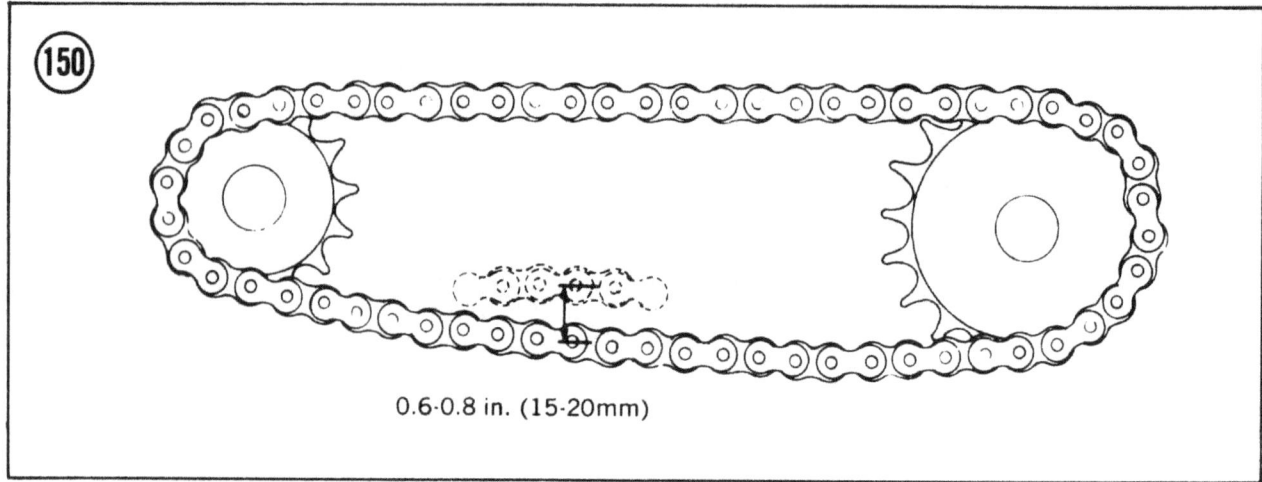

0.6-0.8 in. (15-20mm)

If the chain has become so worn that adjustment is not possible, replace the chain with a new one.

Install the master link so that the clip opening faces opposite to the direction of chain movement (**Figure 152**). Failure to do so may result in the loss of the clip and consequent chain breakage. The H2 model does not have a master link.

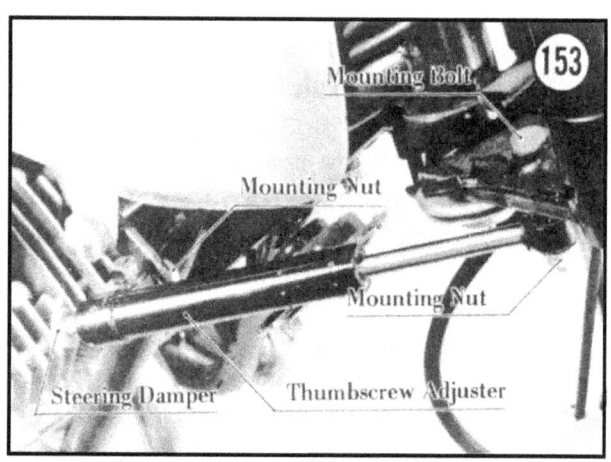

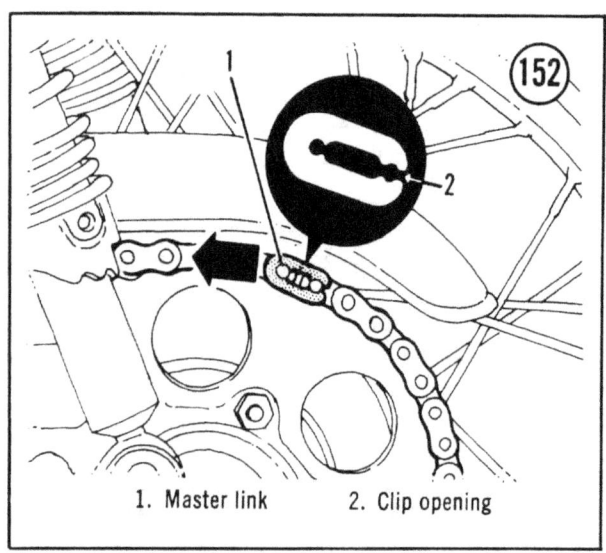

1. Master link   2. Clip opening

HYDRAULIC STEERING DAMPER

The hydraulic steering damper (**Figure 153**) is connected between the frame and steering head. The damper absorbs handlebar vibration during high speed riding.

As the steering stem moves, the damper piston moves back and forth within the damper cylinder. As the piston moves, oil is forced through a small orifice in the piston, thereby preventing rapid motion of the steering stem.

To remove the oil damper, remove the attaching hardware.

Check the condition of the damper by alternately compressing and extending it quickly. If little or no resistance is encountered as you operate it, or if any oil leakage is evident, replace the unit. The steering oil damper is not serviceable.

FRAME REPAIR

The frame does not require periodic maintenance. However, all welds should be examined immediately after any accident, even a slight one.

Component Removal/Installation

1. Disconnect the negative battery cable. Remove the fuel tank, seat, and battery.

2. Remove the engine as described in Chapter Three.

3. Remove the front wheel, steering and

suspension components as described in Chapter Six.

4. Remove the rear wheel and suspension components. See Chapter Six.

5. Remove the lighting and other electrical equipment. Remove the wiring harness. See Chapter Four.

6. Remove the kickstand and centerstand as described in this chapter.

7. Remove the bearing races from the steering head tube as described in this chapter.

8. Check the frame for bends, cracks or other damage, especially around welded joints and areas which are rusted.

9. Assemble by reversing the removal steps.

Stripping and Painting

Remove all components from the frame. Thoroughly strip off all old paint. The best way is to have it sandblasted down to bare metal. If this is not possible, you can use a liquid paint remover like Strypeeze, or equivalent, and steel wool and a fine, hard wire brush.

> NOTE: *The side panels and chain guard on some models are plastic. If you wish to change the color of these parts, consult an automotive paint supplier for the proper procedure.*

> CAUTION
> *Do not use any liquid paint remover on these components as it will damage the surface. The color is an integral part of the component and cannot be removed.*

When the frame is down to bare metal, have it inspected for hairline and internal cracks. Magnafluxing is the most common process.

Make sure that the primer is compatible with the type of paint you are going to use for the final coat. Spray one or two coats of primer as smoothly as possible. Let it dry thoroughly and use a fine grade of wet sandpaper (400-600 grit) to remove any flaws. Carefully wipe the surface clean and then spray the final coat. Use either lacquer or enamel and follow the manufacturer's instructions.

A shop specializing in painting will probably do the best job. However, you can do a surprisingly good job with a good grade of spray paint. Spend a few extra bucks and get a good grade of paint as it will make a difference in how well it looks and how long it will stand up. One trick in using spray paints is to first shake the can thoroughly — make sure the ball inside the can is loose; if not, return it and get a good one. Shake the can as long as is stated on the can. Then immerse the can *upright* in a pot or bucket of *warm water (not hot — not over 120°F)*.

> WARNING
> *Higher temperatures could cause the can to burst.* **Do not** *place the can in direct contact with any flame or heat source.*

Leave the can in for several minutes. When thoroughly warmed, shake the can again and spray the frame. Several light mist coats are better than one heavy coat. Spray painting is best done in temperatures of 70-80°F; any temperature above or below this will give you problems.

After the final coat has dried completely, at least 48 hours, any overspray or orange peel may be removed with *a light application* of rubbing compound and finished with polishing compound. Be careful not to rub too hard and go through the finish.

Finish off with a couple of good coats of wax prior to reassembling all the components.

CHAPTER SEVEN

PERIODIC SERVICE AND MAINTENANCE

To gain the utmost in safety, performance, and useful life from your machine, it is necessary to make periodic inspections and adjustments. It frequently happens that minor problems are found during such inspections that are simple and inexpensive to correct at the time, but which could lead to major problems later.

Table 1 is a suggested maintenance schedule. The procedures for performing these services are described in the applicable chapters.

Table 1   MAINTENANCE SCHEDULE

Maintenance Item	Initial 500	Miles 2,000	4,000
Tighten nuts and bolts	X	X	
Lubricate			X
Check tires	X	X	
Check, tighten spokes	X	X	
Check, adjust brakes	X	X	
Check brake fluid	X	X	
Adjust, clean, oil chain	X	X	
Check wheel alignment		X	
Check sprockets		X	
Clean, check brakes			X
Check steering		X	
Check, adjust clutch	X	X	
Change transmission oil	X	X	
Service battery		X	
Clean air cleaner		X	
Remove carbon			X
Check, adjust carburetors and oil pump	X	X	
Clean points, check ignition timing	X	X	
Clean, set spark plugs	X	X	
Clean fuel filter		X	
Clean gas and oil tanks		X	
Check fork oil level		X	
Change front fork oil			X

CHAPTER EIGHT

TROUBLESHOOTING

Diagnosing mechanical problems is relatively simple if you use orderly procedures and keep a few basic principles in mind.

The troubleshooting procedures in this chapter analyze typical symptoms, and show logical methods of isolating causes. These are not the only methods. There may be several ways to solve a problem, but only a systematic, methodical approach can guarantee success.

Never assume anything. Do not overlook the obvious. If you are riding along and the bike suddenly quits, check the easiest, most accessible problem spots first. Is there gasoline in the tank? Is the shutoff valve in the ON or RESERVE position? Has a spark plug wire fallen off? Check ignition switch. Sometimes the weight of keys on a key ring may turn the ignition off suddenly.

If nothing obvious turns up in a cursory check, look a little further. Learning to recognize and describe symptoms will make repairs easier for you or a mechanic at the shop. Describe problems accurately and fully. Saying that "it won't run" isn't the same as saying "it quit on the highway at high speed and wouldn't start," or that "it sat in my garage for three months and then wouldn't start."

Gather as many symptoms together as possible to aid in diagnosis. Note whether the engine lost power gradually or all at once, what color smoke (if any) came from the exhaust, and so on. Remember that the more complicated a machine is, the easier it is to troubleshoot because symptoms point to specific problems.

After the symptoms are defined, areas which could cause the problems are tested and analyzed. Guessing at the cause of a problem may provide the solution, but it can easily lead to frustration, wasted time, and a series of expensive, unnecessary part replacements.

You do not need fancy equipment or complicated test gear to determine whether repairs can be attempted at home. A few simple checks could save a large repair bill and time lost while the bike sits in a dealer's service department. On the other hand, be realistic and do not attempt repairs beyond your abilities. Service departments tend to charge heavily for putting together a disassembled engine that may have been abused. Some won't even take on such a job — so use common sense, don't get in over your head.

OPERATING REQUIREMENTS

An engine needs three basics to run properly: correct gas/air mixture, compression, and a spark at the right time. If one or more are missing, the engine won't run. The electrical system is the weakest link of the three basics.

More problems result from electrical breakdowns than from any other source. Keep that in mind before you begin tampering with carburetor adjustments and the like.

If a bike has been sitting for any length of time and refuses to start, check the battery for a charged condition first, and then look to the gasoline delivery system. This includes the tank, fuel shutoff valve, lines, and the carburetors. Rust may have formed in the tank, obstructing fuel flow. Gasoline deposits may have gummed up carburetor jets and air passages. Gasoline tends to lose its potency after standing for long periods. Condensation may contaminate it with water. Drain old gas and try starting with a fresh tankful.

TROUBLESHOOTING INSTRUMENTS

Chapter One lists many of the instruments needed and detailed instructions on their use.

EMERGENCY TROUBLESHOOTING

When the bike is difficult to start or won't start at all, it does not help to grind away at the starter or kick the tires. Check for obvious problems even before getting out your tools. Go down the following list step-by-step. Do each one; you may be embarrassed to find your kill switch off, but that is better than wearing out your leg. If the bike still will not start, refer to the appropriate troubleshooting procedures which follow in this chapter.

1. Is there fuel in the tank? Do not trust the fuel gauge. Remove the filler cap and rock the bike; listen for fuel sloshing around.

WARNING
Do not use an open flame to check in the tank. A serious explosion is certain to result.

2. Is the fuel tap in the ON position? Turn it to RES to be sure you get the last remaining gas.
3. Is the engine stop switch in the ON position?
4. Are spark plug wires on tight?
5. Is the engine start lever in the right position? It should be pulled up for a cold engine and down for a warm engine.
6. Is the battery dead? Check it with a hydrometer.
7. Has the main fuse blown? Replace it with a good one.

CHARGING SYSTEM

Troubleshooting an alternator system is somewhat different from troubleshooting a generator. For example, *never* short any terminals to ground on the alternator, voltage regulator, or rectifier. The following symptoms are typical of alternator charging system troubles.

1. *Battery requires frequent charging* — The charging system is not functioning or is undercharging the battery. Test the alternator and voltage regulator/rectifier (Chapter Four).

2. *Battery requires frequent additions of water or lamps require frequent replacement* — The alternator is probably overcharging the battery. Check the voltage regulator/rectifier as described in Chapter Four.

ENGINE

These procedures assume the kickstarter cranks the engine over normally.

Poor Performance

1. *Engine misses erratically at all speeds* — Intermittent trouble like this can be difficult to find. The fault could be in the ignition system, exhaust system (exhaust restriction), or fuel system. Follow troubleshooting procedures for these systems carefully to isolate the trouble.

2. *Engine misses at idle only* — Trouble could exist anywhere in ignition system. Refer to *Ignition System* in Chapter Four. Trouble could exist in the carburetor idle circuits.

3. *Engine misses at high speed only* — Trouble could exist in the fuel system or ignition system. Check the fuel lines, etc., as described under *Fuel System* troubleshooting. Also check spark plugs and wires. Refer to *Ignition System* in Chapter Four.

4. *Poor performance at all speeds, lack of acceleration* — Trouble usually exists in ignition or fuel system. Check each with the appropriate troubleshooting procedure.

5. *Excessive fuel consumption* — This can be caused by a wide variety of seemingly unrelated factors. Check for clutch slippage, brake drag, and defective wheel bearings. Check ignition and fuel systems as described later in this chapter.

ENGINE NOISES

1. *Knocking or pinging during acceleration* — Caused by using a lower octane fuel than recommended. May also be caused by poor fuel available at some "discount" gasoline stations. Pinging can also be caused by spark plugs of the wrong heat range. Refer to *Spark Plugs* in Chapter Four.

2. *Slapping or rattling noises at low speed or during acceleration* — May be caused by piston slap, i.e., excessive piston-cylinder wall clearance.

3. *Knocking or rapping while decelerating* — Usually caused by excessive rod bearing clearance.

4. *Persistent knocking and vibration* — Usually caused by excessive main bearing clearance.

5. *Rapid on-off squeal* — Compression leak around cylinder head gasket or spark plugs.

EXCESSIVE VIBRATION

This can be difficult to find without disassembling the engine. Usually this is caused by loose engine mounting hardware or worn engine or transmission bearings.

FUEL SYSTEM

Fuel system troubles must be isolated to the carburetor, fuel tank, fuel tap, or fuel lines. These procedures assume that the ignition system has been checked and properly adjusted.

1. *Engine will not start* — First determine that the fuel is being delivered to the carburetor. Turn the fuel tap to the OFF position; remove the flexible fuel line to the carburetor. Place the loose end into a small container; turn the fuel tap to the ON or RESERVE position. Fuel should run out of the tube. If it does not, remove the fuel tap and check for restrictions within it or the fuel tank. Refer to Chapter Six.

2. *Rough idle or engine miss with frequent stalling* — Check carburetor adjustment. See Chapter Five.

3. *Stumbling when accelerating from idle* — Check idle speed adjustment. See Chapter Five.

4. *Engine misses at high speed or lacks power* — This indicates possible fuel starvation. Clean main jets and float needle valves.

5. *Black exhaust smoke* — Black exhaust smoke means a badly overrich mixture. Check that manual choke disengages. Check idle speed. Check for leaky floats or worn float needle valves. Also check that jets are proper size.

CLUTCH

All clutch troubles, except adjustments, require partial engine disassembly to identify and solve the problem. Refer to Chapter Three for procedures.

1. *Slippage* — This is most noticeable when accelerating in a high gear at relatively low speed. To check slippage, shift to second gear and release the clutch as if riding off. If the clutch is good, the engine will slow and stall. If the clutch slips, continued engine speed will give it away. Slippage results from insufficient clutch lever free play, worn discs or pressure plate, or weak springs.

2. *Drag or failure to release* — This trouble usually causes difficult shifting and gear clash, especially when downshifting. The cause may be excessive clutch lever free play, warped or bent pressure plate or clutch disc, or broken or loose linings.

3. *Chatter or grabbing* — Check for worn or warped plates.

> NOTE: *Clutch wear is accelerated if the transmission is habitually left in gear with the clutch disengaged while waiting for long-duration traffic lights. Instead, shift the transmission to neutral and release the clutch until the cross-traffic amber light indicates that the light is about to change. In addition to reducing*

clutch wear, a measure of safety is gained in that it precludes a cable failure, most certain to occur when the clutch lever is pulled in.

TRANSMISSION

Transmission problems are usually indicated by one or more of the following symptoms.

a. Difficulty shifting gears
b. Gear clash when downshifting
c. Slipping out of gear
d. Excessive noise in neutral
e. Excessive noise in gear

Transmission symptoms are sometimes hard to distinguish from clutch symptoms. Be sure that clutch is not causing the trouble before working on the transmission.

POOR HANDLING

Poor handling may be caused by improper tire pressures, a damaged frame or swinging arm, worn shocks or front forks, weak fork springs, a bent or broken steering stem, misaligned wheels, loose or missing spokes, worn tires, bent handlebar, worn wheel bearing, or dragging brakes.

Poor handling is also caused by the steering head being adjusted too tight or too loose, or by the races and balls being excessively worn. Also, if the frame has been recently repainted, overspray on the bearing races will prevent the bearings from seating correctly and making accurate adjustment impossible.

Worn or frozen swing arm bearings will also cause handling problems. They can be checked by removing the wheel and shocks, and then moving the arm right and left by hand. If the free play is greater than 1mm (0.04 in.) replace the bearings.

> NOTE: *A worn or loose swing arm pivot will usually be felt through a tendency for the motorcycle to weave from side to side. A high-rate wobble indicates front end trouble.*

In addition to the checks mentioned, make certain the tires are mounted correctly and that the beads are seated evenly on the rims. Tires have alignment indicator ribs around the bead and an incorrectly seated bead will be visually apparent. If this condition exists, deflate the tire and reseat the bead before inflating it.

The increasingly common practice of cutting rain grooves into road surfaces has added a totally new handling problem for most motorcycles, no matter how well tuned the suspension. It is most easily solved by using tires that do not have a center groove. If the motorcycle tends to snake, as though the swing arm pivot were loose or worn, the problem usually lies with the rear tire. If the steering is imprecise and mushy, the front tire is at fault. If all other handling factors are correct, a change of tread pattern will almost always correct the situation.

BRAKES

1. *Brake lever or pedal goes all the way to its stop* — There are numerous causes for this including excessively worn linings or pads, air in the hydraulic system, leaky brake lines, leaky calipers, or leaky or worn master cylinder. Check for leaks and thin brake linings or pads. Bleed the brakes. If this does not cure the trouble, rebuild the calipers and/or master cylinder. Also, improper cable or rod adjustment may be a cause.

2. *Spongy lever* — Normally caused by air in the system; bleed the brakes.

3. *Dragging brakes* — Check for swollen rubber parts due to improper brake fluid or contamination, and obstructed master cylinder bypass port. Clean or replace defective parts. Check for broken or weak return springs.

4. *Hard lever or pedal* — Check brake linings or pads for contamination. Also check for restricted brake line and hose and brake pedal needing lubrication.

5. *High speed fade* — Check for glazed or contaminated brake linings or pads. Ensure that recommended brake fluid is installed. Drain entire system and refill if in doubt.

6. *Pulsating lever or pedal* — Check for out-of-round drums or excessive brake disc runout. Undetected accident damage is also a frequent cause of this.

LIGHTING SYSTEM

Bulbs which continuously burn out may be caused by excessive vibration, loose connections that permit sudden current surges, poor battery connections, or installation of the wrong type bulb.

A majority of light and horn or other electrical accessory problems are caused by loose or corroded ground connections. Check those first, and then substitute known good units for easier troubleshooting.

TROUBLESHOOTING GUIDE

Table 1 is a quick reference guide which summarizes part of the troubleshooting process. Use it to outline possible problem areas, then refer to the specific chapter or section involved.

Table 1 TROUBLESHOOTING GUIDE

Item	Problem or Cause	Things to Check
Loss of power	Poor compression	Piston rings and cylinder Head gaskets Crankcase leaks
	Overheated engine	Lubricating oil supply Oil pump Clogged cooling fins Ignition timing Slipping clutch Carbon in combustion chamber
	Improper mixture	Dirty air cleaner Starter lever position Restricted fuel flow Gas cap vent hole
	Miscellaneous	Dragging brakes Tight wheel bearings Defective chain Clogged exhaust system
Steering	Hard steering	Tire pressures Steering damper adjustment Steering stem head Steering head bearings Steering oil damper

(continued)

Table 1 TROUBLESHOOTING GUIDE (continued)

Item	Problem or Cause	Things to Check
Steering (continued)	Pulls to one side	Unbalanced shock absorbers Drive chain adjustment Front/rear wheel alignment Unbalanced tires Defective swing arm Defective steering head Defective steering oil damper
	Shimmy	Drive chain adjustment Loose or missing spokes Deformed rims Worn wheel bearings Wheel balance
Gearshifting difficulties	Clutch	Adjustment Springs Friction plates Steel plates
	Transmission	Oil quantity Oil grade Return spring or pin Change lever or spring Drum position plate Shift drum Shift forks
Brakes	Poor brakes	Worn linings or pads Brake adjustment Oil or water on brake linings or pads Loose linkage or cables Low brake fluid level
	Noisy brakes	Worn or scratched lining or pads Scratched brake drums or disc Dirt in brakes
	Unadjustable brakes	Worn linings or pads Worn drums or disc Worn brake cams

APPENDIX

SPECIFICATIONS

This chapter contains specifications and performance figures for the various Kawasaki models covered by this book. The tables are arranged in order of increasing engine size.

SPECIFICATIONS, MODEL S1

DIMENSIONS
- Length — 79.1 in.
- Width — 31.5 in.
- Wheelbase — 52.4 in.
- Road clearance — 5.9 in.
- Weight — 326 lbs.

PERFORMANCE
- Maximum speed — 105 mph
- Fuel consumption — 89 mpg/30 mph
- Climbing ability — 40 degrees
- Braking distance (feet/mph) — 39/31

ENGINE
- Bore and stroke (inches) — 1.77 x 2.06
- (millimeters) — 45 x 52.3
- Displacement (cubic inches) — 15.2
- (cubic centimeters) — 249
- Compression ratio — 7.5 to 1
- Horsepower/rpm — 32/8,500
- Torque (foot-pounds/rpm) — 19.5/7,000

FUEL SYSTEM
- Carburetor — Mikuni VM22SC
- Fuel tank capacity — 3.7 gal.

LUBRICATION SYSTEM
- Type — Superlube
- Oil tank capacity — 1.6 qt.

IGNITION SYSTEM
- Type — Battery
- Ignition timing — 23 degrees BTDC
- Spark plug — NGK B-9HCS

TRANSMISSION
- Primary reduction ratio — 2.22 to 1
- Gear ratios
  - 1st — 2.86 to 1
  - 2nd — 1.79 to 1
  - 3rd — 1.35 to 1
  - 4th — 1.12 to 1
  - 5th — 0.96 to 1

FRAME
- Steering angle — 42 degrees
- Caster — 62 degrees
- Trail — 4.3 in.
- Tire size
  - Front — 3.00-18 4PR
  - Rear — 3.25-18 4PR

BRAKES
- Type — Drum
- Diameter x width
  - Front — 7.1 x 1.2 in.
  - Rear — 7.1 x 1.2 in.

SPECIFICATIONS, MODEL KH250

DIMENSIONS
- Length — 79.5 in.
- Width — 32.3 in.
- Wheelbase — 54.1 in.
- Road clearance — 6 in.
- Weight — 393 lbs.

PERFORMANCE
- Maximum speed — 90 mph
- Fuel consumption — 83 mpg/25 mph
- Climbing ability — 40 degrees
- Braking distance (feet/mph) — 39/31

ENGINE
- Bore and stroke (inches) — 1.77 x 2.06
- (millimeters) — 45 x 52.3
- Displacement (cubic inches) — 15.2
- (cubic centimeters) — 249
- Compression ratio — 7.5 to 1
- Horsepower/rpm — 28/7,500
- Torque (foot-pounds/rpm) — 19.5/7,000

FUEL SYSTEM
- Carburetors — Mikuni VM22SC
- Fuel tank capacity — 3.7 gal.

LUBRICATION SYSTEM
- Type — Superlube
- Oil tank capacity — 1.6 qt.

IGNITION SYSTEM
- Type — Battery
- Ignition timing — 23 degrees BTDC
- Spark plugs — NGK B-9HS

TRANSMISSION
- Primary reduction ratio — 2.22 to 1
- Gear ratios
  - 1st — 2.86 to 1
  - 2nd — 1.79 to 1
  - 3rd — 1.35 to 1
  - 4th — 1.12 to 1
  - 5th — 0.96 to 1

FRAME
- Steering angle — 42 degrees
- Caster — 62 degrees
- Trail — 4.3 in.
- Tire size
  - Front — 3.25-18 4PR
  - Rear — 3.50-18 4PR

BRAKES
- Type — Drum
- Diameter x width
  - Front — 7.1 x 1.2 in.
  - Rear — 7.1 x 1.2 in.

SPECIFICATIONS, MODEL S2

DIMENSIONS
- Length — 79.1 in
- Width — 31.5 in.
- Wheelbase — 52.4 in.
- Road clearance — 6.3 in.
- Weight — 330 lb.

PERFORMANCE
- Maximum speed — 111 mph
- Fuel consumption — 75 mpg at 30 mph
- Climbing ability — 40 degrees
- Braking distance (feet mph) — 39.4/31

ENGINE
- Bore and stroke (inches) — 2.09 x 2.06
- (millimeters) — 53.0 x 52.3
- Displacement (cubic inches) — 21.2
- (cubic centimeters) — 346.2
- Compression ratio — 7.3 to 1
- Horsepower/rpm — 45/8,000
- Torque (foot-pounds/rpm) — 30.7/7,000

FUEL SYSTEM
- Carburetor — Mikuni VM24SC
- Fuel tank capacity — 3.7 gal.

LUBRICATION SYSTEM
- Type — Superlube
- Oil tank capacity — 1.6 qt.

IGNITION SYSTEM
- Type — Battery
- Ignition timing — 23 degrees BTDC
- Spark plug — NGK B-9HC

TRANSMISSION
- Primary reduction ratio — 2.22 to 1
- Gear ratios
  - 1st — 2.86 to 1
  - 2nd — 1.79 to 1
  - 3rd — 1.35 to 1
  - 4th — 1.12 to 1
  - 5th — 0.96 to 1

FRAME
- Steering angle — 42 degrees
- Caster — 62 degrees
- Trail — 4.3 in.
- Tire size
  - Front — 3.00-18 4PR
  - Rear — 3.50-18 4PR

BRAKES
- Type — Front, disc/Rear, drum
- Diameter x width
  - Front — 8.9 in. disc diameter
  - Rear — 7.1 x 1.2 in.

SPECIFICATIONS, MODEL S3

DIMENSIONS
- Length — 79.7 in.
- Width — 32.3 in.
- Wheelbase — 53.7 in.
- Road clearance — 6 in.
- Weight — 353 lbs.

PERFORMANCE
- Maximum speed — 102 mph
- Fuel consumption — 75 mpg/25 mph
- Climbing ability — 40 degrees
- Braking distance (feet/mph) — 39/31

ENGINE
- Bore and stroke (inches) — 2.24 x 2.06
- (millimeters) — 57 x 52.3
- Displacement (cubic inches) — 24.43
- (cubic centimeters) — 400.4
- Compression ratio — 6.5 to 1
- Horsepower/rpm — 47/7,000
- Torque (foot-pounds/rpm) — 31.2/6,500

FUEL SYSTEM
- Carburetor — Mikuni VM26SC
- Fuel tank capacity — 3.7 gal.

LUBRICATION SYSTEM
- Type — Superlube
- Oil tank capacity — 1.6 qt.

IGNITION SYSTEM
- Type — Battery
- Ignition timing — 23 degrees BTDC
- Spark plug — NGK B-9HCS

TRANSMISSION
- Primary reduction ratio — 2.22 to 1
- Gear ratios
  - 1st — 2.86 to 1
  - 2nd — 1.79 to 1
  - 3rd — 1.35 to 1
  - 4th — 1.12 to 1
  - 5th — 0.96 to 1

FRAME
- Steering angle — 42 degrees
- Caster — 62 degrees
- Trail — 4.4 in.
- Tire size
  - Front — 3.25-18 4PR
  - Rear — 3.50-18 4PR

BRAKES
- Type
  - Front — Disc
  - Rear — Drum
- Diameter x width
  - Front — 10.9 in. disc diameter
  - Rear — 7.1 x 1.2 in.

SPECIFICATIONS, MODEL KH400

DIMENSIONS
- Length — 79.7 in.
- Width — 32.3 in.
- Wheelbase — 53.7 in.
- Road clearance — 5.9 in.
- Weight — 357 lbs.

PERFORMANCE
- Maximum speed — 102 mph
- Fuel consumption — 75 mpg/25 mph
- Climbing ability — 40 degrees
- Braking distance (feet/mph) — 39/31

ENGINE
- Bore and stroke (inches) — 2.24 x 2.06
- (millimeters) — 57.0 x 52.3
- Displacement (cubic inches) — 24.43
- (cubic centimeters) — 400.4
- Compression ratio — 6.5 to 1
- Horsepower/rpm — 38/7,000
- Torque (foot-pounds/rpm) — 28.2/6,500

FUEL SYSTEM
- Carburetors — Mikuni VM26SC
- Fuel tank capacity — 3.7 gal.

LUBRICATION SYSTEM
- Type — Superlube
- Oil tank capacity — 1.6 qt.

IGNITION SYSTEM
- Type — Capacitor discharge
- Ignition timing — 23 degrees BTDC at 4,000 rpm
- Spark plugs — NGK B-8HS

TRANSMISSION
- Primary reduction ratio — 2.22 to 1
- Gear ratios
  - 1st — 2.86 to 1
  - 2nd — 1.79 to 1
  - 3rd — 1.35 to 1
  - 4th — 1.12 to 1
  - 5th — 0.96 to 1

FRAME
- Steering angle — 42 degrees
- Caster — 62 degrees
- Trail — 4.4 in.
- Tire size
  - Front — 3.25-18 4PR
  - Rear — 3.50-18 4PR

BRAKES
- Type
  - Front — Disc
  - Rear — Drum
- Diameter x width
  - Front — 10.9 in. disc diameter
  - Rear — 7.1 x 1.2 in.

SPECIFICATIONS, MODEL H1

DIMENSIONS
- Length — 82.5 in.
- Width — 33.1 in.
- Wheelbase — 55.1 in.
- Road clearance — 5.3 in.
- Weight — 384 lbs.

PERFORMANCE
- Maximum speed — 118 mph
- Fuel consumption — 78 mpg at 31 mph
- Climbing ability — 40 degrees
- Braking distance (feet/mph) — 34.5/31

ENGINE
- Bore and stroke (inches) — 2.36 x 2.31
- (millimeters) — 60.0 x 58.8
- Displacement (cubic inches) — 30.4
- (cubic centimeters) — 498.0
- Compression ratio — 6.8 to 1
- Horsepower/rpm — 60/7,500
- Torque (foot pounds/rpm) — 42.3/7,000

FUEL SYSTEM
- Carburetor — Mikuni VM28SC
- Fuel tank capacity — 4.0 gal.

LUBRICATION SYSTEM
- Type — Injectolube
- Oil tank capacity — 2.5 qt.

IGNITION SYSTEM
- Type — Battery or CDI
- Ignition timing — 25 degrees BTDC
- Spark plug — NGK BUHX

TRANSMISSION
- Primary reduction ratio — 2.41 to 1
- Gear ratios
  - 1st — 2.20 to 1
  - 2nd — 1.40 to 1
  - 3rd — 1.09 to 1
  - 4th — 0.92 to 1
  - 5th — 0.81 to 1

FRAME
- Steering angle — 42 degrees
- Caster — 61 degrees
- Trail — 4.3 in.
- Tire size
  - Front — 3.25-19 4PR
  - Rear — 4.00-18 4PR

BRAKES
- Type
  - Front — Drum or disc
  - Rear — Drum
- Diameter x width
  - Front drum — 7.9 x 1.4 in.
  - Rear — 7.1 x 1.4 in.
  - Disc diameter — 11.65 in.

SPECIFICATIONS, MODEL KH500

DIMENSIONS
- Length — 82.5 in.
- Width — 32.9 in.
- Wheelbase — 55.5 in.
- Road clearance — 5.7 in.
- Weight — 42.3 in.

PERFORMANCE
- Maximum speed — 118 mph
- Fuel consumption — 78 mpg/31 mph
- Climbing ability — 40 degrees
- Braking distance (feet/mph) — 34.5/31

ENGINE
- Bore and stock (inches) — 2.36 x 2.31
- (millimeters) — 60.0 x 58.8
- Displacement (cubic inches) — 30.4
- (cubic centimeters) — 498
- Compression ratio — 6.8 to 1
- Horsepower/rpm — 52/7,000
- Torque/rpm — 39.1 ft.-lb./6,500

FUEL SYSTEM
- Carburetors — Mikuni VM28SC
- Fuel tank capacity — 4.2 gal.

LUBRICATION SYSTEM
- Type — Injectolube
- Oil tank capacity — 2.5 qt.

IGNITION SYSTEM
- Type — Capacitor discharge
- Ignition timing — 23 degrees BTDC at 4,000 rpm
- Spark plugs — NGK B-9HS-10

TRANSMISSION
- Primary reduction ratio — 2.41 to 1
- Gear ratios
  - 1st — 2.20 to 1
  - 2nd — 1.40 to 1
  - 3rd — 1.09 to 1
  - 4th — 0.92 to 1
  - 5th — 0.81 to 1

FRAME
- Steering angle — 39 degrees
- Caster — 63 degrees
- Trail — 4.3 in.
- Tire size
  - Front — 3.25-19H 4PR
  - Rear — 4.00-18H 4PR

BRAKES
- Type
  - Front — Disc
  - Rear — Drum
- Diameter x width
  - Front — 9.7 in. disc diameter
  - Rear — 7.1 x 1.4 in.

SPECIFICATIONS, MODEL H2

DIMENSIONS
- Length — 83.1 in.
- Width — 32.7 in.
- Wheelbase — 57.0 in.
- Road clearance — 5.5 in.
- Weight — 452 lbs.

PERFORMANCE
- Maximum speed — 126 mph
- Fuel consumption — 45 mpg/50 mph
- Climbing ability — 40 degrees
- Braking distance (feet/mph) — 39.4/31

ENGINE
- Bore and stroke (inches) — 2.80 x 2.48
- (millimeters) — 71.0 x 63.0
- Displacement (cubic inches) — 45.6
- (cubic centimeters) — 748.0
- Compression ratio — 7.0 to 1
- Horsepower/rpm — 71/6,800
- Torque (foot-pounds/rpm) — 57.1/6,500

FUEL SYSTEM
- Carburetor — Mikuni VM30SC
- Fuel tank capacity — 4.5 gal.

LUBRICATION SYSTEM
- Type — Injectolube
- Oil tank capacity — 2.1 qt.

IGNITION SYSTEM
- Type — CDI
- Ignition timing — 23 degrees BTDC at 4,000 rpm
- Spark plug — NGK B-9HS-10

TRANSMISSION
- Primary reduction ratio — 1.88 to 1
- Gear ratios
  - 1st — 2.17 to 1
  - 2nd — 1.47 to 1
  - 3rd — 1.11 to 1
  - 4th — 0.92 to 1
  - 5th — 0.81 to 1

FRAME
- Steering angle — 39 degrees
- Caster — 63.5 degrees
- Trail — 4.1 in.
- Tire size
  - Front — 3.25-19H 4PR
  - Rear — 4.00-18H 4PR

BRAKES
- Type — Front, disc/Rear, drum
- Diameter x width
  - Front — 9.7 in. disc diameter
  - Rear — 7.9 x 1.4

KAWASAKI TRIPLES
Supplement for United Kingdom

This supplement points out special design features of bikes delivered to the United Kingdom.

LUBRICANTS AND PETROL

U.K. models use the same lubricants and petrol as U.S. models. **Table 1** indicates recommended types and capacities in Imperial measure.

HEADLAMP

United Kingdom models use a prefocused headlamp bulb and a city (pilot) lamp.

Headlamp Bulb Replacement

1. Remove 2 retaining screws holding reflector unit in place (work from back of lamp).
2. Lift out reflector unit and twist bulb retain-

Table 1   RECOMMENDED LUBRICANTS AND PETROL

	Capacity	Type
Engine oil		
Models S1, KH250, S2, S3, KH400	1.33 Imp. qt.	2-stroke engine oil
Models H1, KH500	2.08 Imp. qt.	
Model H2	1.75 Imp. qt.	
Transmission oil	0.97 Imp. qt.	SAE 10W-30, 10W-40
Front forks		
Models S1, KH250	210cc	SAE 10W non-detergent
Models S2, S3	200cc	
Model KH400	145cc	
Model KH500	170cc	
Model H1 (drum brake)	230cc	
Models H1 and H2 (disc brake)	160cc	
Petrol		
Models S1, KH250, S2, S3, KH400	3.08 Imp. gal.	85 octane or higher
Models H1, KH500	3.33 Imp. gal.	
Model H2	3.75 Imp. gal.	
Brake fluid	—	J-1703

ing socket counterclockwise to remove it from reflector. See **Figure 1**.

3. To remove bulb from its socket, push in on bulb and twist counterclockwise.

4. Discard old bulb and install new one by pushing bulb into its socket and twisting clockwise. Refer to **Figure 1**.

5. Insert bulb retaining socket into the reflector and twist clockwise to lock it.

6. Position the reflector unit and install 2 retaining screws (work from back of lamp).

City (Pilot) Lamp Replacement

The city (pilot) lamp bulb bayonets into a bulb holder, which in turn bayonets into the headlamp reflector. To replace the bulb, use the following procedure.

1. Twist bulb holder counterclockwise and remove it from headlamp reflector (**Figure 2**).

2. Twist bulb counterclockwise and remove it from bulb holder.

3. Discard old bulb. To install a new one, insert bulb into holder and twist clockwise.

4. Insert bulb holder into headlamp reflector and twist clockwise. Refer to **Figure 2**.

High Beam Indicator Lamp Replacement

1. Slide the rubber sleeve back and pull the high beam indicator bulb holder out of the headlamp shell.

2. Remove and discard the old bulb. Install a new bulb and insert bulb holder into headlamp shell. Slide rubber sleeve firmly in place.

BULB TYPES

Table 2 lists bulbs used in United Kingdom models.

HORN/PASSING SWITCH

On United Kingdom models, there is a combination horn/passing switch. When depressed, it activates the horn; when pushed sideways, it activates the headlight high beam whether the headlight switch is on or off. The switch cannot be repaired. If defective, the entire switch housing must be replaced.

HEADLAMP SWITCH

The United Kingdom and European headlamp switch has 3 positions; OFF, city (pilot) lamp, and headlight. The switch cannot be repaired; if defective, the entire switch housing must be replaced.

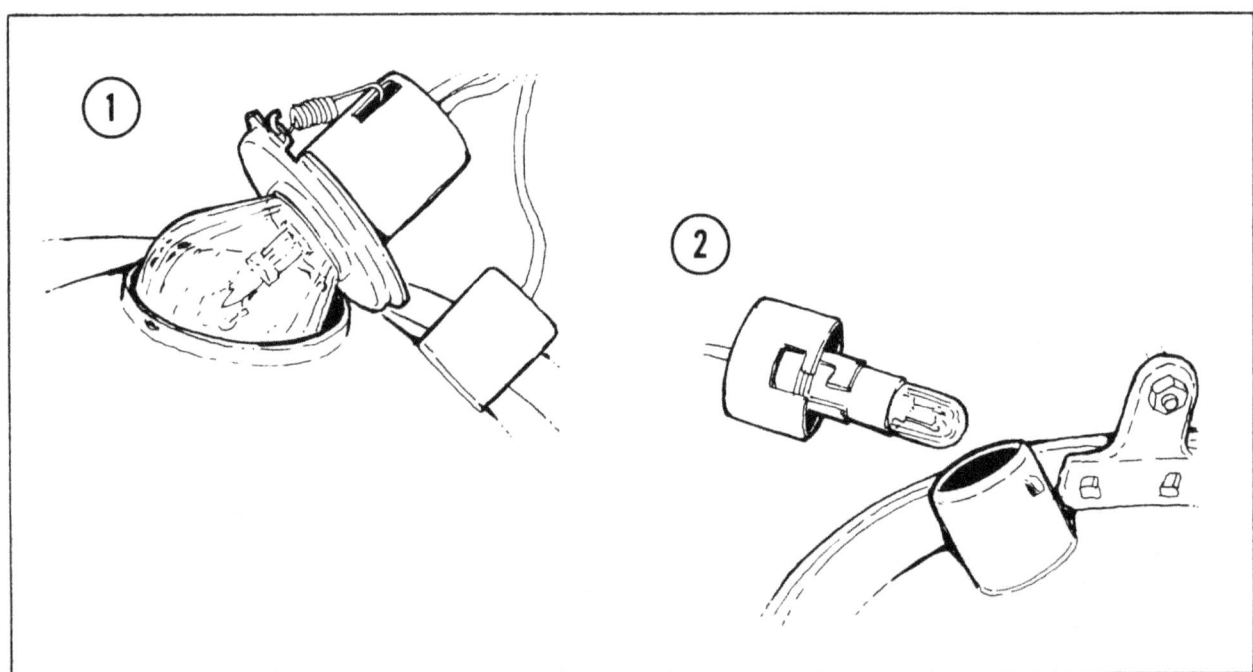

Table 2 BULB TYPES

Application	Rating
Headlamp	
Models S1, S2	12V 35W/25W
Remaining models	12V 35/35W
Tail/stop lamp	
Models S1, S2	12V 8W/23W
Remaining models	12V 5/21W
Turn signal lamps	
Models S1, S2	12V 23W
Remaining models	12V 21W
City (pilot) lamp	12V 4W
Horn	12V 2.5A
Instrument lamps	
All except high beam indicator lamp	12V 3W
High beam indicator lamp	12V 1.5W

NOTES

INDEX

A

Air cleaner 21-23
Air screw setting 25
Alternator
    Removal and installation 42-43
    Troubleshooting 80-85

B

Battery 89-92
Battery ignition system 11-14, 72-75
Brake light 93
Brakes, drum
    Adjustment 132-134
    Description 129
    Disassembly 130
    Inspection 130-131
    Reassembly 132
    Specifications 131
    Troubleshooting 161, 163
    Ventilator (rear) 129-130
Brakes, front disc
    Bleeding 127
    Caliper assembly 126, 127-129
    Disc 126, 129
    Line 129
    Master cylinder 122-125
    Pads 125-127
    Tools 121-122
    Torque specifications 122
    Troubleshooting 161, 163
Breaker points 10-11

C

Capacitor discharge ignition system
    (see Ignition system, CDI)
Carbon removal 6-7, 34, 36
Carburetor
    Adjustment 102-104
    Components 104-105
    Float mechanism 94
    Main fuel system 95-97
    Miscellaneous problems 105
    Overhaul 98-102
    Pilot system 95
    Specifications 105
    Starter system 97-98
    Tune-up adjustment 24-27
Centerstand 152

Charging system 159
Clutch
    Adjustment 27-28
    Description and operation 46-50
    Overhaul 50-54
    Troubleshooting 160-161, 163
Coil, ignition 74
Compression test 5-6
Condenser 74-75
Countershaft sprocket 41-42
Crankcase 57-60
Crankcase covers
    Left cover 40-41
    Right cover 43-44
Crankshaft 60-63
Cylinder and cylinder heads 34-36

D

Distributor, CDI system
    Adjustment (H series) 76
    Removal and installation 44-45
Drive chain 153-154

E

Electrical system
    Alternator 42-43, 80-85
    Battery 89-92
    Battery ignition system 11-14, 72-75
    Capacitor discharge ignition system 14-21, 75-80
    Distributor 44-45
    Horn 93, 162
    Lights 92-93, 162
    Rectifier 85-87
    Spark plugs 7-10, 80
    Voltage regulator 86-89
Engine
    Crankcase 57-60
    Crankshaft 60-63
    Cylinders and cylinder heads .. 34-36
    Left crankcase cover 40-41
    Lubrication 30-32
    Operating principles 29-30
    Piston, piston pin, and piston rings 36-40
    Removal 32-34
    Right crankcase cover 43-44
    Sprocket 41-42
    Troubleshooting 159-160
    Washing 5
Exhaust pipes and mufflers 152-153

F

Float mechanism 94, 102
Fork, front 134-142
Frame 107, 154-155
Fuel system 95-97, 160
Fuel tank 149-151

G

Gearshift mechanism 54-57, 163
General information 1-4

H

Handlebar 107-110
Headlight 92, 162
Horn 93, 162
Hubs 112, 113-117
Hydraulic steering damper 154

I

Idle speed 25, 103-104
Ignition coil 74
Ignition system, battery 11-14, 72-75
Ignition system (CDI)
   H1 .... 19-21, 75-77
   H1E 16-19
   H2 .... 14-16, 77-80
   KH400 21
   KH500 .... 16-19, 75-77

K

Kickstand 152
Kickstarter 68-71

L

Lights 92-93, 162
Lubrication system 30-32

M

Maintenance schedule 156-157
Master cylinder, brake 122-125
Mufflers 152-153

O

Oil pump
   Adjustment 27
   Checking 31-32
   Output 32
   Removal and installation 46
Oil tank 150-152

P

Pilot system 95
Piston, pin, and rings 36-40
Primary drive gear 54

R

Rectifier 85-87
Rims 111

S

Safety hints 4, 89-90
Service hints 1
Shock absorbers 145
Spark plugs 7-10, 80
Specifications
   H1 170
   H2 172
   KH250 166
   KH400 169
   KH500 171
   S1 165
   S2 167
   S3 168
Spokes 111
Sprocket, rear 148-149
Sprocket, countershaft 41-42
Starter system 97-98
Steering system 141-144, 162-163
Swinging arm 145-148

T

Tachometer gear 45-46
Timing
   Breaker point models 11-14
   CDI models 14-21
Tires 110-111
Tools 1-3
Transmission 63-68, 161, 163
Tune-up
   Air cleaner 21-23
   Breaker points 10-11
   Carbon removal 6-7
   Carburetor 24-27
   Clutch 27-28
   Compression test 5-6
   Engine washdown 5
   Ignition timing (breaker point models) ... 11-14
   Ignition timing (CDI) 14-21
   Oil pump 27
   Spark plugs 7-10
Turn signals 93
Troubleshooting
   Alternator 80-85

Battery ignition 72-74	Steering 162-163
Brakes 161, 163	Transmission 161, 163
Carburetor 96, 104	Vibration 160
CDI (battery) 76	Voltage regulator 86-89
CDI (magneto) 79	
Charging system 159	

V

Vibration, excessive 160
Voltage regulator 86-89

Clutch 160-161, 163
Emergency 159
Engine 159-160
Fuel system 160
General information 158-159
Guide 162-163

W

Handling 161
Lighting system 162
Rectifier 85-87

Wheels 110-121
Wiring diagrams 180-195

KAWASAKI S1, S1A, S2, S2A (1972-1973)

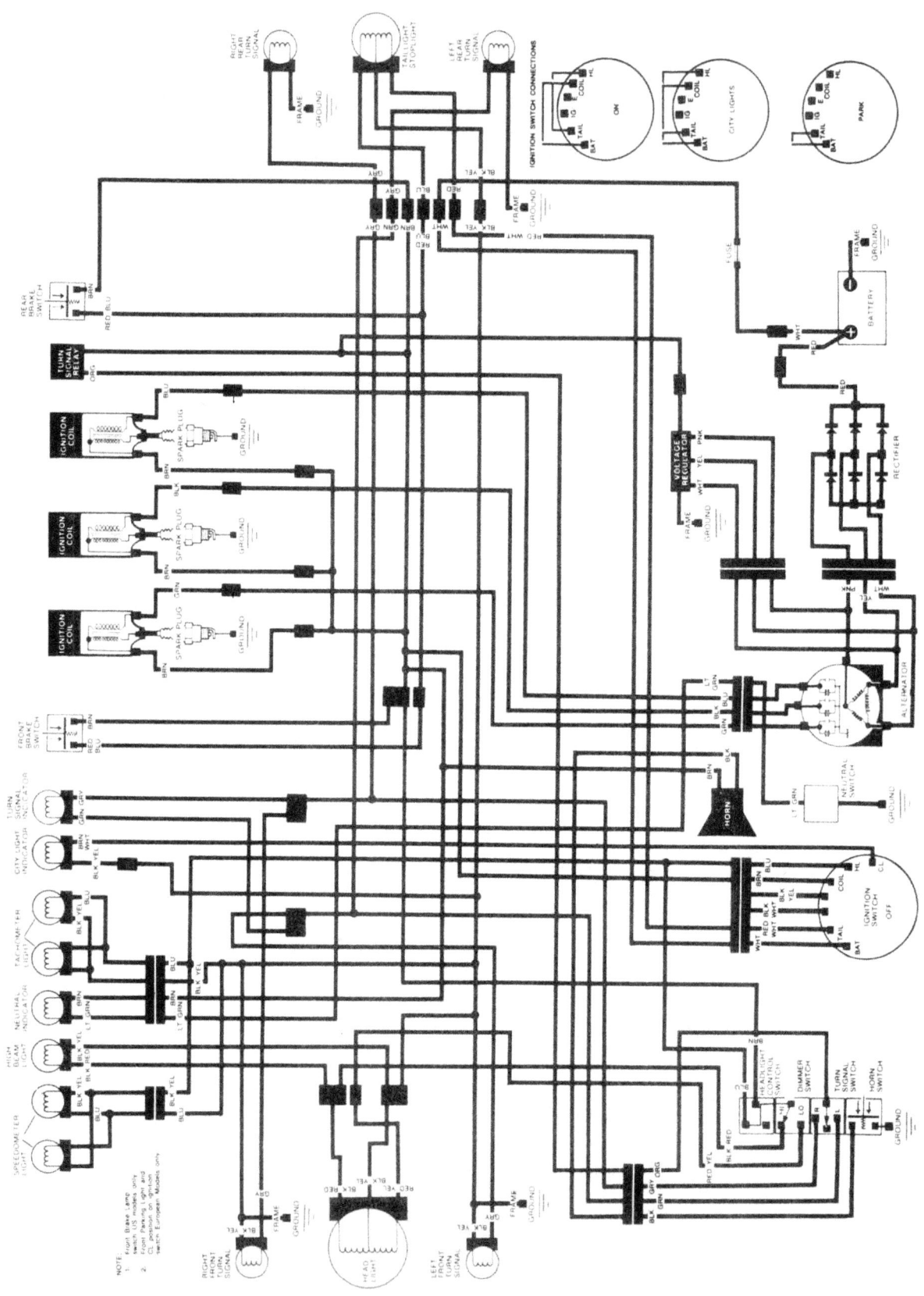

KAWASAKI S1B, S1C, S3, S3A — U.S. & EUROPE (1974-1975)

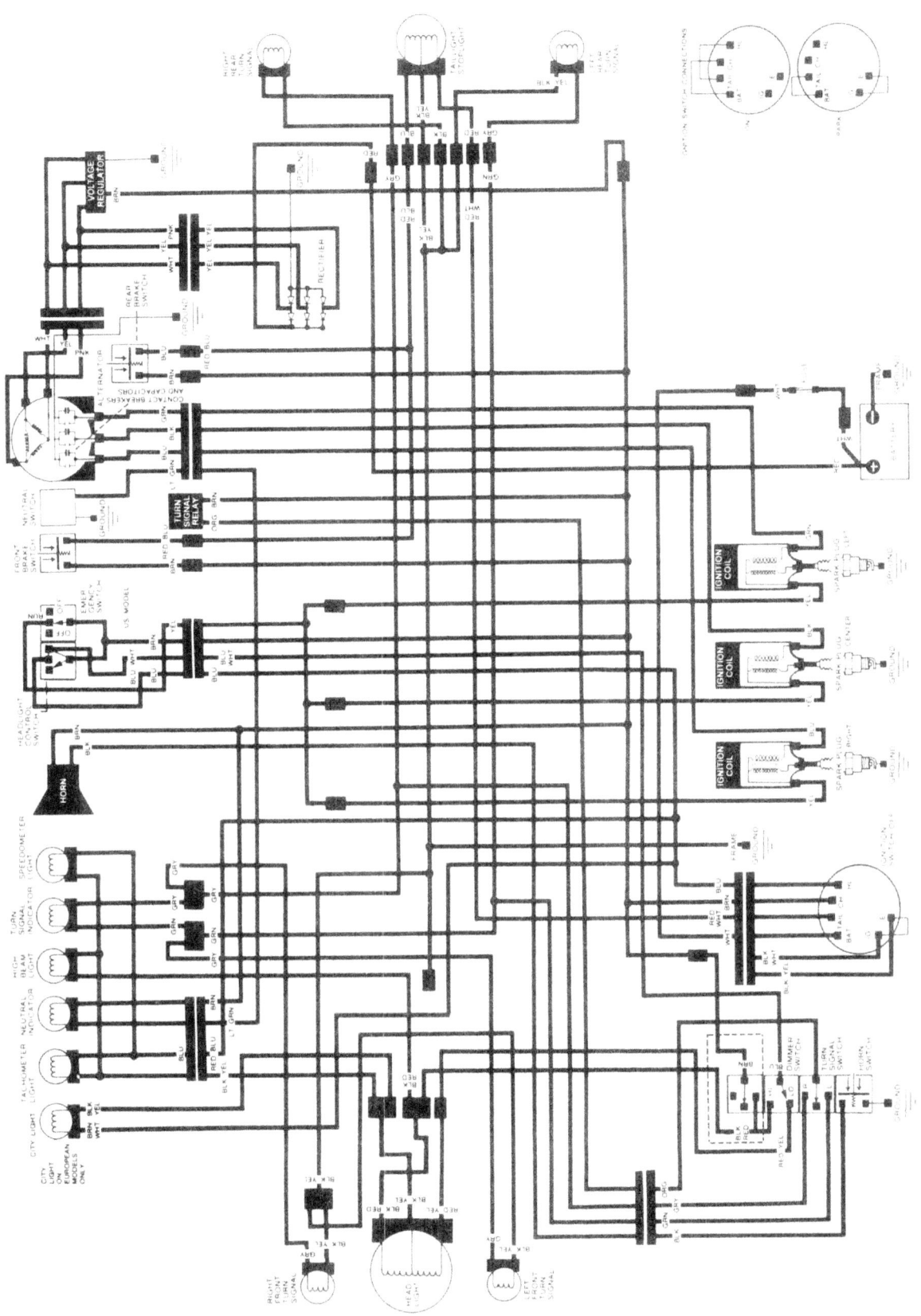

KAWASAKI KH250A5 — U.S. & CANADA

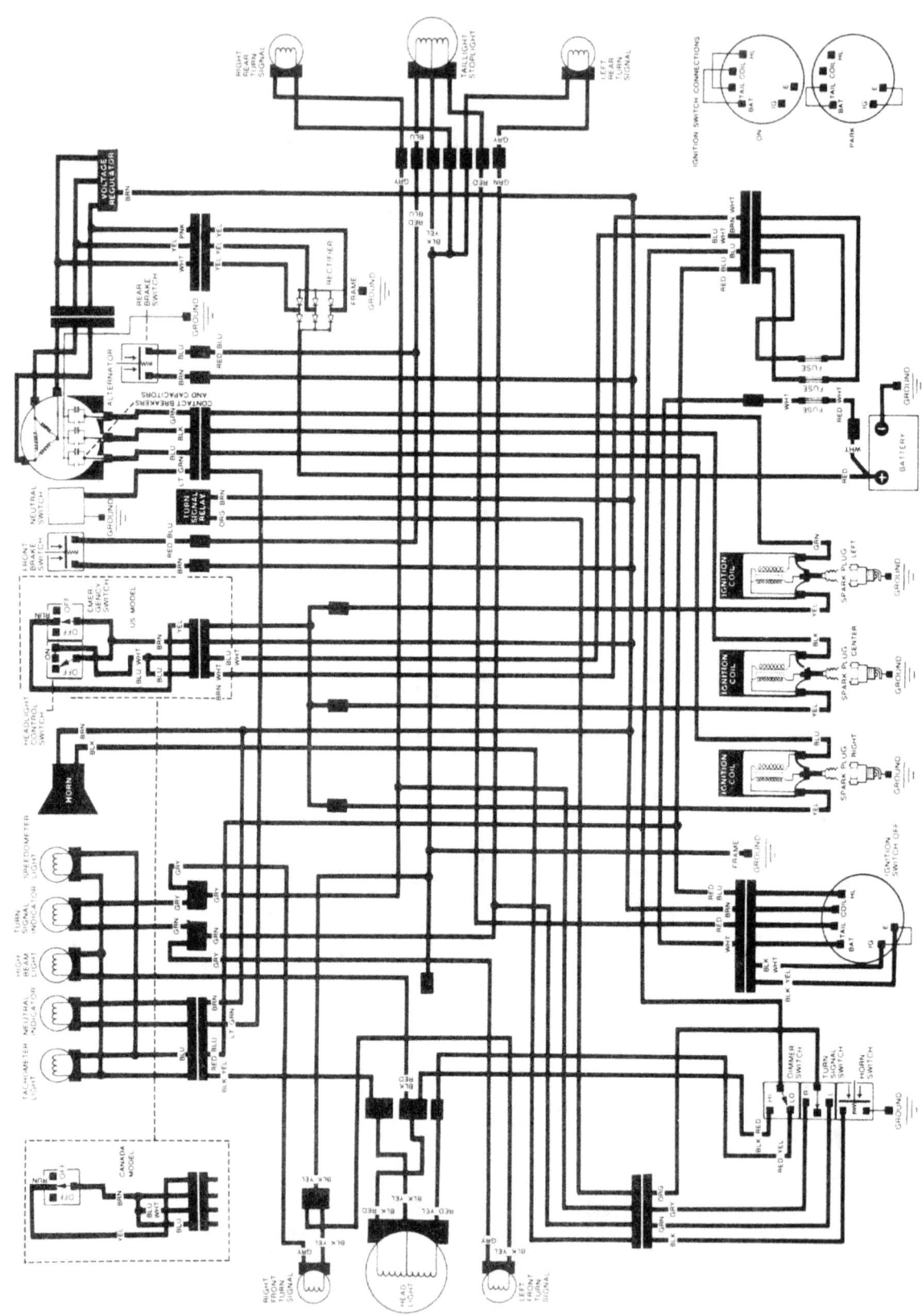

KAWASAKI KH250B1 — EUROPE

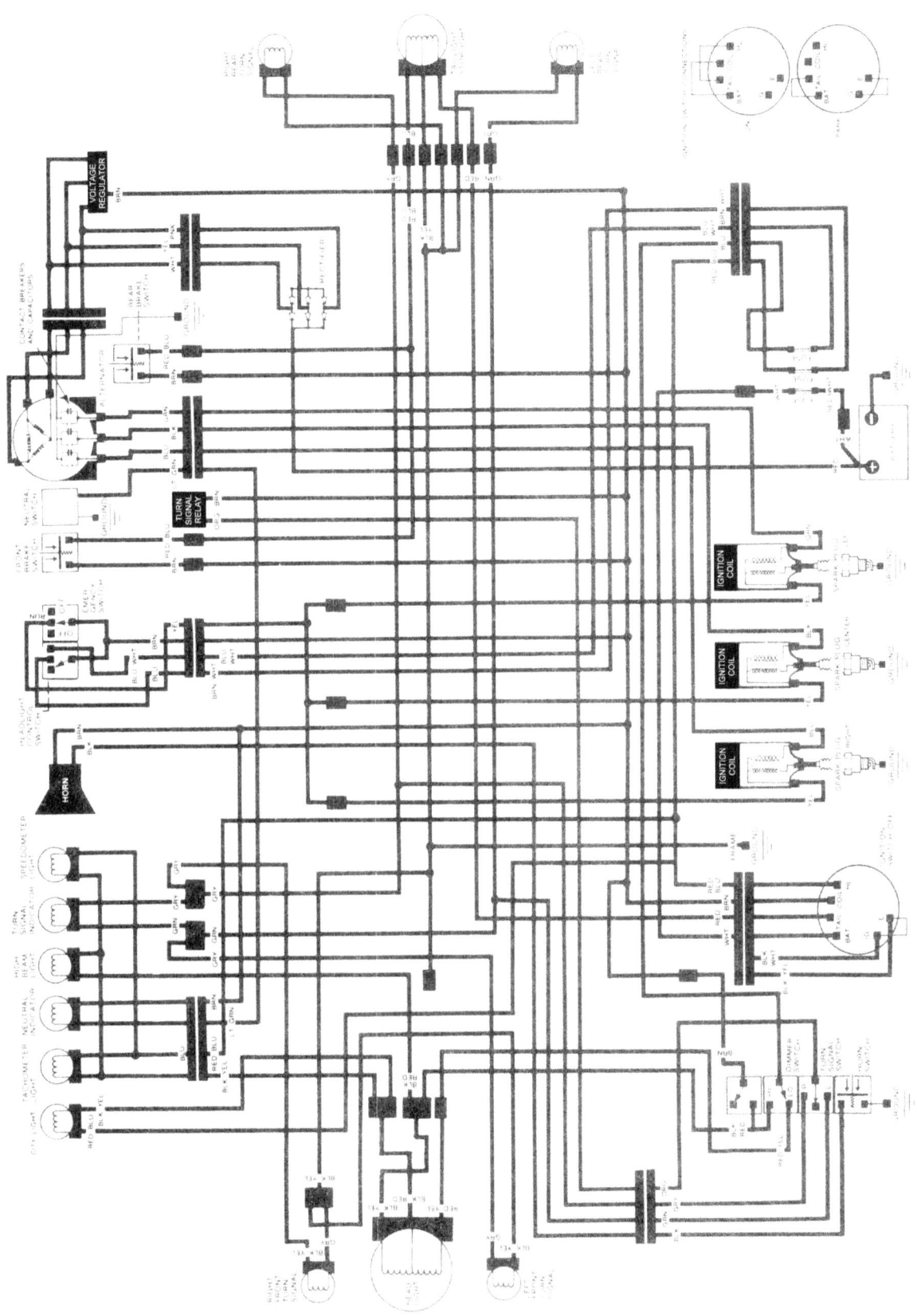

KAWASAKI KH400A3 — U.S. & CANADA

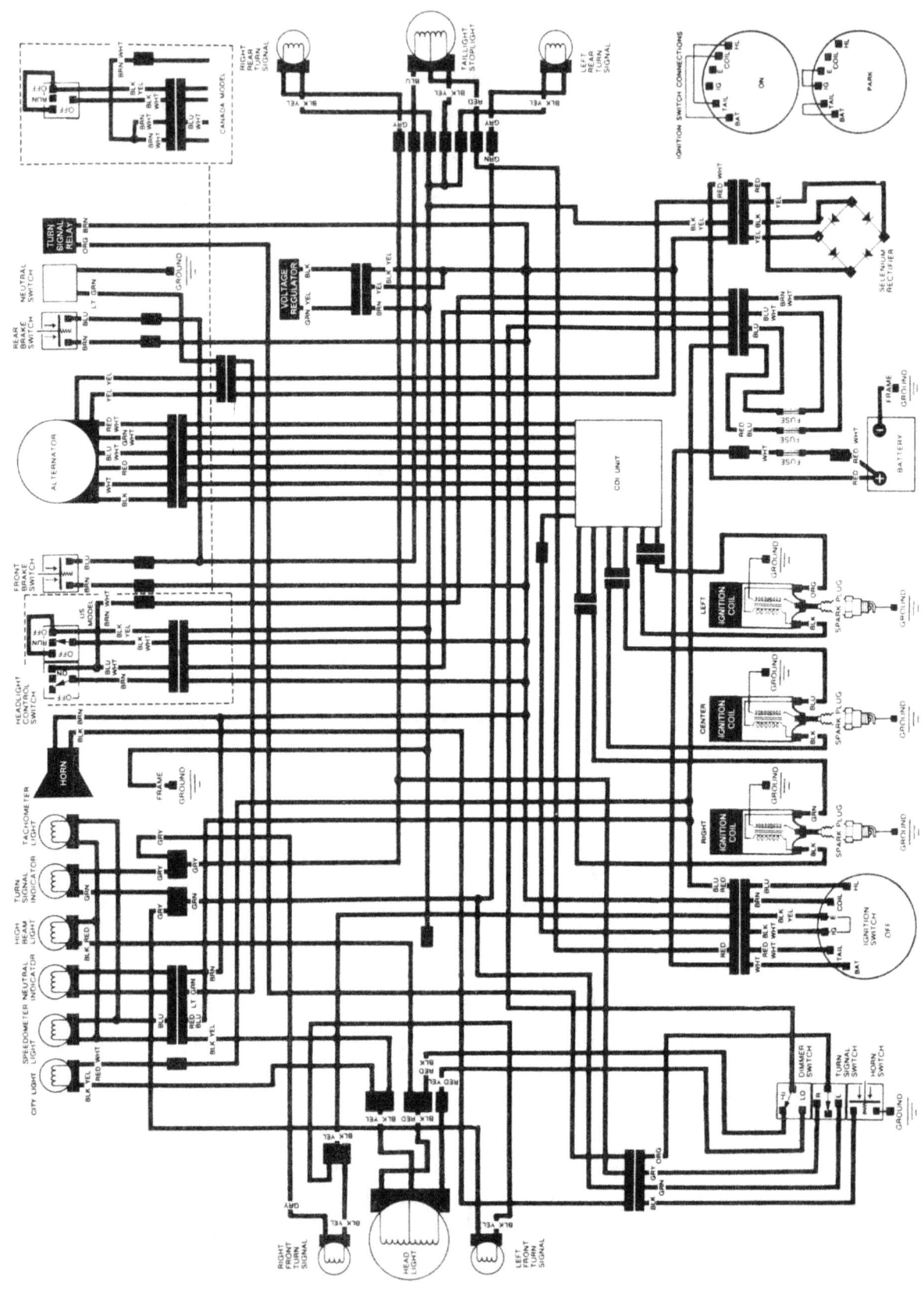

KAWASAKI KH400A3 — EUROPE

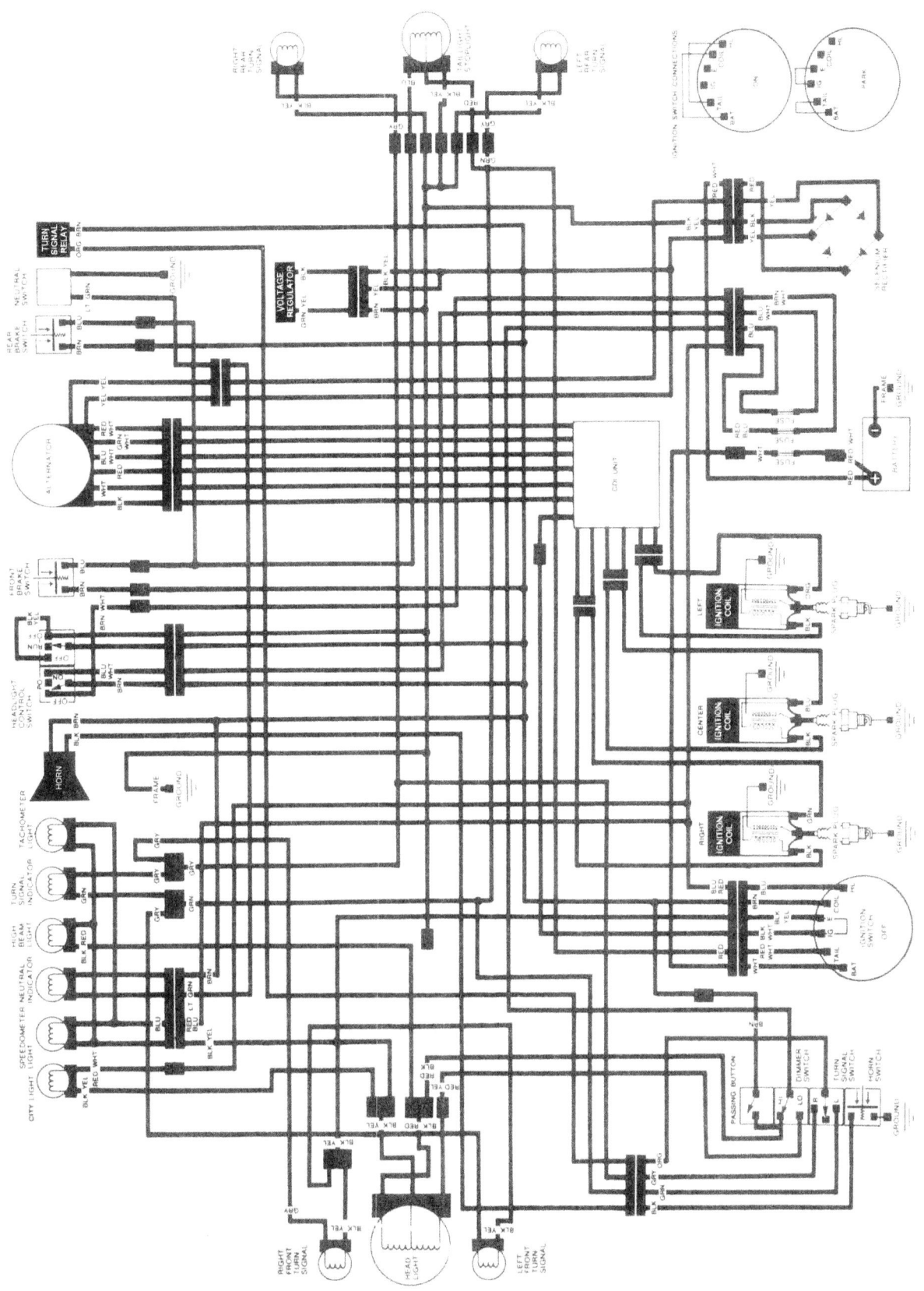

KAWASAKI H1 WITH CAPACITOR DISCHARGE IGNITION

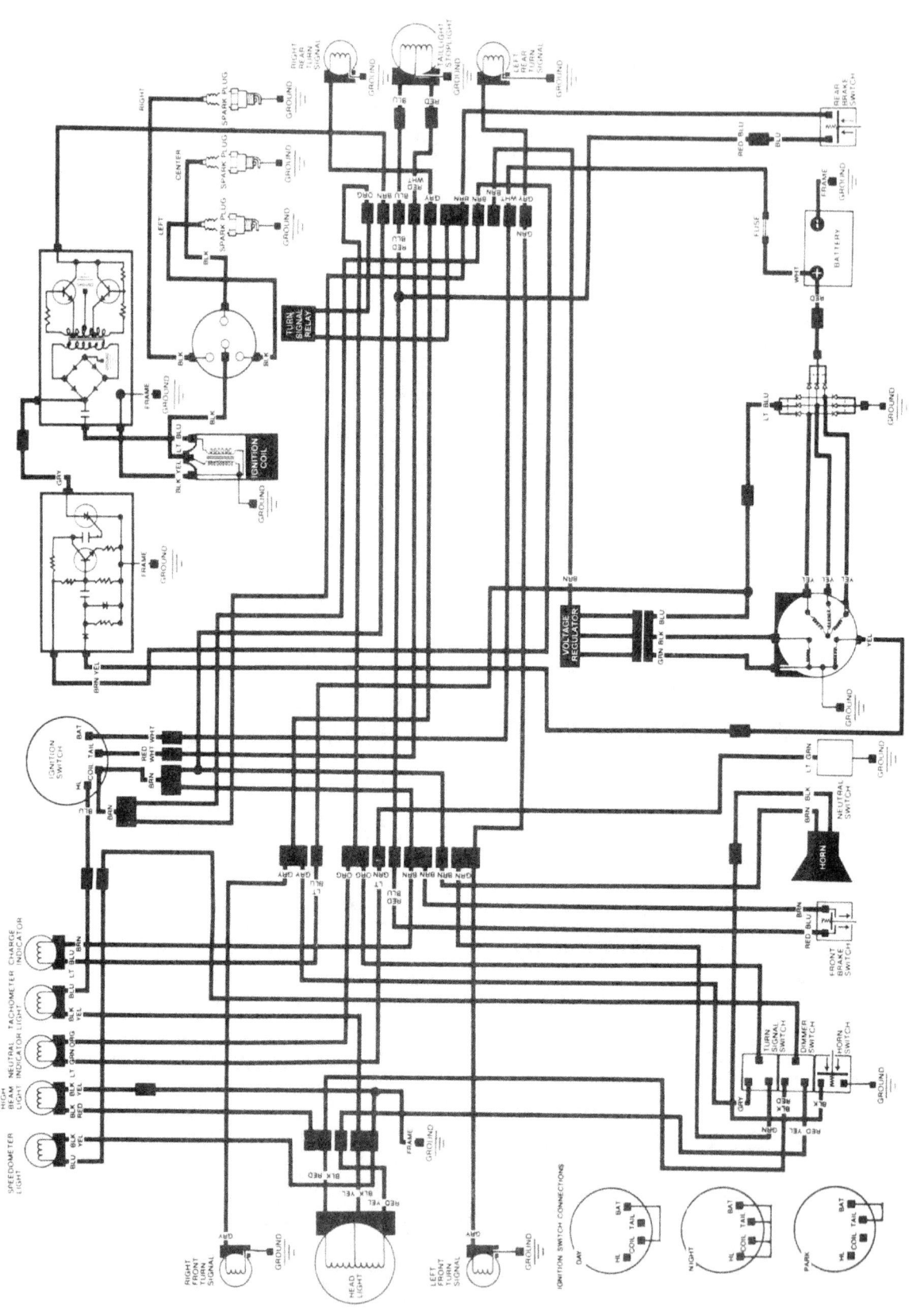

KAWASAKI H1 WITH DISC BRAKES

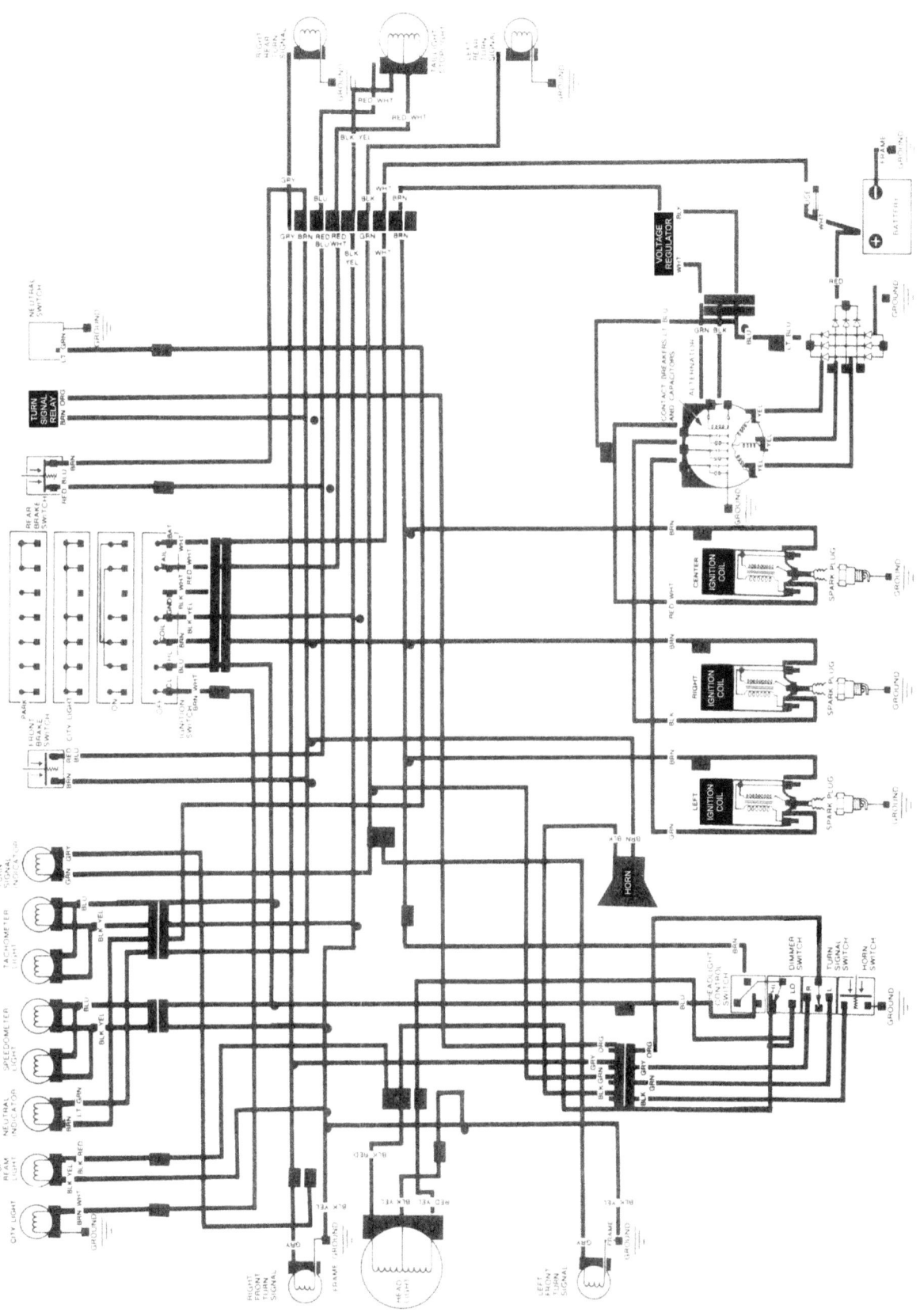

KAWASAKI H1 — EUROPE (1969-1971)

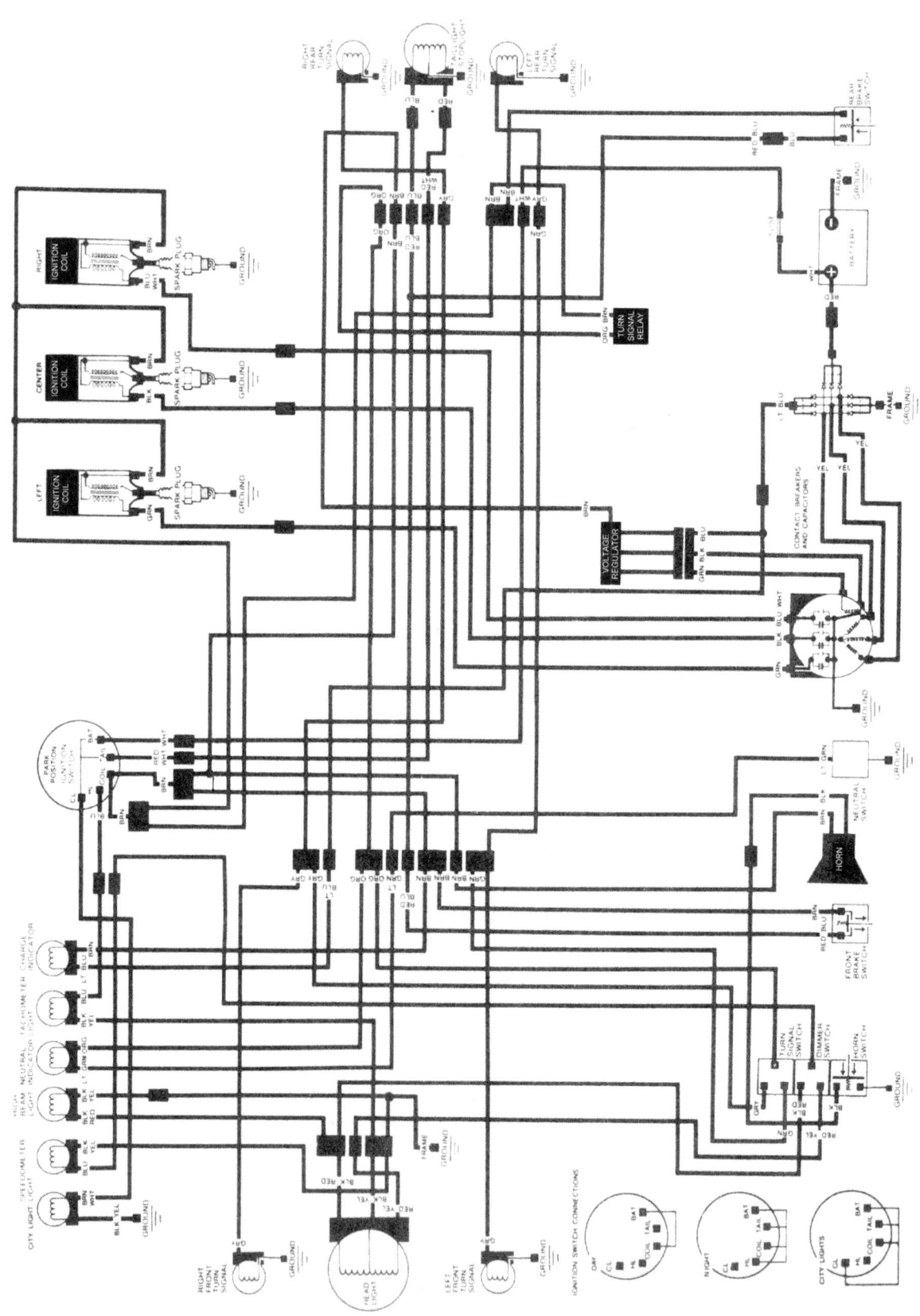

KAWASAKI H1E — U.S.

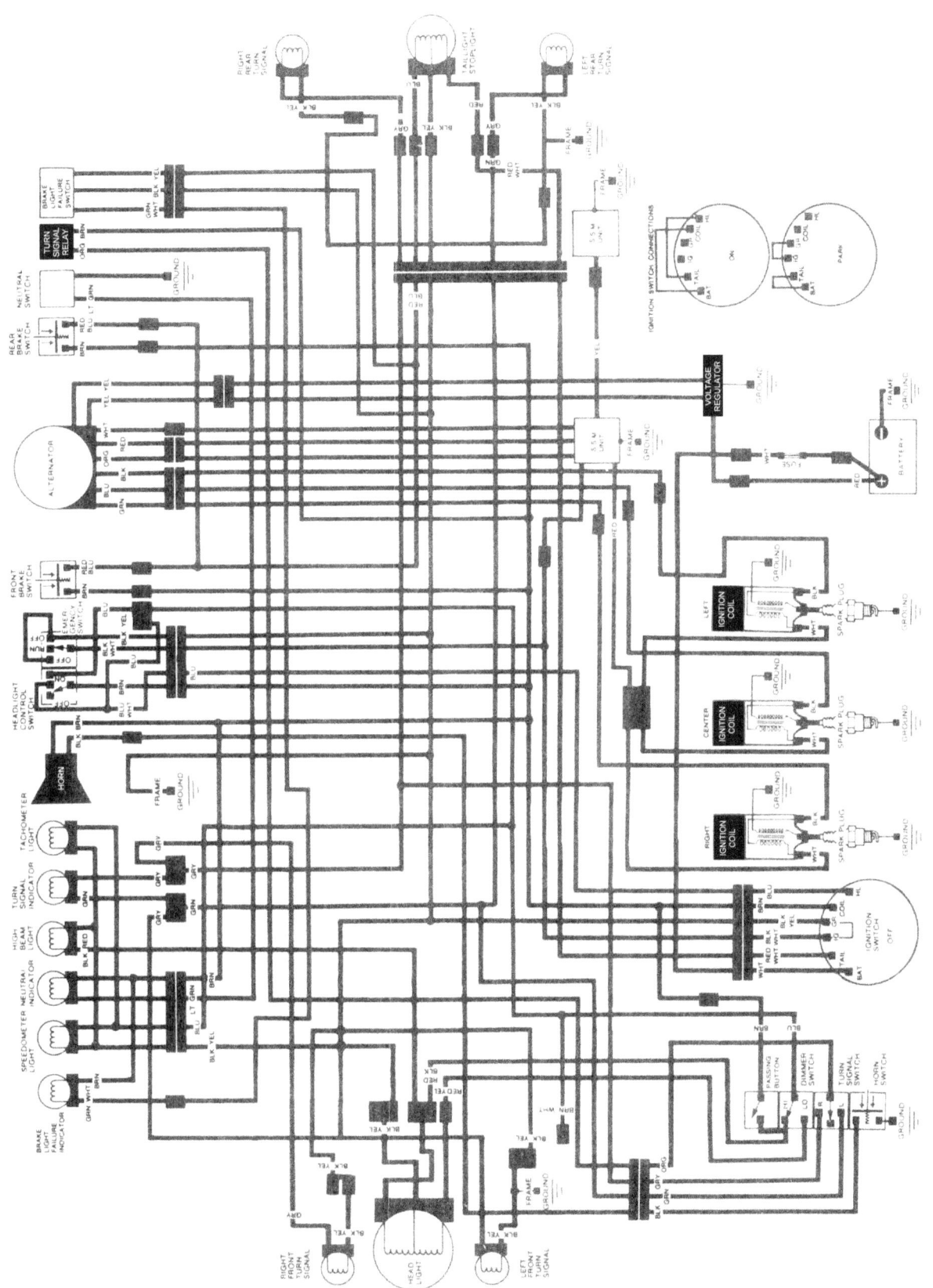

KAWASAKI H1E — EUROPE

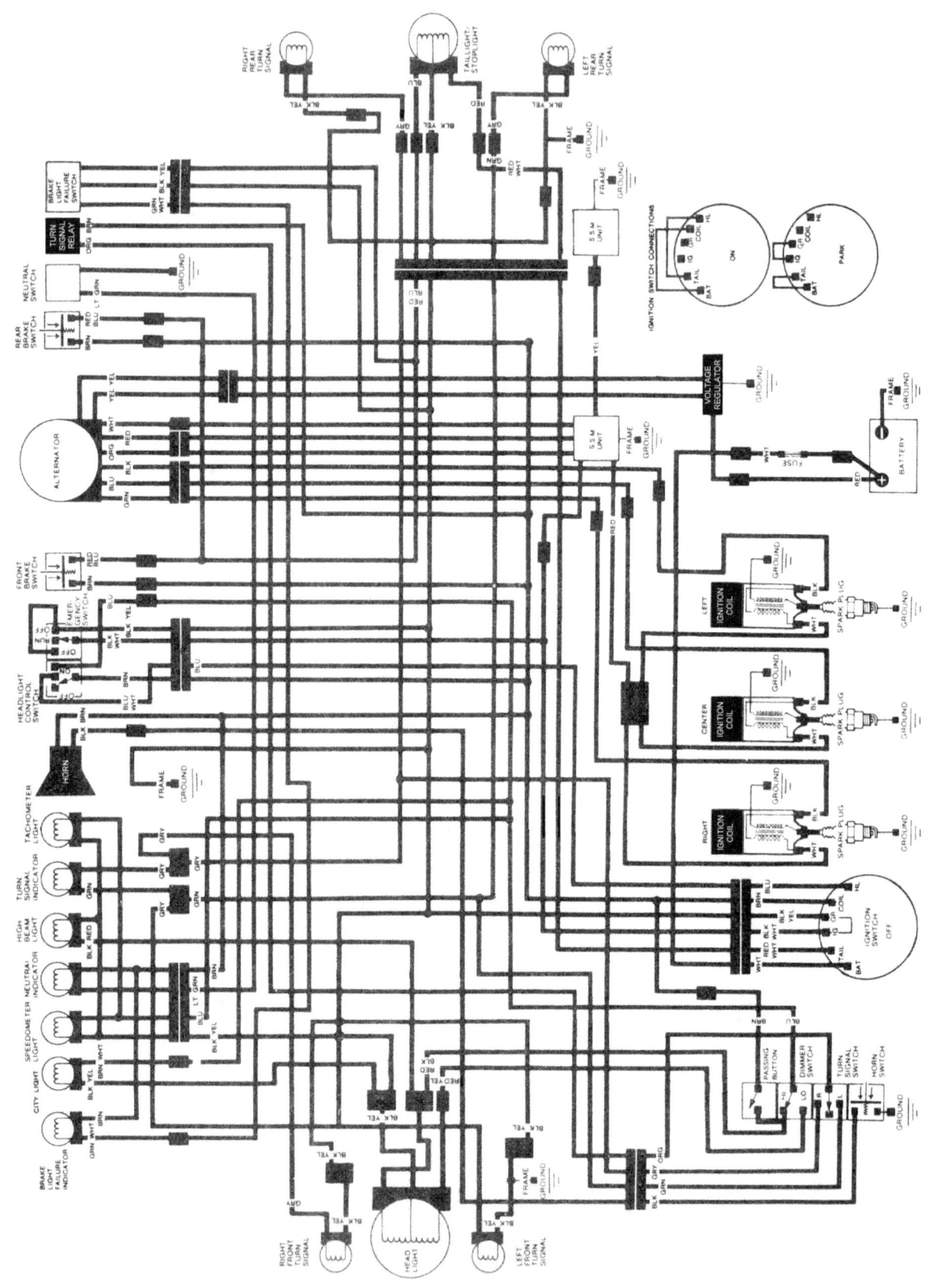

KAWASAKI KH500A8 — U.S.

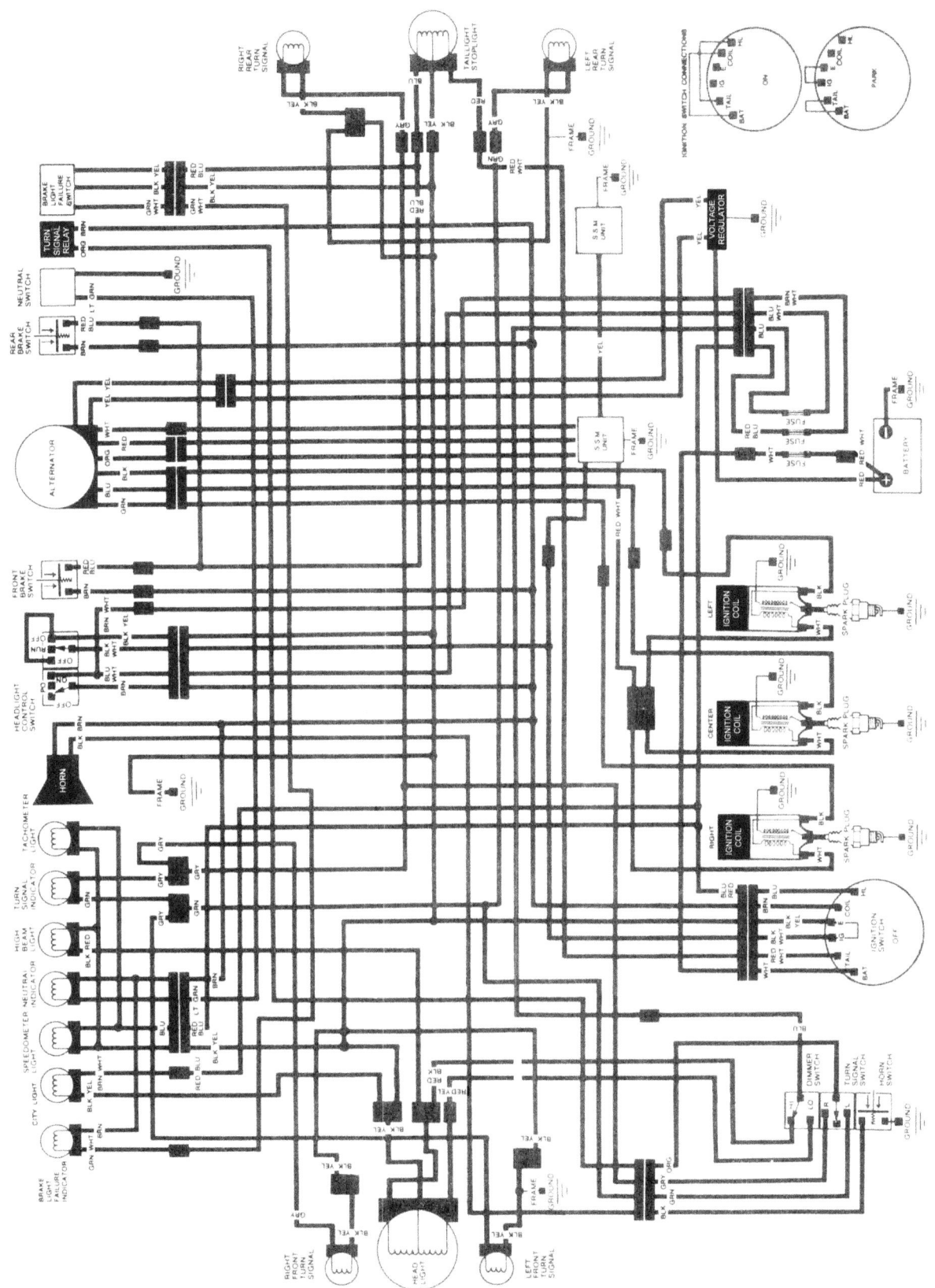

KAWASAKI KH500A8 — EUROPE

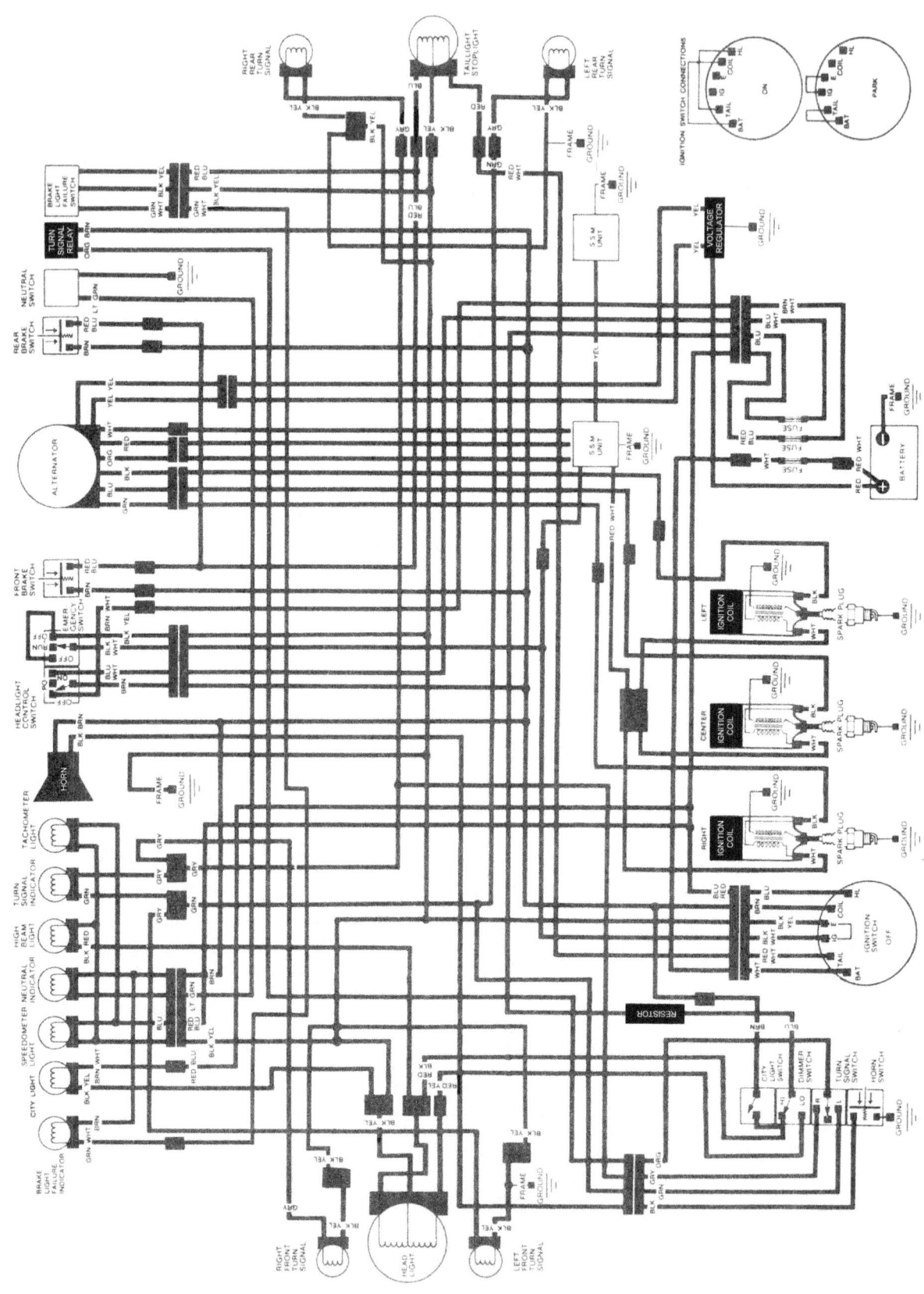

KAWASAKI H2

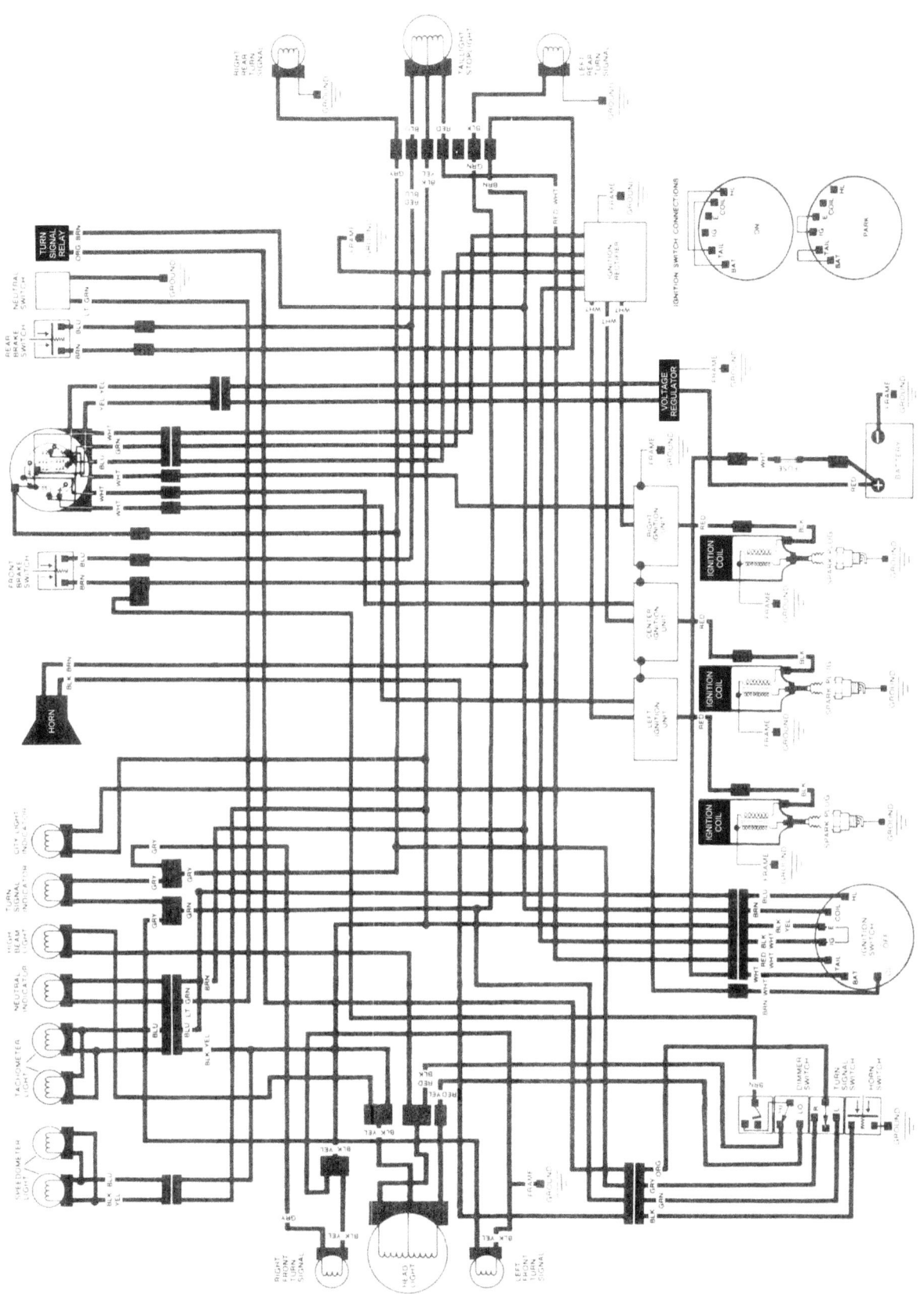

KAWASAKI H2B — U.S.

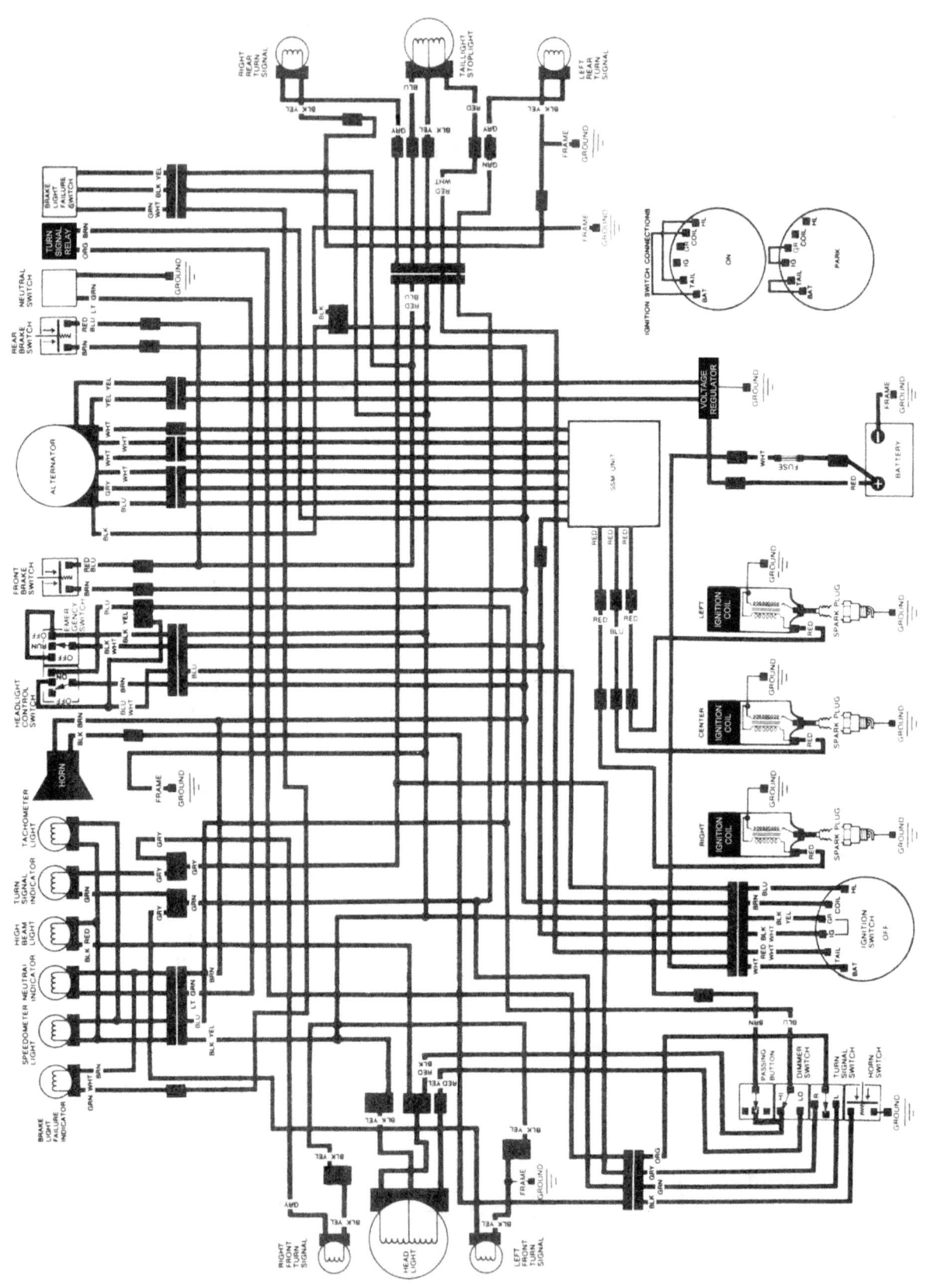

KAWASAKI H2B — EUROPE

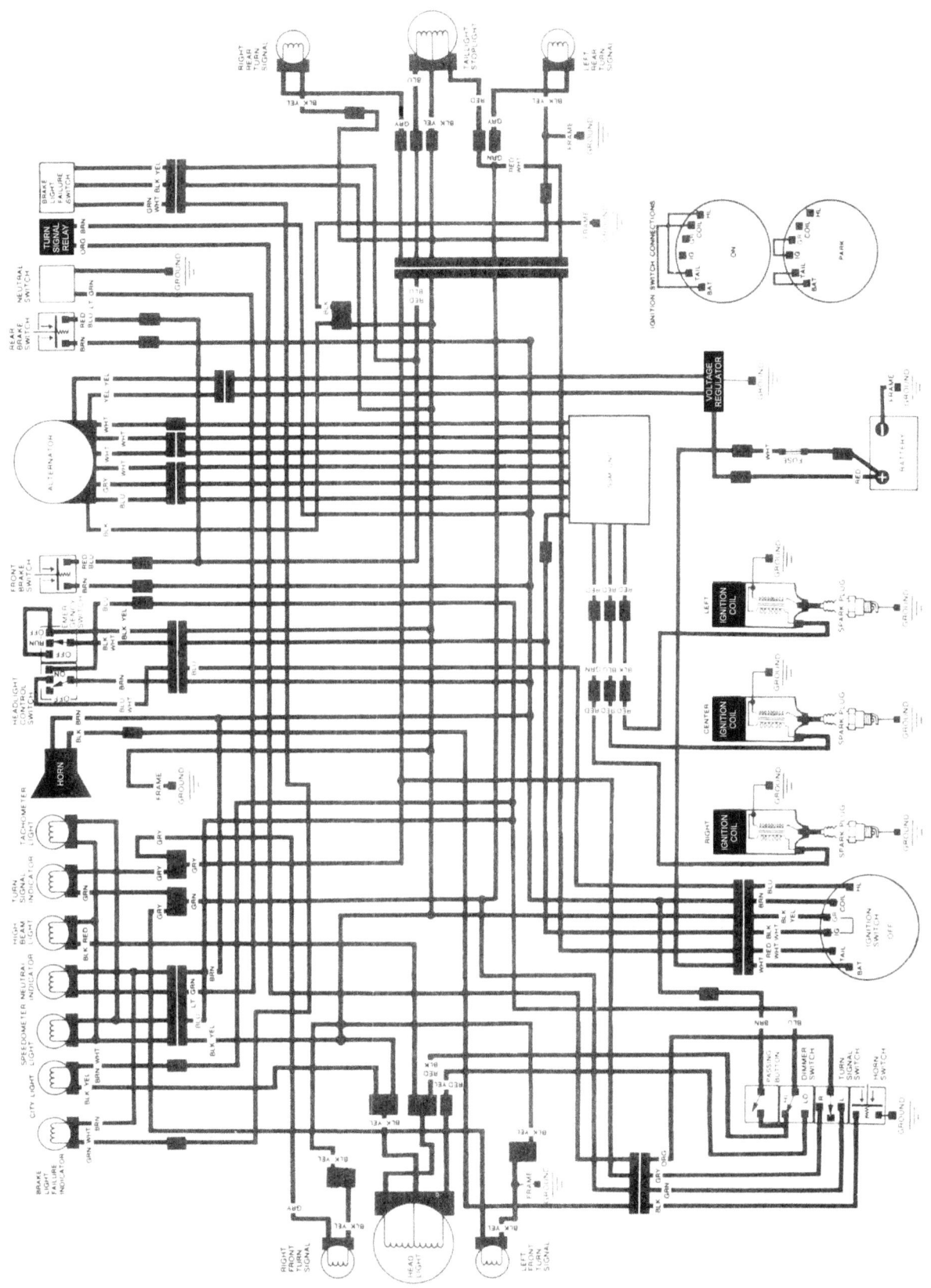

VELOCEPRESS MANUALS – MOTORCYCLE BY MAKE

AJS 1932-1948 SINGLES & TWINS 250cc THRU 1000cc (BOOK OF)
AJS 1945-1956 SINGLES RIGID & SPTRING FACTORY WSM & PARTS
AJS 1945-1960 SINGLES MODELS 16 & 18 350cc & 500cc (BOOK OF)
AJS 1948-1956 TWINS MODELS 20 & 30 FACTORY WSM & PARTS
AJS 1955-1965 SINGLES MODELS 16 & 18 350cc & 500cc (BOOK OF)
AJS 1957-1966 SINGLES & TWINS (ALL) FACTORY WSM
AJS 1959-1969 G80CS G85CS & P11 OFF ROAD FACTORY WSM
AJS 1968-1974 STORMER FACTORY WSM & PARTS LIST
ARIEL UP TO 1932 (BOOK OF)
ARIEL 1932-1939 PREWAR MODELS (BOOK OF)
ARIEL 1933-1951 (WORKSHOP MANUAL)
ARIEL 1939-1960 4 STROKE SINGLES (BOOK OF)
ARIEL 1958-1964 LEADER & ARROW FACTORY WSM & PARTS LIST
ARIEL 1958-1964 LEADER & ARROW (BOOK OF)
BMW R26 R27 (1956-1967) FACTORY WORKSHOP MANUAL
BMW R50 R50S R60 R69S (1955-1969) FACTORY WORKSHOP MANUAL
BMW R50/5 R60/5 R75/5 (1969-1973) FACTORY WORKSHOP MANUAL
BRIDGESTONE 90 SERIES FACTORY WSM & PARTS CATALOGUE
BRIDGESTONE 175 SERIES FACTORY WSM & PARTS CATALOGUE
BRIDGESTONE 350 SERIES FACTORY WSM & PARTS CATALOGUES
BSA SERVICE SHEETS MASTER CATALOGUE ALL MODELS 1945-1967
BSA BANTAM D1 TO D7 1948-1966 FACTORY SERVICE SHEETS MANUAL
BSA BANTAM ALL MODELS FROM 1948 ONWARDS (BOOK OF)
BSA BANTAM D14 FACTORY SERVICE MANUAL
BSA DANDY FACTORY WORKSHOP MANUAL (COMPILATION)
BSA SINGLES & V-TWINS UP TO 1926 inc. 1927 SUPPLEMENT (BOOK OF)
BSA SINGLES & V-TWINS UP TO 1930 (BOOK OF)
BSA SINGLES & V-TWINS UP TO 1935 (BOOK OF)
BSA SINGLES & V-TWINS 1936-1939 (BOOK OF)
BSA C10, C11 & C12 1945-1958 FACTORY SERVICE SHEETS MANUAL
BSA OHV & SV SINGLES 250-600cc 1945-1959 (BOOK OF)
BSA C15 & B40 1958-1967 FACTORY SERVICE SHEETS MANUAL
BSA OHV & SV SINGLES 250cc (ONLY) 1954-1970 (BOOK OF)
BSA B31, B32, B33 & B34 1945-60 FACTORY SERVICE SHEETS MANUAL
BSA OHV SINGLES 350 & 500cc 1955-1967 (BOOK OF)
BSA M20, M21 & M33 1945-1963 FACTORY SERVICE SHEETS MANUAL
BSA TWINS A7 & A10 1948-1962 FACTORY SERVICE SHEETS MANUAL
BSA TWINS A7 & A10 1948-1962 (BOOK OF)
BSA TWINS A50 & A65 1962-1965 FACTORY WORKSHOP MANUAL
BSA TWINS A50 & A65 1962-1969 (SECOND BOOK OF)
BULTACO 125cc to 37cc SINGLES 1968-1979 WORKSHOP MANUAL
CZ 125cc to 380cc SINGLES 1967-1974 WORKSHOP MANUAL
DOUGLAS 1929-1939 PREWAR ALL MODELS (BOOK OF)
DOUGLAS 1948-1957 POSTWAR ALL MODELS FACTORY SHOP MANUAL
DUCATI 160cc, 250cc & 350cc OHC MODELS FACTORY SHOP MANUAL
HODAKA 90cc, 100cc & 125cc SINGLES 1964-1978 WORKSHOP MANUAL
HONDA 50cc ALL MODELS UP TO 1970 INC MONKEY & TRAIL (BOOK OF)
HONDA 90cc ALL MODELS UP TO 1966 (BOOK OF)
HONDA TWINS & SINGLES 50cc THRU 305cc 1960-1966 (BOOK OF)
HONDA TWINS ALL MODELS 125cc THRU 450cc UP TO 1968 (BOOK OF)
HONDA C100 50cc SUPER CUB O.H.C. 1959-1962 FACTORY WSM
HONDA C110 50cc SPORT CUB O.H.C. 1960-1962 FACTORY WSM
HONDA 50-65-70-90cc O.H.C. SINGLES 1959-1983 WSM
HONDA 100-125cc SINGLES CB/CD/CL/SL/ 1970-1984 FACTORY WSM
HONDA 125-150cc TWINS C/CS/CB/CA 1959-1966 FACTORY WSM
HONDA 125-160-175-200cc TWINS 1965-1978 WORKSHOP MANUAL
HONDA 250-305cc TWINS C/CS/CB 1961-1968 FACTORY WSM
HOHDA 250-350cc TWINS CB/CL/SL 1968-1973 FACTORY WSM
HONDA 250-360cc TWINS CB/CL/CJ 1974-1977 FACTORY WSM
HONDA 350F & 400F 4-CYLINDER 1972-1977 FACTORY WSM
HONDA 450cc TWINS CB/CL 1965-1974 K0 TO K7 WORKSHOP MANUAL
HONDA 500cc & 550cc 4-CYL 1971-1978 FACTORY WORKSHOP MANUAL
HONDA 750cc SHOC 4-CYL 1969-1978 K0~K8 WORKSHOP MANUAL
HUSQVARNA 125cc to 450cc SINGLES 1965-1975 WORKSHOP MANUAL
INDIAN PONYBIKE, BOY RACER & PAPOOSE ILL PARTS LIST & SALES LIT

VELOCEPRESS MANUALS – SCOOTERS BY MAKE

BSA SUNBEAM SCOOTER WORKSHOP MANUAL 1959-1965
BSA SUNBEAM SCOOTER 1959-1965 (BOOK OF)
LAMBRETTA 1947-1957 ALL 125 & 150cc MODELS (BOOK OF)
LAMBRETTA 1957-1970 LI & TV MODELS (SECOND BOOK OF)
NSU PRIMA 1956-1964 ALL MODELS (BOOK OF)
TRIUMPH TIGRESS SCOOTER WORKSHOP MANUAL 1959-1965
TRIUMPH TIGRESS SCOOTER (BOOK OF)
VESPA 1951-1961 (BOOK OF)
VESPA 1955-1963 125 & 150cc & GS MODELS (SECOND BOOK OF)
VESPA 1955-1968 GS & SS (BOOK OF)
VESPA 1963-1972 90, 125 & 150cc (THIRD BOOK OF)

VELOCEPRESS MANUALS – MOPEDS & MOTORIZED BICYCLES

CYCLEMOTOR (BOOK OF)
NSU QUICKLY 1953-1963 ALL MODELS (BOOK OF)
PUCH MAXI N & S MAINTENANCE & REPAIR (3 MANUAL COMPILATION)
RALEIGH MOPEDS 1960-1969 (BOOK OF)

J.A.P. ENGINES 1927-1952 & MOTORCYCLES 1934-1952 (BOOK OF)
KAWASAKI TRIPLES 1968-1980 ALL MODELS 250cc to 750cc WSM
MAICO 250cc to 501cc 1968-1978 WORKSHOP MANUAL
MATCHLESS 1931-1939 ALL MODELS 250cc THRU 990cc (BOOK OF)
MATCHLESS 1945-1956 RIGID & SPRING FACTORY WSM & PARTS
MATCHLESS 1945-1956 SINGLES G3 & G80 350cc & 500cc (BOOK OF)
MATCHLESS 1948-1956 TWINS G9 & G11 FACTORY WSM & PARTS
MATCHLESS 1955-1966 SINGLES G3 & G80 350cc & 500cc (BOOK OF)
MATCHLESS 1957-1966 SINGLES & TWINS (ALL) FACTORY WSM
MONTESA 1962-1978 125cc to 360cc ALL MODELS WORKSHOP MANUAL
NEW IMPERIAL ALL SV & OHV FROM 1935 ONWARDS (BOOK OF)
NORTON 1932-1939 PREWAR MODELS (BOOK OF)
NORTON 1932-1947 (BOOK OF)
NORTON 1938-1956 (BOOK OF)
NORTON 1945-1963 MODELS 16H, Big4, ES2, 19 & 50 WSM'S & PARTS
NORTON 1955-1963 MODELS 19, 50 & ES2 (BOOK OF)
NORTON 1948-1970 DOMINATOR TWINS FACTORY WSM'S & PARTS
NORTON 1955-1965 DOMINATOR TWINS (BOOK OF)
NORTON 1960-1970 TWIN CYLINDER FACTORY WORKSHOP MANUAL
NORTON 1970-1975 COMMANDO 850 & 750cc FACTORY WSM
NORTON 1975-1978 MK 3 COMMANDO 850 cc FACTORY WSM
PANTHER 1932-1958 LIGHTWEIGHT MODELS 250 & 350cc (BOOK OF)
PANTHER 1938-1966 HEAVYWEIGHT MODELS 600 & 650cc (BOOK OF)
PENTON-KTM-SACHS 1968-1975 100cc & 125cc WORKSHOP MANUAL
PENTON-KTM 1972-1975 175cc, 250cc & 400cc WSM & PARTS MANUALS
PENTON-KTM 1972-1979 125cc to 400cc ENGINE WSM & PARTS MANUAL
RALEIGH MOTORCYCLES 1919-1933 (BOOK OF)
ROYAL ENFIELD 1934-1946 SINGLES & V TWINS (BOOK OF)
ROYAL ENFIELD 1937-1953 SINGLES & V TWINS (BOOK OF)
ROYAL ENFIELD 1946-1962 SINGLES (BOOK OF)
ROYAL ENFIELD 1948-1962 350cc & 500cc PRE-UNIT BULLET WSM
ROYAL ENFIELD 1948-1963 500cc TWINS FACTORY WORKSHOP MANUAL
ROYAL ENFIELD 1952-1963 700cc TWINS FACTORY WORKSHOP MANUAL
ROYAL ENFIELD 1956-1966 250cc CRUSADER & 350cc NEW BULLET WSM
ROYAL ENFIELD 1958-1966 250cc & 350cc SINGLES (SECOND BOOK OF)
ROYAL ENFIELD 1962-1970 INTERCEPTOR WSM'S & PARTS (Compilation)
RUDGE 1933-1939 (BOOK OF)
SACHS 1968-1975 100cc & 125cc ENGINES WSM & M/CYCLE PARTS LIST
SUNBEAM 1928-1939 (BOOK OF)
SUNBEAM 1946-1957 S7 & S8 (BOOK OF)
SUZUKI 50cc & 80cc UP TO 1966 (BOOK OF)
SUZUKI T10 1963-1967 FACTORY WORKSHOP MANUAL
SUZUKI T20 & T200 1965-1969 FACTORY WORKSHOP MANUAL
SUZUKI TWINS 1962 ONWARDS 125-500cc WORKSHOP MANUAL
TRIUMPH 1935-1949 SINGLES & TWINS (BOOK OF)
TRIUMPH 1937-1961 SINGLES SV & OHV 250cc-600cc + TERRIER & CUB
TRIUMPH 1945-1955 PRE-UNIT 350cc, 500cc & 650cc TWINS WSM No.11
TRIUMPH 1945-1959 TWINS (BOOK OF)
TRIUMPH 1956-1969 TWINS (BOOK OF)
TRIUMPH 1956-1962 PRE-UNIT 500cc & 650cc TWINS WSM No.17
TRIUMPH 1957-1963 UNIT CONSTRUCTION 350-500cc WSM No.4
TRIUMPH 1963-1974 UNIT CONSTRUCTION 350-500cc FACTORY WSM
TRIUMPH 1963-1970 UNIT CONSTRUCTION 650cc FACTORY WSM
TRIUMPH 1968-1974 TRIDENT T150 & T150V FACTORY WSM
TRIUMPH 1971-1973 650cc OIL-IN-FRAME FACTORY WSM
TRIUMPH 1973-1978 750cc BONNEVILLE & TIGER FACTORY WSM
TRIUMPH 1979-1983 750cc T140, TR7 & TR65 FACTORY WSM
VELOCETTE 1925-1970 ALL SINGLES & TWINS (BOOK OF)
VELOCETTE 1933-1952 MOV-MAC-MSS RIGID FRAME FACTORY WSM
VELOCETTE 1953-1960 MAC SPRING FRAME WSM & ILL PARTS LIST
VELOCETTE 1954-1971 MSS-VENOM-THRUXTON-VIPER FACTORY WSM
VILLIERS ENGINE UP TO 1959 INC. 3 WHEELERS (BOOK OF)
VILLIERS ENGINE UP TO 1969 (BOOK OF)
VINCENT 1935-1955 (WORKSHOP MANUAL)
YAMAHA 1961-1967 YA5 & YA6 (WORKSHOP MANUAL & ILL PARTS LIST)
YAMAHA 1968-1971 DT1 & MX SERIES Inc. GYT WORKSHOP MANUAL
YAMAHA 1971-1972 JT18 & JT2 (WORKSHOP MANUAL & ILL PARTS LIST)

VELOCEPRESS MANUALS - THREE WHEELER'S

BOND MINICAR THREE WHEELER 1948-1967 (BOOK OF)
BMW ISETTA FACTORY WORKSHOP MANUAL
BSA THREE WHEELER (BOOK OF)
RELIANT REGAL THREE WHEELER 1952-1973 (BOOK OF)
VINTAGE MORGAN THREE WHEELER (BOOK OF)

VELOCEPRESS TECHNICAL BOOKS – MOTORCYCLE

1930'S BRITISH MOTORCYCLE CARBS & ELEC COMPONENTS (BOOK OF)
1930'S BRITISH MOTORCYCLE ENGINES (OVERHAUL & MAINTENANCE)
1930'S BRITISH MOTORCYCLE GEARBOXES & CLUTCHES (BOOK OF)
CATALOG OF BRITISH MOTORCYCLES (1951 MODELS)
LUCAS ELECTRONICS BRITISH M/CYCLES REPAIR & PARTS (1950-1977)
MOTORCYCLE ENGINEERING (P.E. Irving)
MOTORCYCLE ROAD TESTS 1949-1953 (Motor Cycle Magazine UK)
SPEED AND HOW TO OBTAIN IT (Motor Cycle Magazine UK)
TUNING FOR SPEED (P.E. Irving)
WIPAC (COMBO) MANUAL NUMBER 3 + M/CYCLE & SCOOTER MANUAL